The English Village Constable
1580–1642

A Social and
Administrative Study

JOAN R. KENT

CLARENDON PRESS · OXFORD
1986

Oxford University Press, Walton Street, Oxford OX2 6DP
Oxford New York Toronto
Delhi Bombay Calcutta Madras Karachi
Petaling Jaya Singapore Hong Kong Tokyo
Nairobi Dar es Salaam Cape Town
Melbourne Auckland
and associated companies in
Beirut Berlin Ibadan Nicosia

Oxford is a trade mark of Oxford University Press

Published in the United States
by Oxford University Press, New York

© Joan R. Kent 1986

British Library Cataloguing in Publication Data
Kent, Joan R.
The English village constable 1580–1642: a social
and administrative study.
1. Constables—England—History—16th century
2. Constables—England—History—17th century
I. Title
363.2952950942   HV8196.A2
ISBN 0–19–822913–5

Library of Congress Cataloging in Publication Data
Kent, Joan R.
The English village constable 1580–1642.
Bibliography: p.
1. Constables—England—History—16th century.
2. Constables—England—History—17th century.
I. Title.
HV7899.K46 1986   363.2950942   86–3070
ISBN 0–19–822913–5

Set by Hope Services, Abingdon
Printed in Great Britain
at the University Printing House, Oxford
by David Stanford
Printer to the University

IN MEMORY OF MY MOTHER
MILDRED ROBBINS KENT
1901–1981

Preface and Acknowledgements

In the course of this work I have incurred many obligations. I would like to thank the Canada Council for a grant which helped to finance the very early stages of the research. I am indebted to Sweet Briar College for a number of Summer research grants; for the Sweet Briar Faculty Fellowship, which made possible an early sabbatical leave in 1980–1; and for a grant toward the cost of preparing the final typescript. I am indebted to many archivists for their unfailing helpfulness in answering my queries and making available documents in their care. Special thanks are due to the staffs of the county record offices of Hertfordshire, Leicestershire, Norfolk, Staffordshire, and Worcestershire. I would also like to thank the librarians of the Institute of Historical Research for their many courtesies over the years. A number of colleagues at Sweet Briar and elsewhere have offered encouragement during the course of this project, and I hope that they will not be too disappointed with the result. I owe special acknowledgements to Murray Tolmie, who sparked my undergraduate interest in Tudor-Stuart history and who remains a valued mentor and friend; to the late Joel Hurstfield who was generous with his time and support long after I completed my Ph.D. research; to Conrad Russell and Keith Thomas for their encouragement of this project; to Lynda Price for sharing with me her knowledge of Middlesex constables; and to Edward Drayer of the Department of Anthropology and Sociology at Sweet Briar College who has offered a willing ear and some helpful insights during my many 'struggles' with the constables. I would like to thank Mrs Anita Hildebrandt for typing both preliminary and final drafts of the manuscript, and for coping so ably with my rather indecipherable scrawl.

Quotations from Crown-copyright records in the Public Record Office appear by permission of the Controller of HM Stationery Office. Some of the material presented in chapters 1, 2, 3, 5, and 7 appeared originally, in a much more abbreviated form, in *Journal of British Studies*, xx, no. 2 (1981), pp. 26–49; some material in chapter 6 in *Local Population Studies*, xxvii (1981), pp. 35–51; and some material in chapter 7 in *Midland History*, viii (1983), pp. 70–85. The

Pattingham Constable's Accounts are now in the custody of the Staffordshire Record Office, reference D3451/2/2.

I have modernized capitalization and extended abbreviations in quotations from manuscripts and printed sources, but have retained the spelling of the original. Dates are given in Old Style, except that the year has been taken to begin on the first of January.

JOAN R. KENT

May 1985

Contents

Abbreviations

Add. MS	Additional Manuscripts
BL	British Library
E	Exchequer
Essex RO	Essex Record Office
Herts. RO	Hertfordshire Record Office
HMC	Historical Manuscripts Commission
HWRO	Hereford and Worcester Record Office
Leics. RO	Leicestershire Record Office
Norf. Arch. Wills	Norfolk Archdeaconry Wills
Norw. Cons. Wills	Norwich Consistory Wills
NNRO	Norfolk and Norwich Record Office
P and P	*Past* and *Present*
PR/I	Probate Records/Inventories (Leics.)
PRO	Public Record Office
PR/T	Probate Records/Testaments (Leics.)
QS/O	Quarter Sessions Order Books (Staffs.)
QS/B	Quarter Sessions Books (Herts.)
Salop RO	Shropshire Record Office
Somerset RO	Somerset Record Office
SP	State Papers
STAC 8	Star Chamber Proceedings, James I
Staffs. RO	Staffordshire Record Office
VCH	Victoria County History

I

Introduction

THE petty constable of late sixteenth- and early seventeenth-century England was a major official of the village or parish; but despite the attention which historians of the period have long devoted to local history, there exists no detailed study of the office or its occupants. The constableship did receive brief treatment in some late nineteenth- and early twentieth-century works on local government, and within the last two decades a renewed interest in the localities, and in some cases in society at the village level, has resulted in increased attention being given to such officers. The constable has usually received a rather bad press, and in order to provide a context for this study it is necessary to consider briefly earlier evaluations of such officers.

The constableship received some attention in the late nineteenth and early twentieth centuries from constitutional and legal historians, who were interested primarily in the nature of the office, and their work remains useful in considering the origins of the position and the powers of such officials.[1] However, the portrayal of constables which long held sway derived largely from the discussions of village or parish government by some of the early editors of local records, and from more general surveys of English government such as those of the Webbs and E. P. Cheyney.[2] The rather positive assessments of both

---

[1] See esp. H. B. Simpson, 'The Office of Constable', *English Historical Review*, x (1895), 625–41; W. S. Holdsworth, *A History of English Law*, iv (London, 1924), pp. 123–5.

[2] J. C. Cox, *Three Centuries of Derbyshire Annals*, 2 vols. (London, 1890), esp. i. 95–112; and his *Churchwardens' Accounts* (London, 1913), ch. 22, which deals with constables' accounts; W. E. Tate, *The Parish Chest*, 3rd edn. (Cambridge, 1969), ch. 7 (first published in 1946); J. Whitehead and W. E. Tate, 'The Parish Constable', *Amateur Historian*, i, no. 2 (1952), 38–42; Sidney and Beatrice Webb, *English Local Government from the Revolution to the Municipal Corporation Act*: v. i. *The Parish and the County* (London, 1906), esp. pp. 15–29; E. P. Cheyney, *A History of England from the Defeat of the Armada to the Death of Elizabeth*, 2 vols. (New York, 1926), ii. ch. 41. Also see T. A. Critchley, *A History of Police in England and Wales*, rev. edn. (London, 1978), pp. 1–17, whose description of the constableship in this period is based largely on the work of the Webbs. For an early study of local government in a particular township see Arthur Redford, *The History of Local Government in Manchester*, i (London, 1939), and esp. pp. 51–62 for a discussion of the constables.

the qualifications and conduct of constables provided by Eleanor Trotter in her study of Yorkshire, and later by Mildred Campbell in her work on the yeomen of Elizabethan and early Stuart England, seem to have gone largely unnoticed.[3] Shakespeare's Dogberry, Dull, and Elbow dominated historians' views of constables as well as those of literary scholars who discussed the constableship.[4] They found 'comic constables' in historical records as well as in seventeenth-century dramatic works, and portrayed such officers as both reluctant and incompetent agents of royal authority. Most historians attributed the failings of constables largely to their lowly social position, claiming that more substantial villagers sought exemption from the office or employed substitutes. The Webbs contended that the office was so unpopular that it was 'abandoned to humble folk' who were attracted by its perquisites or were too poor to employ deputies, while T. A. Critchley added a new twist to their argument when he claimed that by the seventeenth century the office was regarded as suitable only for 'the old, idiotic, or infirm', and that wealthier merchants, tradesmen, and farmers paid their way out of serving.[5] J. Whitehead and W. E. Tate too had indicated that increasing numbers sought exemption from the office, and they suggested that the constable was often a 'slow-witted villager of the commoner sort'.[6] Such views reached their culmination in the work of E. P. Cheyney who employed the words 'uneducated', 'untrained', 'ignorance', 'stupidity', 'incompetency', and 'failure' in describing constables and their conduct in office.[7] He claimed that they frequently failed in the performance of their duties, while W. E. Tate suggested that many of them made no attempt to discharge even half of their obligations. Tate described constables as being content 'with levying a modest rate, whipping an occasional vagrant, leaving rogues alone so long as they made no attempt to interfere with the constable, upon the principle laid down by the most distinguished member of their class — Dogberry, — and submitted at quarter sessions the gratifying, but not wholly veracious presentment, which appears in the records as *omnia bene*'.[8]

---

[3] Eleanor Trotter, *Seventeenth Century Life in a Country Parish* (Cambridge, 1919), ch. 5; Mildred Campbell, *The English Yeoman under Elizabeth and the Early Stuarts* (New Haven, 1942), pp. 318–25.

[4] See Hugh C. Evans, 'Comic Constables — Fictional and Historical', *Shakespeare Quarterly*, xx (1969), 427–33 for one such piece by a literary scholar.

[5] The Webbs, *The Parish and the County*, p. 18; Critchley, *History of Police*, pp. 10–11.

[6] Whitehead and Tate, 'The Parish Constable', 41–2, 38.

[7] Cheyney, *History of England*, ii. 408.   [8] Tate, *The Parish Chest*, p. 187.

Such views of constables have been increasingly challenged during the last two decades. Studies of local government have shed new light on such officers, while recent work in social history has also increased historians' understanding of the nature of English villages in the sixteenth and seventeenth centuries. A number of county studies, some of them inspired by 'the gentry controversy' and others by an interest in the interaction between the rulers of the county and the central government, have focused attention on the provinces.[9] Although most of these works are concerned primarily with social élites and with the higher officials of the county, some of them do give brief attention to the officers of the manor, township, and parish.[10] There has also been a growing interest in village histories. The work of W. G. Hoskins on Leicestershire villages, although primarily economic and demographic in emphasis, gave some attention to village

[9] Three earlier county studies should be mentioned: William B. Willcox, *Gloucestershire: A Study in Local Government, 1590 to 1640* (New Haven, 1940); Joel Hurstfield, 'County Government: Wiltshire, *c.*1530–*c.*1660' (1957), repr. in Hurstfield, *Freedom, Corruption and Government in Elizabethan England* (Cambridge, Mass., 1973), pp. 236–93; T. G. Barnes, *Somerset, 1625–40: A County's Government during 'The Personal Rule'* (Cambridge, Mass., 1961); for county studies which have appeared during the last two decades see Alan Everitt, *The Community of Kent and the Great Rebellion 1640–60* (Leicester, 1966); J. S. Morrill, *Cheshire, 1630–1660: County Government and Society During the English Revolution* (London, 1974); A. Hassell Smith, *County and Court: Government and Politics in Norfolk, 1558–1603* (Oxford, 1974); Anthony Fletcher, *A County Community in Peace and War: Sussex, 1600–1660* (London, 1975); S. J. Watts, *From Border to Middle Shire: Northumberland, 1586–1625* (Leicester, 1975); Peter Clark, *English Provincial Society from the Reformation to the Revolution: Religion, Politics and Society in Kent, 1500–1640* (Hassocks, 1977); Clive Holmes, *Seventeenth-Century Lincolnshire* (History of Lincolnshire, vii (London, 1980); and M. E. James, *Family, Lineage and Civil Society: A Study of Society, Politics and Mentality in the Durham Region* (Oxford, 1974). Also see the following unpublished Ph.D. theses: B. W. Quintrell, 'The Government of the County of Essex, 1603–42' (University of London, 1965); G. L. Owen, 'Norfolk, 1620–1641: Local Government and Central Authority in an East Anglian County' (University of Wisconsin, 1970); R. H. Silcock, 'County Government in Worcestershire, 1603–1660' (University of London, 1974); Julie Calnan, 'County Society and Local Government in the County of Hertford, *c.*1580–*c.*1630, with Special Reference to the Commission of the Peace' (Cambridge University, 1979); and two articles by Ann L. Hughes, 'Warwickshire on the Eve of Civil War: A "County Community"?', *Midland History*, vii (1982), 42–72, and 'The King, the Parliament, and the Localities during the English Civil War', *Journal of British Studies*, xxiv, no. 2 (1985), 236–63, which present material from her Ph.D. thesis, 'Politics, Society and Civil War in Warwickshire 1620–1650' (University of Liverpool, 1980).

[10] See Hurstfield, 'Wiltshire *c.*1530–*c.*1660', pp. 283, 288; Barnes, *Somerset*, esp. pp. 76–7, 182–4, 222, 228–30, 241; Willcox, *Gloucestershire*, pp. 49–55; Fletcher, *Sussex*, pp. 141–7, 223, 226–7; Clark, *English Provincial Society*, esp. pp. 116, 176–7, 250–1; Quintrell, 'The Government of the County of Essex', esp. pp. 25–6, 50–5, 78, 195–8, 230; Silcock, 'County Government in Worcestershire', esp. pp. 63–5; Calnan, 'County Society and Local Government in the County of Hertford', 185–8.

government, and his study of Wigston Magna became a model for
other histories of local communities.[11] More recently such studies have
also been shaped by the work of Peter Laslett and the Cambridge
Group for the History of Population and Social Structure.[12] Alan
Macfarlane, whose study of witchcraft was based in part on a detailed
examination of several villages,[13] became a major advocate of the
historical study of small communities, of the total history of a
settlement, though he denied that English villages were 'communities'
in the accepted sense of the word.[14] Local studies such as those of
Margaret Spufford on three Cambridgeshire villages,[15] and of Keith
Wrightson and David Levine on an Essex village,[16] reflect some of
these influences and provide new insights into village society and
government. Wrightson's and Levine's study of Terling also demon-
strates another development in local history, which has been of major
significance in the re-evaluation of constables, the recent interest in
the history of crime. J. S. Cockburn's extensive work on the assizes and
assize records has proved to be but one product of a growing attention
to legal history.[17] A number of books and articles have appeared which

[11] W. G. Hoskins, *The Midland Peasant* (London, 1957); also see D. G. Hey, *An
English Rural Community: Myddle under the Tudors and Stuarts* (Leicester, 1974).

[12] See Peter Laslett, *The World We Have Lost* (London, 1965), which first dealt with
many of the topics being pursued by the Cambridge Group.

[13] Alan Macfarlane, *Witchcraft in Tudor and Stuart England* (New York, 1970).

[14] Alan Macfarlane, *Reconstructing Historical Communities* (Cambridge, 1977); also see
his *The Origins of English Individualism: The Family, Property and Social Transition*
(Oxford, 1978). For a response to his comments about English 'communities', originally
published as 'History, anthropology and the study of communities', *Social History*, ii
(1977), 631–52, see C. J. Calhoun, 'History, anthropology and the study of
communities: some problems in Macfarlane's proposal', *Social History*, iii (1978),
363–73 and his 'Community: towards a variable conceptualization for comparative
research', *Social History*, v (1980), 105–29.

[15] Margaret Spufford, *Contrasting Communities: English Villagers in the Sixteenth and
Seventeenth Centuries* (Cambridge, 1974).

[16] Keith Wrightson and David Levine, *Poverty and Piety in an English Village: Terling,
1525–1700* (New York, 1974). For a recent study of an English town see John T. Evans,
Seventeenth Century Norwich: Politics, Religion and Government (Oxford, 1979) and for a
local study that is primarily political in emphasis see Frank F. Foster, *The Politics of
Stability: A Portrait of the Rulers of Elizabethan London* (London, 1977).

[17] J. S. Cockburn, *A History of English Assizes, 1558–1714* (Cambridge, 1972);
Cockburn has edited the following volumes of assize records: *Calendar of Assize Records:
Hertfordshire Indictments, Elizabeth I* (London, 1975); *Calendar of Assize Records:
Hertfordshire Indictments, James I* (London, 1975); *Calendar of Assize Records: Sussex
Indictments, Elizabeth I* (London, 1975); *Calendar of Assize Records: Sussex Indictments,
James I* (London, 1975); *Calendar of Assize Records: Essex Indictments, Elizabeth I* (London,
1978); *Calendar of Assize Records: Kent Indictments, Elizabeth I* (London, 1979); *Calendar
of Assize Records: Kent Indictments, James I* (London, 1980); *Calendar of Assize Records:*

deal with crime and punishment in various English counties,[18] and in a
few cases with law enforcement at the village level;[19] and many of these
studies have given some attention to the constable in his capacity as a
police officer.[20] In addition, Keith Wrightson has devoted an article
specifically to the roles of constables and jurymen in the enforcement
of the law.[21]

As historians' knowledge about English local society and government

Surrey Indictments, Elizabeth I (London, 1980). Also see T. G. Barnes, ed., *Somerset Assize Orders, 1629–1640* (Somerset Record Society, lxv, 1959); J. S. Cockburn, ed., *Western Circuit Assize Orders, 1629–1648* (Camden Society, 4th series, xvii, 1976).

[18] Joel Samaha, *Law and Order in Historical Perspective: The Case of Elizabethan Essex* (New York, 1974); J. S. Cockburn, 'The Nature and Incidence of Crime in England 1559–1625: A Preliminary Survey', in J. S. Cockburn, ed., *Crime in England 1550–1800* (Princeton, 1977), pp. 49–71; M. J. Ingram, 'Communities and Courts: Law and Disorder in Early-Seventeenth Century Wiltshire', in *Crime in England 1550–1800*, pp. 110–34; T. C. Curtis, 'Quarter Sessions Appearances and Their Background: A Seventeenth-Century Regional Study', in *Crime in England 1550–1800*, pp. 135–54; J. A. Sharpe, *Crime in Seventeenth Century England: A County Study* (Cambridge, 1983); and Cynthia Herrup, 'New Shoes and Mutton Pies: Investigative Responses to Theft in Seventeenth-Century East Sussex', *Historical Journal*, xxvii (1984), 811–30 and her 'Law and Morality in Seventeenth-Century England', *P and P*, cvi (1985), 102–23. Also see T. C. Curtis and F. M. Hale, 'English Thinking about Crime', in L. A. Knafla, ed., *Crime and Criminal Justice in Europe and Canada* (Calgary, 1981); T. Curtis, 'Explaining Crime in Early Modern England', *Criminal Justice History*, i. (1980), 117–37; Walter J. King, 'Vagrancy and Local Law Enforcement: Why Be a Constable in Stuart Lancashire?', *Historian*, xlii (1980), 264–83; Alan Macfarlane, *The Justice and the Mare's Ale: Law and disorder in seventeenth-century England* (Oxford, 1981); J. Walter, 'Grain riots and popular attitudes to the law', in John Brewer and John Styles, eds., *An Ungovernable People: The English and their Law in the Seventeenth and Eighteenth Centuries* (New Brunswick, New Jersey, 1980), 47–84. There has also been a good deal of work on crime and punishment in the eighteenth century; see esp. J. M. Beattie, 'The Pattern of Crime in England, 1660–1800', *P and P*, lxii (1974), 47–95; D. Hay *et al.*, *Albion's Fatal Tree: Crime and Society in Eighteenth-Century England* (London, 1975); D. Hay, 'War, Dearth and Theft in the Eighteenth Century: The Record of the English Courts', *P and P*, xcv (1982), 117–60; John Langbein, ' "Albion's" Fatal Flaws', *P and P*, xcviii (1983), 96–120.

[19] Wrightson and Levine, *Poverty and Piety in an English Village*, ch. 5; J. A. Sharpe, 'Crime and Delinquency in an Essex Parish 1600–1640', in Cockburn, ed., *Crime in England*, pp. 90–109; and his 'Enforcing the Law in the seventeenth-century English village', in V. A. C. Gattrell, B. Lenman, and G. Parker, eds., *Crime and the Law: The Social History of Crime in Western Europe since 1500* (London, 1980), pp. 97–119.

[20] See esp. Samaha, *Law and Order*, pp. 84–8; Curtis, 'Quarter Sessions Appearances and Their Background', pp. 144–8; Sharpe, 'Crime and Delinquency in an Essex Parish', pp. 94–8; Sharpe, 'Enforcing the Law', pp. 101–2, 108–9; King, 'Vagrancy and Local Law Enforcement', 269–76; Herrup, 'New Shoes and Mutton Pies'.

[21] Keith Wrightson, 'Two concepts of order: justices, constables and jurymen in seventeenth-century England', in Brewer and Styles, eds., *An Ungovernable People*, pp. 21–46; on juries also see J. S. Morrill, *The Cheshire Grand Jury 1625–59* (Leicester, 1976).

has increased,[22] the portrayal of constables provided by earlier historians has been subjected to growing criticism. Although T. G. Barnes in 1961 still described constables as 'illiterate', 'ignorant', 'lazy', 'timorous', 'powerless', 'disobedient', and 'negligent',[23] some historians since that time have challenged such views. Joel Samaha and J. A. Sharpe have suggested that constables, at least in Essex, were not as lowly as previous historians assumed,[24] but little specific evidence has been provided about the social position of such men. Samaha also challenged the portrayal of constables as ineffective in fulfilling their duties, at least in the area of law enforcement. Anthony Fletcher too suggested that 'negligence and inefficiency' were 'the exception rather than the rule' among such officers, while William Willcox contended that constables were deserving of greater sympathy than they had usually received.[25] However, none of them offers a detailed analysis of constables' conduct in office and their performance of their duties. Finally, and perhaps most important, A. Hassell Smith, Keith Wrightson, and J. A. Sharpe have employed approaches to the constableship rather different from those of most earlier writers, who focused on the personal and social characteristics of those who held the position. Sharpe suggests that historians have described constables as inefficient because they applied twentieth-century standards in assessing the behaviour of such officers, and failed to appreciate that the assumptions and expectations which prevailed during the seventeenth century were different from those in the modern world. He is concerned particularly with constables' police duties, and he contends that their conduct can be understood only in terms of the assumptions about law enforcement which were in operation during the seventeenth century, and particularly the belief that 'the peace . . . should . . . be kept with minimal interference from agencies outside the parish'. Smith and Wrightson both direct attention to the conflicting pressures which constables experienced, and Wrightson suggests that the conduct of such officers must be viewed in light of the 'strains of their mediating

[22] For a synthesis of much of the recent work on English social history of the early modern period see Keith Wrightson, *English Society 1580–1680* (New Brunswick, 1982).

[23] Barnes, *Somerset*, pp. 76–7.

[24] Samaha, *Law and Order*, p. 87; Sharpe, 'Crime and Delinquency in an Essex Parish', p. 95.

[25] Samaha, *Law and Order*, pp. 85–8; Fletcher, *Sussex*, p. 223; Willcox, *Gloucestershire*, p. 55; also see Calnan, 'County Society and Local Government in the County of Hertford', p. 187.

position between their communities and the law'. He suggests that local concepts of order which conflicted with 'the order of the law' sometimes led to 'studied negligence' by constables in the performnance of their police duties.[26]

Recent work has thus called in question the assessment of constables as lowly and bumbling officials, and suggested that different criteria must be employed in evaluating the conduct of such officers. At the same time some historians have argued that the deficiencies which constables did display are explained less by the personal inadequacies of the incumbents than by the structural constraints of the position itself.[27] However, the evidence presented to date is not sufficient to create a new social profile of constables nor to rescue them from charges of laziness, negligence, and incompetency. Moreover, recent evaluations of their conduct have been confined largely to their performance as police officers, and this may or may not provide an accurate guide to the manner in which they executed their other duties. Wrightson's analysis of the 'mediating role' of constables is also restricted to their law enforcement duties, and this concept should be applied in examining their other functions as well. If the conduct of constables is to be fully understood it is necessary to consider further the very nature of the office, and to examine its origins and its development prior to the sixteenth century. The character of the position was shaped in part by the manner in which constables were selected for office, and this matter too requires further exploration.

The aim of this study is to provide a detailed examination of the constableship in order to shed light on the character and personnel of village government, and on the interaction between the central government and local communities, in the sixty years or so before the Civil War. Consideration will be given to the duties, selection, and social characteristics of constables, to their performance in office, and

[26] Sharpe, 'Enforcing the Law', p. 108 and his 'Crime and Delinquency in an Essex Parish', p. 96; Smith, *County and Court*, pp. 112–3; Wrightson, 'Two concepts of order', esp. pp. 21–32. Despite his comments about the personal deficiencies of constables, Barnes, *Somerset*, pp. 77, 210, 222, 228–30, directs attention to the conflicting pressures which constables faced in a particular instance, the collection of ship-money. Also see Cheyney, *History of England*, ii. 415; Morrill, *Cheshire Grand Jury*, pp. 30, 32; Clark, *English Provincial Society*, pp. 116, 251.

[27] In addition to Wrightson, 'Two concepts of order', see my article 'The English Village Constable, 1580–1642: The Nature and Dilemmas of the Office', *Journal of British Studies*, xx, no. 2 (1981), 26–49, which was in publication when Wrightson's article appeared in print.

to the factors which shaped their conduct. The evidence presented here indicates that recent challenges to the traditional portrayal of constables are well placed, and that such officers were neither as socially inferior nor as negligent in performing their duties as earlier historians had contended. It will also be suggested that their conduct was more often shaped by the very nature of the position than by the particular qualities of individual incumbents; and that both their successes and their failings should be viewed in light of their dual relationship with their superiors and their local public.

A study of the constableship, and of the way in which it functioned as a link between the central government and the localities during the sixteenth and seventeenth centuries, also affords another perspective on state-formation during this period. A number of works concerned with state-building in early modern Europe have appeared during the last decade, works which vary considerably in their approaches and interpretations.[28] Some scholars view state-formation largely as a question of ideology, and while giving some attention to the realities of power they focus on the development of the 'state-idea' as a means of legitimating authority. Others place greater emphasis on structural change and power relationships. These studies also disagree about the particular dynamics of state-building in early modern Europe. While some regard external pressures, whether military, economic, or religious, as the decisive factor in the development of states, others view state-formation as a process that was shaped largely by internal social configurations. However, such scholars are not agreed about the nature of European society in the early modern period, nor about the precise relationships between social dynamics and state development. Some argue that central authority was strengthened as a result of growing ambivalence and tension between social classes or 'leading functional groups', particularly between the nobility and the bourgeoisie. Although recent Marxist scholars see the early modern state as being

---

[28] The following discussion is based primarily on Perry Anderson, *Lineages of the Absolutist State* (London, 1974); J. H. Shennan, *The Origins of the Modern European State 1450–1725* (London, 1974); V. G. Kiernan, *State and Society in Europe 1550–1650* (New York, 1980); Perez Zagorin, *Rebels and Rulers 1500–1660*, 2 vols. (New York, 1982); Norbert Elias, *Power and Civility* (New York, 1982), an English translation of a work first published in 1939, and his *Court Society* (New York, 1983), esp. ch. 1. Also see the collection of articles in Charles Tilly, ed., *The Formation of National States in Western Europe* (Princeton, 1975), and the older article by J. A. Maravall, 'The Origins of the Modern State', *Journal of World History* vi (1960–1), 789–808. In a brief summary it is not possible to explore fully all the arguments of these scholars, nor to do justice to the intricacies of some of their points.

shaped by the rise of the bourgeoisie, they claim that the upper reaches of this stratum were 'aristocratized' and that the nobility retained its social ascendency. They regard the absolute state as an instrument of this 'feudal' class, which employed state power to maintain its dominance during a period of transition from feudalism to capitalism. Those who conceive of early modern Europe as a 'society of orders' may agree with Marxist scholars that the absolute state rested primarily on aristocratic social foundations, but they deny that such states were class instruments or that they were 'feudal' in character. While there is agreement that early modern state-building entailed conflict, there is not accord about its character. Marxist writers argue that advances in agrarian and mercantile capitalism in some parts of Europe led to the emergence of power groups which challenged state rule because it no longer served their interests, but others contend that political conflict was occasioned by the growth of central power, against which various groups reacted.

Although differing in their interpretations of state-formation, these analyses have in common the fact that they give little attention to processes of state-building at the lowest level and to the problem of assimilating semi-autonomous local communities into a centralized structure.[29] Norbert Elias refers briefly to the fact that the formation of absolute states sometimes entailed the absorption of 'organs of autonomous local administration', but he does not show how this was achieved.[30] V. G. Kiernan points out that in many parts of Europe there was still 'a lively village community, often electing its own headman and forming the lowest rung on the ladder up to the throne'. However, the means by which these communities were integrated into a state structure is not considered. Such units of power do not fit well into his theory of a 'centralized landowners' state' designed for the subjection of the lower orders, and Kiernan quickly adds that 'the villager was dropped behind, failing to secure a place in a society in flux'.[31] Although Perez Zagorin portrays the 'village community' as an entity which was concerned with many local matters, particularly of an agrarian nature, in its relations with the state the village appears only as

[29] Peter Clark has pointed out that, in the case of England, historians have recognized that it was not a 'wholly integrated national community' in the pre-industrial period, but that they have been slow to appreciate that the country was divided not only into 'county societies' but also into a host of local communities, possessing their own customs (*English Provincial Society*, pp. 120–1).
[30] Elias, *Power and Civility*, p. 110.
[31] Kiernan, *State and Society*, p. 7.

an 'institutional cellule of revolt'.[32] Many students of early modern
state-formation do not seem to entertain the possibility that village
communities, as well as 'the feudal class' or 'leading functional groups'
or 'élites of the society of orders', participated in power relationships;
and their studies do not take sufficient account of processes of
interaction between these local units and the central government. A
study of the office of constable in sixteenth- and seventeenth-century
England provides evidence about the interrelationship between village
and state hierarchies of authority in one European country in the early
modern period, and thus sheds light on ongoing processes which
appear to be central to an understanding of state-formation.

The approach and methods employed in this examination of the
constableship were determined in part by the character of the sources,
and the limitations which they impose. The study was also shaped by
general conceptions about the nature of the office which owe much to
anthropologists' studies of similar positions in non-Western societies,
though some medieval historians, as well as Keith Wrightson, have
viewed the office in rather similar terms.[33]

Basic materials for an investigation of the office of constable in the
late sixteenth and early seventeenth centuries are not very plentiful,
few constables' records of this period having survived. This study
began with villages and village records, and a number of communities
in several counties were selected for detailed consideration simply on
the basis of extant materials which shed light on the constableship.[34]
Many references will be found to Pattingham, Staffordshire; Branston,
Waltham, and Melton Mowbray, Leicestershire; Salwarpe and Stone,
Worcestershire; Bushey and Little Munden, Hertfordshire; and
Gissing, Norfolk. The officers of these nine settlements in five
counties provide the basis for a social profile of those who served as

---

[32] Zagorin, *Rebels and Rulers*, i. esp. pp. 85–6 and ch. 7. For more detailed
examination of 'village communities' during the early modern period see two articles by
Jerome Blum, 'The European Village as Community: Origins and Functions',
Agricultural History, xlv (1971), 157–78 and 'The Internal Structure and Polity of the
European Village Community from the Fifteenth to the Nineteenth Century', *Journal of
Modern History*, xliii (1971), 541–76; and the discussion of French 'territorial
communities' in Roland Mousnier, *The Institutions of France under the Absolute Monarchy
1598–1789: Society and the State*, trans. Brian Pearce (Chicago, 1979), i, ch. 12.
[33] See Helen M. Cam, *The Hundred and the Hundred Rolls* (New York, 1930), esp.
p. 193; Wrightson, 'Two concepts of order'; also see Holdsworth, *History of English Law*,
iv. 124. See below, n. 39 for the anthropological works.
[34] Although the term 'village' is employed throughout this study, one of the
settlements included, Melton Mowbray, Leicestershire, was a small market town.

constable. Other sections of the study make use of constables' records from other villages in the same counties: Gayton, Staffordshire; Wymeswold and Stathern, Leicestershire; Shelton, East Harling, Carleton Rode, and Stockton, Norfolk; and from some villages in other counties, Stockton, Salop; Millington, Yorkshire; Manchester, Lancashire; West Monkton and Cheddar, Somerset; and Great Easton, Essex. The Midlands are certainly best represented, and the Home Counties in particular inadequately covered, especially since the materials for the Hertfordshire villages do not include any constables' accounts.

Local sources relating directly to the constable's office include court leet rolls, town books which record the selection of such officers, and sometimes summary accounts, precepts, and receipts, rating lists which constables compiled for the collection of various local levies and their accounts, as well as the presentments which they made to quarter sessions. Such materials are very uneven in quantity and quality and not all of these records exist for each community considered here. Constables' accounts, which are the single most important source, vary considerably in their character and completeness. Some consist of rather brief entries, while others are very detailed in nature and the accounts for a single year sometimes occupy several closely written pages. Only scattered accounts, on loose sheets of paper, survive for some villages; those for Gissing, East Harling, Carleton Rode, Salwarpe, and Melton are of this type.[35] Such records are more likely to be extant for an extended period of time if they were entered in a book, as was the case, for example, in Pattingham, Branston, Waltham, Wymeswold, Manchester, Shelton, and Stockton, Salop. Accounts for these villages survive for a number of years during the early seventeenth century, and in the case of Pattingham almost continuously from 1582 to 1640.[36]

Other kinds of local sources were employed in the study of the social characteristics of constables. Parish registers or Bishop's Transcripts

[35] See NNRO, PD 50/36L (Gissing); PD 219/126 (East Harling); PD 254/63, 112 (Carleton Rode); HWRO, 850 SALWARPE, BA 1054/2, Bundle D; Leics. RO, DG 36/186–9; DG 25/39/1/1–4.

[36] The Pattingham accounts are contained in a volume with those of the churchwardens, and are found in the parish church; they will be referred to simply as Pattingham Constables' Accounts. For the other accounts see Leics. RO, DE 720/30 (Branston); DE 625/60 (Waltham); BL Add. MS 10457 (Wymeswold); J. P. Earwaker, ed., *The Constables' Accounts of the Manor of Manchester* (Manchester, 1892), i and ii; NNRO, PD 358/33 (Shelton); Salop RO, 3067/3/1 (Stockton).

of the registers were used to identify the men who served as constable
and for some elementary family reconstitution. Wills and inventories
provide information on the economic position and social status of
those who held the office. Local rating lists, as well as the subsidy rolls,
also shed light on the relative wealth of constables. Lists or accounts of
churchwardens, overseers, and surveyors, and sometimes other
officers of the manor or parish, provide information about constables'
experience in other local offices. Many of these same materials, and
particularly wills and inventories, local rating lists, and Bishop's
Transcripts, which usually were signed by the churchwardens, were
used as a source of information on the literacy of constables. The court
rolls of the manor of Pattingham form the basis for a study of the
obedience to the law of the men chosen as constable in that village.

An examination of court records was confined largely to the five
counties in which the sample villages are located, although some
materials from other shires have been included. Sessions records are
not extant for Leicestershire for the period under consideration, and it
was not possible to examine systematically all the manuscript
sessions materials for the other four counties. For these reasons
printed sessions records from additional counties were employed in
considering some questions, such as the selection of constables and
their performance of some of their duties.[37] The printed assize records
for all the Home Counties, and not just Hertfordshire, were used in

[37] Many of the Norfolk quarter sessions records for the 1630s were unavailable
because they required repairs; and for some years the surviving materials consist entirely
or largely of recognizances, which were not examined. The following materials were
consulted: NNRO, Sessions Records, Boxes 10 (beginning in 1587–8), 11, 12, 12A,
13A, 14, 16, 17 pts. i and ii, 18–23, 24, pts. i and ii, 25, 27 (1629–30), 31, and 31A
(1636–7). The printed sessions rolls for Staffordshire were employed for the period
1586–1608, S. A. H. Burne, ed., *The Staffordshire Quarter Sessions Roll for 1586*
(Staffordshire Historical Collections, 1927); S. A. H. Burne, ed., *Staffordshire Quarter
Sessions Rolls*, vols. i–v (Staffordshire Historical Collections, 1929–40); D. H. G. Salt,
ed., *Staffordshire Quarter Sessions Rolls, Easter 1608 to Trinity 1609* (Staffordshire
Historical Collections, 1948–9). Transcripts of the rolls, found in Staffs. RO, were used
for the period 7 Jac I (Roll 16) to 9 Car. I (Roll 34); due to the kindness of the archivist,
Mr F. B. Stitt, I was permitted to make use of these materials outside the regular hours
of the record office. The original Staffordshire Quarter Sessions Order Books, vol. ii–v,
were examined. In the case of Worcestershire only the printed calendar to the sessions
records has been used, J. Willis Bund, ed., *Calendar of Quarter Sessions Papers
1591–1643* (Worcestershire Historical Society, 1900). The Hertfordshire sessions
order books were used, Herts. RO, QS/B, 2A and 2B, as well as the printed materials in
W. J. Hardy, ed., *Notes and Extracts from the Sessions Rolls, 1581 to 1689* (Hertford County
Records, i, 1905), and William Le Hardy, ed., *Calendar to the Sessions Books and Sessions
Minute Books 1619–57* (Hertford County Records, v, 1928). Printed sessions records
from other counties will be cited in the course of the study.

examining the kinds of legal suits brought against constables. There are also some references to Exchequer suits which involved constables from other counties. The Star Chamber records for the Jacobean period, which are so accessible due to the quality of the manuscript index and a more recent computerized one,[38] were searched for all cases in which constables were primary plaintiffs or defendants. An investigation of the State Papers, which contain orders from the central government affecting constables, reports from higher officials about the conduct of such officers, and some presentments which constables made to monthly meetings in the 1630s, were confined largely to materials relating to the five counties. However, some other records which shed particular light on the activities of constables were utilized.

The sources are problematic, and they do not lend themselves to precise statistical analysis. Wherever possible arguments are supported with figures, though the extent to which they provide an accurate measure remains doubtful owing to the incompleteness of the records from which they were compiled. In many cases illustration and example must serve, and questions can be raised as to how representative these are. It is hoped that evidence from court records and other sources, which cover entire counties, provides at least some counterbalance to the detailed information derived from the study of the constableship in particular communities. Deficiencies in the surviving evidence, and the fact that it will never be possible to investigate the qualities and performance of more than a small proportion of constables, preclude any absolute conclusions about such officials. Perhaps the examination of officers in other villages in other counties will modify the picture presented here.

In considering a local office such as the constableship much can be learned from the work of anthropologists on 'village headmen' in non-Western societies, particularly from their discussion of the role of such officers after they were made agents of colonial powers. English villages of the seventeenth century were in some respects rather different from local communities in British Africa in the late nineteenth and early twentieth centuries; and the effects on local officers of the expansion of royal government in medieval and early modern England were not strictly comparable to those resulting from the penetration of imperial government into previously autonomous

---

[38] The detailed manuscript index is found in the PRO, and the computerized index, in 3 vols., was prepared by T. G. Barnes, *List and Index to the Proceedings in Star Chamber for the Reign of James I*, American Bar Foundation (Chicago, 1975).

African villages. None the less, there are structural similarities in the positions of constable and headman, due to the fact that they both were in origin local officers who subsequently were made agents of the state as well. Such positions thus came to interlink two distinct hierarchies of authority; and, as a result, such officers had dual obligations and there were dual sanctions on them.[39]

In order to appreciate the 'interhierarchical'[40] nature of the position occupied by constables under Elizabeth and the early Stuarts, it is necessary to consider briefly the origins of the constableship and its development during the Middle Ages. Although the petty constable was the oldest of the royal officials at the village level, the office was originally a local one and it continued to be shaped by its local roots long after constables had become agents of the state.

The precise origins and sources of constables' powers are somewhat obscure, but their initial authority appears to have derived from the fact that they were chiefs and representatives of local bodies. Authorities on the office in the sixteenth and seventeenth centuries claimed that the word 'constable' was Saxon in origin and that such a title had been held first by the Constable of England.[41] However, they

[39] The approach to the constableship adopted here has been influenced by anthropological studies of headmen, especially in central and southern Africa, and particularly by the work of Max Gluckman. See Max Gluckman, 'Interhierarchical Roles: Professional and Party Ethics in Tribal Areas of South and Central Africa', in Marc J. Swartz, ed., *Local-Level Politics* (Chicago, 1968), esp. pp. 70–2; Gluckman, *Custom and Conflict in Africa* (repr. Oxford, 1970), esp. pp. 34–7, 51–2; Gluckman, *Politics, Law and Ritual in Tribal Society* (Oxford, 1965), pp. 165–6; J. A. Barnes, J. C. Mitchell, and Max Gluckman, 'The Village Headman in British Central Africa', in Gluckman, ed. *Order and Rebellion in Tribal Africa* (London, 1963), pp. 146–70. Similar approaches to such positions are found in J. A. Barnes, *Politics in a Changing Society* (repr. Manchester, 1967), and J. C. Mitchell, *The Yao Village* (Manchester, 1956). A somewhat different perspective on such positions is employed in Lloyd Fallers, 'The Predicament of a Modern African Chief: An Instance from Uganda', *American Anthropoligist*, lvii (1955), 290–302, and in his *Bantu Bureaucracy* (Cambridge, n.d.), esp. pp. 17–19, 141–3, 155–78. Yet another approach to such positions is found in Harriet J. Kupferer's study of Cree chiefs and New Guinea headmen, 'Impotency and Power: A Cross-Cultural Comparison of the Effects of Alien Rule', in Marc J. Swartz, Victor Turner, and Arthur Tuden, eds., *Political Anthropology* (Chicago, 1966), pp.61–71. Also see the brief discussion of 'village headmen' in various parts of Europe, including England, in Blum, 'The Internal Structure and Polity of the European Village Community', 556–62, 568–9.

[40] See Gluckman, 'Interhierarchical Roles', pp. 70–2.

[41] William Lambard, *The Dueties of Constables, Borsholders, Tythingmen, and such other lowe and lay Ministers of the Peace* (London, 1599), pp. 4–5; William Sheppard, *The Offices and Duties of Constables, Borsholders, Tythingmen, Treasurers of the County-Stock, Overseers of the Poore and other Lay-Ministers* (London, 1641), pp. 9–11; R[obert] G[ardiner], *The*

traced the petty constable's powers, as opposed to his title, to the police duties for which the medieval vill or tithing had been responsible.[42] In the early Middle Ages a man elected by the township or tithing, whether he was called tithingman or borsholder or headborough or reeve, led a delegation of four able inhabitants which represented these local communities and was answerable for their police duties at the hundred court, and particularly at the sheriff's biannual tourn. In this office lay the origins of the constableship.[43] The representative functions of such officials probably extended to matters other than law enforcement, on which the township was consulted by or accountable to higher authorities. The reeve, or in some areas the tithingman, seems to have been a kind of village headman, a leader of the township who enjoyed various responsibilities within its bounds, often of an agrarian nature, and who acted as its agent in its dealings with outsiders.[44]

During the course of the Middle Ages these local officials, whose original powers derived from the fact that they were the elected representatives of local communities, also became agents of the central government and often known as constables. Sixteenth- and seventeenth-century writers were not agreed as to whether the constableship had developed directly from these ancient offices or whether a new position had been created and added to the old during the course of the Middle Ages. Some claimed that many of these officers continued to be known by their ancient titles and enjoyed only the powers of the 'old office', while others had acquired additional powers, 'a second office', and sometimes a new title, 'constable'. They dated this 'latter made office' from the reign of Edward III, and suggested that just as constables of the hundred had been created in the reign of Edward I as assistants to

---

Compleat Constable, 2nd edn. (London, 1700), pp. 1–2; Michael Dalton, *The Countrey Justice* (London, 1635), p. 46.

[42] Lambard, *Dueties of Constables*, pp. 6–9; Sheppard, *Offices and Duties of Constables*, pp. 11–12, 28–32; E. W., *The Exact Constable: with his Original and Power in the Offices of Church wardens, Overseers of the Poor, Surveyors of the Highwayes, Treasurers of the County Stock, and other inferior officers as they are established, both by the Common Laws and Statutes of this Realm*, 2nd edn. (London, 1660), pp. 3–6; R. G., *Compleat Constable*, pp. 2–4, 15.

[43] F. W.. Maitland, *The Constitutional History of England* (Cambridge, 1961), pp. 47–52; Cam, *The Hundred and the Hundred Rolls*, pp. 19, 119–20, 126, 176, 184, 189–90, 192–3; George C. Homans, *English Villagers in the Thirteenth Century* (New York, 1970), pp. 297–305, 324–6, 333–7; Helen Jewell, *English Local Administration in the Middle Ages* (New York, 1972), pp. 60–1, 129–33, 158–69. Also see Simpson, 'Office of Constable', pp. 625–36.

[44] Homans, *English Villagers*, pp. 300–1, 325, 333–6.

the Constable of England, so petty constables had been created at a later date to aid the constable of the hundred.[45] However, other seventeenth-century commentators did not accept that a new office had been created during the reign of Edward III. They claimed that the constable's authority derived from 'the ancient common laws and customs of this kingdom practiced long before the conquest'. The legislation of Edward III's reign, which some interpreted as creating a new office with new authority, they regarded as but 'a recitall of the ancient common lawes', as confirming powers which such officers already enjoyed.[46] Although some local headmen did receive a new title, the government does not seem to have created a new office. Rather it took over an existing official and gave him royal duties, while leaving him with his original powers and functions as the leader and representative of the township.

The title 'constable' seems to have been military in origin. It probably was as a result of new military functions conferred on local officials by the state during the thirteenth century that some village headmen were first called constables. During the reign of King John officials of the hundred who already had obligations for peacekeeping were given responsibilities for mustering the armed men within their jurisdictions; and they were called constables and, by the reign of Edward I, high constables. In Henry III's reign villages too apparently were required to have one or two officials, also called constables, who were to have the duty of assembling the local militia for the inspection of arms. This task seems to have fallen to the elected officials who already represented the township in police matters. It was thus in connection with communal military obligations that the representatives of townships and tithings were first formally considered agents of the central government.[47]

During the fourteenth century village chiefs, by whatever name,

[45] Lambard, *Dueties of Constables*, pp. 9–10; Sheppard, *Offices and Duties of Constables*, p. 28; E. W., *Exact Constable*, p. 5; R. G., *Compleat Constable*, p. 15; Vincent Prince, *The Constables Calendar: or An Almanack for the year of our Lord God, 1660* (London, 1660), sig. B3.

[46] Edward Coke, *The Fourth Part of the Institutes of the Laws of England* (London, 1671), p. 265; Dalton, *Countrey Justice*, p. 47; Francis Bacon, 'The Answers to Questions Touching the Office of Constable' (1608), in J. Spedding *et al.*, eds., *The Works of Francis Bacon*, vii (London, 1859), p. 749, R. G., *Compleat Constable*, pp. 2–3, cites both arguments about the constable's origins.

[47] Cam, *The Hundred and the Hundred Rolls*, pp. 86, 189–92; Maitland, *Constitutional History*, p. 276; Simpson, 'Office of Constable', pp. 630–1, 632–3; 13 Ed. I (Statute of Winchester).

were also recognized as having obligations to the state as well as to the township in police matters. Legislation of Edward III's reign, viewed by some seventeenth-century writers as creating the office of constable, appears to have formalized their responsibilities for peacekeeping and to have subordinated them to the crown. An act of 1328 specifically empowered borough-holders and constables to enforce its provisions against affrays and those riding armed, while the Statute of Westminster in 1330 referred jointly to 'constables and townships' as those responsible for apprehending thieves and turning them over to sheriffs or gaolers. An act of the following year, which extended the provisions of the Statute of Winchester, made constables responsible for apprehending and delivering to the sheriff any suspicious persons appearing in their townships. Whereas the vill or tithing collectively had been responsible for police duties, and the constable or tithingman or borsholder had acted merely as its agent, the Edwardian legislation recognized the constable as well as the township as having obligations to the state for keeping the peace. Such officials thus became police officers of the crown.[48]

Constables' duties during the Middle Ages were not, however, to be confined to the traditional police functions which had rested with the vill, nor to responsibilities in connection with the township's provision of soldiers and arms. During the course of the fourteenth and fifteenth centuries the royal duties of such officers were expanded by two means. Just as statutes of Edward III's reign formalized their responsibilities in matters of law enforcement, so other statutes further amplified the office. Secondly, their duties were enlarged as a result of their general subordination to higher officials of the crown and their obligations to execute the commands of such officers.

Additional duties in the area of law enforcement were conferred on constables by economic and social legislation of the fourteenth and fifteenth centuries. An act of Henry VI's reign made them responsible for the standard weights and measures which every township containing a constable was required to possess. They were also charged with enforcing statutory provisions regulating servants and labourers, being required to apprehend any who defied stipulations concerning wages and conditions of labour and to certify such offences to the justices of the peace. Other medieval statutes which forbade servants from playing certain sports and games, and at the same time

---

[48] 2 Ed. III, c. 3; 4 Ed. III, c. 10; 5 Ed. III, c. 14; also see Simpson, 'Office of Constable', pp. 633–4.

ordered them to engage in archery practice, made constables responsible for the enforcement of such provisions.[49]

Acts of Parliament also gave constables duties in connection with taxation, although in some cases this legislation perhaps merely confirmed powers which they had long enjoyed as representatives of the township. The functions accorded them by several fourteenth- and fifteenth-century acts on purveyance were in part those of a policeman, but they were also recognized as agents of the local community, charged with protecting its rights and interests. Statutes of Edward III's reign empowered the constable and four discreet men of each township to appraise the true value of commodities taken by purveyors and ordered that the agreement between the owner and the purveyor be concluded, and the tallies sealed, in the presence of the constable. An act of Henry VI's reign extended such powers in instances when purveyance involved the taking of carts and horses. The taker was required to procure the constable's consent (or that of the mayor, sheriff, or bailiff) and to secure the delivery of the cart or horse from him, as well as having the permission of the owner. It was both as representative of the local community and as the state's policeman that constables were given duties in connection with purveyance by another act of Henry VI. This statute, which authorized owners to resist the demands of purveyors in instances when they refused to make ready payment for goods under 40s. in value, ordered 'every constable, tythingman or chief pledge of every town or hamlet' to aid the owners in such resistance 'for the peace better to be kept'.[50] Constables also had responsibilities in connection with the levying of fifteenths which, as in the case of purveyance, seem to have derived from their position as the chief of the township. As late as Henry VII's reign acts granting fifteenths reveal constables acting only as agents of local communities and not of the state. They apparently were responsible for protecting the interests of the township and complaining of any wrongs committed by the collectors, and the acts ordered that their complaints be heard and determined by the justices of the peace.[51] However, the beginning of a significant change in constables' responsibilities for tax collecting seems to have occurred during the course of Henry VII's

[49] 8 H. VI, c. 5, 11 H. VII, c. 4; 23 Ed. III, c. 1, 25 Ed. III, c. 1, 25 Ed. III, Stat. 2, cc. 2, 5; 12 R. II, c. 6, 11 H. IV, c. 4.

[50] 4 Ed. III, cc. 3, 4; 5 Ed. III, c. 2; 10 Ed. III, Stat. 2, c. 1; 25 Ed. III, Stat. 5, c. 1; 36 Ed. III, c. 2; 28 H. VI, c. 2; 20 H. VI, c. 8.

[51] e.g. 7 H. VII, c. 11; 12 H. VII, c. 12; 3 H. VIII, c. 3; 4 H. VIII, c. 19.

reign. They were ordered to 'favour, helpe and assiste' the collectors within their townships, and thus they were obliged to serve the central government as well as the local community.[52]

Constables' duties during the Middle Ages were also enlarged as a result of their obligations to execute the commands of higher officials, the sheriff, the coroner, and especially the justices of the peace. It is not clear when constables first were expected to act as servants of the justices. However, an act of 1485 recognized such a duty when it made them the justices' agents in implementing provisions against unlawful hunting, and probably their functions under the Statute of Labourers had been similar in nature.[53] When an act of 1536 created justices in Wales it specifically stated that both high constables and petty constables were to be attendant on them, and no doubt this was already established practice in England.[54] By the seventeenth century some of the authors of handbooks on the office suggested that constables' police powers had been transformed by the creation of the justices of the peace. They argued that the authority of constables was now derived largely from the precepts and warrants of the justices rather than from their own original powers as 'conservators of the peace'. William Sheppard in his handbook on the constableship claimed that at one time 'the constables of every village had a kinde of rule within the same village and were to keep the peace there; and therefore the constable was called ruler of the village'. However, he believed that their 'primitive' and independent powers had largely disappeared when they became subservient to the justices in their peacekeeping duties.[55] Although constables could still act on their own authority in preserving the peace, even after the creation of the justices, many of their duties in law enforcement did come to derive from the commands of others, and especially the justices. However, their obligations to execute the warrants and precepts of these and other higher officials increased rather than diminished their police duties. In the sixteenth century such subordination to the crown's officials was also to add to their military functions and to their responsibilities in the area of taxation.[56]

The source of constables' authority was thus twofold. Such officers

---

[52] 12 H. VII, c. 13, #VIII; 19 H. VII, c. 32, #VIII.   [53] 1 H. VII, c. 7.
[54] 27 H. VIII, c. 5; also see Simpson, 'Office of Constable', p. 635.
[55] Sheppard, *Offices and Duties of Constables*, pp. 26–7, 63–4 also see E. W., *Exact Constable*, pp. 15–19; R. G. *Compleat Constable*, p. 18; Dalton, *Countrey Justice*, pp. 3–5.
[56] See below, ch. 2.

enjoyed certain powers derived from ancient custom and rooted in
their original position as leaders and representatives of local communities;
and some of these powers were recognized at law during the course of
the Middle Ages. Other duties were conferred on them by the state,
either directly by statute or indirectly by virtue of their being made
agents of the Crown's ministers.

The fact that constables became royal officials did not, however,
mean that the local origins of their position were completely
overshadowed by their new duties to the state. Constables continued to
have responsibilities to represent the township, even while they
acquired obligations to serve the central government. Moreover, at
least some of them retained purely local functions as 'village
headmen'.[57]

Nor did the fact that such village officers had become royal officials
result in uniformity in their titles or in the number of officers in a
township, and these matters continued to be determined by local
custom. In some areas, such as the west of England, where the tithing
rather than the vill had been the original police unit, local officers who
enjoyed the same duties as constables continued to be known as
tithingmen. In Kent, where the early peacekeeping divisions were
known as borshes, local officers retained the title of borsholder.
Normally there were either one or two such officers, whatever their
titles, within a township. However, in instances when the chief officials
did become known as constables there sometimes were others who
bore such ancient titles as tithingman, headborough, or thirdborough
who acted as their assistants and who were inferior to them in
authority. There was thus very considerable local diversity. While
some townships possessed a single constable or tithingman or
borsholder, others contained two chief officers, and yet others were
also served by lesser officials with various titles.[58]

The term of office too was a matter of custom, though subject to less
variation than the number and title of such officers. The constableship
was most often an annual position, and officers usually chosen at either
Michaelmas or Easter, though occasionally they seem to have been
selected at the beginning of January. However, in some villages the

[57] This was true even in the seventeenth century; see below, ch. 2.

[58] The diversity of arrangements in different parts of the country is reflected in the
records of local officials and in quarter sessions materials, and is also discussed by the
authors of handbooks; see Lambard, *Dueties of Constables*, pp. 4, 7–10; Sheppard,
Offices and Duties of Constables, pp. 11–13; E. W., *Exact Constable*, p. 4; R.G., *Compleat
Constable*, pp. 4–5. Also see Simpson, 'Office of Constable', pp. 631–2.

office was held for two years; and in these cases officers sometimes served staggered terms, with one new constable being chosen each year.[59]

The selection of constables was also governed by local custom, and the fact that they had become royal officials in most cases did not alter the method of their appointment. Originally elected by the inhabitants of the vill or tithing, such officers continued to be selected by local bodies rather than by the state or by their administrative superiors. They were thus formally accountable to the township as well as to higher authorities.[60]

The origins of the constableship and the course of its development prior to the sixteenth and seventeenth centuries thus resulted in its being a dual position, such officers having obligations both to the state and to the local community. Like village headmen in non-Western societies who were made agents of colonial powers in the nineteenth and twentieth centuries, constables too enjoyed an 'interhierarchical' role, and were required to function in two different capacities.[61] On the one hand, as the lowest officer in a hierarchy of authority which stretched from the monarchy to the village, they were bound to serve the king and higher officials of the Crown. On the other hand, they also had obligations to the local community and were required to represent its interests to the state; they were still agents of the township in its dealings with the Crown's officials. There were thus dual sanctions on them, and if villagers' interests clashed with those of the state the constableship would become a focus of conflict.

Historians have drawn attention to the growing penetration of the state into the provinces in late sixteenth- and early seventeenth-century England, and some have suggested that local communities were more fully integrated into a national structure during that period. In part this is ascribed to the growing administrative pressures which the central government exerted in the localities. Keith Wrightson also attributes the state's success in expanding its control over local

---

[59] Constables' accounts reveal variations in the term of office and the authors of handbooks also indicated that the term was a matter of custom; see E. W., *Exact Constable*, p. 7; Sheppard, *Offices and Duties of Constables*, p. 14. Constables of Gissing, Norfolk, and Little Munden, Hertfordshire, at some periods served staggered two-year terms; see NNRO, PD 50/36L and Herts. RO, D/P71/5/1, from which lists of constables were compiled.

[60] See below, ch. 3.

[61] See esp. Gluckman, 'Interhierarchical Roles', and Barnes, Mitchell, and Gluckman, 'The Village Headman', pp. 151–2.

government to economic and social changes within local communities. He argues that the wealth, interests, and values of the 'local notables' who held parish offices distanced them from their poorer neighbours, and that they became 'willing auxiliaries of the magistrates and ministers' in the enforcement of many of the government's policies.[62] There is evidence that constables experienced increasing demands and pressures from above, a fact reflected in the expansion of their duties and in the growing number of occasions on which they were formally accountable to higher authorities for the fulfilment of their responsibilities. The extent of the government's supervision of such officers, particularly in some counties and during certain periods, probably did have an impact on their performance. It will be shown that the village notables who served as constable often co-operated with the central government, and possibly some of them did so because they identified with the interests of the state and its representatives.

However, evidence from a number of counties would suggest that the constable's position remained an 'interhierarchical' or 'mediating' one even during the early seventeenth century. Such officers continued to act as representatives of local communities as well as agents of the central government, and they were subjected to local pressures which sometimes conflicted with those exerted by the state and their superiors. As village communities increasingly felt the weight of central authority, there was a greater probability of conflict between local customs and interests and the state's demands, and constables were more likely to experience incompatible pressures. Although they often co-operated in implementing policies imposed from above, their actions sometimes continued to be affected by local pressures and local loyalties. Moreover, despite the state's increasing control over the localities, it will be shown that in most cases this did not extend to the appointment of constables. Not only were they local men, but even in the early seventeenth century they usually continued to be chosen for office by their fellow villagers. This fact too made them subject to local influences. In addition, a certain informality of arrangements continued to characterize local government at the level of the township or parish. Constables in many instances were still 'village headmen' who were dependent upon the assistance of other inhabitants if they were to fulfil the demands which the state placed upon local communities. In short,

[62] Wrightson, 'Two concepts of order', pp. 32–3, 35–46; and his *English Society*, esp. pp. 149–73, 222–8.

it will be argued that the constableship in the late Tudor and early Stuart period continued to be rooted in local custom as well as being part of a national structure of authority, and that the actions of such officers were often shaped by the duality of the position.

2

Powers and Duties of the Office: The Functions of Constables, 1580–1642

HISTORIANS have recognized that constables were major local officials during the Middle Ages, but suggest that their importance declined during the sixteenth and seventeenth centuries. Some contend that by 1600 the churchwardens had replaced them as the primary local officers, and that the creation of surveyors of the highways and overseers of the poor also detracted from their former dominance.[1] These parish officials did perform tasks which might in an earlier period have fallen to constables, and in other cases they were made joint or alternate authorities with them. However, it will be argued that constables remained the most important local officers throughout the late sixteenth and early seventeenth centuries.

Despite the duties acquired by the new officials of the parish, the functions of constables also increased very markedly during this period. They retained many of the original police functions which they had performed as leaders of the township, but at the same time they acquired many new regulatory duties as a result of the social and economic legislation enacted under the Tudors and the early Stuarts. They also received additional police responsibilities because they were servants to the justices and because of administrative changes of the seventeenth century which brought them under more regular supervision by these officials. Like their medieval predecessors, constables of early modern England had duties in connection with the communal armour and common soldiers, but in military matters they also became the agents of the Lords Lieutenant and their deputies and responsible for the impressment of soldiers as well as for attendance upon the militia. Furthermore, constables acquired new responsibilities for the assessment and collection of a wide variety of taxes and rates. At the same

[1] See esp. the Webbs, *The Parish and the County*, pp. 18–19 and n. 3, 20, 25–6; and for other suggestions that constables were not as important by the end of the sixteenth century as they once had been, see Cheyney, *History of England*, ii. 403; Critchley, *History of Police*, p. 10; Simpson, 'Office of Constable', p. 638.

time that their royal duties increased very substantially, they also
retained their obligations, as leaders of the township, to represent the
local community to higher authorities. Moreover, some of them
continued to have various functions of a purely local character. A
detailed examination of constables' duties, which will draw attention to
a few local variations in their tasks as well as to the growing number of
responsibilities which fell to all constables, will suggest the continuing
importance of the constableship during the late sixteenth and early
seventeenth centuries and the extent to which it remained the chief
link between the central government and local communities. A
consideration of the increasing demands which the state made of such
officers during this period also reveals how burdensome the position
could be.

I. LAW ENFORCEMENT AND ADMINISTRATIVE DUTIES

In their partial inheritance of the police duties of the vill or tithing
constables had acquired wide-ranging responsibilities for law enforcement. As conservators of the peace it was their duty to prevent and
suppress breaches of the peace such as affrays and riots, and also to
apprehend offenders who had committed more serious criminal
offences categorized as felonies. In such cases they could act on their
own authority, without any command from others. They were
responsible too for setting watch and ward for the apprehension of
suspicious persons, for sending out hues and cries after offenders, and
for seizing the goods of suspected felons who had fled, and keeping
them safe. On their own authority they could also conduct searches for
felons or for stolen goods; and in these cases, as well as in pursuit of an
'affrayor' or to pacify an affray, they could break down the doors of a
house to gain admittance if this proved necessary. Constables had
responsibility too for the maintenance of such local instruments of
justice as the stocks, the cage, the pillory, the whipping-post, and the
cuckstool.[2]

There was little change in these traditional responsibilities during
the late sixteenth and early seventeenth centuries; but in police matters
constables were also very much the servants of higher officials, and

[2] See the following for a discussion of the peacekeeping duties which constables were
expected to perform on their own authority, without command from others: Lambard,
Dueties of Constables, pp. 11–18; Bacon, 'Office of Constable', pp. 751–3; Sheppard,
Offices and Duties of Constables, pp. 33–63; E. W., *Exact Constable*, pp. 15–25; R. G.,
Compleat Constable, pp. 15–20.

particularly the justices of the peace. Although they could make arrests on their own authority, warrants from the justices also obliged them to apprehend offenders and to bring them before higher authorities and in some cases to convey them to gaol. Precepts from the justices sometimes instructed constables to inflict punishment on minor offenders. Their responsibilities at common law for setting watch and ward were also supplemented by directives from above which ordered special watches or directed that the watch be doubled or sometimes merely reminded them of their traditional duties in this area.[3] Constables were also subject to the commands of coroners, summoned to attend their hearings, and sometimes required to assure the appearance of a villager or two to serve on coroners' juries.[4]

Although constables had in a sense become accountable to higher authorities for police duties which had once been attached to the vill or tithing,[5] the township still shared in such obligations and many traces of collective responsibilities survived from the Middle Ages. Even in the early seventeenth century constables were still in many ways merely 'headmen' of local communities in police matters, and other inhabitants were required to assist them in their duties. They were supposed to keep watch and ward and to pursue hue and cry, and if a thief was not apprehended the villages in each hundred were collectively accountable for compensating the victim just as they had been since the enactment of the statute of Winchester in 1285.[6] Although constables were responsible for assuring that the stocks and other instruments of punishment were kept in repair, they did so as village agents and the

---

[3] The discussion of the peacekeeping duties which constables fulfilled at the behest of higher officials is based on evidence in quarter sessions materials and constables' accounts, as well as on the discussions by authors of handbooks. Numerous references could be given to sessions materials, but see for example, Bund, ed., *Sessions Papers*, pp. 103, 156, 185, 313, 334, 347, 363, 365, 366, 580, 638, 651; Staffs. RO, QS/O, iv. 71ᵛ, 106; Transcripts Sessions Rolls, Jac I, Roll 27, no. 14; Roll 64, no. 56; and precepts in Norfolk sessions materials, for example NNRO, Sessions Records, Box 27, which contains a number of such items. For orders from the justices for keeping watch and ward see, for example, Staffs. RO, QS/O, ii. 68; iii. 19ᵛ, 124, 125, 143ᵛ, 149, 165; v. 47; HWRO, 850 SALWARPE, BA 1054/1, Bundle A, nos. 9, 110, 138, 158, 169, 176, 180, 283. Many orders concerning watches are found in other sessions records as well. For the handbooks see Lambard, *Dueties of Constables*, pp. 18–23; Sheppard, *Offices and Duties of Constables*, pp. 63–80; E. W., *Exact Constable*, pp. 25–7; R. G., *Compleat Constable*, pp. 61–7; Price, *Constables Calendar*, sig. B4ᵛ–5.

[4] See, for example, HWRO, 850 SALWARPE, BA 1054/2, Bundle D, no. 8; Leics. RO, DE 625/60, fo. 6; DE 720/30, fo. 17; Pattingham Constables' Accounts, 1622–3, 1637–8 (2), 1639–40; Borthwick Institute, PR MIL. 10, 1637; Salop RO, 3067/3/1, p. 47.   [5] See above ch. 1, n. 48.

[6] This provision was reconfirmed in an act of 1584, 27 Eliz. I, c. 13.

whole community was likely to bear the fine if they were found in decay.[7] Constables could also call upon their fellow inhabitants to assist them in serving warrants, making arrests, guarding prisoners, and conveying them before a justice or to gaol. Those who refused to aid them could be fined or imprisoned.[8] Village recognition of such collective duties sometimes was reflected in local by-laws. For example, the jury in the manor of Manchester in 1596 directed every inhabitant of the township to be ready 'at the constables commandemente' to aid them in the crown's service 'either daye or nighte'; while the manorial court in Pattingham in 1605 ordered every household to have a 'sufficient club' for the purpose of assisting the constables in their police duties.[9] Although constables were 'king's men' in local communities and held accountable for enforcing the peace, the responsibility thus did not rest exclusively with such officers. If they were to fulfil their duties properly they needed to procure assistance from their fellow inhabitants.

It has been noted that social and economic regulations enacted during the fourteenth and fifteenth centuries augmented constables' traditional peacekeeping duties, and a number of these tasks continued to fall to them under the Tudors and Stuarts. Medieval legislation had made them responsible for assuring that the township possessed standard weights and measures;[10] and during the sixteenth and seventeenth centuries it was their duty to appear annually before the clerk of the market to have these weights and measures inspected.[11] Constables' obligations during the Middle Ages to enforce laws concerning servants and labourers were continued by the Elizabethan statute of artificers. This act empowered them to compel artificers to engage in agricultural work at harvest time. It also required them,

---

[7] Constables' accounts contain numerous entries for the repair of such facilities; see below, ch. 6 n. 83. For an example of a fine being imposed on a constable when, at the command of neighbours, he had not repaired the stocks, see Burne, ed., *Sessions Rolls*, ii. 296, 339.

[8] The authors of handbooks of the constableship all drew attention to this fact; see Lambard, *Dueties of Constables*, p. 12; Bacon, 'Office of Constable', p. 751; Sheppard, *Offices and Duties of Constables*, pp. 165–6; E. W., *Exact Constable*, p. 25; R. G., *Compleat Constable*, p. 16.

[9] J. P. Earwaker, ed., *The Court Leet Records of the Manor of Manchester* (Manchester, 1884–6), ii. 119; Staffs. RO, Pattingham Court Rolls, D 1807/178.

[10] See above, ch. 1, n. 49.

[11] Entries concerning appearances before the clerk of the market occur regularly in constables' accounts; see below, ch. 6, nn. 2–3. For example of precepts ordering constables to appear before the clerk and to bring in all those using weights and measures see HWRO, 850 SALWARPE, BA 1054/1, Bundle A, nos. 156, 159.

along with two other 'honest householders', to witness the testimonials of servants who were changing masters, and to assure that servants arriving in the village possessed testimonials.[12] Their earlier obligations to enforce legislation against games and sports which distracted men from archery practice were continued by an act of Henry VIII's reign 'for the maintenance of artillery and debarring unlawful games'. Throughout the late sixteenth and early seventeenth centuries constables continued to have responsibilities for searching out such forbidden games.[13] The duties they acquired during Henry VII's reign to act as the justices' agents in enforcing provisions against illegal hunting were continued by a Jacobean act on this matter. The statute empowered constables or headboroughs who possessed a warrant from two justices to enter and search the house of any person suspected of illegally possessing 'setting dogges or netts' for taking pheasants or partridge and to seize the same and keep them for their own use.[14]

However, in addition to these duties, many new regulatory responsibilities were conferred upon constables during the late sixteenth and early seventeenth centuries. They were made administrative agents of the justices in their supervision of certain occupations and trades, and servants of the justices, or sometimes the parish, in the enforcement of local obligations concerning the relief of the poor and the repair of highways. The creation of a number of new statutory misdemeanours during this period also added to their responsibilities. Both statutes and instructions from their superiors often brought them into association with the officers of the parish, and particularly the churchwardens, in the presentment of offenders and in the collection of fines from those who had committed misdemeanours.

Constables were made the administrative agents of higher officials in their oversight of servants and, during the early seventeenth century, of alehouse keepers and victuallers as well. In some counties, if not in all, orders from either the justices or the high constables obliged them to bring servants to annual or biannual sessions where the period of service could be extended for another year or the servant given a testimonial authorizing him to depart. On such occasions they also seem to have been required to submit lists of masters and servants and to report on the servants' wages.[15] In the early seventeenth century

[12] See above, ch. 1, n. 49 and 5 Eliz. I, c. 4.

[13] See above, ch. 1, n. 49 and 33 H. VIII, c. 9.

[14] See above, ch. 1 n. 53 and 7 Jac. I, c. 11.

[15] Constables' appearances before higher officials with servants are recorded in their accounts; see below, ch. 6 nn. 11–13. Also see a precept from the justices on this matter, NNRO PD 50/36L no. 21

constables also became the justices' agents in the licensing of alehouses. Not only were they, along with churchwardens and high constables, to inform the justices how many alehouses should be permitted in their communities and who was most suited to keep them, but in practice they became responsible for bringing all the ale-keepers within their jurisdictions to yearly meetings of the justices for relicensing and rebinding.[16] By the early seventeenth century victuallers and butchers were also required to appear annually before the justices to enter recognizances binding them not to dress or sell flesh during Lent, and constables were made responsible for assuring their attendance on such occasions.[17]

Constables also acquired administrative duties in connection with the parish's obligations for the repair of the highways and the relief of the poor, some of these responsibilities being conferred on them by statute and others by order of the justices. The sixteenth-century legislation which made the parish responsible for the repair of roads and created new officers, the surveyors, to oversee this work, gave to constables and churchwardens the duty to call the parishioners together yearly in Easter week for the purpose of choosing surveyors. They were also responsible for designating the days for common work on the roads.[18] Perhaps it was constables' functions under this legislation which suggested to the justices that they could also be employed to assure that overseers of the poor gave up their accounts and that new overseers were selected. Precepts required constables to

[16] Licensing had been regulated by 5 & 6 Ed. VI, c. 25 which required only an initial licence to be granted by two justices and which empowered them 'from tyme to tyme' to bind keepers to maintain good order in their houses. For the new regulations of 1607, some changes implemented by a proclamation of 1619, and other related documents see BL Cotton MS Titus B. III, ff. 2–21ᵛ. Also see a set of proposals for a new licensing system in BL Salisbury MS 142/189, M485/35; and additional materials on the licensing of inns and alehouses, particularly on the patents issued under James I, in W. Notestein, F. H. Relf, and H. Simpson, *The Commons Debates, 1621* (New Haven, 1935), vii. 311–22, 379–87, 553–6. Also see S. K. Roberts, 'Alehouses, brewing and government under the early Stuarts', *Southern History*, ii (1980), 45–71. Constables' accounts reflect their new duties in connection with alehouses; see below, ch. 6, nn. 6–8. For precepts from the justices ordering them to bring ale-keepers and their sureties before them for relicensing and rebinding see HWRO, 850 SALWARPE, BA 1054/1, Bundle A, nos. 11, 20, 76, 176, 272, BA 1054/2, Bundle H (one unnumbered item); NNRO, PD 50/36L, no. 57. Dalton, *Countrey Justice*, p. 360 contains a copy of a warrant for alehouse keepers to renew their recognizances.

[17] Entries concerning the appearance of victuallers and butchers before the justices occur in constables' accounts; see below, ch. 6, nn. 9–10. Also see precepts sent to constables, HWRO, 850 SALWARPE, BA 1054/1, Bundle A, nos. 9, 60, 64, 106, 285; NNRO, PD 50/36L, no. 64; and a warrant printed in Dalton, *Countrey Justice*, pp. 261–2.

[18] 2 & 3 P. & M., c. 8; 5 Eliz. I, c. 13; 18 Eliz. I. c. 10.

bring the churchwardens and overseers before the justices annually to render account, and warrants were directed to them for the selection of new overseers. Presumably it was their responsibility to make sure that the parishioners did meet in Easter week in accordance with the statutory provisions to choose such officers.[19] Although the church-wardens and overseers were primarily responsible for the actual administration of the Poor Law, an act of 1610 did give constables, along with churchwardens, overseers, and vicars, a role in the employment of charitable bequests for binding out poor apprentices.[20]

Legislation from the early sixteenth century onward had given constables responsibilities for the idle and wandering poor who fell within the vagrancy acts.[21] During the period under consideration several statutes defined their obligations and added to their duties. An act of 1576 required them to apprehend and deliver to the next constable all those idle wanderers defined as vagrants by an act of 1572, and such offenders were to be conveyed from officer to officer to the gaol or a House of Correction. A new act in 1598, which provided the basis for constables' authority throughout the early seventeenth century, extended their duties by altering the punishment that was to be meted out to vagrants. They were to be apprehended, whipped, and conveyed to the next constable, along with a pass directing them from officer to officer to their place of birth or last residence. Incorrigible rogues, and any whose place of birth or last residence could not be determined, were to be conveyed to the House of Correction or the common gaol, and this duty too fell to constables. Their responsibility for the apprehension of vagrants was extended by an act of 1610 which empowered the justices to order privy searches for rogues and idle persons twice a year, and which required constables to bring those arrested during the search before the justices.[22]

However, the duty of apprehending and punishing vagrants fell not only to constables. Just as their fellow inhabitants had responsibilities at common law to assist them in the arrest of other offenders, so they

---

[19] See precepts sent to constables, HWRO, BA 1054/1, Bundle A, nos. 11, 20, 76, 176; BA 1054/2, Bundle H (2 unnumbered items). NNRO, PD 50/36L, no. 57. Entries in constables' accounts also record their appearance before the justices with the churchwardens and overseers and their receipt of warrants for the selection of new overseers; see below, ch. 6, nn. 6–8.

[20] 7 Jac. I, c. 3.

[21] See 22 H. VIII, c. 12; 27 H. VIII, c. 25; 1 Ed. VI, c. 3; 3 & 4 Ed. VI, c. 16; 14 Eliz. I, c. 5 for earlier legislation on vagrancy.

[22] 18 Eliz. I, c. 3; 39 Eliz. I, c. 4; 7 Jac. I, c. 4.

were obliged by statute to aid constables in bringing vagrants to justice. An act of 1604 was most explicit in making it obligatory for all persons in the community to assist in the apprehension of rogues, and provided that anyone who neglected to arrest a wanderer and convey him to the nearest constable or tithingman was to be fined 10s. 'Sufficient men' of the village were also obliged to assist constables in the privy search for rogues. The passport or testimonial given to such offenders was to be signed not only by the constable but either by another officer (a justice, headborough, or tithingman) or by the minister of the parish, and the minister was to record the substance of the testimonial in a book to be provided for that purpose.[23]

Restrictions on travel during this period were not limited to the begging poor and others who fell within the vagrancy acts. There were attempts to prevent, or at least control, population mobility among the poorer sort by requiring passports for travel, and this provided further work for constables. Not only were they responsible for issuing and inspecting vagrants' passes, but it seems to have been their duty to police the whole 'passport system' through which the justices and other officials authorized travel. The diseased poor, who under the law of 1598 were required to have licences to travel to the baths, had to submit their documents to constables, who seem to have been obliged to convey such travellers to the next village just as they did in the case of vagrants. Seamen who had suffered shipwreck and maimed soldiers returning from the wars, whom the justices could authorize to travel to their own parishes and to seek relief during the journey, apparently were required to report to the constables of each village on the route to procure endorsement for their passes and the aid to which they were entitled. There were others on the roads for whose passes there was no specific statutory basis, and they too seem to have been obliged to present their credentials to constables as they passed from village to village, and in some cases such officers may have been required to aid and assist them. Constables' duties in such matters were nowhere clearly defined. However, in practice they apparently had a general responsibility for keeping an eye on strangers who entered the village, assuring that they had proper authorization to be on the roads, and apprehending them if they did not.[24]

[23] 14 Eliz. I, c. 5; 39 Eliz. I, c. 4; 1 Jac. I, c. 7; 7 Jac. I, c. 4.
[24] For passes granted to the disabled and to the shipwrecked and maimed soldiers see 39 Eliz. I, c. 3; 39 Eliz. I, c. 17. Constables' accounts are filled with entries concerning travellers of various sorts; see below, ch. 6. Dalton, *Countrey Justice* (1635 edn.),

Legislation was also directed against particular categories of idle and disorderly people, and in the implementation of these acts too constables had some responsibilities. Lewd and wandering persons who pretended to be soldiers and mariners were the subject of special legislation in 1598, and constables made responsible for conveying them to the next constable, with a pass directing them to their own parishes.[25] An act of 1601 'to prevent misdemeanours in lewd and idle people', which concerned petty offences such as 'unlawfull cuttynge or taking aways of corne and grayne growynge, robbynge of orchards or gardens, dygginge upp or takinge aways fruite trees, breakynge of hedges, poles or other fences, cuttynge or spoiling of woodes and underwoodes', conferred upon constables the duty to whip such offenders.[26] Constables were often responsible too for inflicting upon the parents of bastards the penalties meted out by the justices under the provisions of an act of 1576. It also fell to them to convey the mothers of bastards to the House of Correction after this punishment was established by an act of 1610.[27]

Early seventeenth-century laws regulating alehouse keepers and victuallers made constables, on direction from the justices, responsible for the enforcement of the penalties provided by these acts. A statute of 1604 empowered them, jointly with the churchwardens, to levy fines from keepers who broke the assize or allowed excess tippling in their houses. Further legislation in 1627 conferred on either constables or churchwardens the responsibility of inflicting penalities on those who operated alehouses without a licence. If the offender could not pay the fine, or possessed insufficient goods for it to be levied by distraint, the constable was to punish him by whipping. For second or further offences under the act, unlicensed keepers were to be committed to a House of Correction, and in practice constables rather than church-wardens probably were expected to impose that penalty.[28] During the early seventeenth century they also became responsible for enforcing regulations which prohibited victuallers from dressing and selling flesh during Lent. Constables were included in a list of officers who were

pp. 101–2, 124, 127, 380, discusses the supposed restrictions on the issuing of passes, and prints copies of such passes, pp. 380–1. The passport for travel included in *The Countrey Justice* (1618 edn.), p. 337, indicated that constables should aid and assist such travellers.

[25] 39 Eliz. I, c. 17.   [26] 43 Eliz. I, c. 7.

[27] 18 Eliz. I, c. 3; 7 Jac. I, c. 4; court records indicate that constables were made responsible for carrying out such punishments.

[28] 1 Jac. I, c. 9; 3 Car. I, c. 4.

empowered by an act of 1604 to enter victualling houses where they suspected offences against these provisions, and if they found any flesh killed or dressed they were to seize it and give it to 'prisoners and other poore folkes by theire discretion'.[29]

Statutes against drunkenness and swearing also made constables the agents of the justices in imposing penalties on such offenders. An act against drunkenness in 1607, reconfirmed in 1624, gave constables and churchwardens jointly the duty of levying the fines or carrying out the alternative penalty of imprisonment in the stocks.[30] A statute of 1624 against profane swearing and cursing empowered constables, along with churchwardens and overseers, to collect the shilling penalty, by distraint if this proved necessary. If the offender did not possess sufficient goods to cover the fine he was to be placed in the stocks, probably by the constable, who was also charged with administering punishment to those under twelve years of age who were to be whipped.[31]

Sabbatarian legislation passed during the reign of Charles I gave constables new duties in enforcing provisions against games and sports, and made them responsible for regulations against other kinds of activities on the Sabbath. An act of 1625 restricting sports on Sunday designated either constables or churchwardens as collectors of the fines from offenders and empowered them to distrain if necessary. Any who had insufficient goods to meet the fine were to be placed in the stocks for three hours, and the implementation of this penalty probably fell to constables rather than churchwardens. Further legislation in 1627 which prohibited travel on Sundays by itinerants such as carriers, waggoners, and drovers of cattle, and which forbade the sale of flesh by butchers, also conferred on either constables or churchwardens the duty to levy fines from offenders.[32]

Constables also acquired responsibilities for implementing provisions concerning public health when an act of 1604 empowered them to order those infected with plague to keep to their own houses;[33] and they had duties too for enforcing upon parishioners their obligations for repair of the highways. The Tudor acts which charged the parish with the upkeep of the roads not only made constables responsible for assuring that the parishioners assembled to select surveyors, but also required them to see that the inhabitants carried out the 'common

[29] 1 Jac. I, c. 29.
[30] 4 Jac. I, c. 5; 21 Jac. I, c. 7.
[31] 21 Jac. I, c. 20.
[32] 1 Car. I, c. 1; 3 Car. I, c. 2.
[33] 1 Jac. I, c. 31.

work' on the roads. The initial act, passed in Mary's reign, had
provided that constables and churchwardens receive the fines collected
by high constables and bailiffs from parishioners who refused to fulfil
their obligations to work on the highways. However, an Elizabethan
statute made either constables or churchwardens responsible for
collecting such fines if the surveyors of the highways had not done so.[34]

Legislation of the late sixteenth and early seventeenth centuries also
required constables to report to the justices on their enforcement of
certain laws, and to return to higher authorities the names of those
who had breached social and economic regulations. The act of 1610
which authorized privy searches for vagrants not only ordered
constables to return to the justices the names of those whom they had
arrested during the search, but also to report on how many vagrants
they had apprehended between searches and the punishments they
had imposed on them.[35] Although the act of 1604 regulating ale-
keepers and that of 1607 against drunkenness had made constables
responsible only for levying fines from offenders, a further statute in
1624 explicitly required them (and also churchwardens, headboroughs,
tithingmen, 'alecunners', and sidesmen) to present to the justices or to
the court leet both ale-keepers who committed illegalities and
drunkards.[36] Other acts obliged constables to return to the justices the
names of those who defied the state's religious provisions. A statute of
1593 ordered popish recusants to 'register' with the minister and the
constable, headborough, or tithingman. The minister was to enter this
information in a book, while constables were to return the names of
recusants to the justices at the next quarter sessions. Under an act of
1606 constables were given joint responsibility with the churchwardens
for making annual presentments to the justices of those who failed to
attend church once a month.[37]

Constables' duties to make presentments on social and economic
matters did not rest only on statute, but also derived from the orders of
higher officials. Directives from their superiors, and especially the
justices, required constables to submit such returns on an increasing
number of occasions during the early seventeenth century. Moreover,
they were called upon to make presentments on a variety of questions
in addition to those for which they had explicit statutory responsibility.

---

[34] 2 & 3 P. & M., c. 8; 18 Eliz. I, c. 10.
[35] 7 Jac. I, c. 4.
[36] 1 Jac. I, c. 9; 4 Jac. I, c. 5; 21 Jac. I., c. 7.
[37] 35 Eliz. I, c. 2; 3 Jac. I, c. 4.

By the early seventeenth century, if not before, they were being sent specific lists of articles on which to base their returns.

Constables had long been responsible for submitting presentments to the sheriff's tourn or the court leet in manor or hundred; and where such courts survived they continued to have such obligations during the late Tudor and early Stuart period. Their accounts not only provide evidence that they were required to attend the tourn or leet, but they sometimes record payments for writing articles to be submitted there.[38] However, it was to higher officials and their courts that they were obliged, on an increasing number of occasions, to return the names of offenders and to report on their enforcement of various statutes. Throughout the later sixteenth and early seventeenth centuries constables received orders from the justices to make presentments to quarter sessions, though the particular procedures varied from county to county. Sometimes they may have been required to attend sessions for the purpose of making presentments, but usually they were instructed to deliver such returns either to the high constable or to the justices of the division prior to the meeting of the court.[39] From the early years of the seventeenth century, and perhaps before that time, constables were also required to make presentments to assizes, and to submit such returns to the high constable or the justices.[40] In addition to these regular presentments, the justices from time to time also ordered special returns on a particular question, sometimes apparently being prompted to do so by a royal proclamation or by general orders handed down by the judges of assize.[41]

Constables' duties to make presentments were greatly increased

[38] e.g., NNRO, PD 219/126 (East Harling) 1618, 1619, 1624, 1627, 1630, 1637; PD 358/33 (Shelton), 1626, 1637, 1639; PD 50/36L (Gissing), no. 92; Staffs. RO, D/705/PC/1/1 (Gayton), pp. 11, 13, 14, 22, 24, 26, 27; Pattingham Constables' Accounts, 1613–14, 1614–15, 1616–17, 1622–3, 1628–9. 1638; also see more regular entries in the Branston accounts, Leics. RO, DE 720/30, and in those of Millington, whose constables attended the sheriff's tourn, Borthwick Institute, PR MIL. 10. The constables of Stockton, Salop, also appear to have been required to make regular presentments to the hundred court, which probably enjoyed leet jurisdiction, Salop RO, 3067/3/1.

[39] For precepts ordering such presentments see HWRO, 850 SALWARPE, BA 1054/1, Bundle A, nos. 54, 56, 59, 61, 81, 110, 168, 197; BA 1054/2, Bundle H (2 unnumbered items); NNRO, PD 50/36L, nos. 10, 25, 26, 29. Constables' accounts also provide evidence that they made such presentments; see below, ch. 6.

[40] For precepts ordering such presentments see HWRO, 850 SALWARPE, BA 1054/1, Bundle A, nos. 4, 92, 96, 116, 138, 152, 169, 171, 270, 276; also see below, ch. 6.

[41] Constables' accounts record a number of special presentments and these will be discussed below; see ch. 6.

during the 1630s as a result of the administrative changes growing out of the Book of Orders in 1631.[42] The justices were directed to hold monthly meetings in their divisions and to summon constables, churchwardens, overseers, and surveyors to make presentments to them. Such orders once again associated constables with the officers of the parish, and made them jointly answerable for the enforcement of economic and social regulations. During the 1630s precepts from the justices were sometimes directed to all of these officials, a procedure which was not entirely new, at least in some counties. The Norfolk justices had sent their orders for sessions presentments to the parish officers as well as to constables during the first decade of the seventeenth century, and precepts for assize presentments often seem to have been directed jointly to constables and churchwardens.[43] Although all these officials were supposed to appear before the justices at their monthly meetings, the role of constables still seems to have been the most important. In some counties they were responsible for passing on the justices' orders to the churchwardens and the overseers, and occasionally their accounts indicate that they paid the charges for drafting the presentments of these officials. Sometimes they delivered presentments from the parish officers to the justices, and it seems possible that some magistrates required only constables to attend their monthly meetings.[44]

Not only were constables called upon to make more frequent presentments during the course of the early seventeenth century, but they were required to make returns on many matters other than those for which they had explicit statutory obligations. In the counties examined in detail here they were expected to respond to specific

[42] For the Book of Orders see BL Add. MS 12496, ff. 263–90, esp. ff. 281–281ᵛ; also see B. W. Quintrell, 'The Making of Charles I's Book of Orders', *English Historical Review*, xcv (1980), 553–72, and Paul Slack, 'Books of Orders: The Making of English Social Policy 1577–1631', *Transactions of the Royal Historical Society*, 5th series, xxx (1980), 1–22.

[43] For precepts to make presentments to monthly meetings see HWRO, 850 SALWARPE, BA 1054/1, Bundle A, nos. 51, 54, 145, 275, 282; for Norfolk precepts for sessions presentments see NNRO, PD 50/36L, nos. 25, 26; and for precepts for assize presentments directed to constables and churchwardens see HWRO, 850 SALWARPE, BA 1054/1, Bundle A, nos. 92, 96, 152, 276; also see below, ch. 6.

[44] For evidence of constables being responsible for ordering the churchwardens and overseers to appear see the Hertfordshire returns in PRO, SP 16/344/30 III, V; SP 16/418/21 III, V; the Branston constables recorded payments for writing presentments for the parish officials, Leics, RO, DE 720/30, ff. 31ᵛ, 33, 38, 48 and there is evidence from Pattingham that the constables made presentments on behalf of the churchwardens on some occasions, Pattingham Churchwardens' Accounts, 1634 (4 entries).

articles in making their returns to quarter sessions and assizes and to the justices at their monthly meetings. The items included breaches of various economic and social regulations, and in such cases constables' returns provided the basis for the prosecution of offenders. However, the justices also demanded information on questions which might not require any legal action, and such presentments thus constituted administrative reports as well as judicial returns.

The articles sent to constables varied in their number and content, reflecting the addition of new statutory offences, the shifting concerns of the central government and the judges of assize, and variations from county to county in the interests of the justices. Attorney–General Coke drew up a list of eighteen articles on which high constables were to make presentments to assizes in the late sixteenth century,[45] while those addressed to petty constables and other local officers in the early seventeenth century ranged from as few as four to as many as a dozen items. Recusants and illegalities in alehouses usually seem to have been included among the articles for assize presentments. In addition, Worcestershire constables and churchwardens in July 1622 were ordered to make presentments to assizes on their punishment of vagrants, another common item, and on provisions made for the poor. A long list of items sent to them in March 1634 included drunkards, inmates, illegal cottages, the decay of highways and bridges, the keeping of watch and ward, hues and cries, riots, routs, and unlawful assemblies as well as recusants, alehouses, and provisions for the poor.[46] Similar matters were included in the articles for presentments to sessions and monthly meetings. For example, a precept to the constables, churchwardens, and overseers of Gissing in 1607 ordered them to make sessions presentments on the enforcement of the following statutes: labourers, assize of bread and ale, rogues and vagabonds, the Poor Law, recusants and sectaries, artificers, alehouses, and drunkenness.[47] A number of the same items were mentioned in a precept for sessions presentments sent to the constable and church-wardens of Salwarpe in 1623, though it also included unlawful gaming, decay of highways, watch and ward, and illegal cottages, which did not appear in the Norfolk directions.[48] Despite the instructions contained

[45] PRO, SP 12/276/72.
[46] HWRO, 850 SALWARPE, BA 1054/1, Bundle A, nos. 270, 96; also see nos. 171, 169, 152.
[47] NNRO, PD 50/36L, no. 10; also see nos. 25, 26, 29.
[48] HWRO, 850 SALWARPE, BA 1054/1, Bundle A, no. 197; also see nos. 158, 54, 56, 59, 61, 110, 81; BA 1054/2, Bundle H (24 March 1634, 12 September 1642).

in the Book of Orders in 1631, the articles issued by the justices of different counties for presentments to monthly meetings showed some variations in content, just as did those for sessions and assizes. The articles issued by the Hertfordshire justices followed rather closely the printed directions they received from the Government, and those to be answered by constables included highways, vagrancy, alehouses, masterless men, unlawful games, cottages and inmates, drunkenness, night walkers, watch and ward, and the sufficiency of constables.[49] The Staffordshire justices at Easter 1631 ordered presentments to monthly meetings on the profaning of the Sabbath, swearing, and bastardy as well as on more common items such as drunkenness, alehouses, absence from church, vagrants, cottages and inmates, and watch and ward. Similar articles were contained in the directions issued by the Worcestershire justices in December 1634.[50]

Although the responsibility for making presentments rested upon the shoulders of constables and other local officers, such returns often seem to have been a communal matter, with such officials acting as representatives of local bodies. Just as the reeve or the tithingman and his delegation had represented the township at the sheriff's tourn during the Middle Ages,[51] and just as those on hundred juries still acted as representatives of their localities in the sixteenth and seventeenth centuries, so too do constables seem to have functioned as agents of the village or parish in making presentments. H. B. Simpson probably is correct to suggest that constables' returns were accepted as true presentments because such officers were originally regarded as lawful representatives of local communities, giving voice to collective accusations.[52] Further support for the contention that the return of offenders was often a communal matter, whatever its status at law, is found in the kinds of accusatory documents which villagers sometimes submitted to the justices. Petitions to the magistrates which charge that an inhabitant had committed a misdemeanour often contain the

---

[49] See PRO, SP 16/344/30; 347/67; 418/21; and mention of the justices' use of two books of articles sent to them in SP 16/351/113.

[50] Staffs. RO, QS/O, iv. 5ᵛ–6; HWRO, 850 SALWARPE, BA 1054/1, Bundle A, no. 51; also see nos. 275, 282, 54, 145. Constables' accounts in Leicestershire also make reference to the articles which they obtained as a basis for their presentments for sessions, assizes, and monthly meetings; see Leics. RO, DE 720/30, ff. 10, 10ᵛ, 11ᵛ, 12ᵛ, and DE 625/60, ff. 12, 35ᵛ, 36ᵛ. For other references to such articles see Borthwick Institute, PR MIL. 10, 1642; Salop RO, 3067/3/1, pp. 6, 39; NNRO, PD 254//112, 1623–4, 1639–40; J. C. Atkinson, ed., *Quarter Sessions Records* (The North Riding Record Society, i–iv, 1884–6), i. 118.

[51] See above, ch. 1.   [52] Simpson, 'Office of Constable', pp. 629–30.

signatures and marks of a number of villagers, as well as the endorsement of the constable.[53] Although the justices may have regarded the return of presentments as an official responsibility of constables, villagers probably viewed this as a duty in which other inhabitants also had a part to play.

Constables' administrative and police duties thus increased very considerably during the late Tudor and early Stuart period as new regulatory responsibilities, conferred on them both by statute and by the orders of higher officials, were added to their traditional obligations for peacekeeping. Not only were they responsible for setting watches, pursuing hue and cry, and apprehending offenders, but also for presenting to assizes, quarter sessions, and monthly meetings those who had breached a wide variety of statutory regulations and for levying the fines or meting out other penalties under these acts. Furthermore, they became administrative agents of the justices in their regulation of certain occupations and in their supervision of the overseers of the poor, and administrative agents of the parish in the matter of highway repairs. Although constables were royal officials, and held accountable by their superiors for an increasing number of law enforcement duties, they had not entirely absorbed the police functions which had once been the collective responsibility of the township; and their fellow villagers were obliged to assist them in many of their tasks. Constables still functioned in part as 'headmen' of local communities in fulfilling the collective obligations of such bodies to pursue and apprehend offenders, and as their representatives in making presentments to higher officials. At the same time the social and economic legislation of the period, and orders from their superiors, also brought constables into association with the officials of the parish both in making presentments and in collecting fines from offenders.

II. MILITARY DUTIES

The military duties from which constables probably derived their very title remained an important part of the office during the late Tudor and early Stuart period. They continued to be responsible for the

---

[53] e.g. NNRO, Sessions Records, Boxes 13A, 17 (pts. i and ii), 20, 21, 22, 24, (pts. i and ii) which contain a number of such items. Also see the discussion of the 'communal' role in presenting offenders in Curtis, 'Quarter Sessions Appearances and Their Background', pp. 138–40, 147, 149–50.

village armour, the soldiers' appearance at musters, and for the maintenance of the shooting butts. In military matters, as in their police functions, constables acted as agents of local communities, because these obligations continued to be communal in character.[54] Although they were in charge of the armour and responsible for keeping this equipment and the shooting butts in repair, if the arms or the butts were found defective the village as a whole was penalized.[55] The fact that the churchwardens sometimes shared in military responsibilities further attests to the communal nature of such tasks, and to the importance of local custom in determining the allocation of responsibilities that were collective in nature.[56] By the sixteenth and seventeenth centuries constables were also the agents of the Lords Lieutenant and their deputies. Many of their military duties derived from the orders of these officials, just as in law enforcement their responsibilities often arose from the warrants and precepts of the justices.[57]

During the late Tudor and early Stuart period constables' primary military duties were in connection with musters, whether they entailed merely a showing of the armour or the actual training of the bands. Precepts issued on the authority of the Lords Lieutenant or their deputies directed constables themselves to attend musters and to assure the appearance of the trained soldiers from their communities, properly equipped and armed.[58] In order to meet this obligation they had to arrange for the storing, repair, and cleaning of the communal armour, for replacing it when it became worn or obsolete, and for transporting it to musters.[59] It is not clear just what functions they were expected to perform at the showing or training itself, but perhaps they were called upon to help preserve order during such gatherings.[60]

[54] 4 & 5 P. & M., c. 2, #5; for a detailed discussion of the militia and military provisions during this period see Lindsay Boynton, *The Elizabethan Militia 1558–1638* (London, 1967).   [55] e.g. Leics. RO, DE 720/30, ff. 22ᵛ, 29, 30ᵛ, 33, 47ᵛ, 49ᵛ.

[56] See George A. Carthew, 'Extracts from a Town Book of the Parish of Stockton in Norfolk', *Norfolk Archaeology*, i (1847), 171, 172, 175, 176, 178, 179; F. J. Western, 'Churchwardens' Accounts of Stathern, 1630 to 1677', *Transactions Leicestershire Archaeological Society*, xxiii (1947), 79, 82, 89; and HWRO, 850 STONE, BA 5660/3 (i).

[57] Precepts issued to the constables indicate that they were based on the authority of the Lords Lieutenant or their deputies; for some examples see n. 58 and n. 62 below.

[58] See precepts to constables in HWRO, 850 SALWARPE, BA 1054/2, Bundle H (27 August 1626); NNRO, PD 50/36L, nos. 33, 40, 67, 68. Constables' accounts also provide evidence about such duties; see below, ch. 5.

[59] Constables' accounts contain evidence about such duties; see below, ch. 5.

[60] For some suggestions about the functions of high constables at musters see Owen, 'Norfolk, 1620–41', ch. 4, esp. pp. 80–1 and n. 34.

Although small settlements were required to supply only two or three soldiers to the trained bands, all able-bodied men from sixteen to sixty were obliged to do military service if such need arose, and occasionally constables were ordered to draw up full muster rolls for their townships and to submit them to the Lords Lieutenant.[61]

Constables of the late sixteenth and early seventeenth centuries were also 'press-men', and obliged to supply a specific number of soldiers from their townships for active military duty.[62] In this instance it was the constable, and not the community as a whole, who was held responsible for furnishing such recruits. None the less, officers required assistance from their fellow inhabitants in taking up soldiers, guarding them, and assuring their safe delivery to higher officials, just as they needed local co-operation in meeting their obligations in connection with the militia. Although this duty was more irregular than their responsibilities in connection with musters, constables were required to press soldiers on a number of occasions during the late sixteenth and early seventeenth centuries: for Ireland and for continental expeditions during the 1590s, and in the case of Ireland into the early years of the next century, for Count Mansfeld and the Cadiz expedition and other continental engagements in the later 1620s, and for the wars against the Scots in 1639–40.[63]

Although some aspects of constables' military duties were less consistently demanding than their responsibilities for law enforcement, in the 1590s, the later 1620s, and the final years of the 1630s they can have been in little doubt that their military obligations constituted one of their major responsibilities. Such duties may in origin have been but an adjunct to their police powers, but by the sixteenth and seventeenth centuries they constituted a separate sphere of activity and formed an important part of the office. However, the origins of their military powers had not entirely been lost from sight. While constables had become agents of the Lords Lieutenant and their deputies, they still were executive agents of the township as well. They acted on its behalf

---

[61] e.g. HWRO, 850 SALWARPE, BA 1054/2, Bundle H (27 August 1626); and entries in constables' accounts which indicate that they were required to draw up such rolls, e.g. Earwaker, ed., *Constables' Accounts*, i. 170; ii. 60; Salop RO, 3067/3/1, pp. 25, 36, 42; Pattingham Constables' Accounts, 1634–5.

[62] See precepts in NNRO, PD 50/36L, nos. 61, 69, and HWRO, 850 SALWARPE, BA 1054/1, Bundle A, no. 170. Constables' accounts also contain evidence about their duties to press soldiers; see below, ch. 5.

[63] Constables' accounts provide evidence about their duties during these periods; see below, ch. 5.

in maintaining the communal armour and in assuring the provision of 'common' soldiers to serve in it, and they were dependent upon the assistance of other inhabitants if they were to meet such obligations.

III. TAX COLLECTING

Constables' duties in connection with taxation, like their police and military functions, probably arose from the fact that they were leaders of local communities. They could thus be called upon to lead a delegation which represented the township and which possessed authority to commit it to certain tax burdens. Although medieval constables had responsibilities as representatives of their townships and as policemen in the levying of purveyance and fifteenths,[64] in the sixteenth and seventeenth centuries such officers became tax-collectors as well, charged with gathering an ever-increasing number of national, county, and local rates.

Although constables had long been associated with purveyance, in the reign of Mary Tudor just as in the fourteenth century their duties were only of a supervisory nature.[65] Apparently it was only in the later sixteenth century when county rates had replaced, at least in part, the gathering of produce from the township that these officers acquired responsibility for levying provision for the royal household.[66] The extent of their duties varied somewhat from county to county, depending upon the nature of local obligations and the arrangements that had been made within the shire to fulfil them. Constables were required to collect an annual rate for provision that was paid to the high constable,[67] but for many their duties did not end there. Some were obliged to levy additional rates for particular commodities, wax, oats, wheat, poultry, and sometimes for carts, while others had to supply actual produce such as wheat, oats, hay, straw, and butter to the

---

[64] See above, ch. 1, nn. 50–2.

[65] 2 & 3 P. & M., c. 6.

[66] On the subjecct of provision and county compositions arranged during the later sixteenth century see Allegra Woodworth, *Purveyance for the royal household in the reign of Queen Elizabeth* (Transactions American Philosophical Society, new series, xxxv, pt. 1, Philadelphia, 1945).

[67] See precepts ordering payment of provision money in HWRO, 850 SALWARPE, BA 1054/1, Bundle A, nos. 4, 57, 69, 77, 87, 92, 93, 117, 118, 133, 167, 267, 268, and many receipts for such payments in BA 1054/2, Bundle G; NNRO, PD 50/36L, nos. 4, 17, 18, 20, 31, 33, 36, 39, 59. Such payments are entered in constables' accounts of all the villages examined; see below, ch. 5, n. 4.

royal household.[68] Constables had further duties when the monarch was on progress or for some other reason present in the county. Some were required to collect special rates for progresses, while others were called upon to furnish produce and carts to transport it, and also to assist in the carriage of the monarch's household and possessions. These duties seem to have varied considerably and probably depended largely on a village's location.[69]

Two other burdens in kind imposed on local communities also created responsibilities for constables, the obligation to supply horses and sometimes oats and coals to the postmaster, and the duty to render assistance to saltpetre men in carrying their tubs and fuel and the saltpetre itself. Constables were obliged to procure goods or services from other villagers in order to meet the demands of these officials. Such obligations too seem to have fallen rather unevenly, depending in part on a village's location. Nor were the requisitions made by such officials constant over time, and in the case of saltpetre men they tended to parallel the level of military preparations. However, in some villages and in some years constables' duties were increased very considerably by the demands of such officials.[70]

Constables' responsibilities in connection with national parliamentary taxes, like their duties in regard to purveyance, had not originally involved the collection of the state's taxes but rather the representation of the township's interests.[71] However, by the reign of Henry VIII they were also charged with levying such revenues. The poll tax of 1513 conferred on them responsibility for the assessment and collection of the levy.[72] The procedures established in this act, with a few modifications, were to be used in connection with the major

[68] For reference to levies for wax see Pattingham Constables' Accounts, and those of Stockton, Salop, Salop RO, 3067/3/1; for oats, the Pattingham accounts and those of Gayton, Staffs. RO, D/705/PC/1/1; for both oats and wheat, those of Great Easton, Essex RO, D/P 232/8/1; for poultry those of Branston and Waltham, Leics. RO, DE 720/30, DE 625/60. For evidence of produce being supplied to the royal household see the materials for Bushey and Little Munden in Herts. RO, D/P26/7/1; D/P26/10/1; D/P71/5/1; D/P71/5/2; accounts for Gissing, Shelton, East Harling, and Carleton Rode, NNRO, PD 50/36L; PD 358/33; PD 219/126; PD 254/112; and precepts in PD 50/36L, nos 4, 19, 28, 38, 60.

[69] For examples of levies for progresses sees Staffs. RO, QS/O, ii. 48ᵛ, iv. 231 and Pattingham Constables' Accounts, 1618–19, 1619–20, 1623–4; Earwaker, ed., *Constables' Accounts*, i. 33. The accounts of Branston and Waltham reveal that constables there were required to supply produce and carts; see below, ch. 5, nn. 15–18.

[70] Constables' accounts indicate that they were required to perform such duties; see below, ch. 5, nn. 20–4.

[71] See above, ch. 1.   [72] 4 H. VIII, c. 19.

parliamentary tax of the sixteenth and seventeenth centuries, the subsidy. Two kinds of duties accrued to constables under the provisions of the subsidy acts. In the first place they were to lead a delegation to meet with the subsidy commissioners about the assessment of the tax, though this responsibility was not exclusive to constables and the delegation could be headed by another substantial inhabitant. Precepts were to be delivered to subconstables, tithingmen, borsholders, bailiffs or similar officers, and to other 'substantiall, discreet and honest persones', ranging in number from two to eight depending on the size of the community, ordering them to appear before the commissioners. They were charged to inquire into the wealth of persons in their communities, and then they were to appear before the commissioners a second time to return a certificate of the names and wealth of those to be taxed. A further day was appointed for finalizing the assessments and the local delegation was again to appear before the commissioners, along with any other inhabitants who had been summoned for examination about their wealth. The responsibility for the assessment of the tax thus fell not to constables alone, and they acted merely as leaders of delegations which represented local communities at meetings with the commissioners. Once the assessments had been drawn up constables had a second responsibility. They were to act as the commissioners' agents in gathering the levy and returning it to the collectors, though this task too could be performed by another substantial inhabitant rather than the constable.[73]

Constables were also charged with gathering the prerogative taxes imposed during the early seventeenth century. It was their duty to lead village delegations which conferred with the commissioners about benevolences in 1614 and 1622, and about a benevolence for Ireland in 1642, and they were responsible for collecting the money.[74] They were the government's agents in the imposition of the 'forced loan' in 1627, and were obliged to appear before the commissioners with the

---

[73] 6 H. VIII, c. 26, and successive subsidy acts.

[74] There are references in constables' accounts to benevolences in 1614–15 and 1622, and these make it clear that the same procedures were followed as in the case of the subsidy; see, for example, Leics. RO, DE 720/30. ff. 10, 19ᵛ; DE 625/60, ff. 9ᵛ, 10ᵛ; Pattingham Constables' Accounts, 1621–2. Their accounts also record such meetings concerning the benevolence for Ireland in 1642; see Leics. RO, DE 625/60, fo. 65ᵛ, DE 720/30, ff. 51, 51ᵛ; Salop RO, 3067/3/1, p. 51; Borthwick Institute, PR MIL. 10, 1642. The poll tax of 1641 involved similar consultations, e.g. Leics. RO, DE 625/60, fo. 60; DE 720/30, fo. 50; Salop RO, 3067/3/1, p. 49; Borthwick Institute, PR MIL. 10, 1641, 1642.

subsidy men of the village who were called upon to 'lend' money.[75] The duty of assessing and collecting ship-money also fell to constables. Once again they were required to lead a village delegation, and to confer with the high constable about the distribution of this rate among the settlements within the hundred. Then constables and their fellow delegates were to assess the ship-money within their townships. Having procured approval of the local rating list, it was their duty to collect the money.[76] Constables in some counties were responsible too for collecting 'contributions' for the repair of St. Paul's church, another rate imposed by prerogative authority during the 1630s; but in other shires the justices, who were commissioners for this tax, directed their precepts to churchwardens.[77]

The collection of various county and local rates also fell to constables. Although their duties in this area increased considerably during the late sixteenth and early seventeenth centuries, some of these rates were of earlier provenance. They had probably long collected the hundred rate for compensating victims of robbery in cases when a thief was not apprehended. When the liability of the hundred to make compensation for robberies was reconfirmed in a statute of 1584 constables and headboroughs were explicitly made responsible for assessing this rate within their townships, gathering the money, and paying it to the justices.[78] An act of Henry VIII's reign gave them duties in connection with county rates for the repair of bridges. Either constables or two substantial inhabitants of every town and parish were to represent their communities at meetings with the justices about the assessment of such rates, and on behalf of the inhabitants to consent to the levy. While the act left to the justices the appointment of collectors, constables in fact became responsible for gathering rates for bridges.[79]

[75] See precepts in HWRO, 850 SALWARPE, BA 1054/1, Bundle A, nos. 204, 273, 183, 65. Constables' accounts also contain entries on this matter.

[76] See precepts in HWRO, BA 1054/1, Bundle A, nos. 171, 172, 173, 180; a village assessment for ship-money in Bushey in 1636, Herts. RO, D/P26/10/1, p. 24. Constables' accounts also contain references to their duties in connection with ship-money; see below, ch. 5.

[77] For the commission for the repair of St. Paul's see PRO, SP 16/188/37 and materials contained in SP 16/213. Examples of constables being required to collect this levy are found in Leics. RO, DE 625/60, ff. 42, 42ᵛ, 45ᵛ, 46, 54ᵛ, 56ᵛ; DE 720/30, ff. 35, 36, 42ᵛ.

[78] 27 Eliz. I, c. 13.

[79] 22 H. VIII, c. 5; also see precepts in HWRO, 850 SALWARPE, BA 1054/1, Bundle A, nos. 150, 184c; BA 1054/2, Bundle G (one precept dated 26 March 1611 and receipts for the payment of such rates); NNRO, PD 50/36L, nos. 16, 32.

Constables were also obliged to gather a variety of county and local rates for military purposes. By the early seventeenth century they were required to return annual payments to the high constable for the muster master, and sometimes for the repair or watching of the beacons and for the drum major's pension or the marshal's wages. Rates also had to be collected for powder, match, and bullets, while the township's obligations to provide common armour necessitated local levies to cover the purchase and maintenance of such equipment.[80] Constables' responsibilities for military rates were considerably increased when soldiers were sent on active duty, and they were obliged to collect coat and conduct money, and sometimes other special levies as well.[81]

The social legislation of the late sixteenth and early seventeenth centuries, which has already been discussed in connection with an increase in constables' administrative and police duties, also added to their responsibilities in the area of taxation. Sometimes the acts themselves designated constables as collectors, while in other instances they were called upon by the justices to gather such funds. An act of 1604 required them to levy rates for the relief of victims of plague, and added considerably to their tax-collecting duties during certain years.[82] Statutes which provided for the support of maimed soldiers also made them responsible for those collections.[83] The act of 1593 specified that churchwardens were to gather such funds, and the role of constables was limited to assisting these officers when it was necessary to distrain. However, a statute in 1598 claimed that there had been negligence in the collection of the rate because the penalty for failure was too small and applied only to churchwardens; and it provided that constables and churchwardens 'joyntlye and severallye shall have like aucthoritye and meanes to levye, collect and gather the sommes'.

---

[80] See precepts in HWRO, 850 SALWARPE, BA 1054/1, Bundle A, nos. 3, 25, 28, 56, 58, 89, 97, 99, 167, 168, 176, 181, 184a, 196, 220, 271, 286, 288; and receipts in BA 1054/2, Bundle G; NNRO, PD 50/36L, nos. 5, 15, 24, 41, 68. Also see local tax lists in Herts, RO, D/P71/5/1 and Leics. RO, DG 36/191, 219; DG 25/1/1, p. 37.

[81] See precepts in HWRO, 850 SALWARPE, BA 1054/1, Bundle A, nos. 271, 134, 82, 174, 170; NNRO, PD 50/36L, nos. 5, 66, 69, 76. Such entries also appear in constables' accounts; see below, ch. 5.

[82] 1 Jac. I, c. 31; also see precepts ordering such payments in HWRO, 850 SALWARPE, BA 1054/1, Bundle A, nos. 7, 10, 72, 73, 74, 163, 185, 218, and receipts in BA 1054/2, Bundle G. Such payments are also entered in constables' accounts; see below, ch. 5, nn.5–7.

[83] 35 Eliz. I, c. 4; 39 Eliz. I, c. 21; 43 Eliz. I, c. 3.

Other Elizabethan acts authorized rates for relief of prisoners in the King's Bench and Marshalsea prisons, for county hospitals, almshouses, and prisoners in the county gaol, and they designated churchwardens as responsible for these collections; but precepts ordering their payment sometimes were sent to constables.[84] Statutes which empowered the justices to levy funds for the support of Houses of Correction did not specify how the money was to be collected, but the duty often fell to constables.[85] In addition to county rates established by statute, the justices imposed a host of miscellaneous rates which varied from shire to shire; and it was usually constables who had to collect such levies.[86]

The division of responsibilities between constables and church-wardens in making collections for charitable purposes illustrates the extent of regional diversity in the duties of local officers, and the importance of custom in such matters. By the early seventeenth century a number of these levies were lumped together and paid quarterly to the high constable just before each of the quarter sessions. However, there were variations in the rates included; and while 'quarteridge' was sometimes collected and returned by constables, in other cases it was paid by churchwardens. The constables of both Pattingham and Gayton were responsible for making payments for the county gaol and the House of Correction; but, while the Gayton officers also delivered payments for the King's Bench and Marshalsea prisons, in Pattingham this rate was usually paid by the churchwardens, who also made the collections for maimed soldiers. However, in the Leicestershire villages of Branston, Waltham, Wymeswold and Stathern, and in the town of Melton Mowbray, the quarter rates for which constables were responsible included maimed soldiers as well as hospitals and the county gaol, but there is no evidence in these communities of regular payments for the maintenance of the House of Correction. In Gissing, on the other hand, constables' duties were restricted to levies for the House of Correction, and churchwardens gathered the other funds for charitable purposes. In the neighbouring villages of Shelton, Bunwell, and Carleton Rode constables were responsible for 'quarteridge', as they were in Salwarpe, and in that

---

[84] 14 Eliz. I, c. 5; 39 Eliz. I, c. 3; 43 Eliz. I, c. 2; also see n. 87 below.

[85] 18 Eliz. I, c. 3; 7 Jac. I, c. 4; also see n. 87 below.

[86] Evidence of constables being obliged to collect such rates is found in their accounts and will be discussed more fully below; see ch. 5. For orders from higher authorities for the payment of such rates see, for example, HWRO, 850 SALWARPE, BA 1054/1, Bundle A, no. 22; Staffs. RO, QS/O, iii. 155ᵛ, 185ᵛ.

village the levy included maimed soldiers, the county gaol, and the House of Correction.[87]

Finally, constables were authorized to collect rates to cover the expenses of the office. An act of 1606 empowered them to obtain reimbursement for costs incurred in conveying prisoners to gaol. When an offender lacked sufficient goods for the constable to procure the money by distraint, he could secure a warrant from the justices authorizing him, along with the churchwardens and two or three other honest inhabitants, to impose a rate on the township to meet such charges.[88] Between 1572 and 1598, when the statutory punishment of vagrants required that they be conveyed to gaol or a House of Correction, constables were also entitled, on a warrant from the justices, to levy rates on the parish to cover 'reasonable chardges for themselves and the prisoner'. These provisions were repealed in 1598, when the punishment was altered, and it was not until 1662 that another act empowered constables to levy rates to cover their expenses in apprehending and punishing vagrants and conveying them to the next officer.[89] In addition to these special rates authorized by statute, it was common practice for villages to authorize constables to collect local levies to cover their official expenses. Known as 'constables' lewnes' in some counties, such funds often seem to have been used not only to pay officers' expenses but also to meet a number of the local and county levies for which they were responsible. Rather than separate collections being made for 'quarteridge', or the repair of bridges, or the muster master's wages, some constables levied general lewnes from which they paid these sums.[90]

In the case of all the county rates, and ship-money which followed the same procedure, specific sums were allocated to each township;

[87] See Pattingham Constables' Accounts; Pattingham Churchwardens' Accounts; Staffs. RO, D 705/PC/1/1; Leics. RO, DE 720/30; DE 625/60; BL Add. MS 10457; Everard L. Guilford, 'The Accounts of the Constables of the Village of Stathern, Leicestershire', *Archaeological Journal*, 2nd series, lxix (1912), 125–60, and esp. 126–33; Leics. RO, DG 36/197, 202, 215, 217, 218, 219, 227; NNRO, PD 50/36L, nos. 12, 27, 30, 43, 44, 45, 46, 54; PD 358/33; PD 254/113; HWRO, 850 SALWARPE, BA 1054/1, Bundle A, nos. 11, 21, 22, 23, 24, 54, 55, 56, 59, 61, 81, 88, 97, 110, 114, 117, 147, 153, 168, 179, 220, 256, 281, and many receipts issued to the constables in BA 1054/2, Bundle G.

[88] 3 Jac. I, c. 10.   [89] 14 Eliz. I, c. 5; 14 Car. II. c. 12.

[90] Local tax lists for constables' 'lewnes' are found with their accounts or among village materials; see several such assessments among the Pattingham Constables' Accounts; many such lists among the Wymeswold accounts, BL Add. MS 10457; constables' rating lists for Little Munden in Herts. RO, D/P71/5/1; D/P71/5/2; and for Branston in Leics. RO, DE 720/30.

and the distribution of the rate within the township was the responsibility of local authorities. Although constables received the precepts ordering the collection of such levies, and were held responsible for their payment, they could not impose them on their own authority alone. Practices varied from village to village, but whether it was a levy for a county rate or for constables' lewnes, it was necessary for them to consult at least a few other inhabitants who were familiar with men's abilities and who would consent to the local distribution of the tax.[91] In the assessment of local and county rates, just as in the assessment of the subsidy, officers were thus dependent upon procuring the co-operation and aid of other residents.

Constables' duties did not end with their attempts to levy a tax or rate, because if they encountered difficulties in gathering the money they were expected to collect it by distraint. The statutes which conferred tax-collecting duties on them usually stipulated that they were to distrain in cases when inhabitants refused to pay, and this principle applied to all levies that fell within their jurisdiction, whether statutory or not. If some residents proved uncooperative, constables were required to seize sufficient goods or cattle to recover the money, or they might be obliged to pursue charges against them. Even when they were not the primary collectors of a rate sometimes they were given responsibilities if the money had to be levied by distraint. Originally this was their only role in the collections for maimed soldiers. They continued to have similar obligations, jointly with the churchwardens, to distrain for the poor-rate if the overseers had been unable to collect it.[92]

As tax-collectors, constables' duties were almost as numerous and as demanding as their police and administrative functions, although subject to some regional variations. These were due largely to local differences in the allocation of responsibilities between constables and churchwardens for levying county rates and the contributions for the repair of St. Paul's, and to the effects of location and local arrangements on a township's obligations to supply the royal household and to meet the demands of saltpetre men and postmasters. Constables' tax-collecting duties too underwent considerable expansion

---

[91] For example, see rating lists in Herts. RO, D/P 71/5/1, D/P71/5/2; D/P26/10/1; Leics. RO DG 36/207, 214; NNRO, PD 358/33, p. 214, which give the names of those who had approved them.

[92] For statutes which ordered constables to distrain for levies see 35 Eliz. I, c. 3; 43 Eliz. I, c. 2; 39 Eliz. I, c. 4; 39 Eliz. I, c. 21; 43 Eliz. I, c. 3.

during the late sixteenth and early seventeenth centuries. Both statutes and the orders of their superiors made them responsible for gathering a number of additional county rates, while they also acquired the duty to levy provision and not just to be present when purveyors made their collections in a township. Their duties in collecting national taxes had also increased since the early sixteenth century when they first became the state's agents in gathering these revenues. More frequent subsidies between 1590 and 1611, when they sometimes were obliged to collect more than one payment during a year, added to their burdens. So did the prerogative taxes, and particularly ship-money. Although constables' obligations in tax collecting were those of royal officers, they were not only agents of the state. They also functioned as representatives of local communities. They led a delegation from the township in negotiations with higher authorities about the assessment and distribution of such levies, and they acted on its behalf to meet collective obligations to such officials as postmasters and saltpetre men.

IV. OTHER DUTIES

There were a few duties which brought constables into the arena of national politics. On occasions when the state required the engagement of townsmen and villagers in the political process they were responsible for assuring such participation. One instance of this kind was the election of Members of Parliament, when sheriffs apparently directed to constables precepts requiring them to bring in the freeholders of their townships to participate in county elections.[93] The issue of the Protestation Oath in 1642 provided another occasion when ordinary Englishmen, and not just the freeholders among them, were formally brought within the confines of national politics. In that instance constables were responsible for the appearance of the inhabitants of their townships to take the oath, and sometimes they were required to accompany first the parish officers and then the rest of the residents when they went to be sworn.[94] While such duties did not constitute a very large, or perhaps very significant, part of the office, they further attest to the role of constables in providing a link between the central government and local communities.

[93] e.g. HWRO, 850 SALWARPE, BA 1054/1, Bundle A, no. 2, and a case in which a constable of the West Riding was accused of intimidating voters at the 1620 county elections, *HMC Twelfth Report*, part iv, p. 457.

[94] See a precept in HWRO, 850 SALWARPE, BA 1054/1, Bundle A, no. 9; and entries in constables' accounts, e.g. Leics. RO, DE 625/60, fo. 65; DE 720/30, fo. 51.

At the opposite extreme from such national functions were the local duties enjoyed by some officers, many of them agrarian in character. Responsibilities of this kind were determined by local custom, and they displayed considerable variation. Some constables apparently had few or no such duties within the township, while functions that in some villages were attached to the constable's office were in other cases the responsibility of churchwardens. In primarily pastoral and forest areas, often characterized by scattered settlements and weak manorial structures, constables may never have functioned as leaders of local communities to the same extent that they did in 'fielden' villages.[95] Furthermore, in settlements affected by enclosure, where the communal fields had been subdivided, constables by the seventeenth century may no longer have performed local agricultural duties for which they had once been responsible. However, constables' accounts from several Midland villages indicate that these officers still had a number of such obligations.

In the Leicestershire villages of Branston, Waltham, and Wymeswold constables in the early seventeenth century were responsible to the township for the execution of many local tasks, though they did not perform all of them personally. Such duties included custody of the communal bull; maintenance of village gates, waterings, weirs, sheep dams, pinfolds, and hedges; fetching 'setts' for planting; 'trenching' and sowing fields; and thatching the herdsman's house.[96] Constables were also in charge of guarding crops from village animals and from deer and crows, and were responsible for the eradication of vermin such as foxes and moles.[97] The position of local leadership enjoyed by

[95] For a discussion of some of the differences in settlement patterns and social organization, as well as in economic structures, between 'pastoral' and 'fielden' or 'champion' areas, see Joan Thirsk, ed., *The Agrarian History of England and Wales*, iv (Cambridge, 1967), pp. 1–15, 109–12; and her 'Seventeenth-Century Agriculture and Social Change', in Paul Seaver, ed., *Seventeenth Century England* (New York, 1976). For a more detailed study of pastoral farming in one of the counties included here see Thirsk, 'Horn and Thorn in Staffordshire: The Economy of a Pastoral County' *North Staffordshire Journal of Field Studies*, ix (1969), 1–16.

[96] See fairly regular entries concerning such matters in the Branston, Waltham, and Wymeswold accounts, Leics. RO, DE 720/30, DE 625/60, BL Add. MS 10457. There are some similar entries in the accounts of Millington, Borthwick Institute, PR Mll. 10 and in those of Stockton, Salop RO, 3067/3/1, and the Melton Mowbray accounts also mention repairs to the pinfold, Leics. RO, DG 25/39/1/3, pp. 2, 2ᵛ. For examples of churchwardens being responsible for such agrarian tasks see Western, 'Churchwardens' Accounts of Stathern', 79, 84, 93, 99, 107; J. C. Cox, 'The Registers and Churchwardens' and Constables' Accounts of the Parish of Repton', *Journal of the Derbyshire Archaeological and Natural History Society*, i. (1879), 30.

[97] For examples of guarding crops see Leics. RO, DE 625/60 ff. 5ᵛ, 7, 13, 14ᵛ, 16ᵛ,

some constables, and not only in Leicestershire villages, is also reflected in their role in communal rituals and festivities. Their accounts record payments for 'drawinge the feild' on 'Plow Mondaye', for 'drink' for those who 'gote wood to make a bonefier on the kings holydaie', and for 'expenses when we came from the perambulation'.[98] Not only did constables remain the executive agents of local communities and their representatives to higher authorities, but some officers thus continued to have purely local duties as well.

V. THE CONSTABLE'S OATH: A REFLECTION OF GROWING ROYAL DUTIES

The expansion of constables' duties during the late sixteenth and early seventeenth centuries, and their increasing subordination to higher officials, is reflected in the changing content of the oath administered to such officers. Although these documents were confined largely to a definition of their obligations in law enforcement, and therefore provide little evidence about their responsibilities in other areas, the changes in the description of their police duties are none the less indicative of the growing demands of the office. Revisions to the oath reflect changes in their statutory duties and in their responsibilities for presenting offenders, as well as recognition of their subordination to the justices.

A document found among the North Riding sessions materials may be a copy of the oath administered to constables when they first were recognized as royal officials, as Eleanor Trotter has suggested.[99] It specified only that they should exercise the office within their townships, present 'all mannour of bloodsheddes, assaltes and affreys and outcryes' against the king's peace, execute all writs and precepts lawfully directed to them, and personally do all in their power to conserve the peace. This brief oath was perhaps still being employed in

17, 21, 41, 44ᵛ, 52, 56; DE 720/30, ff. 7ᵛ, 38, 47ᵛ; and for the eradication of vermin see DE 625/60, ff. 2ᵛ, 4, 14, 16ᵛ, 17ᵛ, 23, 33, 45ᵛ, 51, 56, 58ᵛ; DE 720/30, ff. 7, 7ᵛ, 8ᵛ, 13, 14ᵛ, 16ᵛ, 18, 47ᵛ. For examples of the churchwardens being responsible for such tasks see Western, 'Churchwardens' Accounts of Stathern', 77, 79, 82, 87, 90, 91, 96; Pattingham Churchwardens' Accounts; Cox, 'Registers, Churchwardens' and Constables' Accounts', 30.

[98] See Leics. RO, DE 625/60, fo. 14; Pattingham Constables' Accounts, 1603–4; Leics. RO, DE 625/60, fo. 10ᵛ, and also see fo. 31 for reference to expenses on 'Crosse Munday'.

[99] Atkinson, ed., *Sessions Records*, i. 183; Trotter, *Seventeenth Century Life*, p. 85.

Yorkshire during the early seventeenth century. However, in some areas it was revised and expanded to incorporate statutory duties conferred on constables during the reigns of Elizabeth and the early Stuarts, and to make explicit their obligations to carry out the warrants of the justices of the peace.

An oath cited by Francis Bacon in 1608 required constables to swear to 'well and truly serve the King, and the lord of this law-day', and such duties were set out more fully than in the Yorkshire document. They were bound to keep watch and ward and to pursue hue and cry, to apprehend those commiting riots and affrays and to arrest felons, and to make presentment of all 'bloodsheds, out-cries, affrays and rescues'. The oath also mentioned their duties to enforce statutes against vagrants and those who played unlawful games, and it obliged them to 'have regard unto the maintenance of artillery', thus making at least brief mention of their military functions. Finally, it specifically bound them to execute the precepts of the justices of the peace.[100] The oath printed in the 1635 edition of Dalton's *Countrey Justice*, and similar ones found in handbooks of the mid-seventeenth century, reflect further expansion in constables' duties. These documents not only set out in greater detail their obligations at common law to 'well and truly serve our sovereign lord the king', without any mention of the lord of the law-day, but they also incorporated statutory duties which had accrued to such officers during the early seventeenth century. They were bound not only to enforce the laws against vagrancy and unlawfull games, but also to present to assizes, sessions, or the leet offences under the statutes regulating alehouses, for the repression of drunkenness and against profane swearing, as well as to make annual presentments to sessions of recusants and absences from church. These oaths too made specific reference to constables' obligations to implement the warrants and precepts of the justices.[101]

An examination of constables' duties during the late sixteenth and early seventeenth centuries makes it difficult to accept arguments that the office was declining in importance during that period, or that such officers had been superseded by more recently created parish officials. Although they were associated with the churchwardens, overseers, and surveyors in the performance of some of their duties, constables

---

[100] Bacon, 'Office of Constable', pp. 753–4.
[101] Dalton, *Countrey Justice*, pp. 363–4; also see E. W., *Exact Constable*, pp. 76–9; R. G., *Compleat Constable*, pp. 10–12.

remained the chief link between the central government and local communities. Sometimes they acted as the justices' agents in their dealings with the officials of the parish or even as executive agents of the parish itself. W. S. Holdsworth detected the importance of constables in linking parish and township, and in turn in the subordination of these units of local government to royal authority, when he stated:

... in the hundred and the township the constables were the officials through whom these medieval communities were connected with the new civil functions of that old ecclesiastical community — the parish; and it was through them that the activities of this new civil unit were linked up and subordinated to the organized rule of the justices of the peace.[102]

A consideration of constables' functions during the late sixteenth and early seventeenth centuries also reveals that they were made answerable to the state and to higher officials for a growing number of duties. Parliament gave them new regulatory tasks, primarily in the economic and social sphere, and made them responsible for levying some additional taxes and rates; but they also acquired further obligations in law enforcement, tax collecting, and military matters as a result of their duty to execute the warrants and precepts of higher officials. Such orders account for many of their responsibilities in making presentments, as well as for their duties to levy the prerogative taxes imposed under the early Stuarts and to impress soldiers. In addition, their administrative and police duties were augmented by new procedures, particularly the monthly meetings during the 1630s, which made them more frequently accountable to higher authorities for the execution of the office. Moreover, in many counties, if not in all of them, the early seventeenth century saw growing formalization of constables' presentments, whether to assizes, sessions, or monthly meetings, and they were called upon to submit returns in response to specific questions. There is no doubt that constables' duties were more numerous and more onerous in the 1630s than they had been during the 1580s.

Although there were many tasks for which all constables were responsible, there were a few regional variations in their duties. In some communities other officials, and particularly the churchwardens, were called upon to perform tasks that elsewhere were among

---

[102] Holdsworth, *History of English Law*, iv. 125.

constables' obligations. Some sixteenth- and seventeenth-century statutes contributed to such local variations by making constables and churchwardens alternate authorities in enforcing economic and social regulations, levying fines from offenders, and collecting county rates. However, these acts probably only reinforced regional differences which already existed. Such local diversity is evidence of the continuing importance of custom in determining the allocation of responsibilities at the local level, and is suggestive of the degree of informality which still governed local institutional arrangements. The divergence in local traditions is most clearly apparent in the kinds of duties which constables performed at the behest of the township alone. In some villages they had a number of such responsibilities, largely agrarian in nature, even during the Tudor and early Stuart period. However, in other communities such tasks were performed by the churchwardens, while in yet other settlements these functions apparently were no longer, and may never have been, communal in nature.

In spite of the fact that constables' royal duties expanded very considerably, and that they increasingly were subordinated to higher officials, their original position as 'village headmen' had not been completely overshadowed by their responsibilities as 'king's men'. Law enforcement, tax collecting, and the provision of armour and soldiers entailed obligations that were not exclusively those of constables, and they acted on behalf of the whole community in responding to the state's demands. Moreover, they still required, and were entitled to, the assistance of other inhabitants in carrying out many of the tasks for which they were responsible. They also continued to function as leaders of village delegations, and as representatives of local communities, in negotiations between those bodies and higher authorities. Even in the early seventeenth century the responsibilities of constables as agents of the central government had not entirely superseded their original obligations as leaders and representatives of local communities.

The relationship between the state and village communities in early modern England cannot be fully understood unless this duality in the character of the constable's office is kept in mind. The government's agent in the localities, who was given an increasing number of responsibilities during the late sixteenth and early seventeenth centuries, was an official who continued to possess rights and duties as leader and representative of the village; and in this lay both the strengths and the weaknesses of the office. The fact that the constable occupied a position where two distinct hierarchies of authority intersected probably enhanced his ability to mediate between them, but it also made his position a focus of conflict.[103]

[103] See below, chs. 5–7.

3

Filling the Office: Procedures and Problems

THE headmen of English villages, whether they were called headboroughs or tithingmen or borsholders or constables, originally were
chosen for the position by their fellow inhabitants; and even when they
became recognized as royal officials they continued to be selected
locally by those owing suit to courts leet. However, some suggest that
by the late sixteenth and early seventeenth centuries the justices
frequently appointed such officers.[1] The magistrates were responsible
for general supervision of the constabulary, including appointments,
and they often seem to have administered the oath to such officers; but
in most of the counties examined in this study there is suprisingly little
evidence that they appointed constables. Despite the fact that these
officers were the crown's representatives in local communities, and
more immediately the agents of the justices, they usually were chosen
for the position by a local body. Evidence from a number of counties
suggests that there were considerable variations from township to
township, even within a county, in the proportion of residents
considered eligible to serve as constable, the methods for choosing
such officers, and who had a voice in their selection. One of the most
striking facts about the constableship is the extent to which local
custom governed appointments during most of the late sixteenth and
early seventeenth centuries. However, during the 1630s the governmnt
attempted to discourage traditional procedures; and in some counties
the justices more often intervened in the selection of constables during
that decade.

Some contend that, whatever the methods for choosing constables,
the office was unpopular and that men sought to avoid it if at all

[1] e.g. the Webbs, *The Parish and the County*, pp. 27–8; A. Hassell Smith, 'Justices at
Work in Elizabethan Norfolk', *Norfolk Archaeology*, xxxiv (1967), 105; Critchley, *History
of Police*, pp. 16–17; Barnes, *Somerset*, p. 48. For other brief discussions of the selection
of constables see Willcox, *Gloucestershire*, p. 50; Fletcher, *Sussex*, pp. 141–2, 146;
Quintrell, 'The Government of the County of Essex', pp. 195, 198; Hurstfield,
'Wiltshire', *c.*1530–*c.*1660', p. 283; Cox, *Derbyshire Annals*, i. 105; Trotter, *Seventeenth
Century Life*, pp. 106–11; Campbell, *The English Yeoman*, pp. 319–20, 324; Holdsworth,
History of English Law, iv. 123–4; Wrightson, 'Two concepts of order', p. 26; King,
'Vagrancy and Local Law Enforcement', 272–3.

possible.[2] Historians suggest that many who were selected for the position claimed exemption or offered other reasons for not serving, and some argue that those who could afford to do so hired substitutes. The difficulties of filling the office have been attributed in part to the fact that incumbents were obliged to remain in the position for years on end. There is some evidence of reluctance to hold the constableship, and in view of the rather onerous duties which it entailed it probably was not eagerly sought after. However, it will be suggested that attempts to escape service were less common than often supposed. Claims about men's reluctance to fill the office, as well as about the length of the terms they were obliged to serve, seem to be exaggerated.

I. THE SELECTION OF CONSTABLES: CRITERIA AND PROCEDURES

Seventeenth-century commentators claimed that by law those chosen as constable should meet certain criteria of 'fitness', that they should possess 'honesty', 'knowledge', and 'ability'; but in fact there appear to have been few uniform regulations governing eligibility for the office.[3] Probably most would have agreed with such writers that the mentally defective, 'infants', and women were unsuitable for the position. It also seems to have been generaly accepted that those in certain professions — clergymen, higher officials such as justices and sheriffs, lawyers, attorneys, and physicians — were personally exempt from serving as constable.[4] Particular individuals might not be required to fill the office, but the responsibility attached not so much to persons as to properties. In most cases it was not the possession of land alone but the habitation of a particular tenement within a township which carried

[2] The Webbs, *The Parish and the County*, pp. 18–19; Critchley, *History of Police*, pp. 10–11; Trotter, *Seventeenth Century Life*, pp. 104, 108–9, 113; Campbell, *The English Yeoman*, pp. 321, 324–5; Cheyney, *History of England*, ii. 408; Barnes, *Somerset*, pp. 48, 76, 241; Hurstfield, 'Wiltshire *c.*1530–1660', pp. 283, 287–8; Quintrell, 'The Government of the County of Essex', p. 196; Whitehead and Tate, 'The Parish Constable', 41–2; Wrightson, 'Two concepts of order', pp. 26–7, though he cautions against 'too sweeping a dismissal' of constables as 'shanghaied village paupers'; King, 'Vagrancy and Local Law Enforcement', 269, 270–2, 276; Clark, *English Provincial Society*, p. 116.

[3] Bacon, 'Office of Constable', p. 751; Dalton, *Countrey Justice*, p. 47; *The Reports of Sir Edward Coke* (London, 1738), viii. 41; Sheppard, *Offices and Duties of Constables*, pp. 15–17; E. W., *Exact Constable*, pp. 8–10; R. G., *Compleat Constable*, p. 7.

[4] Sheppard, *Offices and Duties of Constables*, pp. 16, 18–19; E. W., *Exact Constable*, pp. 10–2; R. G., *Compleat Constable*, p. 7.

with it the obligation of providing a constable. Men, or even women, who were personally exempt from holding the position might still be required to supply someone to serve for the tenements which they inhabited.[5] Originally constables were probably chosen from among those who owed suit to the sheriff's tourn, or to the court leet in manor or hundred in cases where such jurisdiction had fallen into private hands.[6] However, by the late Tudor and early Stuart period it was a matter of custom as to which houses within a particular settlement were required to provide a constable, and there was considerable local diversity. In some instances officers were drawn from only six or seven houses, while in other cases a large proportion of the male heads of household were eligible to serve in the office.[7]

The procedures for choosing the constable from among those obliged to fill the office were also based on local custom. As the authors of handbooks pointed out, such officers traditionally had been elected in the tourn or the leet; and in many cases they continued to be selected, or at least confirmed in office, by such bodies during the sixteenth and early seventeenth centuries. However, other arrangements had developed in some settlements, and the authors of handbooks recognized alternate procedures which had become 'customary'. William Sheppard, for example, endorsed selection in the leet as the best way of choosing constables where that continued to be the custom, but he added that 'where custome is otherwise there it may be otherwise'.[8]

Constables in many of the villages considered in detail in this study do appear to have been confirmed, if not actually chosen, in the leet in either manor or hundred.[9] However, this apparent uniformity masks a

---

[5] Sheppard, *Offices and Duties of Constables*, pp. 20–1; R. G., *Compleat Constable*, p. 8.

[6] Disputes over constableships found in quarter sessions records indicate that custom determined which houses were required to provide a constable; see below, nn. 57–61.

[7] Differences in the number of tenements required to provide a constable become evident in disputes over the constableship that were referred to the justices and judges of assize; see below, nn. 57–61.

[8] Sheppard, *Offices and Duties of Constables*, pp. 14–15; also see Bacon, 'Office of Constable', p. 751; Dalton, *Countrey Justice*, p. 47; E. W., *Exact Constable*, p. 7; R. G., *Compleat Constable*, p. 8.

[9] Gissing, Norfolk: NNRO, PD 50/36L; Francis Blomefield, *An Essay Toward a Topographical History of the County of Norfolk*, i. (London, 1805), p. 181; Waltham and Branston, Leicestershire: Leics. RO, DE 625/60; DE 720/30; John Nichols, *The History and Antiquities of the County of Leicester*, II, pt. i (London, 1795), p. 8; Stockton, Salop: Salop RO, 3067/3/1; Gayton, Staffordshire: Staffs. RO, D/705/PC/1/1; Pattingham, Staffordshire: Staffs. RO, D/1807; Bushey, Hertfordshire: Herts. RO, Bushey Court Rolls and *VCH Hertfordshire*, ii. 142, 182; Manchester, Lancashire:

diversity of local practice. In some cases the office passed from house to house, and the court merely confirmed in office the man whose turn it was to serve. The constableship in Branston, Leicestershire, seems to have rotated among about thirteen houses in the village.[10] In Gayton, Staffordshire, the office was probably held in turn by the ten households liable to provide a constable prior to 1642. In that year the inhabitants agreed to increase the number to seventeen and stipulated that the office would rotate among those on the list.[11] Other instances of selection by 'house-row' are found in quarter sessions records, and occasionally such procedures are mentioned in other court records as well.[12] Sometimes constables were selected by the members of the jury in the leet, and they seem to have enjoyed a free choice from among those eligible for the position. In Bushey, Hertfordshire, the officers were chosen by the jury, and selection apparently limited only by the fact that one constable was to represent the 'town', and the other the remainder of the parish. An order of the leet in 1623 specified which houses were to be regarded as lying within the town, and designated the remainder as belonging to the parish of Bushey.[13] The constables of Manchester too seem to have been chosen freely by the jury of the court leet in that manor. In Pattingham, Staffordshire, the selection also appears to have involved a real choice by the leet, though probably with the limitation that one be chosen for the 'town' and the other for the outlying hamlets.[14] Quarter sessions records reveal the existence of other procedures by which constables were chosen within the leet. Sometimes the jury apparently selected the officer from among several

Earwaker, ed., *Court Leet Records*, i–iii; Shelton, Norfolk: Blomefield, *Norfolk* v. 270 and NNRO, PD 358/33; Carleton Rode, Norfolk: NNRO, PD 254/112; East Harling, Norfolk: NNRO, PD 219/126.

[10] Such a pattern is revealed in the list of constables, compiled from their accounts, Leics. RO, DE 720/30.

[11] Staffs. RO, D 705/PC/1/1, p. 41.

[12] For some examples of election by house-row see Staffs. RO, QS/O, iii. 187ᵛ; iv. 7; Transcripts Sessions Rolls, Jac. I, Roll 56, no. 20; S. C. Ratcliff and H. C. Johnson, eds., *Quarter Sessions Order Books* (Warwick County Records, i–ii, 1935–6), i. 40–1, 167; H. H. Copnall, ed., *Notes and Extracts from the Nottinghamshire County Records of the Seventeenth Century* (Nottingham, 1915), p. 19. Also see PRO, STAC 8/43/13.

[13] Herts. RO, Bushey Court Rolls, no. 6403.

[14] When two constables elected in Manchester in 1603 refused to serve two others were chosen in a second election; see Earwaker, ed., *Court Leet Records*, ii. 191. There is no evidence in the leet records or in the constables' accounts of selection by house-row or any other special means of choosing constables. The information concerning the Pattingham constables is derived from a list of their names between 1582 and 1640, compiled from their accounts and from court leet rolls, Staffs. RO, D/1807.

names suggested by the previous constable. In other instances the steward made the choice, possibly from names suggested by the jury or by the retiring constable. Occasionally a particular landowner seems to have enjoyed the responsibility of naming a constable who would be confirmed in the leet.[15]

Courts leet in either manor or hundred continued to be held during the late sixteenth and early seventeenth centuries in many of the areas considered in detail in this study, but this was not true in all parts of England. Sometimes it was probably the decline of the leet which led to the development of other procedures for choosing constables. In some areas where such courts no longer met, the inhabitants assembled for the specific purpose of choosing a constable, and sometimes they were ordered to do so by the justices.[16] Even when leets continued to be held, but such jurisdiction was attached to a hundred court, villages within the hundred probably often selected their constables locally by some means, these officers merely being confirmed in the leet. Although the constables of Waltham apparently took office in the court leet of the hundred of Framland, their accounts regularly indicate that they were selected by 'the inhabitants of Waltham', and it is possible that the townsmen assembled especially for this purpose prior to the leet.[17]

The most common alternative to choosing constables in the leet was selection by the parish vestry. This was a product not merely of the decline of the leet but also of the Tudors' adoption of the parish as the chief unit of local government. When they gave secular duties to existing ecclesiastical officials, the churchwardens, and created new parish officers, the surveyors of the highways and the overseers of the poor, they added further complexities to a system of local government which already displayed considerable regional diversity. It has already been noted that by the early seventeenth century constables had been associated with the officials of the parish in the conduct of a number of their duties.[18] The existence of parish officers with secular tasks none the less raised questions about their relationship to a much older royal

---

[15] e.g. Staffs. RO, Transcripts Sessions Rolls, Jac. I, Roll 26, nos. 38–9; QS/O, v. 31–2; E. H. Bates Harbin, ed., *Quarter Sessions Records for the County of Somerset*, 2 vols. (Somerset Record Society, xxiii–xxiv, 1907–8), ii. 147; Barnes, ed., *Somerset Assize Orders*, p. 40; James Tait, ed., *Lancashire Quarter Sessions Records* (Chetham Society, lxxvii, 1917), pp. 223, 283.

[16] Staffs. RO, QS/O, iv. 13, 14; Ratcliff and Johnson, eds., *Sessions Order Books*, i. 99; Copnall, ed., *Notes and Extracts*, p. 18.

[17] Leics. RO, DE 625/60.   [18] See above, ch. 2.

official, the constable, and about his relationship to the parish. In origin he had no connection with this local unit but with the township and the manor. While parishes and townships sometimes were coterminous, in other instances a parish might contain several townships. The territory over which a constable traditionally had jurisdiction might be equivalent to a parish, or it might be only part of a parish. However, once this old ecclesiastical division also became a unit of secular administration, and the constable often associated with its officials in the conduct of his office, contemporaries frequently did not make a clear distinction between the two jurisdictions. Petty constables were often called parish constables, even when they were not really officers of the parish; although sometimes this was an accurate description since they were selected by parish vestries. In some instances the vestry probably made the choice because a leet no longer was held, but this was not always the case. Some constables appear to have been chosen by the parishioners, though formally confirmed in the leet. The fact that constables' relationships with the parish differed from one part of the country to another thus contributed further to the local diversity which characterized their appointment.

Evidence from several areas suggests that the parish had come to enjoy a role in the selection of constables by the late sixteenth century. Both F. G. Emmison and B. W. Quintrell indicate that Essex constables were chosen by parish vestries.[19] Frank F. Foster's work on Elizabethan London reveals that the vestries in the city also selected constables, although they were officials of the ward and not the parish, and continued to be confirmed in the wardmotes.[20] The constables of a number of Norfolk communities probably were selected by the parish, even in cases when they were confirmed in the leet.[21] The officers of Little Munden, Hertfordshire, may also have been chosen by the parish vestry. Their selection is recorded in a book which listed the churchwardens, overseers, sidesmen, and surveyors too, while decisions

---

[19] F. G. Emmison, *Catalogue of Essex Parish Records*, 2nd edn. (Chelmsford, 1966), p. 17; Quintrell, 'The Government of the County of Essex', pp. 195, 198.

[20] Foster, *The Politics of Stability*, pp. 29–32, 37–8. Also see R. G., *Compleat Constable*, ch. 23, who also indicates that London constables were nominated in the vestry though confirmed in the wardmote.

[21] Shelton: NNRO, PD 358/33 (see the accounts for 1616–17 for a reference to constables of the 'parish'); Stockton: see Carthew, 'Town Book of the Parish of Stockton', 167–87; Watton: Thomas Barton, 'Notices of the Town and Parish of Watton', *Norfolk Archaeology*, iii (1852), 406–11; East Harling: NNRO, PD 219/126.

in regard to the constableship sometimes were referred to as those of 'the parish'.[22] The town book of Melton Mowbray, Leicestershire, also records the selection of constables and townwardens as well as churchwardens and surveyors, and all of these officers apparently were chosen by the same body.[23]

The fact that constables' accounts sometimes are found in the same volume with those of parish officers, and that they are referred to as 'parish' officials even when they clearly were not chosen by the parish, introduces further confusion into an already complex picture. The constables of Pattingham were selected in the court leet of the manor, and this township was not coterminous with the parish which contained a second township, Rudge. Although the authority of these officials did not extend to the entire parish, their accounts none the less are contained in a volume with those of the churchwardens, and decisions in regard to the constableship are recorded as being made by 'the parisheners'.[24] In Bushey too, where constables were officers of the leet, which passed by-laws governing their selection, their names and those of the headboroughs, and sometimes even the alecunners of the manor, are listed in the same book with those of the parish officers, while it was the vestry which sometimes authorized levies connected with the constable's office.[25]

Not only were constables usually chosen by local bodies, but they were also formally accountable to the local community. While they were answerable to the justices and other higher officials for the execution of many of their duties, it was to their fellow inhabitants that they were obliged to render account at the end of their term. The constables of Manchester not only were selected by the leet, but that body required an accounting from them. An order of 1578 directed that they give up their accounts within fourteen days of leaving office, either to the jury or their successors; but in 1595 the option was removed and they were ordered to present their accounts to the jury in the open leet at Michaelmas, on pain of a fine of 40s. This was reaffirmed in 1612, when it was stipulated that such accounts be entered in a book to be purchased for that purpose.[26] The records of Shelton, Norfolk, too contain a specific order concerning constables' obligations to render account. In 1628 'the inhabitants' agreed to

[22] Herts. RO, D/P71/5/2.   [23] Leics. RO, DG 25/1/1.
[24] Staffs. RO, D/1807; Pattingham Constables' Accounts, 1582–1640.
[25] Herts. RO, Bushey Court Rolls, no. 6403; D/P26/7/1.
[26] Earwaker, ed., *Court Leet Records*, i. 202, 261; ii. 102, 277.

require constables to account within a month of completing their terms, on pain of forfeiting their allowances of 2s. 6d.[27] Other officers too were obliged to account locally, sometimes to the vestry or the parishioners, while in other cases terms such as 'the townsmen' or 'the inhabitants' are used to describe those who reviewed their reckonings.

The records are sometimes explicit in specifying that constables' accounts had been reviewed by one body or another. The Shelton parish book indicates that in 1617 'a trew accoumpte of the constableshipp was given unto the townesmen of Shelton', while some of the Pattingham accounts reveal that they had been accepted by 'the parisheners'. In 1602–3, for example, the retiring officers paid over funds remaining in their hands to the new constables 'by the consent of a greate number of the parisheners'.[28] Some of the Wymeswold accounts also contain notations that they had been approved, as in 1603 when the retiring constable paid the remaining funds to his successor in the presence of the vicar, who registered that this had been done with the 'consent of the whole parish of Wymeswould'.[29] Sometimes the names of a few of those who were present and who had allowed the constables' bills were recorded on these documents, as was the case in Lessingham, Norfolk, in 1613 and in Wymeswold in 1631.[30] In other instances inhabitants actually signed the accounts to show that they had approved them. This apparently was regular practice in Melton Mowbray, and the names of six to eight townsmen who had 'seen and allowed' the accounts appear on such documents.[31] The East Harling accounts of 1627 and those for Great Easton in 1623 also contain a few signatures, while the members of the jury in Manchester, or some of them, also signed the constables' accounts to show that they had approved them.[32] Whether they were described as 'inhabitants' or 'neighbours' or 'townsmen' or 'parishioners', the local residents who usually selected constables thus demanded an accounting from them, and these officers were thus answerable to the local community as well as to their superiors.

---

[27] NNRO, PD 358/33, 1628.

[28] NNRO, PD 358/33, 1616–17; Pattingham Constables' Accounts, 1602–3; also see these accounts for the years 1596–7, 1610–11, 1614–15.

[29] BL Add. MS 10457, fo. 22; also see fo. 27 for a reference in 1624 to the accounts being taken by 'neighbours'.

[30] NNRO, PD 274/13, 1613; BL Add. MS 10457, fo. 42ᵛ.

[31] Leics. RO, DG 25/39/1/1, 3; DG 36/188, 189.

[32] NNRO, PD 219/126, 1627; Essex RO, D/P232/8/1, 1623; Earwaker, ed., *Constables' Accounts*, i and ii.

Although the authors of handbooks emphasized the importance of local custom in the selection of constables, they also indicated that the justices of the peace sometimes appointed such officers and that they frequently gave them the oath of office. Michael Dalton claimed that it was common practice for the justices both to choose and to swear constables. However, other writers suggested that the magistrates enjoyed the power to appoint constables only in special circumstances, when a candidate had refused to assume office or when the constableship was left vacant because an incumbent had died or moved from the village. Some of them also argued that the justices could remove a man whom they deemed unfit for the office and appoint another in his place. However, there was disagreement about this matter; and some claimed that the magistrates had no voice in the selection of constables but must leave the choice to the leet, even if this resulted in the appointment of a man who was unfit for the office.[33]

The handbooks accurately mirror the legal confusion surrounding the justices' powers to select constables. A case tried in King's Bench in 1612 was decided against the justices who had removed from office a constable of Stepney and appointed another in his place. The judges on that occasion declared that although the justices could choose and remove high constables they had 'no power nor authority' to elect or displace petty constables.[34] This ruling perhaps was superseded, as some of the authors of handbooks suggested, by opinions handed down by the judges at the winter assizes in Norfolk in 1633. They declared that the magistrates could remove unfit officers chosen by a leet, and that sessions, or if that was 'too far off' the nearest justice, could also select a constable if a leet had failed to replace an incumbent who had died or moved from the village.[35] In 1640 the judges on the Oxford circuit directed both justices and stewards of leets to refuse to swear constables who were insufficient, but they did not authorize the magistrates to appoint such officers.[36] While the government in the 1630s seems to have encouraged the justices to take a more active role in the selection of constables, it was not until 1662 that their powers in the appointment of constables were clarified by an act of Parliament.

[33] Dalton, *Countrey Justice*, p. 47; Sheppard, *Offices and Duties of Constables*, pp. 22–4; E. W., *Exact Constable*, pp. 7, 12–13; R. G., *Compleat Constable*, pp. 8–9.
[34] *The Report of Edward Bulstrode of Cases in the Court of King's Bench* (London, 1657), p. 174.
[35] Barnes, ed., *Somerset Assize Orders*, p. 69; also see PRO, SP 16/255/48 (also printed in Barnes, p. 71).
[36] Staffs. RO, QS/O, v. 47.

The statute authorized two justices to select such officers, subject to later confirmation in quarter sessions, in instances when a leet had not been held or when the office was vacant because an incumbent had died or moved. However, the act made no provision for the justices to remove and replace constables whom they deemed unsuitable for office.[37]

Some historians argue that in practice the justices, either in their official capacities or through the powers which they enjoyed as large landholders and lords of leets, regularly appointed constables.[38] On some occasions such men probably did exert their influence through informal channels. Although actions of this kind, due to their very nature, are likely to leave little mark on the records, an occasional incident comes to light in the correspondence of the period. In a letter of the late sixteenth century Sir Thomas Holland reported to Bassingbourn Gawdy that he had 'made' a man constable of Kenninghall, Norfolk, 'against the will of some chief inhabitants'. The town reportedly was the scene of excessive drinking and disorderly conduct and Holland indicated that he had selected as constable a man who was 'severe against ale-houses'.[39] Although justices sometimes may have exerted their influence individually and informally, quarter sessions records provide very little evidence of official intervention in the selection of constables, though there were some variations from county to county. At least until the 1630s magistrates usually seem to have upheld local customs governing the eligibility and choice of such officers, and very seldom seem to have made appointments themselves.

The justices often did give constables the oath of office, and this fact is sometimes recorded in sessions records. The Bench also ordered men to repair to the nearest justice to be sworn, and that probably was the more usual procedure unless there had been some dispute about the selection of an officer.[40] Constables' accounts too occasionally

---

[37] 14 Car. II, c. 12, #XV.

[38] See esp. the Webbs, *The Parish and the County*, pp. 27–8; Smith, 'Justices at Work in Elizabethan Norfolk', 105; and Emmison, *Catalogue of Essex Parish Records*, p. 16. For a summary of differing opinions on this question see Critchley, *History of Police*, pp. 16–17.   [39] *HMC Tenth Report*, pt. ii (Gawdy MSS), p. 33.

[40] e.g. Staffs. RO, QS/O, ii. 97, 98ᵛ; iv. 205ᵛ; Transcripts Sessions Rolls, Jac. I, Roll 56, no. 20; Roll 58, no. 104; Roll 69, no. 20; Tait, ed., *Sessions Records*, pp. 119, 143, 155, 191, 224; John Lister, ed., *West Riding Sessions Records*, 2 vols. (The Yorkshire Archaeological and Topographical Association, Record Series, iii. liv, 1888 and 1915), i. 58; Atkinson, ed., *Sessions Records*, i. 217; iv. 102; B. H. Cunnington, ed., *Records of the County of Wiltshire, being Extracts from the Quarter Sessions Great Rolls of the Seventeenth Century* (Devizes, 1932), p. 102.

provide evidence of the justices swearing constables. The Pattingham officers were ordered to certify to the high constables where they had taken their oaths in 1615–16 and in 1625–6, and on the second occasion they appear to have been sworn by a justice. There are also references to oath-taking before the justices in the accounts of Gayton, Gissing, Shelton, and Branston.[41] The justices may increasingly have superseded the leet's jurisdiction in swearing constables, and while this perhaps reflects the growing subordination of these officers to the crown and its ministers, as H. B. Simpson suggests,[42] the practice was not universal even by the early seventeenth century. Constables sometimes still took their oaths in the leet. For example, the officers of Branston were sworn at Framland court, the hundred court which enjoyed leet jurisdiction, in 1616–17, 1639–40, and 1640–1, and probably in other years as well, although they are known to have taken their oaths before a justice in 1614–15, 1617–18, and 1621–2.[43] The officers of Stockton, Salop, regularly took their oaths in the hundred court, which presumably enjoyed leet jurisdiction, and it seems probable that the constables of Manchester usualy were sworn into office by the steward of the court leet in that manor.[44] Moreover, the magistrates themselves sometimes ordered that a constable be sworn in the leet.[45] The justices had thus not replaced the leet entirely in swearing constables into office, even though these officials were directly responsible to them for carrying out many of the duties to which the oath bound them. In any case, it seems to be going too far to suggest, as Simpson does, that the mere swearing of constables by the justices signified their complete subordination to the central government, and that 'the local origin of their office had passed out of sight'.[46]

[41] Pattingham Constables' Accounts, 1615–16, 1625–6; Staffs. RO, D 705/PC/1/1, pp. 25, 26; NNRO, PD 50/36L, no. 89, PD 358/33, 1622; Leics. RO, DE 720/30, ff. 9, 13, 18ᵛ.

[42] See Simpson, 'Office of Constable', p. 639 where it is suggested that the administration of the oath by the justices can be 'considered as the characteristic mark of the final subordination of local to central government in rural districts, of the conversion of a local administrative officer into a ministerial officer of the crown'.

[43] Leics. RO, DE 720/30, ff. 11ᵛ, 45ᵛ, 47ᵛ; and also see n. 41 above.

[44] Salop RO, 3067/3/1, pp. 29, 33, 36, 39, 41; while it seems probable that the Manchester constables usually took their oaths in the leet, in 1604 quarter sessions ordered that the sheriff and the hundred constable take the oath of a Manchester officer, Tait, ed., *Sessions Records*, p. 238.

[45] e.g. Atkinson, ed., *Sessions Records*, iii. 150; Staffs. RO, QS/O, iv. 226–226ᵛ; v. 31–2; Bates Harbin ed., *Sessions Records*, ii. 87–8 (a hundred court which probably enjoyed leet jurisdiction).

[46] Simpson, 'Office of Constable', p. 639.

The justices in quarter sessions also exercised general supervision over the selection of constables, and while they responded to appeals and petitions of various kinds they seldom seem to have taken the initiative in such matters. There is little evidence of magistrates intervening to remove 'unfit' constables and replace them. However, there are some notable exceptions to this, and the justices in a few counties seem to have been unusually thorough in their oversight of the constabulary. Keith Wrightson has drawn attention to the fact that the Essex justices removed and replaced a number of 'insufficient' constables during the years 1629 to 1631. The Lancashire justices too apparently discharged some constables, as well as rejecting men who were nominated for the position.[47] Among the counties whose sessions records have been examined for this study, only the Hertfordshire materials provide evidence of the justices removing officers whom they deemed unsuitable and appointing others. Two such cases are found in their order book in 1628–9, while the remaining seven cases date from the 1630s and early 1640s.[48] In some instances the nature of the deficiency is specified. They discharged one constable on grounds of poverty, another because he was infirm, while a third was removed because of his advanced age. The Bench also deemed unsuitable the leet's selection of a man who lived with his father as a servant, and they replaced another officer who was in debt and as a result did not dare to go abroad to execute the office. Sometimes it was noted only that officers were 'unfitting' and that new ones were to be sworn. The removal of unsuitable constables by the Hertfordshire justices seems to lend further support to Julie Calnan's portrayal of the magistrates of that county as unusually diligent in fulfilling their duties.[49]

Justices also took action when they discovered that villages had failed to select a constable; but in very few cases did they remedy the deficiency by appointing an officer. While it does not seem to have been common in most counties for settlements to be without a constable, in the North Riding of Yorkshire indictments were brought against a number of townships which lacked officers.[50] The Bench fined the inhabitants for their negligence in amounts ranging from 10s.

[47] Wrightson, 'Two concepts of order', pp. 37–8; King, 'Vagrancy and Local Law Enforcement', 273–4.

[48] Herts. RO, QS/B, 2A, ff. 91, 108ᵛ, 163, 182, 194; 2B, ff. 14, 28d; also see n. 55 below.

[49] Calnan, 'County Society and Local Government in the County of Hertford'.

[50] Atkinson, ed., *Sessions Records*, i. 1, 3, 25, 91, 98, 196, 232, 266; ii. 41, 100–1, 104, 196, 234; iii. 151, 170, 191, 237, 258, 268; iv. 110, 174.

to £10, and ordered such communities to select constables. In only one instance between 1604 and 1640 is there evidence that the justices appointed a constable when one was lacking. On another occasion they threatened a village that if the inhabitants could not agree on an officer before the next sessions the Bench would choose one.[51]

Usually the justices became involved in the selection of constables only as a result of petitions from others, from individuals who wanted to be released from office or who offered reasons why they should not be obliged to serve, or from inhabitants complaining that someone had refused to assume the position. In these cases too it was rare for them to resolve the issue by choosing a constable. When they received complaints that men had refused to serve, they usually ordered them to do so and to take the oath of office, or else be bound over to sessions. Sometimes they fined them or threatened them with a fine.[52] The justices allowed the claims of some of those who asserted that they were personally exempt from holding the office, and they sometimes accepted pleas of men who urged their unsuitability to be constable. In such cases they normally directed the leet or the inhabitants to select a new officer.[53] Usually they ordered new elections too in response to petitions from men who had fulfilled their terms and asked to be relieved of office.[54] However, the Hertfordshire justices may have replaced constables whose terms had expired. They did so in one instance in 1628, and their order book contains seven other directives during the late 1620s, and twelve during the 1630s, for the swearing of new officers. There is no evidence in these instances that they were removing constables whom they deemed unsuitable, and perhaps they were replacing men who had completed their service.[55] In Warwickshire there are some instances in which the justices discharged an incumbent who had completed his term, and also appointed a new officer. They usually summoned two or three villagers from whom to

---

[51] Atkinson, ed., *Sessions Records*, iii. 170; ii. 101.

[52] e.g. Staffs. RO, QS/O, ii. 97, 98ᵛ, 102, 147, 147ᵛ; Transcripts Sessions Rolls, Jac. I, Roll 66, nos. 41, 42; Bund, ed., *Sessions Papers*, pp. 605, 606, 672; Atkinson, ed., *Sessions Records*, i. 177, 217; iv. 18, 102, 186; Copnall, ed., *Notes and Extracts*, p. 19, Tait, ed., *Sessions Records*, p. 214; Bates Harbin, ed., *Sessions Records*, i. 111, 339; ii. 149; Lister, ed., *West Riding Sessions*, i. 144; ii. 212–3.

[53] e.g. Staffs. RO, QS/O, iii. 198ᵛ; iv. 151ᵛ, 157, 226–226ᵛ; Lister, ed., *West Riding Sessions*, iii. 352.

[54] e.g. Staffs. RO, QS/O, iii. 185ᵛ; iv. 13, 14, 157; v. 96–7; Cunnington, ed., *Sessions Great Rolls*, p. 138.

[55] Herts. RO, QS/B, 2A, ff. 32ᵛ, 36–36ᵛ, 42ᵛ, 54ᵛ, 60, 67, 78, 103, 108, 109, 120, 139, 142, 150, 153ᵛ, 211; 2B, ff. 8ᵛ, 9.

make the choice, though sometimes the incumbent or the township made a preliminary selection of several inhabitants.[56]

Not only did the justices seldom settle disputed constableships by appointing new officers, but they usually upheld local customs governing eligibility for the position. When magistrates received petitions from men who claimed that their tenements were exempt from providing a constable, these normally seem to have been allowed if it could be proved that the tenement had not been required to provide a constable in the past. Sometimes such cases were carried over from sessions to sessions, or referred to the judges of assize, in order that local custom could be determined.[57] Even when villagers complained to the justices that customary arrangements limited the office to only a few men, when there were others of greater ability capable of serving, the justices often ordered that custom be maintained. When three residents of a Staffordshire village petitioned quarter sessions in 1607 claiming that the office was continually limited to one of them, and urged that other fit persons be required to serve, the justices ordered that the existing arrangements be continued. In 1620 when the Staffordshire justices were informed that the election of the constable of Knightley was limited to twenty-two houses that by custom served in the office, the justices also ordered that the procedure be maintained. On another occasion, in 1631, when the Staffordshire Bench discharged a widow who had been selected constable by house-row, they pointed out in a subsequent order that their decision was not to be prejudicial to ancient custom, and they stipulated that the person next in line by house-row was to assume the office.[58]

There are, however, some signs during the 1630s that the justices were becoming less respectful of traditions which restricted the office to certain tenements, and that they also began to deny the validity of some of the customary procedures used in selecting constables. Their change of attitude was probably prompted in part by directives from the central government and the judges of assize which encouraged

---

[56] Ratcliff and Johnson, eds., *Sessions Order Books*, i. 12, 17, 196, 231–2; ii. 7, 40–1.

[57] For cases where consideration was given to the exemption of certain tenements see Staffs. RO, QS/O, iii. 64; Bates Harbin, ed., *Sessions Records*, i. 307; ii. 87–8, 147, 172–3, 192–3, 267; Atkinson, ed., *Sessions Records*, i. 103; iv. 111; Tait, ed. *Sessions Records*, pp. 108, 223, 271, 283; and for similar cases before the judges of assize see Barnes, ed., *Somerset Assize Orders*, pp. 3, 23, 26–7, 28–9.

[58] Staffs. RO, Transcripts Sessions Rolls, Jac, I, Roll 37, no. 44; QS/O, ii. 88; v. 7ᵛ.

them to intervene in the selection of constables, and by the judges' decisions on disputed constableships in which they overruled previous customs and exemptions.[59] In Staffordshire, where the justices during an earlier period had upheld local customs in the selection of constables, some of their decisions in the later 1630s and early 1640s denied the validity of such practices. For example, in 1640 the Bench directed the inhabitants of Sandon to put aside the tradition which had confined the constableship to only seven tenements, and to proceed to elect a fit, able, and substantial villager for the office. Similarly, in 1642, when they were informed that only eleven inhabitants of Mavesyn Ridware, some of them the poorest in the village, had furnished a constable while others of better estate never held the office, the justices ordered that in future no cottager was to serve and no person of ability to be exempted by former custom.[60] A directive of the Nottinghamshire justices in 1642 displayed a similar disregard for local traditions. In response to a petition from some villagers of Lowdham who complained that the constableship was imposed on only seven farmers, on grounds of custom, when the community contained forty inhabitants able to serve, the justices forbade this arrangement. They ordered that in future the constable should be chosen in the court leet, if one existed, or otherwise selected by the inhabitants without regard to any previous usage.[61]

Although there are indications by the later 1630s that the justices in some counties were making inroads into the local customs which had governed the selection of constables, in most shires they appear to have exercised little influence over the actual appointment of such officers. The primary concern of most justices seems to have been that every village have a constable. Among the counties whose records have been examined here, only those of Hertfordshire provide evidence that the magistrates tried to assure the quality of such officers by replacing men whom they deemed unsuitable, and most such cases in that county date from the 1630s or later. The justices usually became involved in the selection of constables only when a petition required their

---

[59] The Book of Orders in 1631 instructed the justices that constables should be chosen from among the 'abler sort of parishoners' (BL Add. MS 12496, fo. 287ᵛ), while the judges of assize had directed them in 1633 to remove insufficient constables, and in 1640 to refuse to swear those chosen by house-row if this procedure produced men who were unfit for office (Barnes, ed., *Somerset Assize Orders*, p. 69; Staffs. RO, QS/O, v. 47). For decisions in which the judges overruled custom see Barnes, ed., *Somerset Assize Orders*, pp. 35, 39, 40, 47.

[60] Staffs. RO, QS/O, v. 11, 116.   [61] Copnall, ed., *Notes and Extracts*, p. 18.

attention, and they normally filled the position only when customary means of choosing an officer had been unsuccessful. Their apparent respect for local custom, at least prior to the 1630s, even in cases when this resulted in the office being imposed on only a few inhabitants or in substantial residents being exempted from service, is one of the most striking features of magisterial decisions about disputed constableships.[62]

II. DIFFICULTIES IN FILLING THE OFFICE

Some of the disputes about the selection of constables which were referred to the justices seem to substantiate the arguments of those who claim that the office was unpopular. Contemporary comment adds further weight to such contentions. No less a body than the Privy Council believed that men were so anxious to avoid service as constable that they would be willing to compound in order to be free of the office for life. A project designed by Sir Henry Neville, which was accepted by the king and the Council in 1608, focused primarily on releasing men from jury service in return for a payment of £5; but it also proposed exempting from the constable-ship a certain number in each parish who were prepared to compound. Neville claimed that this office, like jury duty, was 'very often imposed unequally' and that 'some men are pinched and others spared', and he suggested that many would be eager to compound.[63] Despite some indications that the office of constable was unpopular, there is not a great deal of evidence of attempts to avoid service. There may, however, have been greater difficulties in filling the position during the 1630s than in earlier years.

Although quarter sessions records contain petitions and orders which reveal or suggest a reluctance to hold the office, the total number of such cases in any of the sessions materials examined is not very large. There are few recorded instances of men openly refusing to serve as constable. For example, only six such cases appear in the

[62] Also see Quintrell, 'The Government of the County of Essex', p. 195, who suggests that the Bench had little control over the appointment of constables; and Fletcher, *Sussex*, pp. 141–2, 146, who draws attention to the importance of custom in the selection of constables in that county, and who claims that the nomination of constables and tithingmen at sessions was unusual before the 1650s.

[63] PRO, SP 14/31/55, for Neville's proposal; SP 14/31/57 for another document in support of it; SP 14/31/56 for a draft of a commission to compound, which was issued on 28 February 1608.

order book of the Staffordshire justices between 1619 and 1642.[64] The lack of a constable in some townships may be due to the fact that nobody would take on the office unless forced to do so. If that was the case, there does seem to have been fairly widespread refusal to serve in the North Riding of Yorkshire.[65] There the problem was sufficiently great that the justices issued two general orders on the matter in 1609 and 1614.[66] However, the North Riding was the only area examined where there were more than one or two instances of villages lacking constables. Petitions in which individuals claimed exemption from service,[67] or contended that they were unfit for office,[68] may also indicate reluctance to hold the position; but once again such appeals do not seem to have been very numerous.

Only occasionally do leet records and town books provide evidence that men had refused to assume office, or hints that they were reluctant to do so. Two men selected in Manchester in 1603 refused to serve, allegedly 'without anie juste cause', and they were fined and two others chosen for the position.[69] On several occasions the Manchester leet seems to have anticipated that men would be reluctant to assume the constableship, and the court ordered them to take the oath by a certain date on threat of penalties ranging from £5 to £13. 6s. 4d.[70] The Little Munden records contain one case of a man who was not eager to assume the position, and who seems to have feared that once in office he might be obliged to serve for several terms. William Risdaile agreed

---

[64] Staffs. RO, QS/O, ii. 88, 97, 98ᵛ, 147, 147ᵛ; iv. 157; for some cases in other counties see Bates Harbin, ed., *Sessions Records*, i. 87, 111, 288, 339; ii. 149, 218; Atkinson, ed., *Sessions Records*, i. 177, 217; iv. 18, 102, 186.

[65] Atkinson, ed., *Sessions Records*, i. 1, 3, 25, 91, 98, 196, 232, 266; ii. 41–2, 100–1, 104, 108, 196, 234; iii. 151, 170, 191, 237, 252, 258, 268; iv. 110, 174. Critchley, *History of Police*, p. 17, indicates that thirty-one townships in Hampshire were without constables in 1612.

[66] Atkinson, ed., *Sessions Records*, i. 172; ii. 47.

[67] For cases involving personal exemptions see Staffs. RO, QS/O, iii. 26ᵛ, 198ᵛ; Tait, ed., *Sessions Records*, pp. 53, 109, 118; Atkinson, ed., *Sessions Records*, i. 25; Copnall, ed., *Notes and Extracts*, p. 18; Bates Harbin, ed., *Sessions Records*, ii. 186; Ratcliff and Johnson, eds., *Sessions Order Books*, i. 27, 40–1. For cases involving disputes over whether or not certain tenements were required to provide a constable see Bates Harbin, ed., *Sessions Records*, i. 307; ii. 87–8, 147, 172–3, 267.

[68] For cases of men claiming to be unfit for service see Staffs. RO, QS/O, iv. 244ᵛ, 226–226ᵛ; Cunnington, ed., *Sessions Great Rolls*, p. 116; Lister, ed., *West Riding Sessions*, ii. 352; Bates Harbin, ed., *Sessions Records*, ii. 85–6; Staffs. RO, Transcripts Sessions Rolls, Jac. I, Roll 26, nos. 38–9; Roll 42, no. 38.

[69] Earwaker, ed., *Court Leet Records*, ii. 191, 197.

[70] Earwaker, ed., *Court Leet Records*, iii. 160, 195, 247, 262, 319.

to become constable only on the condition that he be excused from the office for the next four years.[71]

The extent of substitutions has been used as one of the chief measures of the unpopularity of the constableship and of the difficulties encountered in filling the position.[72] Both men and women who were considered personally exempt from serving sometimes were ordered to find deputies for their tenements, and incumbents occasionally appointed a deputy if they were incapacitated or obliged to be absent from the village;[73] but the records provide very little other evidence of substitutions. The accounts of Waltham, Branston, Melton Mowbray, Wymeswold, Bushey, Gissing, Shelton, Salwarpe, and Manchester contain no mention of substitutes, though it must be admitted that all of these materials are incomplete.[74] Other such records reveal only a few deputies. The nearly complete Pattingham accounts for the period 1582 to 1640 register only two substitutions. A possible third comes to light in the court leet records, and in the early 1640s a woman employed a deputy.[75] There are four cases of substitution listed in the Little Munden materials, three of them instances in which gentlemen employed others to serve for them, and also four cases noted in the accounts of Stockton, Salop.[76] One substitution is found in the Millington records of the 1630s.[77] If the number employing deputies provides a measure of the unpopularity of the office, this evidence does not suggest that men attempted to escape the position as often as sometimes is supposed.

There are not many cases either in which men petitioned the justices because they had been in office for more than a year and were

[71] Herts. RO, D/P71/5/2.

[72] See esp. the Webbs, *The Parish and the County*, p. 18; Critchley, *History of Police*, pp. 10–11.

[73] For some cases of temporary deputies see Leics. RO, DE 625/60, ff. 15, 20, 22ᵛ; and fo. 54, a case in which a deputy served for six weeks and took the oath of office; for contemporary opinions on deputies see Sheppard, *Offices and Duties of Constables*, p. 25; E. W., *Exact Constable*, pp. 13–14; Bacon, 'Office of Constable', p. 754.

[74] Leics. RO, DE 625/60; DE 720/30; DG 25/39/1/1–4; DG 36/186–9; DG 25/1/1; BL Add. MS 10457; Herts. RO, D/P26/7/1; D/P26/10/1; NNRO, PD 50/36L, PD 50/35; PD 358/33; HWRO, 850 SALWARPE, BA 1054/2, Bundle D; Earwaker, ed., *Constables' Accounts*, i and ii.

[75] Pattingham Constables' Accounts, 1638–9, 1639–40; Staffs. RO, D/1807/ 245, 246, 247, 248, 254a, substitution possibly occurred in 1635–6 when the leet roll indicates that Martin Hardwicke and William Pitt were chosen constables, while the names of Henry Johnson and William Pitt appear on the constables' accounts; see Staffs. RO, D/1078/237, 238.

[76] Herts. RO, D/P71/5/2; Salop RO, 3067/3/1.

[77] Borthwick Institute, PR MIL. 10.

unable to get relief from their duties. Historians cite examples of officers who had served for a number of years, sometimes as many as fifteen or seventeen terms without a break; but such instances seem to have been rather unusual.[78] The Warwickshire materials, which contain the most evidence of men being unable to procure release from the office, include only eight petitions of this kind between 1625 and 1642. A few of these constables had served for several years, one for four, one for three, and another for two, but the remaining five officers had held the position for only a year and a half or a year and a quarter or more than a year.[79] The order book of the Staffordshire justices contains only six orders between 1619 and 1642 concerning constables who had served beyond their terms. In one of these cases it was the inhabitants and not the incumbent who made the complaint. They claimed that he had been in office for four years and that the steward had ignored their choice and ‚sworn him for a fifth term. The constables of one town protested that they had been in office for over two years, but the remaining four petitions came from men who had served only a year and asked to be discharged.[80] There is a mere scattering of such cases among other sessions materials, though some of the unexplained interventions by the Hertfordshire justices, which were more numerous, may be cases in which they were replacing men who had served beyond their terms.[81]

Nor do the constables' accounts examined provide much support for contentions that men were burdened with the office for several years and unable to find anyone to replace them. There are very few cases of multiple terms, except in villages where this was accepted practice during some periods. The two men who took office in Little Munden in 1630 did serve for three terms, and one of them held the position again in 1638; those chosen in Shelton in 1619 served for two years and an officer of Salwarpe held office for three years, from 1634 to

---

[78] Campbell, *The English Yeoman*, p. 325; Trotter, *Seventeenth Century Life*, p. 113; the Webbs, *The Parish and the County*, p. 19; Hurstfield, 'Wiltshire *c*.1530–*c*.1660', p. 288; King, 'Vagrancy and Local Law Enforcement', 270; Willcox, *Gloucestershire*, p. 50, cites an example of a man who was hired as constable for seventeen years. Quintrell, 'The Government of the County of Essex', p. 196 claims that elections were held annually and that it was rare for a man to continue in office for more than two or three years.

[79] Ratcliff and Johnson, eds., *Sessions Order Books*, i. 12, 17, 196(2), 231–2; ii. 7, 40–1, 119.

[80] Staffs. RO, QS/O, iii. 185^v; iv. 5, 13–14, 29^v, 157; v. 31–2, 96–7.

[81] e.g. Bund, ed., *Sessions Papers*, p. 689; Cunnington, ed., *Sessions Great Rolls*, p. 138; Bates Harbin, ed., *Sessions Records*, i. 307; and for possible Hertfordshire cases see n. 55 above.

1636.[82] Two other cases in which constables served consecutive terms, in Little Munden for the years 1642 and 1643 and in Manchester for the years 1641–2 to 1644, probably are explained by the special circumstances of the Civil War.[83]

Frequent service might have contributed as much as consecutive terms to making the office unpopular, so it is also necessary to consider how often men were obliged to hold the constableship. It is difficult to generalize about the matter since there were variations from township to township and within particular communities as well. When the office rotated among only six or seven houses, men would have been obliged to serve more often than in villages where most households were subject to providing a constable. However, even when a high proportion of male householders were deemed eligible for the position, some men were chosen for the office more frequently than others. Of the eighty-one men known to have held the constableship in Pattingham between 1582 and 1640, one served four terms, six of them three terms and eighteen men held the office at least twice.[84] In the smaller village of Branston, Leicestershire, four of the twenty men who filled the constableship between 1611 and 1643 served three times and another six served twice during that thirty-two year period.[85] Two men in Shelton, Norfolk, held the office five and four times, respectively, in the thirty-year period 1610–40; but their record seems to have been exceptional in that village.[86] The lists of constables in most of the villages considered in this study are incomplete, and the time-span covered often rather brief. However, the surviving evidence would suggest that, while many held the office twice or three times during their lives, only a few of them were obliged to serve four or five terms or more. It does not appear that a few men were constantly burdened with the office.

Although examples of refusal or reluctance to serve as constable can be found throughout the period 1580 to 1642, it seems possible that there was greater difficulty in filling the position during the 1630s, and particularly at the end of that decade, than was the case in earlier years.

[82] Herts RO, D/P71/5/2; NNRO, PD 358/33, 1619; HWRO, 850 SALWARPE, BA 1054/2, Bundle G (name recovered from receipts in this bundle) and constables' accounts, BA 1054/2, Bundle D.

[83] Herts. RO, D/P71/5/2; Earwaker, ed., *Constables' Accounts*, ii. 96.

[84] The names are derived from the Pattingham Constables' Accounts, 1582–1640 and the court leet rolls of the manor of Pattingham, Staffs. RO, D/1807.

[85] This evidence is derived from the constables accounts, Leics. RO, DE 720/30.

[86] See the Shelton parish book, NNRO, PD 358/33.

A considerable proportion of the disputed constableships which came before the justices of some counties date from that period, while most of the substitutions found in constables' accounts and other hints of reluctance to serve are also found during those years. T. G. Barnes points out that in Somerset the justices dealt with twelve cases of men unwilling to be constables between 1635 and 1638, as many as during the previous ten years, and that nine of these cases were heard between Epiphany 1637–8 and Epiphany 1638–9.[87] An examination of the Wiltshire quarter sessions records led Joel Hurstfield to suggest that tithingmen in that county were increasingly reluctant to hold the office in the years just prior to the Civil War.[88] The actions taken by the Hertfordshire justices may reflect their growing supervision of the constabulary rather than any change in men's willingness to serve as constable,[89] but they did intervene more often in the 1630s; 24 cases appear in their order book for that period and an additional 7 beween 1640 and 1642, as opposed to 14 such cases between 1620 and 1629.[90] There are fewer differences between the 1620s and 1630s in the number of disputed constableships in the order book of the Staffordshire justices; 11 cases are recorded between 1620 and 1629 as opposed to 12 between 1630 and 1639, though they did deal with 6 more cases between 1640 and 1642.[91] The substitutions recorded in the Pattingham constables' accounts or leet rolls all occurred in the later 1630s or early 1640s, while the orders issued by the Manchester leet which obliged men to take the oath by a certain deadline also date from the 1630s, 1629–30, 1632–3, 1636–7, 1637–8, 1639–40.[92] Perhaps it is not without significance that one of the officers elected in 1637–8, who was subject to such an order, was absent in London at the time of his selection and therefore not in a position to resist the leet's choice.[93] The few cases in which constables are known to have served multiple terms are found mainly during the 1630s; and it was in 1639 that William Risdaile of Little Munden agreed to serve only after obtaining assurance that he would be freed from the office for the next four years.[94] Walter J. King is probably correct to suggest that the major reason for avoiding the office was a financial one; and if there was growing reluctance to serve during the later 1630s, this is probably

[87] Barnes, *Somerset*, p. 241.
[88] Hurstfield, 'Wiltshire *c*.1530–*c*1660', pp. 283, 288.
[89] See below, ch. 7.   [90] Herts. RO, QS/B, 2A and 2B.
[91] Staffs. RO, QS/O, ii–v.   [92] See above, n. 75, n. 70.
[93] Earwaker, ed., *Constables' Accounts*, ii. 40 n. 1.   [94] See above, n. 71.

explained by the added financial liability entailed in the collection of ship-money and unpopular military levies at that time.[95]

Although many were perhaps not eager to serve as constable, both the Jacobean Council and some modern historians seem to have overestimated men's reluctance to hold the position. Some did try to avoid the office; they refused to be sworn, or offered excuses for not serving or hired deputies, and such tactics may have become more prevalent during the 1630s than in earlier years. It is possible that the office was more unpopular than the records would seem to indicate, but in the areas examined here there is not very much evidence of difficulty in filling the position. Mildred Campbell suggests that 'custom and current opinion had made it a public obligation' for yeomen to serve in the constableship; and custom probably helps to explain the acceptance of the position by others as well.[96] After serving a term men normally could expect to be free of the position for some years to come, and that fact too probably helped to make the office more tolerable. Some may even have welcomed the opportunity to hold the constableship. William Hunt suggests that 'the godly' often sought parochial office in order to implement moral and social reform;[97] and a few of the less godly may not have been averse to serving because they hoped to use their official powers to pursue personal ends.[98]

The appointment of constables in the early seventeenth century continued to reflect the local origins of the position. Not only were they usually selected locally, whether in the leet or the vestry or by some other means, and in accord with customs which varied from township to township, but they were also formally accountable to their fellow inhabitants. Although constables were answerable to higher authorities for their royal duties, and especially to the justices of the peace who

[95] King, 'Vagrancy and Local Law Enforcement', 270–2; his evidence from Lancashire would suggest that in that county reluctance to hold the office became marked only during the 1640s and 1650s (p. 269 and n. 13). On the financial burdens of the office see below, ch. 5; and on constables' difficulties in levying ship-money and military rates, see ch. 7.

[96] Campbell, *The English Yeoman*, p. 319; also see King, 'Vagrancy and Local Law Enforcement', 276, who suggests that it was customary to take turns in the office and that many never considered not serving.

[97] William Hunt, *The Puritan Moment: The Coming of Revolution in an English County* (Cambridge, Mass., 1983), ch. 6 and esp. p. 144. See below ch. 7, nn. 154–64 for some constables who may have been motivated by godly concerns, and who met with resistance in trying to enforce legislation against drunkenness and the profaning of the Sabbath.

[98] See below, ch. 5, nn. 77–86, 147–52; ch. 6, nn. 112–15, 117–27, for cases of constables who seem to have abused their powers in order to serve their own interests.

often swore them into office, in theory these officials had no voice in the selection of constables and in practice they seldom seem to have made such appointments. By the 1630s the central government apparently came to believe that traditional procedures for choosing constables, and local customs governing eligibility, were leading to the selection of unqualified men. Instructions from the Privy Council, directives issued by the judges of assize, and the legal opinions which they handed down, all encouraged the justices to take a more active role in supervising the appointment of constables. They were authorized to overrule local custom if it inhibited the selection of able men, to make good the deficiency if a township lacked a constable, and if necessary to remove 'unfit' officers and appoint others in their places. The justices in some counties apparently responded to such orders by showing less regard for custom in their decisions about disputed constableships. However, the Hertfordshire magistrates seem to have been somewhat exceptional in removing insufficient constables and in taking it upon themselves to appoint such officers. It does not appear to have been common practice, even in the 1630s, for the justices to select constables.

Despite the concerns voiced by the central government, local arrangements on the whole seem to have proven adequate in filling the office. Some townships apparently did lack constables until pressure was brought to bear on them to appoint such officers, and local communities sometimes were obliged to appeal to the justices because the men selected claimed to be exempt from serving or simply refused to assume the office. However, there does not seem to be evidence of widespread resistance to holding the constableship. Even if the position was not popular, and perhaps became more unpopular during the later 1630s, most of those chosen do seem to have undertaken their duties without undue protest. 'Custom' probably played as large a part in men's acceptance of this obligation as it did in determining the procedures by which they were selected for the office. A sense of public responsibility or a desire to implement reform, or in some cases more selfish motives, may also help to explain men's willingness to serve as constable.

4

Communities and their Constables: A Social Profile

COMMENTATORS of the sixteenth and seventeenth centuries frequently stated or implied that the methods employed in choosing constables led to the selection of poor and ignorant men.[1] Complaints submitted to the courts and statements of government officials sometimes echoed the charge that the lowly and uneducated were being selected for the position.[2] Historians have often accepted these contemporary assessments of constables, and portrayed such officers as lacking the social position, education, and experience that were required for the proper execution of their duties.[3] Such views have not gone entirely unchallenged, and a growing number of historians in recent years have argued that constables were more substantial and better qualified for the position than earlier writers contended.[4] However, such claims are based on evidence which is rather limited both geographically and chronologically. Possible variations among the constabularies in different kinds of settlements, and the question of changes over time in the social characteristics of constables, have not been fully explored.

Although recent historians appear to be correct in their supposition that most of those who held the constableship were more prosperous and better equipped for the office than many earlier writers had suggested, the calibre of constables did vary. Not only were there differences within a township in the wealth and status of those who

---

[1] Bacon, 'Office of Constable', p. 751; Sheppard, *Offices and Duties of Constables*, pp. A2ᵛ-A3, 16-19; E. W., *Exact Constable*, pp. 8-10; Dalton, *Countrey Justice*, p. 47; Lambard, *Dueties of Constables*, pp. 3-4.

[2] Cockburn, ed., *Sussex Indictments, James I*, p. 55; Barnes, ed., *Somerset Assize Orders*, p. 69; PRO, SP 16/329/9; BL Add. MS 12496, f. 287ᵛ; Staffs. RO, QS/O, v. 47.

[3] The Webbs, *The Parish and the county*, pp. 18-19 and n. 3; Critchley, *History of Police*, pp. 10-11; Willcox, *Gloucestershire*, p. 50; Barnes, *Somerset*, pp. 76-7; Cheyney, *History of England*, ii. 408.

[4] Trotter, *Seventeenth Century Life*, p. 112; Campbell, *The English Yeoman*, p. 318; Hoskins, *Midland Peasant*, p. 208; Samaha, *Law and Order*, pp. 84-8; Sharpe, 'Crime and Delinquency in an Essex Parish', pp. 94-5; Wrightson, 'Two concepts of order', pp. 27-8.

held the office, but it will be shown that the social characteristics of constables varied from village to village. Such diversity is a product, at least in part, of differences in the character of these settlements. Local historians have emphasized the growing social and economic differentiation within English rural communities during the seventeenth century. They suggest that villages were increasingly dominated by 'élites' whose wealth, status, and values distanced them from the growing numbers of labourers and paupers found in these communities.[5] This description may accurately reflect the direction of social change in rural England, but not all villages conformed to such a pattern during the late sixteenth and early seventeenth centuries. Local communities continued to display diversity in their economic and social structures, in the division of wealth as well as in settlement patterns, manorial arrangements, farming types, the relative importance of crafts and trades, and the degree to which they were affected by population mobility, to name some of the factors which shaped their character. In order to understand the variations in the social characteristics of constables, it is necessary to appreciate the diversity among the settlements in which they served.

This chapter will examine in some detail nine townships in five counties, and similarities and differences among them in the social composition of their constabularies.[6] Consideration will be given to the wealth, occupation, and social status of constables, and to whether or not they came from families which had long been established in the village. Attempts will be made to assess the extent of literacy among constables, and attention will also be given to the amount of experience in local government possessed by those who filled the office. In an effort to determine whether or not the men chosen as constable were usually law-abiding inhabitants, some evidence about the court records of those who held office has been assembled for one village.

---

[5] e.g. Wrightson, *English Society*, esp. chs. 2, 5–7; Hunt, *The Puritan Moment*, esp. chs. 2, 3, 6; Clark, *English Provincial Society*, esp. pp. 122, 157, 176–7; Holmes, *Seventeenth-Century Lincolnshire*, ch. 2 and esp. pp. 23–9.

[6] Bushey and Little Munden, Hertfordshire; Salwarpe and Stone, Worcestershire; Branston, Waltham-on-the-Wolds, and Melton Mowbray, Leicestershire; Pattingham, Staffordshire; Gissing, Norfolk. Materials for Shelton, Norfolk, were also examined but the information proved too fragmentary to include this village.

I. THE STATUS OF CONSTABLES: WEALTH, OCCUPATION, AND SOCIAL DESCRIPTION

Perhaps there were some villages in which it was usual for poorer men to hold the constableship, but that was not the case in Bushey and Little Munden, Hertfordshire; Salwarpe and Stone, Worcestershire; Branston, Waltham, and Melton Mowbray, Leicestershire; Pattingham, Staffordshire; or Gissing, Norfolk. Usually constables are listed among those assessed as landholders on local rating lists, and only a handful of cottagers are found serving in the office in these townships. Moreover, evidence from both local tax lists and the subsidy rolls indicates that the wealthiest men in these communities filled the office. There are some variations from village to village in the proportion of the subsidy men known to have served as constable, probably due largely to the incompleteness of the evidence. However, most of the names, exclusive of those of major gentlemen, found on the rolls for all of these communities were those of men who held the constableship or their widows.[7] None the less, there were differences in the relative wealth and the status of the constables in these townships. While in some cases many prosperous yeomen, and even a few gentlemen, held the office, in other instances a majority of constables were farmers of more moderate means. The constabularies of some townships included a substantial number of craftsmen or tradesmen, but others contained very few or none in such occupations. In order to appreciate the variations which existed, it is necessary to consider these communities and their constables in greater detail.

(1) Yeomen and Husbandmen of Little Munden, Salwarpe, Stone, and Gissing

Although Little Munden, Salwarpe, Stone, and Gissing varied in size and farming types, they had similarities in social structure. Of the settlements considered here, they most closely fit historians' models of socially differentiated villages containing prosperous élites and growing numbers of labourers and paupers.[8] None of them contained many resident gentlemen, and those who were present were usually rather minor gentry. Below the level of the gentlemen there were a number of

---

[7] e.g. 15 of 21 names on the Pattingham rolls, and 3 others probably served in the office prior to 1584 (PRO, E 179/178/225, 235, 248, 284, 292, 299, 318); 26 of 33 names in Bushey (E 179/121/259, 279, 314, 329, 331); and probably 25 of 28 names on the rolls for Little Munden (E 179/248/17; E 179/121/260, 263, 269, 304, 337).

[8] See above, n. 5.

very substantial farmers who enjoyed a disproportionate share of the wealth in these agrarian communities. While a few prosperous yeomen occupied the top of the social scale, there were substantial numbers of cottagers and labourers at the bottom. In the middle range there were some husbandmen of rather moderate means and sometimes a few craftsmen and tradesmen. The social structure of these villages was in turn reflected in the particular composition of their constabularies.

Little Munden, in the hundred of Broadwater in central Hertfordshire, contained about sixty-five families during the early seventeenth century, and was served by two constables. It was a village of dispersed settlement, the hamlets of Dane End, Green End, Altwicke, and Potters Green appearing on poor-relief lists of the period, while the place-names Yardley and Windmill End are also mentioned in local records.[9] Cattle raising and dairying were major pursuits, inventories revealing the presence of milkhouses, butter, and cheese. Farmers also possessed sheep and some pigs. However, the crops from the arable were more valuable than animal husbandry, especially the large acreages of wheat.[10]

The village contained two manors, the major one of Munden Freville and a smaller manor, Libury. Although a number of gentlemen, in addition to the lords of these properties, had landed interests in the village, few of them were resident there. By the 1630s both of the manors, 410 acres in Munden Freville and 150 acres in Libury, appear to have been leased by yeomen.[11]

Other yeomen too had amassed substantial estates in Little Munden, and twelve or thirteen very prosperous farmers dominated the economic life of the village in the 1630s. On a churchwardens' rating list of 1637 four men were taxed for 150 acres or more, another four for between 100 and 149 acres and five for between 50 and 99 acres. Below them, and in terms of their landed holdings separated by some distance from these men, were a number of smaller farmers. The rating list of 1637 indicates that four men were taxed for 25 to 49 acres, while fourteen others listed among the landholders possessed only 4 to 14 acres.[12] In addition to the 31–34 villagers in the 1630s

[9] The estimate of population is based on local rating lists in Herts. RO, D/P71/5/1; D/P71/5/2; on settlement patterns see *VCH Hertfordshire*, iii. 129, and for the relevant poor lists, Herts. RO, D/P71/5/2, a parish book which lacks pagination.

[10] Thirsk, ed., *Agrarian History*, p. 51; and information in inventories to which specific references will be given below.

[11] *VCH Hertfordshire*, iii. 131–3; Herts. RO, D/P71/5/1; D/P71/5/2; PRO, E 179/248/17; E 179/121/260, 263, 269, 304, 337.   [12] Herts. RO, D/P71/5/2.

who were taxed as landholders, churchwardens' rating lists of the period also reveal that 26–33 others were not assessed for any lands and were taxed merely as 'inhabitants'.[13] There were thus relatively large numbers of mere cottagers in this village, and many of the names on the tax lists appear, during the same period, on lists of those receiving poor relief. For example, 20 of the 33 'inhabitants' on the churchwardens' rating list of 1637 were receiving poor relief, while another man taxed among the landholders for only four acres also appears on the lists of poor.[14] In view of the arable husbandry of the area probably most of the cottagers were agricultural labourers working on the large farms of the yeomen. Few craftsmen or tradesmen can be identified in Little Munden and probably there were few of them. There was a ploughwright in the village in the 1630s, but he was no mere cottager. Although he does not appear on local tax lists, because he rented land from his father, he left an estate valued at £138 on his death in 1639.[15] The village also contained a maltman, who combined his trade with farming, and he is sometimes listed as a husbandman.[16] Another resident was identified as an innkeeper in assize records, but he too seems to have been a farmer and his son was described as a yeoman.[17] The names of two brickmakers and a bricklayer also appear in the records of the late sixteenth and very early years of the seventeenth century.[18]

Economic life in Salwarpe, a village north of Worcester and adjacent to the large settlement of Droitwich, and in Stone, located in the western part of the county near Kidderminster, was also dominated by a number of prosperous yeomen. Both were small communities, Stone containing about 30–35 families and Salwarpe about 40, and each was served by a single constable.[19] Like Little Munden they were villages

[13] Herts. RO, D/P71/5/2.

[14] Herts. RO, D/P71/5/1, pp. 1–14ᵛ, D/P71/5/2; also see the Bishop's Transcripts, Bundle 111, nos. 2–45.   [15] George Ireland: Herts. RO, 70 HW 39.

[16] John Anthony: Herts. RO, 4 HW 42; Cockburn, ed., *Herts. Indictments, James I*, no. 298.

[17] John Snell: Herts. RO, 119 HW 52; Cockburn, ed., *Herts. Indictments, James I*, nos. 1019, 1049.

[18] Robert Abbot, John Strachie, William Ballham: Herts, RO, Bishop's Transcripts, Bundle 111, no. 9; 3 HW 254; Cockburn, ed., *Herts. Indictments, James I*, no. 651.

[19] Twenty-five names appear on the subsidy list of 16 H. VIII for Stone and 33 names on the hearth tax in 1664, while 32 inhabitants of Salwarpe were taxed for the subsidy of 16 H. VIII and 41 names appear on the hearth tax, PRO, E 179/200/137; E 179/201/312, 325. Although the records of Stone through the early 1620s indicate that the village possessed one constable, by the later 1630s there may have been two officers, Bund, ed., *Sessions Papers*, p. 658.

of dispersed settlement, containing several hamlets. The early nineteenth-century enclosure map of Salwarpe still shows the place-names Copcott, Middleton, Hill End, Boycott, Chauson, High Park, and Oakley which, along with Ladywood and Newland, appear in seventeenth-century documents.[20] Stone contained the settlements of Dunclent, Shenstone, and Hoo.[21] The economy of these townships too was based on mixed farming, but the pattern was different from that in Little Munden. Large acreages of wheat are not to be found in these villages, though inventories reveal substantial crops of rye, barley, oats, and peas, and animal husbandry was relatively more important. Farmers possessed sheep, most of them some cows (and often cheeses in their upper chambers), almost without exception pigs, sometimes in large numbers, and also poultry.[22] Spinning and weaving seem to have been important in both villages. A clothier of Worcester, who on his death in 1613 possessed a lease in Salwarpe valued at £120, and woad houses and woad mills and woad seasoned and unseasoned valued at £600, probably helped to sustain the clothing industry in that village.[23]

Each of these villages contained only one manor. The manor of Salwarpe was in possession of the Talbots, one of the leading royalist families of Worcestershire; and a member of the family was resident in Salwarpe Court during most of the late sixteenth and early seventeenth centuries.[24] Only one other minor gentleman seems to have lived in the village, Thomas Trimnell of Oakley, and he was one of its greatest benefactors,[25] but the Richardson family of Worcester apparently used Chauson in Salwarpe as an occasional residence.[26] The lords of the manor of Stone do not appear to have been resident in that village.[27] Several lesser gentlemen did have connections with Stone and two of them, Edward Broad of Dunclent and William Corfield, who seems to

[20] See HWRO, 850 SALWARPE, BA 252; Bishop's Transcripts, BA 2006/40; also see *VCH Worcestershire*, iii. 205–6.

[21] The information for Stone is derived from the parish register, HWRO, 850 STONE, BA 5660(1), and wills and inventories, to which references will be given below; also see *VCH Worcestershire*, iii. 211.

[22] Specific references to wills and inventories will be given below.

[23] William Coxe: HWRO, BA 3585:164/22; and see below n. 30.

[24] *VCH Worcestershire*, ii. 215–16; iii. 207; and the Bishop's Transcripts, which show baptisms and burials of the Talbots, HWRO, BA 2006/40.

[25] *VCH Worcestershire*, iii. 208, 209; HWRO, 850 SALWARPE, BA 1054/1, Bundle A, nos. 5, 120, 287; BA 1054/2, 'Parchments Belonging to the Parish of Salwarpe', no. VII; BA 3585:133/93.

[26] *VCH Worcestershire*, iii. 208; HWRO, BA 3585:161/113; PRO, E 179/201/311.

[27] *VCH Worcestershire*, iii. 210–11.

have held the lease to the vicarage lands, lived in the village.[28] However, even minor gentlemen are not much in evidence in Salwarpe and Stone and throughout the period under consideration the economic life of these villages was dominated by eight to ten substantial yeoman families. In Salwarpe, and probably in Stone, local taxes were still based on yardlands, suggesting more traditional agrarian patterns than those which prevailed in Little Munden where holdings were listed in acres. Some men held leases to several such properties. However, in these villages the prosperity of many of the yeomen seems to have derived less from the consolidation of holdings within the village than from the fact that they held property in a number of parishes. Their wills are filled with references to lands and houses which they had leased or purchased in neighbouring villages.[29]

Rating lists do not survive for Salwarpe or Stone and precise evidence about the distribution of wealth or the occupational structure of these villages is not available. Wills and inventories and other local records do reveal the presence of a number of smaller farmers, whose wealth did not match that of their yeoman neighbours, and of some who were engaged in the clothing industry.[30] In Salwarpe there were also two tailors, a baker, a smith, and several ale-sellers, while a carpenter and an ale-seller can be identified in Stone. However, aside from the weavers in these villages there is not much evidence of the presence of craftsmen or tradesmen.[31] Finally, at the bottom of the social scale there were a number of labourers. A few of them received bequests in the wills of the gentlemen and yeomen for whom they worked. Some of them, along with a few widows, also appear on lists of

[28] For Edward Broad see HWRO, 850 STONE, BA 5672/2, no. 42; BA 5660/7, nos. 18, 29, 33–7; BA 5672/1, nos. 22a, 22c; BA 5660/1 (i); PRO, E 179/201/237, 242, 254, 292, 305, 311; Bund, ed., *Sessions Papers*, p. 658; and for Corfield, HWRO, BA 3585:156/32; 850 STONE, BA 5660/1 (i); BA 5660/7, nos. 42, 43, 178; BA 5672/1, nos. 22a, 22c. John Gower, esq., though buried in Kidderminster also seems to have had close connections with Stone, and left a bequest to the poor of the parish; see his will, HWRO, BA 3585:156/32.

[29] Subsidy rolls suggest the presence of a number of substantial farmers in these villages; see PRO, E 179/201/237, 242, 254, 292, 305, 311. Specific references to wills and inventories will be given below.

[30] For weavers in Salwarpe see HWRO, BA 3585: 130b/92; 138b/20; 178/262u; and families who seem to have possessed a number of spinning wheels, BA 3585: 136b/122; 149/104e; 133/93; 178/9a; and for Stone see BA 3585: 218a/120; 190/203; 850 STONE, BA 5660/7, no. 38.

[31] HWRO, BA 3585: 130/58; 145/39a; 850 SALWARPE, BA 1054/1, Bundle A, no. 272; BA 3585: 246/119; BA 3585: 127b/122; BA 3585: 235/25; Bund, ed., *Sessions Papers*, p. 658.

those receiving poor relief from stocks bequeathed to the parish.[32]

Gissing, Norfolk, seems to have resembled Little Munden, Salwarpe, and Stone in its social composition, though it differed from these villages in some other respects. Located south of Norwich near the Norfolk–Suffolk border, it too was a rather small village, probably containing about 40 families; but it was served by two constables.[33] Villages in this part of Norfolk in the late sixteenth and early seventeenth centuries are described as consisting of widely scattered family farms. This may well have been true of Gissing, but the records cast little light on the nature of the settlement.[34] It is clear that the economy of the village was based primarily on cattle raising and dairying, inventories revealing the presence of large numbers of milk bowls, tubs, churns, and cheese-presses. The rural weaving industry which apparently flourished in this area has left little trace in the records, though one of the extant wills for Gissing is that of a weaver.[35]

The village contained several manors which, by the beginning of the seventeenth century, had come into the hands of the Kemp family. They bought Gissinghall and Gissing cum Dagworth from Sir Arthur Heveningham in the 1590s and added these to the manors of Hastings and Dawlings which they already possessed.[36] Apart from the Kemps there were few resident gentlemen in Gissing, though a number of men of this status are found among the 'outsitters' on local rating

---

[32] For bequests to servants in Stone wills see HWRO, BA 3585: 156/32; 222a/160; 240/94. An unusual reversal occurred in the case of John Cresser, labourer, who left a will and inventory on his death in 1615, bequeathing most of his £25 worth of goods to his 'master', Mr Edward Broad, as compensation for the charges that Broad had incurred during his sickness (BA 3585: 172/42). The inventory of another labourer of Stone also survives, with a total value of £4. 18s. 10d. (BA 3585: 202a/180). The profit from the £5 left to the poor of Stone by John Gower, esq., in 1612 (BA 3585: 156/32) apparently was distributed yearly on the feast of St. Thomas and several lists of the recipients survive; see HWRO, 850 STONE, BA 5672/1, nos. 22a, 22c; BA 5660/7, nos. 176–9, and some expenditures on the poor found in churchwardens' accounts, 850 STONE, BA 5660/2, no. 219; BA 5660/3 (i).

[33] The estimate of population is based on the local rating lists, NNRO, PD 50/36L, nos. 63, 80, 82, 84; the ecclesiastical census of 1603 which gives 150 communicants, cited in Blomefield, *Norfolk*, i. 179; and the hearth tax, PRO, E 179/154/704.

[34] Thirsk, ed., *Agrarian History*, p. 46; Smith, *County and Court*, p. 5.

[35] Thirsk, ed., *Agrarian History*, pp. 47–9; specific references to the inventories will be given below. For the will and inventory of the Gissing weaver see NNRO, Norw. Cons. Wills, 130 Appleyard and INV. 9/98.

[36] Information on the Kemps is derived from Blomefield, *Norfolk*, i. 167–79; Smith, *County and Court*, esp. pp. 310–11 and Appendix III, PRO, E 179/152/464; E 179/153/558, 585, 614; E 179/154/704; NNRO, Norw. Cons. Wills, 44 Force and 93 Barker.

lists.[37] In the case of two minor gentlemen who did reside in the village there seems to have been little to set them apart from their yeomen neighbours.[38] Gissing contained a number of relatively prosperous yeomen families who formed the apex of the social pyramid, but they seem to have been less wealthy than their counterparts in Little Munden or even in Salwarpe and Stone. They do appear to have possessed a larger proportion of their lands in freehold than did their counterparts in other villages. This property probably had been acquired in the 1580s, when Sir Arthur Heveningham sold off much of the manor of Dagworth to the tenants.[39] However, their prosperity, like that of yeomen in Salwarpe and Stone, also seems to have derived from the fact that they held property in several parishes. Lands in no less than eighteen other villages are mentioned in Gissing wills of the period, and some testators left bequests to the poor of several parishes.[40] Below these yeomen there were other less prosperous inhabitants, probably farmers and labourers, who appear on local rating lists taxed for smaller sums. However, the village does not appear to have contained the number of poor cottagers found in settlements such as Little Munden.[41]

The prosperous yeomen farmers who enjoyed a disproportionate share of the wealth in Little Munden, Salwarpe, Stone, and Gissing probably also dominated local government. They regularly served in the constableship, occasionally being joined in office by a minor gentleman. Such villages provide evidence that some of the farmers who filled the office were very substantial men. The size of their holdings, the value of the personal estates which they left on their deaths, the provisions they made for their children, and in some cases even the size of the families they raised, all indicate that many of the constables in these communities were farmers of more than average means. A number of smaller farmers also held the office, and in Little

[37] The inventory of a Robert Payne, gent., of Gissinghall was taken in 1610, NNRO., INV 23/156a; for gentlemen among the outsitters see NNRO, PD 50/36L, nos. 62, 78, 80, 82, 84, 86, 87, 88.

[38] See below, nn. 70–1.

[39] References to freehold lands in wills will be given below; also see Blomefield, *Norfolk*, i. 174–5.

[40] References to wills which mention lands in several parishes will be given below. For examples of bequests to the poor of several parishes see the will of Nicholas Alden, yeoman, who left funds to the poor of Diss, Winfarthing, and Tibenham (NNRO, Norw. Cons. Wills, 46 Mittings) and the will of Henry Earle, who left bequests to the poor of Diss, Bessingham, Roydon, and Burston (Norw. Cons. Wills, 335 Bate).

[41] NNRO, PD 50/36L, nos. 63, 80, 82, 84.

Munden in the 1630s a few men who appear to have been mere
cottagers. However, in these villages there is little evidence of
craftsmen and tradesmen filling the position.

In Little Munden three gentlemen were chosen for the position, two
in 1629 and another in 1641, but they declined to serve and appointed
deputies.[42] However, the deputies were themselves rather prosperous
men. Stephen Horwood, one of the substitutes in 1629, had also
served as deputy in 1628 and he held the office in 1611 and 1614 as
well. His assessment on a churchwardens' rating list of 1629 was the
tenth highest in the village.[43] John Lanckthone was the other deputy in
1629, probably John senior, yeoman, who died in 1634; while his son,
John Lanckthone of Altwicke, yeoman, was substitute in 1640–1 and
held the office again in 1641–2. The Lanckthones were a very
substantial farming family. On his death in 1660 the younger John left
a personal estate valued at £511. He not only possessed property in
Little Munden but also a house and lands in Great Munden which he
inherited on his father's death in 1634, and some property in the
parishes of Sacombe and Hadham received from his brother-in-law.
His house, which consisted of a hall, kitchen, servants' chamber, and
three upper chambers, seems to have been rather sizeable. He
possessed the largest flock of sheep to appear in the village inventories
of the period, 140 of them, as well as cows, pigs, and horses; but most
of his wealth lay in his crops. He had a total of 97 acres in Little
Munden planted with wheat, barley, peas, and oats, valued at £220,
and crops in other villages, along with his tilth corn, were worth a
further £77. His son John was to inherit his property, and to two other
sons he left substantial bequests of £100 each.[44]

Other substantial farmers also filled the constableship in Little
Munden. At least ten officers, in addition to the Lanckthones, were
described as yeomen. The father of one of these men, six others who
appear on local rating lists taxed for 410, 160, 130, 120, 117, and 96
acres, as well as two men taxed for 60 acres, probably can be classified
as yeomen too. The size of their landed estates, and in some cases

[42] Information on who filled the constableship in Little Munden is derived from
Herts. RO, D/P71/5/1, D/P71/5/2. The list of constables is rather fragmentary prior
to 1628. The names of 21 officers survive for the period 1589 to 1615; 33 names are
missing. There is a gap from 1616 to 1627, but then the list is complete, with 32 names,
for the period 1628–43.
[43] Herts. RO, D/P71/5/2.
[44] Herts. RO, 79 HW 53; 80 HW 24.

evidence from their wills and inventories, attests to the wealth of many of the yeomen who served as constable in this village.[45]

Daniel Nash, who apparently leased the rather substantial 410 acres of the manor of Munden Freville from at least 1636, and who before that was taxed along with widow Martha Kirby for the 120 acres lately held by her yeomen husband, served as constable four times during the 1630s. His partner in the years 1631–3 was another prosperous yeoman, Robert Chapman, who possessed 117 acres in the village. Two members of the Ireland family who held office in the 1630s were also substantial farmers. Michael Ireland, constable in 1633 and 1640, was leasing the 150 acres of Libury manor by 1641, and he had considerable holdings in the village prior to that time. William Ireland, constable in 1633, farmed about 96 acres. John Kempton, constable in 1635, was taxed for 160 acres and his partner in that year, Richard Cocke, held 100 acres.[46]

Wills and inventories provide more explicit information about the wealth of some of the yeomen constables, and not only about those who held office during the 1630s. The estate of John Rowley, yeoman, constable in 1600, was valued at £171 in 1626, and his inventory reveals that he was farming 91 acres.[47] Henry Perry, constable in 1603, was much more prosperous. On his death in 1625 he left very sizeable bequests of £200 each to two sons and £100 to another, and a note on the bottom of his will indicates that his personal estate was valued at £668.[48] John Kirby, who served two terms as constable in 1602 and 1603, farmed 120 acres. His son John, yeoman, who filled the office in 1636, farmed 105 acres and left an estate valued at £300 when he died somewhat prematurely in 1637. His rather curiously arranged house, consisting of a hall, parlour, little buttery, great buttery, dish house, and kitchen on the ground floor, with only lofts above, perhaps contained some comforts. The contents of the parlour alone were valued at £20. However, most of his wealth lay in his crops, corn

---

[45] Information about the status and landed holdings of these men is derived from the Bishop's Transcripts, Bundle 111, nos. 2–45, and rating lists in D/P71/5/1, D/P71/5/2, all in Herts. RO, and from wills and inventories to which references will be given below. The value of personal estates, the size and contents of houses, and other items in the inventories of the men examined in this study can be compared with Margaret Spufford's evidence from Cambridgeshire, *Contrasting Communities*, pp. 72–5, 156–8; and W. G. Hoskins's studies of Leicestershire, esp. *Midland Peasant*, pp. 144–5, 153–4, 157–8, 178; *Essays in Leicestershire History* (Liverpool, 1951), pp. 133–6; *Provincial England* (London, 1965), p. 155.

[46] See rating lists in Herts RO, D/P71/5/2.

[47] Herts. RO, 110 HW 43.

[48] Herts. RO, 100 HW 60.

valued at £156, and in his cows, sheep, horses, and hogs valued at
£47.[49] The Faceys too were a prosperous yeoman family who held the
constableship. John Facey senior served as constable in 1600. His son,
John, who probably held the office, was taxed for 150 acres from at
least 1629 onward, apparently leasing the manor of Libury, and he left
an estate valued at £277 on his death in 1641. His rather substantial
house contained a hall, kitchen, buttery, and servants' chamber, and
three upper chambers, while his six silver spoons indicate that he could
afford a few luxuries. At the time of his death he possessed animals
valued at £45, but like the other prosperous farming constables of this
village the major part of his wealth lay in his crops. About £100 worth
of wheat, rye, barley, oats, and peas were stored in his barns, while the
crops of 28 acres and unsown lands were valued at £64.[50]

The yeomen who occupied the heights of the social structure in
Salwarpe and Stone also filled the constableship in those villages.[51]
Although the precise size of the farms of these yeomen constables is
not known, the wealth of some of them, and some indication of the
extent of their landed interests, is revealed in wills and inventories.
The Hills, Dolittles, Hornblowers, Oldnolls, Clymers, and Thatchers
provide examples of very substantial farmers who filled the office in
Stone, and the Bacons and the Kyndons probably served as constable
too. The Woodhouses, Walfords, Frenches, and Tommeses are
representative of the yeoman constables of Salwarpe, while other
prosperous farmers like the Yarnolds, Smiths, Brookes, and Ellys very
likely held the office.

Three different John Hills probably served as constables of Stone in
the years 1571, 1589, 1607 and 1620, while Humphrey Hill, yeoman,
son of one of these men and brother of another, held the office in
1629. On his death in 1635 Humphrey Hill left a personal estate,

[49] Herts. RO, 74 HW 65; Cockburn, ed., *Herts. Indictments, James I*, nos. 39, 269.
[50] Herts. RO, 41 HW 2.
[51] The lists of constables in Salwarpe and Stone are very incomplete but enough
evidence survives to show that a number of very prosperous yeomen held the office. A
list of 25 names of Salwarpe constables between 1599 and 1642 can be compiled from a
few surviving accounts, HWRO, 850 SALWARPE, BA 1054/2, Bundle D, nos. 1–9;
and from receipts issued to constables, BA 1054/1, Bundle A, no. 72, and the
unnumbered receipts in BA 1054/2, Bundle G; 17 names during the period are missing
from the list. The Stone materials are more fragmentary; the names of 9 constables
between 1560 and 1589 and 12 constables between 1598 and 1629 are known, most of
them traced through receipts issued to them or references to them in churchwardens'
accounts; see HWRO, 850 STONE, BA 5660/7, nos. 12–17, 20, 23–8, 31, 33–7; BA
5660/2, nos. 218, 219, 224; BA 5382; BA 5660/3.

divided between properties in Shenstone and Hoo, valued at about £406. He had eleven children, but his extensive landed interests enabled him to make generous provisions for most of them. One son received a messuage and half yardland in Shenstone, a second lands in Kidderminster, a third a house and yardland in Shenstone, a fourth a messuage and half yardland in the parish of Rushock. The two remaining sons received bequests of £50 and £40, while the one daughter still unprovided for was to receive a portion of £100 at age 21.[52]

The Dolittles were another substantial farming family who held the constableship, and they too had landed interests in more than one parish. John Dolittle of Shenstone, yeoman, probably the John who held the office in 1621–2, left a personal estate valued at £288 when he died in 1640. He possessed a farm in the neighbouring parish of Elmley Lovett as well as his property in Shenstone. At the time of his death his crops were valued at £180 and his livestock, including a yoke of oxen to be paid to the lord as a heriot, at more than £87. He possessed a substantial herd of 22 cows, and had six hundredweight of cheese in the chamber over his parlour. More cheese and butter were stored in Elmley Lovett, along with the tubs, churns, cheese vats, and a cheese-press found there.[53]

The Hornblowers were perhaps not quite as prosperous, but none the less substantial farmers. A Roger Hornblower, yeoman, served as constable in 1562, and there is every reason to believe the later generations of the family also filled the office. Another Roger Hornblower, who shared a farm with his father, left as his half of the estate an inventory value of £235 when he died in 1619. His share of the crops, livestock, and provisions in the house amounted to £98, while he also possessed £23 in money, and there were debts owing to him of £81. To the two daughters for whom he had not yet made provision Roger Hornblower was able to leave £70 each.[54]

Even more impressive in terms of their wealth were the Oldnolls. Nothing is known about Nicholas Oldnoll, constable in 1598; but Roger Oldnoll, yeoman, constable in 1601, 1603, and 1625, left a personal estate valued at £167 in 1635. He had already provided

[52] HWRO, BA 3585: 219c/85 (Humphrey Hill); and for other Hills, see BA 3585: 142a/22; 153/106; 159/180y; 175/56; 231/111; 233/108.
[53] HWRO, BA 3585: 235/36; for John Dolittle the elder of Hoo, BA 3585: 241/22; and for other Dolittles, BA 3585: 74a/57a; 73b/45d.
[54] HWRO, BA 3585: 184/151; for Roger, who died in 608, BA 3585: 146/141; and other Hornblowers, BA 3585: 203/104, 206c/104.

portions to all of his children except one daughter, to whom he left £100. By the time of his death he probably had transferred his land and livestock to his only surviving son, John, who appears to have served as constable in 1638. When John Oldnoll, yeoman, died rather prematurely in 1644, he left an estate valued at £653, and seven young children for whom he had to provide. His house, consisting of parlour, hall, kitchen, and upper chambers, cannot have been any more than adequate for his large family, but it did show a few signs of comfort and even a luxury or two. The linens, bedding, and bedsteads alone were valued at £37, while beef, bacon and other provisions in the house were valued at £25. Oldnoll also possessed two silver bowls valued at £4. His lengthy will reveals that he, like the other wealthy yeomen constables in this village, had landed interests outside Stone, in his case in Chaddesley Corbett. His wife was to enjoy the leases to both properties to maintain the children and raise portions for them. The eldest son was eventually to inherit these leases, and out of the profits he was to pay £300 to one of his brothers when he reached age 14. To another son Oldnoll left £300 at age 21, while two further sons were to receive £200 each. His only daughter was bequeathed £300 at age 30 or on the day of her marriage. However, if she did not marry with the consent of her mother and of Oldnoll's three brothers-in-law, whom he made overseers of his will, the sum was to be reduced to £150. John Oldnoll's rather prosperous state is reflected not only in the sizeable portions he was able to leave his children, but also in the large number of small bequests he made to his servants, several poor neighbours, his sisters, and sisters-in-law, as well as general bequests to the poor of Kidderminster and Chaddesley Corbett. A large proportion of Oldnoll's wealth was accounted for by £295 worth of agricultural produce, and livestock valued at £205. He possessed a sizeable flock of 200 sheep as well as 28 cows and 27 pigs. He had 100 acres planted with rye and 40 acres with peas, in addition to rye, barley, and peas stored in his barns. The size of his farm was thus nearly equal to those of some of the very substantial yeomen who served as constable in Little Munden.[55]

Other yeomen families of Stone who provided constables probably were rather substantial men, if not as prosperous as John Oldnoll, though less is known about them. William Clymer served as constable in 1563, and later generations of this family, who were taxed for the

[55] HWRO, BA 3585: 222a/160 (Roger); 240/94 (John); and for William Oldnoll, a weaver, see 218a/120.

subsidy in Stone, probably held the constableship. Richard Clymer, yeoman, probably son of William, acted as churchwarden on no less than eight occasions between 1580 and 1614 and he no doubt served as constable too. On his death in 1632 his estate was valued at £122. He seems to have been quite elderly by that time and much of his property may has passed to his son, William, who as early as 1624 was to pay part of his father's subsidy assessment. William Clymer, yeoman, also probably served as constable, and is known to have been churchwarden on four occasions.[56] The Thatchers were another yeoman family who provided constables, and they too were subsidy men. John Thatcher held the office in 1566–7, and Francis Thatcher, yeoman, served as constable in 1580–1, 1598–9, and 1601–2. His son, John Thatcher, who acted as churchwarden on at least six occasions, probably filled the constableship too.[57] Three generations of Bacons were subsidy men in Stone, two are known to have served as churchwardens and they probably held the office of constable as well. When John Bacon, yeoman, died in 1620, leaving as orphans one son and four daughters of 'tender years', he was able to make provision for them out of lands and tenements in both Stone and Chaddesley Corbett.[58] The Kyndons too almost certainly held the office. While this family included weavers and husbandmen, Walter Kyndon, who was churchwarden in the 1580s and who probably served as constable during the late sixteenth or early seventeenth century, was described as yeoman. However, by the time of his death in 1631 his estate was valued at only about £46.[59]

The leading families of Salwarpe who served in the constableship were somewhat less wealthy than the Oldnolls or the Hills of Stone, but none the less prosperous yeomen. They too often possessed several properties and were able to make provision for more than one son.

The Woodhouses had several branches in the village and several men in this family held the office during the early seventeenth century. William Woodhouse of Boycott, yeoman, probably served as constable, and is known to have been one of the first overseers of the poor in the

[56] HWRO, BA 3585: 215b/62; BA 5660/7, no. 38; PRO, E 179/201/237, 242, 254, 292, 305, 311.

[57] PRO, E 179/201/237, 242, 254, 292, 305, 311; wills and inventories survive for some Thatchers, HWRO, BA 3585: 178/23; 178/261L; 206c/165.

[58] PRO, E 179/201/237, 242, 254, 305, 311; HWRO, BA 3585: 188/124.

[59] HWRO, BA 3585: 214a/129; for Hugh Kyndon, weaver, see BA 3585: 190/203, and for Simon Kyndon, husbandman, BA 3585: 201/142.

village. His son, John Woodhouse of Boycott, yeoman, held the office in 1607 and 1611, and in turn his son, William Woodhouse of Hill End, yeoman, filled the constableship from 1634 to 1636. The elder William Woodhouse left an estate valued at £201 on his death in 1603. When the younger William died rather prematurely in 1640, leaving six orphaned children all under sixteen years of age, his personal estate was valued at only £95. However, he did hold leases to properties in both Hill End and Ladywood and the profits from these were to be used to educate his family and put them forth to services and trades.[60]

The Frenches were less prolific and more prosperous than the Woodhouses. John French served as constable in 1599 and his son Richard probably held the office during the early seventeenth century. No will or inventory is extant for John, but when Richard, yeoman, died in 1647 he left a personal estate valued at £394 and he was able to make generous provision for his four children. His house was larger than most in the village, apart from the vicarage, with a parlour, hall, kitchen, lower kitchen, 'dayhouse', room next to the 'dayhouse', chambers over the parlour, hall, and kitchen, a chamber for the menservants, and a recent addition referred to as 'the new house'. This dwelling showed some signs of comfort. There were curtained beds in the parlour and one of the chambers, and the linens alone were worth £16. Richard had fairly extensive landed interests in the village and beyond, which enabled him to make provision for his three sons. The lease to a messuage and lands in Ladywood, Salwarpe, was to go to his eldest son, a second son was to inherit a messuage in the neighbouring parish of Hadzor as well as 9 acres of meadow in Droitwich, and a third his interest in two messuages in Middleton, Salwarpe, held in reversion. To his only daughter he bequeathed £200 at age 21, £100 of that sum to be paid by one of her brothers from the profits of the lands he received. The lease which French had purchased from Sherrington Talbot, lord of the manor, was valued at £50 in his inventory, and he also possessed livestock worth £112 and crops worth £83. He seems to have possessed the largest herd of cows in the village. 20 of them, and he is the only villager known to have owned a bull.[61]

The Walfords were another wealthy farming family who held the constableship in Salwarpe. Richard, who died in 1617 leaving a

---

[60] HWRO, Ba 3585: 133/93; 246/167; for other Woodhouse wills and inventories, see 147/146k; 230/226; 230/233.
[61] HWRO, BA 3585: 245/62.

personal estate valued at £227, probably served as constable and his son and heir, Richard, is known to have held the office in 1625. The Walford house, like that of the Frenches, showed some signs of 'the great rebuilding';[62] it contained a new parlour, with a chamber above, as well as the old parlour and a hall. Richard senior no doubt made good use of this space because he raised nine children, while Richard the younger had also produced a family of nine between 1627 and 1643. The elder Richard's inventory reveals such luxuries as a silver mustard bowl, a silver and gilt salt, and nine silver spoons, most of them inherited by Richard the younger on the death of his mother in 1634. However, a lease for forty years to the messuage where he dwelled, valued at £150, accounted for a major portion of the value of Richard Walford's estate.[63]

The Tommeses too seem to have been fairly prosperous farmers. Richard Tommes, yeoman, left an estate valued at only £14 when he died in 1617, probably because he was elderly and had passed on his lands and livestock to his son John. When John, constable in 1609 and 1633, died in 1647, his estate was valued at £183, £80 of that accounted for by leases. Although his landed interests seem to have been confined to the manor of Salwarpe, he did hold considerable property there. He had bought from Sherrington Talbot the leases to a messuage in Middleton, another messuage in Hill End, and a cottage in Salwarpe.[64]

A number of other yeomen families in Salwarpe very likely filled the constableship as well, and some of them too appear to have been rather substantial. Edward Yarnold, yeoman, who served as churchwarden in 1613, and probably as constable, left an estate valued at £220 on his death in 1645.[65] Thomas Smith, yeoman, who was taxed for the subsidy and who acted as one of the local assessors in 1641, was churchwarden on at least five occasions and probably held the constableship too. John Smith, yeoman, another subsidy man and an assessor in 1641, and churchwarden for four terms, probably filled the office as well.[66] John Brooke, yeoman, churchwarden in 1618, no doubt served as constable too. He seems to have been rather prosperous, and possessed a house of seven rooms, though his

[62] W. G. Hoskins, 'The Rebuilding of Rural England, 1570–1640', in *Provincial England*, pp. 131–48; but also see R. Machin, 'The Great Rebuilding: A Reassessment', *P and P*, lxxvii (1977), 33–56.

[63] HWRO, BA 3585: 180/63a (Richard the elder): 220/185 (his widow, Anne).

[64] HWRO, BA 3585: 178/261k; 244/185.

[65] HWRO, BA 3585: 245/93.   [66] PRO, E 179/201/292, 311.

personal estate was valued at only about £100 by the time of his death in 1649.[67] The Elly and Shailer families too probably furnished constables, and both served as churchwardens. William Elly, yeoman, left an estate valued at £155 on his death in 1617, and he possessed leases to two properties in Salwarpe. Thomas Shailer, yeoman, churchwarden in 1622, held lands in Droitwich as well as in Salwarpe. He was probably more substantial than is suggested by his inventory of 1641, which valued his personal estate at only £75.[68]

Gissing provides a final example of a settlement in which a number of substantial farmers served as constable.[69] Nine of the fifteen officers for whom social descriptions survive were identified as yeomen and two as gentlemen, although these men do not seem to have been as wealthy as their counterparts in the villages of Little Munden, Salwarpe, and Stone. Only a few inventories survive for Gissing, but these, along with the wills of a number of the yeomen and minor gentlemen who held the office, are suggestive of the substance of some of them.

Two gentlemen served as constables of Gissing, William Alden in 1632–3 and Thomas Procktor in 1621–2. Alden inherited a personal estate valued at £264 when his yeoman uncle, who probably held the office too, died in 1626. The real estate which came into his hands included freehold and copyhold lands in Gissing, part of a house in Norwich, and other lands in the villages of Great Melton and Fudenhall. On his early death in 1635 many of these lands were to be sold to provide for his wife and for the upbringing of his children. However, he did leave to his heir, who was still a minor, lands in the village of Denton and household goods which included twelve silver spoons, and he provided a portion of £100 to his daughter.[70] The other minor gentleman who held office was a son of the rector of Gissing, Thomas Procktor. On his father's death in 1621 the younger Thomas received lands in Fritton and Morningthorpe as well as the bulk of a personal estate valued at £171. He clearly possessed lands in Gissing as well, and he was taxed for the subsidy there in 1624. However, he

[67] HWRO, BA 3585: 245/21.   [68] HWRO, BA 3585: 180/84; 234/183.

[69] The names of 4 constables who served in 1591 and 1592 are known, and a list of 55 constables can be compiled for the years 1603–43; 26 names are missing from the list. The information is derived from the Gissing Town Book, which contains some summary accounts, NNRO, PD 50/35; and from a few surviving detailed accounts, PD 50/36L, nos. 9–9A, 45, 53–5, 83, 89, 92, 100–1, 103.

[70] NNRO, Norw. Cons. Wills, 46 Mittings, INV 33/19; Norf. Arch. Wills, Register 1635, ff. 73–5.

seems to have moved from the village shortly after that and by 1630 his name appears among the 'outsitters' on local rating lists.[71]

Among the yeomen constables was Anthony Milles, who held the office from 1607–8 to 1609–10. He was taxed for 20s. lands in the subsidy, and left an estate valued at £172 on his death in 1613, including £45 in debts that were owed to him. He possessed a substantial herd of 16 cows and a bull, and apparently was one of the few villagers who also had some sheep. His two posted beds seem to have been common possessions among the yeomen farmers of Gissing, and the cheese, cheese-presses, churns, tubs, and milk bowls which he owned are duplicated in most of the inventories. His son William received the bulk of his personal estate and was to be executor of his will, but he seems to have left the village (he was taxed as an 'outsitter in 1624 and 1631). It was another of Anthony's sons, Thomas, who succeeded his father to the constableship, holding the office in 1625.[72] The inventories of two other yeomen constables do not accurately reflect the wealth of these families. William Kidman, constable in 1607–8 and 1608–9, left a personal estate valued at only £55 on his death in 1638, probably because he was elderly and had already made provision for his sons. He too had three posted beds, which accounted for £12 of the inventory value, but the livestock one would expect to find probably had passed to his heirs. Kidman too was a subsidy man and on a local rating list was taxed for two tenements and a close in the village. He had the fourth highest assessment for local levies in 1624 and was in fifth or sixth place during the early 1630s. This family apparently could afford a few luxuries. William's yeoman father, who probably served as constable too, on his death in 1596 left six silver spoons to one of his grandsons.[73] The estate of another yeoman, John Brown, constable in 1635–6, was valued at only £62 on his death in 1666; but this does not seem to provide an accurate reflection of his means. He too had posted bedsteads, one of them with curtains, and he still had some livestock, along with the cheese in the chamber over the parlour and the usual churns, tubs, and cheese-presses in the dairy. His will suggests a man of greater substance than the inventory

[71] NNRO, Norw. Cons. Wills, 62 Hudd, INV 31/42B; PRO, E 179/153/585; NNRO, PD 50/36L, nos. 63, 78, 80, 82, 84; Blomefield, *Norfolk*, i. 163.

[72] NNRO, Norw. Cons. Wills, 62 Coonney, INV 26/84; PD 50/36L, nos. 62, 84; PRO, E 179/152/464, 558.

[73] NNRO, INV 44/84; Norw. Cons. Wills, 195 Skyppon; PD 50/36L, nos. 63, 80, 82, 84.

reveals, and he held lands in several parishes. He bequeathed freehold and copyhold in Aslacton to one son, houses and lands in Gissing to another son, copyhold and freehold in Gissing to one daughter, and five acres of freehold to another daughter.[74]

Other yeomen constables who seem to have been fairly substantial farmers, and who possessed lands in more than one parish, included Thomas Daynes, constable in 1603–4 and 1604–5, whose will of 1620 mentioned lands in three Norfolk villages and one Suffolk village; and Esdras Taylor, constable in 1612–13 and 1613–14, who possessed lands in Ellingham as well as Gissing.[75] James Freeman, yeoman, constable in 1610–11 and 1611–12, and a subsidy man, was less specific in his will of 1615 referring to all lands, freehold, customary, and copy in Gissing and elsewhere in Norfolk. His son Robert served as constable in 1620–1, 1629–30 and 1636–7, and he too was taxed for the subsidy and appears in seventh or eighth place on local rating lists of the 1630s.[76] Thomas Earle, yeoman, constable in 1591–2 and 1619–20, who was also a subsidy man, inherited lands in both Gissing and Shimpling from his yeoman father, though the elder Earle's estate was valued at only about £22 at the time of his death in 1584.[77]

Less is known about many of the other constables of Gissing, but both the level of their local assessments and the fact that many of them were subsidy men suggest that they too were substantial farmers. John Clipwell, constable in 1624–5, 1629–30, and 1636–7, was taxed for the subsidy and appears in second place on a rating list of 1624. Thomas Froswell, who held office in 1603–4 and 1622, was also a subsidy man and had the third highest assessment on local rating lists in the 1630s. Five other constables of Gissing, Robert Foster, yeoman, constable in 1591–2, Thomas Blome, who served in 1605–6, 1606–7, and 1631–2, Robert Cobbe, yeoman, in office in 1615–6, 1625–6 and 1635–6, Robert Homes, constable in 1606–7, 1607–8, and 1614–15, and Thomas Burde, who served in 1604–5 and 1605–6, are known to have been subsidy men, and they too were probably rather substantial. William Tibenham, constable in 1592–3 and 1621–2 does not appear on any of the surviving subsidy rolls; but he was in third place on a

---

[74] NNRO, Norw. Cons. Wills, 270 Stockwell, INV 52/36.

[75] NNRO, Norf. Arch. Wills, original wills 1621, no. 31; original wills 1615, no. 10.

[76] NNRO, Norf. Arch. Wills, original wills 1615, no. 88; PRO, E 179/152/464, 558, 585; NNRO, PD 50/36L, nos. 80, 82, 84.

[77] NNRO, Norw. Cons. Wills, 355 Bate, INV 2/69 (Henry Earle); Norf. Arch. Wills, original wills 1620, no. 115 (Thomas Earle); PRO, E 179/153/558.

local rating list of 1624, and he too seems to have been a prosperous farmer.[78]

The social heights in villages such as Little Munden, Salwarpe, Stone, and Gissing were occupied by a number of rather prosperous yeomen, and an occasional minor gentlemen, and in such settlements many of the constables were drawn from this social stratum. However, these communities also contained husbandmen of more moderate means and some of these farmers too served in the constableship. They cannot be described as the 'meanest' villagers, because these settlements (with the possible exception of Gissing) contained cottagers who were much less prosperous; but their wealth could not match that of their yeomen neighbours. Some of them seem to have possessed rather small holdings, especially when they are compared with farms of 100 acres or more held by some of the yeomen. The value of their personal estates was usually less than £100, and the portions of £10 or £20 which they provided for their children also point to the fact that they were men of lesser means.

The Hodges, Dugard, and Ellis families of Salwarpe provide good examples of the husbandmen who held the office in such villages. While the size of their holdings is not known, wills and inventories make it possible to contrast their wealth with that of the yeomen constables of this settlement.

John Hodges, husbandman, who served as constable in 1604, left an estate valued at only £85 on his death in 1608, most of the value in agricultural produce and livestock. Hodges transferred his real property to his son, Thomas, but his widow paid £62 to acquire the house and lands, to her 'greate chardge and hinderannce', and on her death in 1619 the estate passed to John Hodges the younger, who served as constable in 1630. The house inhabited by the Hodges consisted only of a hall and a kitchen, with two chambers above the hall, though John the elder raised a family of eight in this dwelling. The house was less crowded when it came into the possession of John the younger, since only four of his seven children survived the hazards of seventeenth-century infancy. Although John Hodges the younger was assessed at 20s. lands for the subsidy, and cannot be classified as a

---

[78] PRO, E 179/152/464; E 179/153/558, 585, 614, 617; NNRO, PD 50/36L, nos. 63, 80, 82, 84. Wills survive for Thomas Froswell (NNRO, Norf. Arch. Wills, original wills 1628, no. 34); Edmund Smith. *c.*1615–16 (Norf. Arch. Wills, original wills 1624, no. 107); Robert Foster (Norf. Arch. Wills, Register 1610, ff. 108ᵛ–109ᵛ); and Robert Cobbe (Norf. Arch. Wills, original wills 1636, no. 44).

poor villager, the prosperity of the Hodges was modest by comparison with that of their yeoman neighbours such as the Frenches, the Walfords, and the Woodhouses. By 1647 the property in Hodges's tenure was held in reversion by Richard French, who had purchased the lease from the Talbots.[79]

The Dugards were another farming family of moderate means. Walter Dugard, husbandman, probably served as constable and his two sons George and John held the office in 1618 and 1619, respectively. Walter left an estate valued at only £67 on his death in 1609. The inheritance of the Dugard sons almost certainly could not match that of some of their yeomen neighbours whose fathers left estates valued at £200 or £300. However, both men, like their father before them, were taxed for the subsidy, George for 26s. 8d. lands and John for 20s. lands.[80]

The Ellis family provides a final example of farmers of middling prosperity who served as constables in Salwarpe. Robert Ellis, husbandman, served as churchwarden in 1615 and probably held the constableship too. His son Robert filled the office in 1639–40 and his son Francis in 1641–2 and 1642–3. None of these men appear on the subsidy rolls of the period, and they apparently were somewhat less prosperous than the Hodges or the Dugards. The value of Robert Ellis's estate is not known, but the bequests in his will of 1635 suggest very modest wealth. His eldest son Robert was to inherit the property on the death of his mother, while his two younger sons, Francis and Thomas, received bequests of £10 each and his daughter ten marks.[81] These sums constitute a very meagre start in life when compared with the bequests of £50 to £300 received by the sons and daughters of some of the yeomen who held the constableship.

Some small farmers held the constableship in Little Munden too, though not much is known about them except the acreage of their farms. There is quite a contrast between Daniel Nash, with his 410 acres, or other yeomen constables with holdings ranging from 60 to 160 acres, and men such as Edmund Walker, husbandman, farming about 20 acres, who held the constableship in 1600 or Thomas Colte

[79] HWRO, BA 3585: 149/104e (John the elder); 195/91 (his widow, Joan); PRO, E 179/201/292, 311; for Richard French see above, n. 61.

[80] HWRO, BA 3585: 149/122; PRO, E 179/201/237, 242, 254, 292, 311. John Dugard was the chief beneficiary of the will of Richard Woodhouse alias Callow (or Calloway), husbandman, who died in 1620 and who referred to John as his kinsman (BA 3585: 187/7).

[81] HWRO, BA 3585: 221b/66.

junior, constable in 1639–40, who was taxed on local rating lists for 30 acres. Two Richard Goodwins served as constable, one in 1597 and the other for three terms, 1635, 1642, and 1643, and they held only about 14 acres. So did Jonas Wood, constable in 1635. Richard Hawkes, constable in 1615, who was described as a husbandman, probably possessed a small holding too.[82]

In villages such as Little Munden, Salwarpe, Stone, and Gissing craftsmen and tradesmen do not appear to have been very numerous and only occasionally is a constable identified as being in one of these occupations. Edward Glover, constable of Salwarpe in 1603, may have been a weaver,[83] and it is possible that two weavers in Stone, John Kyndon and Edward Salisbury, both of whom served as churchwardens, also held the constableship.[84] A maltman, John Anthony, served as constable in Little Munden in 1606–7, as did two brickmakers, John Strachie in 1597 and Robert Abbot in 1610.[85]

During the 1630s there also appear to have been a few men of very slender means who served as constables of Little Munden, along with the prosperous yeomen and occasional husbandmen who also held office during that period. Robert Adams, constable in 1636–7, appears on a local tax list as a landholder, but he was assessed for a mere five acres in the village. John Snell, constable in 1638–9, was also taxed for only five acres, and by 1640 he appears on a local rating list among the 'inhabitants' who were not assessed for any lands. William Risdaile, who held office in 1639–40, having agreed to do so only on the condition that he be exempt from serving for the next four years,[86] also seems to have been a mere cottager. He too was taxed as an inhabitant and apparently held no lands. Simon Mitchell, constable in 1641–2,

---

[82] This information is derived from local rating lists in Herts. RO, D/P71/5/1, D/P71/5/2. A will survives for Edmund Walker, Herts. RO, 3 HW 196; for the identification of Hawkes see Cockburn, ed. *Herts. Indictments, James I*, no. 651.

[83] A John Glover alias Pennis of Ladywood who died in 1617 seems to have been a weaver; and it was probably the constable of 1603, listed as Edward *Pennys*, who witnessed the will and took the inventory of Richard Cowles, weaver, in 1602 (HWRO, BA 3585: 178/262u; 130b/92).

[84] Salisbury is identified as a weaver in a document of 1624 which noted that he was to pay the subsidy with John Kyndon, HWRO, 850 STONE, BA 5660/7, no. 38; John Kyndon was son of Hugh Kyndon, weaver, and inherited his father's looms, BA 3585: 190/203.

[85] See John Anthony's will, Herts. RO, 4 HW 42 and the will of John Strachie, 3 HW 254; for the identification of Robert Abbot see Bishop's Transcripts, Bundle 111, no. 9.

[86] See above, ch. 3, n. 71.

was assessed among the landholders, but for only four acres, and he too must have been a rather poor man.[87]

In Little Munden, Salwarpe, Stone, and Gissing, with their élites of substantial yeomen farmers, the constabulary was characterized by the number of such men who served in the office. The yeomen appear to have held the constableship with greater frequency than other social groups, and sometimes they served several terms within just a few years. Husbandmen too, some of them moderately prosperous and like the yeoman taxed for the subsidy, and an occasional tradesman or craftsman, also filled the constableship in these villages. Some of the husbandmen held office several times during their lives, but the total service of this group in villages such as Little Munden, Salwarpe, and Stone seems to have been less than that of their more substantial farming neighbours. A number of poor men, who appear to have been mere cottagers, held office in Little Munden in the 1630s and early 1640s. However, in almost every case they served in partnership with a substantial yeoman.

(2) Gentlemen, Yeomen, Husbandmen, and Tradesmen of Bushey

The village of Bushey, located in the southern part of Hertfordshire and bordering on Middlesex, was rather different in character from settlements such as Little Munden, Salwarpe, Stone, and Gissing. It contained over 100 households in the 1630s, and is one of the most populous villages considered in this study.[88] Local records sometimes drew a distinction between the 'town' of Bushey, the remainder of the parish, and the hamlet of Leavesden, located in the parish of Watford. These divisions were originally three tithings of the manor of Bushey. Each possessed a constable or equivalent officer, Leavesden being served by a headborough.[89]

The economy of the village was based on mixed farming. The raising of livestock and the breeding of horses were major pursuits in this part of Hertfordshire, and probably in Bushey. Farmers also raised

---

[87] This discussion is based on rating lists and the election of officers in Herts. RO, D/P26/7/1.

[88] Herts. RO, D/P26/7/1 and D/P26/10/1, which contain local rating lists of the period. The largest number of names appears on a churchwardens' rating list of 1636, when 105 were taxed for the levy.

[89] See local rating lists in Herts. RO, D/P26/7/1; D/P26/10/1; Bushey Court Rolls, no. 6403; *VCH Hertfordshire*, ii. 142, 179, 182.

pigs and poultry. However, produce from the arable seems to have
been more valuable. Oats were the largest crop, and hay too was
important, but farmers also grew rye, barley, peas, and the major cash
crop, wheat.[90]

In terms of its social structure Bushey was distinct, in at least one
respect, from all of the other villages under consideration. It contained
more resident gentlemen, while a substantial number of non-residents
of this status also possessed landed interests there for varying periods
of time.[91] The preponderance of gentlemen is accounted for in part by
the presence of three manors, Hartesbourne, Bournhall, and Bushey,
the last divided into three separate interests, and also of two apparently
substantial farms called Pettiplace and Leggats within the hamlet of
Leavesden. Since the manors changed hands several times during the
late sixteenth and early seventeenth centuries, there is some turnover
in the names of gentlemen appearing in the local records.[92] Below the
level of gentlemen, wealth seems to have been more evenly distributed
than in communities such as Little Munden, Salwarpe, Stone, and
Gissing. There were a few yeomen who possessed sizeable holdings.
However, a majority of farmers in the village were of more moderate
means, even though some of them were identified as yeomen. A rating
list of 1632, which gives the acreage on which men were to be taxed for
local levies, shows only three non-gentlemen with 100 acres or more,
while eight other farmers were taxed for 50 to 99 acres. However,
there were 38 farmers holding less than 50 acres, seven of them with
25 to 49 acres, while 31 men were taxed for only 2 to 24 acres.[93] Some
men in this village combined farming with other occupations. Arable
husbandry sustained the related occupations of milling, meal-making,
and malting, while the importance of rearing and fattening livestock is
reflected in the presence of several butchers. Other crafts and trades

---

[90] Thirsk, ed., *Agrarian History*, pp. 50–1; information on the agriculture of Bushey is
also drawn from the local materials in Herts. RO, D/P26/7/1 and D/P26/10/1.

[91] In addition to the gentlemen who will be discussed below, others who appear on
local rating lists or who were taxed for the subsidy in Bushey include Robert Wilbraham,
gent.; Ralph Wilbraham, esq., a Hertfordshire JP; Sir Edward Cary; Sir Edward Alford;
Humphrey Rogers, esq.; Sylas Tito, gent.; Edmund Roydon, gent.; and Richard Right,
gent.

[92] Information about the manors of Bushey and the gentlemen who held them is
found in *VCH Hertfordshire*, ii. 182–4; local documents, particularly rating lists, in Herts.
RO, D/P26/7/1; D/P26/10/1; subsidy rolls, PRO, E 179/120/119; E 179/121/259,
279, 314, 329, 331. Also see the will of Henry Hickman, gent., Herts. RO, 64 AW 11,
and the bond of administration for the estate of George Hickman, 77 AW 34.

[93] Herts. RO, D/P26/10/1. p. 9.

too were represented in the village. The records of the 1630s show the presence of three smiths, a bricklayer, two carpenters, a fuller, a chandler, and a weaver, while a collier and a tailor appear in earlier records along with a cobbler and an ironmonger.[94] The list is probably incomplete, but it does suggest that there was a substantial number of craftsmen and tradesmen in the village. However, few men in this community seem to have been taxed as mere cottagers.

In view of the economy and social structure of the village, it is not surprising that the officers of Bushey display considerable diversity in their wealth and status. In no other village did as many gentlemen hold the office, while there were also some yeomen, larger numbers of small farmers, and some tradesmen who filled the position. Most of the constables were taxed as landholders and not mere cottagers; but a few of those who held office in the 1630s do seem to have been men of rather slender means.[95]

No less than five gentlemen served as constables of Bushey, while several men of this status probably served as headboroughs of Leavesden. The gentlemen constables included George Hickman and his son George, lords of the manor of Bournhall, who were taxed for 170 acres in the village in 1632 and who held office in 1617 and 1636, respectively.[96] William Morgan, gent., served as constable in 1627–8; and although he was assessed for only £2 lands in Bushey in the subsidies of 1625 and 1628, his local assessments during the 1630s were more substantial as was his tax for ship-money in 1636.[97] Robert and Thomas Nicholl, apparently recently arrived gentlemen, also held the office in 1621–2 and 1635, respectively; and more is known about the wealth of this family. Thomas Nicholl senior, who served as constable in 1587–8, was described as a yeoman. However, his son Robert, who was taxed for 108 acres in Bournhall manor in 1632, and

[94] Evidence is derived from the town book and rating lists, Herts. RO, D/P26/7/1; D/P26/10/1; assize records, Cockburn, ed., *Herts. Indictments, Elizabeth I*, nos. 74–5; *Herts. Indictments, James I*, nos. 552, 624, 625, 933; and wills, to which specific references will be given below.

[95] The names of the constables of Bushey are derived from the town book, which gives the selection of these officers, from constables' ratings lists, Herts. RO, D/P26/7/1, D/P26/10/1, and from the Bushey Court Rolls in Herts. RO, nos. 6393, 6395–6, 6398–6407, 37140, 37142, 37148, 37149. The list of constables derived from these sources is somewhat fragmentary. The names of 24 constables between 1585 and 1606 are known; 18 names from this period are missing. There is a gap from 1607 to 1613, but then the list is nearly complete for the period 1614–43, 55 names are known and only 5 are missing from the list.

[96] Herts. RO, D/P26/10/1, p. 9.

[97] PRO, E 179/121/329, 331; Herts. RO, D/P26/10/1.

who seems to have been well provided for even before his father's
death, was designated as gentleman when he was selected surveyor of
the highways in 1632. Although his will of 1633 described him as a
yeoman, he seems to have been regarded as a gentleman by some of his
neighbours; and his bequests suggest that he was a man of
considerable substance. He left £600 to one son, £200 each to two
others, £100 to a fourth son, and a portion of £300 for a daughter. His
son and heir, Thomas, inherited most of his lands, but another son
received a house and nine acres in Bushey and two others jointly
inherited twenty-two acres in the parish of Barnet. The younger
Thomas Nicholl, who served as constable in 1635, was also designated
gentleman. He was an even larger landholder than his father since he
inherited additional property on the death of his grandfather in 1634.[98]

Some men of similar status seem to have served as headboroughs of
Leavesden. The Nicholl family held substantial property there, the
farm called Leggats, as well as their lands in Bushey; and two Nicholls,
who may well have been lesser gentlemen, acted as headboroughs of
that hamlet.[99] Like the Nicholls, the Ewer family of Leavesden also
seems to have risen into the gentry during the early seventeenth
century. William Ewer held Pettiplace farm in Leavesden and in 1632
was also assessed for 32 acres in Bournhall manor. He was designated
'gent.' when he was chosen surveyor of the highways in that year. He,
like the Nicholls, probably served as headborough of Leavesden
during the 1630s, a Thomas Ewer having held the office there in
1624–5.[100] Another of the headboroughs of that hamlet, Thomas
Scott, who served in 1632–3 and 1633–4, and who was taxed for 160
acres in Leavesden, may also have been regarded as a gentleman. He
probably was descended from the family which had held Bournhall
and Hartesbourne manors and Bushey Hall during the late sixteenth
century.[101]

In addition to the gentlemen who filled the constableship or who
served as headboroughs of Leavesden, at least twelve constables of
Bushey were identified as yeomen. Three others, who were in the
direct line of descent in these families and who farmed 120, 61, and 50

---

[98] Herts. RO, D/P26/7/1, pp. 32, 46; D/P26/10/1, p. 9; 75 AW 17; 76 AW 20.

[99] Herts. RO, Bushey Court Rolls, nos. 6402, 6407; D/P26/10/1.

[100] William Ewer was not designated 'gent'. in the 1620s. See Herts. RO,
D/P26/7/1, pp. 32, 46; Bushey Court Rolls, nos. 6403, 6393. A Mr Thomas Ewer of
the Lea appears on local lists from *c.*1608 to 1619 and Henry Ewer, esq., in the 1630s.

[101] Herts. RO, Bushey Court Rolls, nos. 6405, 6406; D/P26/10/1, p. 9; *VCH
Hertfordshire*, ii. 183–4.

acres, respectively, probably can be classified as yeomen too. Some of them, like John Hunt, Henry Francis, Thomas Harte, and the yeomen members of the Blackwell family, whose relatives held two-thirds of Bushey manor, were prosperous men. Hunt, constable in 1632, was taxed for 120 acres in the village on a local rating list of that year. Henry Francis, constable in 1604–5, left bequests of £100 each to four of his children on his death in 1617, and he too seems to have been a man of some substance.[102] Thomas Harte, constable in 1619–20 and 1632–3, appears to have farmed about 75 acres in Bournhall manor, and on his death in 1639, seemingly lacking direct heirs, he left substantial bequests of £250 to a niece and £150 to one Edward Ewer of Abbots Langley.[103] The will of George Blackwell, yeoman, who served as constable on at least four occasions, 1587–8, 1604–5, 1613, and 1624–5, reveals that he possessed considerable holdings in the manor of Bushey and also lands in Hendon, Middlesex. Richard Blackwell, yeoman, constable in 1619–20, also seems to have had a substantial estate and he left a sizeable portion of £100 for a daughter on his death in 1634.[104] However, many of the constables classified as yeomen in this village were men of much more moderate prosperity, middling-sized farmers when their holdings and wealth are compared with those of many of the yeomen constables in settlements such as Little Munden, Salwarpe, Stone, and Gissing.[105]

There were larger numbers of small farmers, and some tradesmen of middling wealth, who filled the constableship in Bushey. Typical of these lesser farmers were four members of the Bonnick family who held the office. Two of them were listed as possessing 12 or 13 acres, and the others too seem to have been rather small landholders. William Fells, constable on three occasions, in 1606, 1614, and 1628, with his 18 acres, Edward Huddell, constable in 1603, and his son Thomas, who held office in 1616 and 1626, who farmed 30 acres, and Nehemiah Knowlton, constable in 1635, with 14 acres, were also farmers of rather moderate means. At least two, and probably more, of

[102] Herts. RO, D/P26/10 1, p. 9; 58 AW 11.
[103] Herts. RO, D/P26/10/1, p. 9; 81 AW 17.
[104] Herts. RO, 73 AW 2; 76 AW 3.
[105] This evaluation is based on the rating lists in Herts. RO, D/P26/7/1 and D/P26/10/1; and on the wills of a number of constables identified as yeomen: Alexander Weedon, c. 1591–2 (52 AW 30); William Weedon, c. 1622–3 (98 AW 19); George Weedon, c. 1600–1, 1617 (69 AW 23); John Fells, c. 1620–1 (82 AW 10); Richard Backer, c. 1630–1 (75 AW 3); Nehemiah Knowlton, c. 1634–5 (136 AW 3Y); and Thomas Adams, who probably served as constable (91 AW 3).

the seven members of the Weedon family who served as constable seem to have been equally small property holders, even though some of them were identified as yeomen. Ralph, who was constable in 1622, held 30 acres, and John, constable in 1630, farmed 15 acres. A number of men who held some land as well as pursuing a trade, most of them in agriculturally related pursuits characteristic of this area of Hertfordshire, also held office. Henry Jorden, mealman, served as constable in 1600; Robert Wood, oatmeal maker, in 1624 and 1635; Thomas Walker, miller, in 1630; and John Fendall, butcher, in 1627. Possibly there were other tradesmen among the constables as well. In addition, a collier held the office in 1592, while Daniel Heyward, who served as constable three times, in 1615, 1623, and 1633, was described at various times as blacksmith, ironmonger, and yeoman.[106]

Information is not available about the property or occupations of all those known to have held the constableship in Bushey, and some perhaps were mere cottagers. A few of those who filled the office in the 1630s, when their relative wealth can be determined from local tax lists, do seem to have been rather poor men. Henry Kinge, constable in 1638–9, was listed for only two acres of meadow on a rating list of 1632, and was taxed only 1s. 6d. for ship-money in 1636, while the assessments of the middling and large farmers in the village ranged from 6s. or 7s. to over £1. His partner in 1638–9, Thomas Buck, also had a rather small ship-money assessment, 2s. 6d., while Francis Heyward, constable in 1630–1, was also taxed 2s. 6d. Daniel Rose, constable in 1633–4, and Richard Ballard, constable in 1635–6, were taxed only 1s. each for ship-money; but perhaps Ballard, who was in office at the time, had managed to keep his own assessment low.[107]

Constables of Bushey thus displayed considerable variety in their backgrounds, reflecting in part the economic and social diversity of this village. While a number of the rather numerous gentlemen with landed interests in this settlement filled the office, as did a few prosperous yeomen, many of the families in Bushey, and many who held the constableship, appear to have been men of middling wealth. Landholders of varying substance were joined in the office by tradesmen and craftsmen, many of them engaged in agriculturally related pursuits

[106] This is based on Herts. RO, D/P26/7/1, D/P26/10/1; also see the wills of Thomas Bonnick (80 AW 8) and Ralph Weedon (77 AW 28) and the wills listed in n. 36 above. A will survives for Robert Warren, collier, c. 1592 (32 AW 25). For identifications of Jorden and Heyward see Cockburn, ed., *Herts. Indictments, James I*, nos. 625, 552, 624, 933; and for Robert Wood, see Bushey Court Rolls, no. 6403.

[107] Herts. RO, D/P26/10/1, pp. 9, 24.

and most of them farmers too. In the 1630s some very small farmers, and perhaps mere cottagers, also held the office.

(3) The Small Farmers of Branston and Waltham

The Leicestershire villages of Branston and Waltham were also dissimilar to communities like Little Munden, Salwarpe, Stone, and Gissing, and they differed from Bushey too. Élites composed of prosperous yeomen and a few minor gentlemen were not to be found in these villages, nor did their economic and social structure display the diversity of wealth and status found in Bushey. They were communities of middling-sized farmers, the kind of villages made familiar by W. G. Hoskins's studies of Leicestershire.[108]

Both Branston and Waltham were located in Framland hundred in the north-eastern corner of the county, just south of Belvoir castle. They were small villages, Branston containing only about 30–35 households and Waltham 50–55 during the early seventeenth century,[109] and each was served by a single constable. The economy of these villages was based primarily on sheep raising and dairying, while the wool grown in the area provided employment for some weavers.[110] These settlements were part of the manorial holdings of the Earls of Rutland and without a resident lord, though he was located nearby at Belvoir castle.[111] Nor did they contain other gentlemen of any great substance. Not a single gentleman appears on the subsidy rolls for Waltham until 1642–3. One man of this status, John Brewer, did reside in Branston in the early seventeenth century, and his widow was still there in the 1640s.[112]

Farms in these villages were described in terms of yardlands, and in Branston, at least, most of them were held on twenty-one year

---

[108] Hoskins, *Midland Peasant*, esp. pp. 142–4, 185–90, 211–15; but also see his articles on Leicestershire farmers of the sixteenth and seventeenth centuries in *Essays in Leicestershire History*, pp. 123–83, and in *Provincial England*, pp. 149–69, which describe villages in which there was greater social and economic differentiation.

[109] Information about the population in these communities found in *VCH Leicestershire*, iii. 166, 168, has been supplemented by local rating lists found amongst the Branston constables' accounts, Leics. RO, DE 702/30, and the hearth tax, PRO, E 179/251/3.

[110] This is based on wills and inventories, to which specific reference will be made below; the parish registers in Leics. RO, DE 720/1; DE 625/1; and on local tax lists in Branston where assessments were based on land, sheep, and cows, DE 720/30.

[111] Nichols, *History and Antiquities*, II, pt. i, pp. 107, 381.

[112] PRO, E 179/134/212, 243, 265, 279, 283, 294, 307, 314; E 179/251/1; SP 16/298/79 (a description of the manor of Branston in 1635); Leics. RO, DE 720/30, ff. 1–2, 55–7.

leases.[113] Holdings in Branston ranged from one to three yardlands, and some farmers no doubt were more prosperous than others, but in both settlements wealth seems to have been more evenly distributed than in villages such as Little Munden, Salwarpe, Stone, and Gissing. A few men were recognized as yeomen, but most of those for whom a social description survives were identified as husbandmen. Even those called yeomen were of rather moderate means when compared with their counterparts in the other villages examined. Some of the farmers combined their husbandry with by-employments such as weaving or selling ale, and this fact too suggests their moderate prosperity.[114]

If there were few substantial farmers in these villages, there also seem to have been fewer poor inhabitants than in communities such as Little Munden, or even in the economically similar village of Wymeswold in the neighbouring hundred of East Goscote, where sheep raising and dairying also predominated. A description of the manor of Branston in 1635 lists only seven cottages. Local rating lists by the early 1640s do contain the names of 14 to 16 villagers who were not taxed for any land, but who did possess varying numbers of sheep and cattle, and perhaps the number of cottagers was on the increase.[115] Local tax lists are not extant for Waltham but the village seems to have been similar to Branston in its composition, and there probably were not many cottagers there either. The churchwardens' accounts reveal that a number of inhabitants were given small amounts in poor relief from bequests left to the parish, but many of them were women (e.g., 11 of 18 in 1609 and 13 of 19 in 1610) and most were probably widows.[116] In contrast to these villages, a Wymeswold rating list of 1608 contained the names of 32 cottagers taxed only for 1 to 5 cows, while 13 farmers were taxed for 80 to 120 acres and two gentlemen possessed 200 to 220 acres.[117] Even when compared with a nearby community in the same county, which engaged in a similar kind of farming, Branston and Waltham do not display much social differentiation.

In rural settlements like Branston and Waltham, where economic and social distinctions do not seem to have been very marked, almost all of those who held the constableship were middling-sized farmers like the Hodges, Dugard, and Ellis families of Salwarpe or the

---

[113] See a description of the manor of Branston in 1635, PRO, SP 16/298/79.
[114] See below, nn. 122–4.
[115] PRO, SP 16/298/79; Leics. RO, DE 720/30, ff. 55–7.
[116] Leics. RO, DE 625/18, ff. 2, 2ᵛ.
[117] BL Add. MS 10457, fo. 4.

husbandmen who held office in Bushey or Little Munden.[118] While some of them constituted the most prosperous men in their own communities, their wealth could not match that of the yeomen described above. The constabulary in these settlements does have a different appearance.

None of the cottagers in Branston is recorded as filling the constableship, and it seems unlikely that cottagers served in Waltham either. However, most of the farming families in these small villages did supply constables, and in Branston the office rotated among them. Of the 13 Branston constables for whom there is information, 2 of them farmed 3 yardlands, 4 of them 2½ yardlands, 4 more farmed 2 yardlands, and 3 held single yardlands.[119] Only Abraham Bishop, constable in 1619, 1631, and 1641, who possessed 2½ yardlands, is identified as a yeoman, while eight other constables are described as husbandmen.[120] Although there presumably were some variations in the wealth of these men, none of them possessed very large holdings when they are compared with those of yeomen who served as constables in some villages. Nor could any of the Branston officers match the substance of such men. Detailed information on landholding does not survive for the Waltham constables, but most of them too seem to have been small farmers. Two of them are known to have farmed single yardlands and another two yardlands, though one man in office in this village in the later 1640s did possess 4½ yardlands.[121]

Some of the husbandmen who held office combined their farming with other employments. One of the Branston officers who held a single yardland, William Robinson, constable in 1616 and 1628, engaged in weaving as well as farming and his will ordered that his sons, to whom he left the weaver's shop, be instructed in that craft. His eldest son William, constable in 1637, supplemented the family income from farming and weaving by selling ale and providing accommodation for travellers. So did another Branston officer, William Morrice, constable in 1618 and 1630, who farmed two

[118] The names of constables of Branston and Waltham are derived from their accounts, Leics. RO, DE 720/30 and DE 625/60, respectively. The names of 33 constables of Branston between 1611 and 1643 are known; only one is missing from the list. The names of 48 constables of Waltham between 1609 and 1660 are known; 9 are missing from the list.

[119] PRO, SP 16/298/79. W. G. Hoskins suggests that yardlands in Leicestershire ranged from 18 to 24 acres; see *Essays in Leicestershire History*, pp. 139–44.

[120] Identifications of constables are based on the parish register, Leics. RO, DE 720/1, and on wills and inventories to which references will be given below.

[121] Leics. RO, DE 73/PR/1: 59/77, 67/105, 69/9, 70/68.

yardlands.[122] They lodged a number of people brought to them by various constables and their houses regularly were used for the conduct of public business.[123] Some of the Waltham constables engaged in similar pursuits. William Hose, constable in 1640, provided lodging for a number of travellers in the 1630s and probably sold ale, while the Goodwins, who provided constables in the 1640s and 1650s, and the Nobles, who possibly served in the office, also seem to have run public houses.[124]

Evidence derived from the wills and inventories of those who held the constableship in Branston and Waltham confirms the impression gained from other sources that they were usually farmers of rather moderate means. W. G. Hoskins's descriptions of the bequests of sheep, household articles, and small monetary sums found in many of the Leicestershire wills of the sixteenth and seventeenth centuries characterize the testaments of Branston and Waltham constables.[125] Inventories have not survived for many of these officers, but the nine extant for Waltham probably provide a fair sample of the wealth of such men. Six of the nine fall within the range of £32 to £90, while five other village inventories of the period range from £28 to £89.[126]

Only a few inventories which date from the 1660s show signs of somewhat greater substance among constables of Waltham. Even then their prosperity was moderate by comparison with that of the yeoman farmers described earlier in this chapter. Thomas Lowe, husbandman,

---

[122] For wills and inventories of the Robinsons and Morrices see Leics. RO, DE 73/PR/T: 1638/51, 1638/70, 1664/72, DE 73/PR/I: 40/252, 41A/70, 62/101, 65/19A (Robinsons); DE 73/PR/I: 1661/C27, PR/I: 55/30 (William Morrice).

[123] For references to the houses of the Robinsons and Morrices in the constables' accounts see Leics. RO, DE 720/30, ff. 25, 31, 45ᵛ, 46ᵛ, 50ᵛ, 51 (3), 52 (2), 52ᵛ, 53ᵛ (2), 54 (3), 54ᵛ (4).

[124] For William Hose see Leics. RO, DE 625/60, ff. 44, 55, 56ᵛ; and Henry Noble, DE 625/60, ff. 35, 44, 58ᵛ, and the inventory of Judith Noble, perhaps his widow, which lists a brewhouse, DE 73/PR/I: 56/134. For references to the Goodwin house see DE 625/60, ff. 44, 44ᵛ, 55ᵛ, 56, 62, 66ᵛ.

[125] Hoskins, *Midland Peasant*, pp. 144–5, 153–4, 157–8, 178; *Essays in Leicestershire History*, pp. 133–6; *Provincial England*, p. 155. For examples see the following wills Leics. RO, DE 73/PR/T: *Branston*: William Robinson, c. 1616, 1628 (1638/51); his widow (1638/70); William Robinson, c. 1637–8 (1664/72); William Morrice, c. 1618, 1630 (1661/C27); Robert George, c. 1617, 1629 (1661/C25); *Waltham*: John Sneath, c. 1615 (1615/61); John Picke, c. 1614 (1615/69); John Hall, c. 1631 (Register Book, 1630–1, fo. 449); William Taylor, c. 1633 (1634/30); Thomas Trowman, c. 1639 (1649/14); Stephen Kellam, c. 1610, 1623, 1642 (1662/VG 58); Edward Hickson, c. 1613 (1634/1).

[126] For constables' inventories see Leics. RO, DE 73/PR/I: 51/15, 53/114, 59/77, 64/92, 64/150, 67/105; and for other Waltham inventories, 41/18, 61/134, 61/159, 84/52, 90/108.

constable in 1636 and 1656, who seems to have farmed two yardlands, left an estate valued at £135 when he died in 1668.[127] Robert Blomfield, constable in 1634, was one of the few villagers taxed for the subsidy in 1642, and this family too seems to have been a little more substantial than most in the village. Robert's son William, husbandman, constable in 1648, farmed 4½ yardlands and left an inventory valued at £317 in 1669. The younger Blomfield had a two-bay house, with two upper chambers, and three of his five beds were 'curtained'. His parlour contained several chairs and three chests, suggesting greater comforts than most farmers in Waltham possessed. However, the bulk of his estate is accounted for by livestock valued at £129 and agricultural produce worth £155.[128] The Bunnis family too probably was more prosperous than most in the village. Edward served as constable in 1612, and he was one of the few inhabitants taxed for the subsidy in 1624. During the dearth of 1623, he was reported by the sheriff as being one of those of greatest wealth who defied the scarcity orders and fed peas to sheep and swine. Even before his death he contributed £5 to be invested for the benefit of the poor, and this too suggests a man of some means. His heirs built on his moderate prosperity. Mr Robert Bunnis, listed on the subsidy roll for 1642, probably was his son, while an Edward Bunnis, gent., known to be grandson of the first Edward, left an estate valued at £355 on his death in 1691.[129] William Brooke, constable in 1609 and 1621, Robert Flower, who held office in 1617, Thomas Trowman, who served in 1639 and who is identified as a yeoman, and Stephen Kellam, constable in 1610 and 1623, were among the few other men in Waltham who were assessed for the subsidy, and they too perhaps were a little more prosperous than some of their fellow farmers.[130]

In Branston there were also a few constables whose inventories were valued at more than £100, and who perhaps were slightly more substantial than most of their farming neighbours. However, their wealth too was moderate by comparison with that of yeomen in other

[127] Leics. RO, DE 73/PR/T: 1669/8, PR/I: 69/9.
[128] PRO, E. 179/134/307; Leics. RO, DE 73/PR/I: 70/68.
[129] PRO, E 179/134/294; SP 14/140/81 II.; Leics. RO, DE 625/18, fo. 29ᵛ; for Mr Bunnis see PRO, E 179/134/307; Leics. RO, DE 625/60, ff. 49ᵛ, 51ᵛ, 52, 53ᵛ, 54, 55, 56, 56ᵛ, 58, 58ᵛ, 60, 61, 61ᵛ, 62ᵛ, 65, 65ᵛ; and for the will and inventory of Edward Bunnis, gent., see Leics. RO, DE 73/PR/T: 1691/73, PR/I: 95/93.
[130] PRO, E 179/134/243, 265, 283, 294, 307; E 179/251/1; also see the wills and inventories of Thomas Trowman and Stephen Kellam, and of a Robert Brooke, son of William, (c. 1656), Leics. RO, DE 73/PR/T: 1649/14, PR/I: 51/15, PR/T: 1662/VG 58, PR/I: 59/77, PR/T: 1665/110, PR/I: 64/150.

villages. William Morrice, constable in 1618 and 1630, who combined farming and ale-selling, left possessions valued at £156 on his death in 1644. His house, which contained five rooms in addition to a buttery and a kitchen, probably was larger than most in the village. However, in his will Morrice left to the one daughter for whom he had not yet provided the rather small portion of £20.[131] Somewhat more prosperous was William Coye, husbandman, constable in 1612 and 1626, who held 2½ yardlands in Branston and about eighteen acres in an enclosed field. In 1611 he possessed a substantial flock of 90 sheep as well as 12 cows, and on his death in 1638 his possessions were valued at £217. There were three rooms on the ground floor of his house, though only one chamber on the second storey had been finished, and the dwelling showed few signs of wealth. To his unmarried daughter Coye left the rather meagre sum of £10 and a long list of household goods. Coye's son and grandson apparently were able to build on the foundation which he had laid. His son, Gervase, constable in 1638, was the most highly rated man in the village on local tax lists of the early 1640s, and he possessed 110–160 sheep and 15–17 cows. He was also one of the four inhabitants, in addition to Mrs Brewer and the clergyman of the village, whose names appear on the subsidy roll of 1642. When his son, another William Coye, died in 1682 his estate was valued at £320, and by that time there were three upper chambers in the house, including one for the menservants.[132] John Worsdale, constable in 1623 and 1635, William Mandefield, constable in 1622 and 1634, Edward George, who held office in 1639, and Peter Hoe, who served in 1620 and 1633, are also among the two to six villagers whose names appear on the subsidy rolls of the early seventeenth century. They too were perhaps a little more substantial than other farmers in the village.[133]

(4) Small Farmers and Craftsmen of Pattingham

Pattingham too was a village of small farmers, but its economy was more diversified than that of Branston or Waltham, and it differed from these settlements in its social structure as a result of that fact. Located in the south-western part of Staffordshire, just west of

[131] Leics. RO, DE 73/PR/I: 55/30, PR/T: 1661/C27.
[132] Leics. RO, DE 73/PR/T: 1638/64, PR/I: 40/257, PR/T: 1682/26, PR/I: 84/35; DE 720/30, ff. 1–2, 55–7; PRO, E 179/134/307.
[133] PRO, E 179/134/243, 265, 279, 283, 294, 307; E 179/251/1; and for Edward George also see Leics. RO, DE 73/PR/T: 1661/C13, C26.

Wolverhampton, Pattingham straddled two counties. While the manor of Pattingham was located entirely within the borders of Staffordshire, a second township in the parish, Rudge, was located in Shropshire. Pattingham manor contained one major settlement, referred to in the records as the 'town', and a number of smaller hamlets containing only a few families. Some of the place-names which occur in sixteenth- and seventeenth-century records still appear on the early nineteenth-century enclosure map: Hardwicke, Clive, Copley, Nurton, Nurton Hill, Little More, Great More, and Woodhouses. Other names found in local records include the Hollies, New Hill, and Brooke, as well as Hale End, Stone Head, Newgate, the Fieldside, and Broadwell, which apparently identified parts of the town of Pattingham.[134] The population of this village was considerably larger than that of Branston and Waltham, and also of Little Munden, Salwarpe, Stone, and Gissing. Pattingham ranks with Bushey as one of the two largest villages considered here, and the population was expanding during the early seventeenth century. While there were about 85 households in the village in 1587, the number had grown to at least 112 by 1649. The increase is explained largely by a growth in the cottage population of the village. By the 1660s the hearth tax identified 41 of the 114 villagers on the list as not chargeable for the levy.[135]

Agriculture in Pattingham was characterized by mixed farming, though as in the Leicestershire villages discussed here and in Salwarpe, Stone, and Gissing, animal husbandry probably predominated. The manorial records and the few surviving inventories reveal the presence of considerable numbers of sheep and some cattle, along with the pigs and poultry that were also found in large numbers in Salwarpe and Stone. The by-laws of the manor regulating the number of sheep which farmers were permitted to place on the commons, and repeated stipulations concerning the 'ringing' of swine, suggest the importance of both sheep and pigs, but also the need for strict controls in a village where the commons probably were limited and arable farming also important. The land transfers reveal the existence of a considerable

[134] For the enclosure map see Staffs. RO, Q/RDc/14; and for local sources of the sixteenth and seventeenth centuries which mention these divisions see H. R. Thomas, *The Pattingham Parish Register, 1559–1812* (Staffordshire Parish Register Society, 1934); the constables' and churchwardens' accounts, contained in a book located in the parish church; Transcripts of Pattingham Court Rolls, Staffs. RO, D/1807, nos. 160–293.

[135] These estimates of population are based on local rating lists found in the same book with the constables' and churchwardens' accounts (see n. 134 above); for the hearth tax see PRO, E 179/256/31.

amount of meadow, and hay was an important crop. The fields of the manor were sown with rye, barley, oats, peas, and probably some wheat.[136]

There were few resident gentlemen in Pattingham, and during the early seventeenth century the manor itself was held by the guardians of a minor, who probably did not reside in the village. Nor do there appear to have been any very wealthy farmers in this settlement, though by the 1640s a few men had amassed estates which set them apart from a majority of their fellows. Most of the lands in the manor were held in customary tenure, and farms here, as in Branston, Waltham, Salwarpe, and Stone, were described in terms of yardlands. However, these traditional units seem to have been breaking up during the early seventeenth century, and on a local rating list of 1649 the classification was abandoned. It was rare for a man to have more than a yardland, 9 to 11 farmers possessing holdings of this size, while 23 to 27 held half yardlands and 10 to 12 quarter yardlands. During most of the late sixteenth and early seventeenth centuries Pattingham, like Branston and Waltham, seems to have been a village of small farmers. In relation to the size of the settlement, very few were taxed for the subsidy, a high of 10 in 1589–90 and only 6 in 1641–2.[137] The increase in the number of cottagers no doubt contributed to growing social differentiation in the village during the course of the early seventeenth century. However, those who occupied the heights of the social structure still seem to have been small farmers, even if many of them did call themselves yeomen.

As important as was farming to the economy of the village,

---

[136] See Staffs. RO, Transcripts Pattingham Court Rolls, D/1807, nos. 160–293; regulations concerning pigs and sheep are found in rolls 178, 179, 270, 274, 276, 282, 292. Pattingham apparently was a 'peculiar' which enjoyed probate authority, and none of the sixteenth- and seventeenth-century wills proved within that jurisdiction have survived (I owe this information to Mr F. B. Stitt, Staffordshire county archivist); but a few wills and inventories of villagers whose holdings lay primarily within the manor of Rudge, and of two vicars of Pattingham, are extant in the Staffordshire Joint Record Office, Lichfield. See the following inventories: William Barber (1559), Roger Hodson, vicar (1582), John Clempson (1583), John Nicholls, husbandman (1591), William Devie, husbandman (1592–3), Thomas Bache (1592), Hugh Alden, husbandman (1608), John Cheese (1631), John Betts, innkeeper (1633), Humphrey Croydon, husbandman (1636), Thomas Keeling (1650).

[137] Staffs. RO, Transcripts Pattingham Court Rolls, D/1807, nos. 160–293, show in whose name the courts were held. The information on landholding comes from local rating lists for the years 1582, 1584, 1587, 1599, 1608, 1623, and 1649, found with the constables' and churchwardens' accounts. For the subsidy rolls see PRO, E 179/178/225, 235, 248, 284, 292, 299, 318. See PRO, E 133/3/539 for a dispute about the customs of the manor of Pattingham.

Pattingham well illustrates 'the partnership between agriculture and industry' which developed in some predominantly pastoral areas during the seventeenth century.[138] Not only did some of the landholders in this village, like those in Branston and Waltham, engage in by-employments, but its inhabitants included substantial numbers of craftsmen and tradesmen who appear on local tax lists among the growing cottage population of the village. Animal husbandry sustained a leather industry whose importance is reflected in the fact that two leather-sealers were selected annually in the manorial court, and in the presence in the village of a number of tanners, shoemakers, and glovers. Cattle raising also provided employment for several butchers, while in other agriculturally related trades there were numerous smiths, a ploughwright, a wheelwright, and a shepherd. The flocks of sheep sustained some weavers and at least one shearsman, and there were also several tailors in the village. One or two carpenters, a joiner, a tiler, and a thatcher also appear in the records. Nailing was another village industry and several cottagers are identified as being engaged in this occupation. Neither travellers nor the villagers themselves can have gone thirsty since at least eight to ten men, and sometimes more, were ale-sellers. Both tanners and smiths often combined their crafts with ale-selling and one tailor too was listed as both a victualler and an ale-seller. A victualler/baker was present at the turn of the seventeenth century and another who combined baking with ale-selling in the 1650s, while several others listed as victuallers/ale-sellers were present in the village during the intervening period. The parish also contained an inn, the New Inn, though it was not located in the township of Pattingham but in the western part of the parish in the township of Rudge.[139]

A majority of constables in Pattingham, like those in Branston and Waltham, were farmers of middling prosperity; and most men in this category served in the office.[140] One gentleman, William Warde, the most highly assessed man in the village in 1608, who was taxed for a yardland and a half, did hold the office in 1608-9 and 1615-16. Of the remaining 80 constables, 21 were identified as yeomen, but they

[138] On the economy of Staffordshire and the importance of industrial by-employments there, see Thirsk, 'Horn and Thorn in Staffordshire', esp. 8, 13-14.

[139] This discussion is based on information from the sources listed in n. 134 above.

[140] Names of the constables are derived from the book containing their accounts for the period 1582-1640 (see n. 134 above) and from court leet rolls, Staffs. RO, D/1807. The list contains 136 names for the period 1581-2 to 1654-5; 10 names are missing.

seem to have possessed rather small farms by comparison with those held by yeomen in Little Munden, Salwarpe, Stone, and Gissing, and not to have matched the substance of the prosperous farmers in those villages. Sixteen of the farmers who held the office were taxed for yardlands, while 34 of them held half yardlands and 11 quarter yardlands. Perhaps some of them possessed more property than is revealed in the Pattingham records, and like farmers in Salwarpe, Stone, and Gissing held lands and tenements in neighbouring parishes or in the manor of Rudge. However, in view of the almost complete absence of wills, which often reveal such possessions, there is little evidence on the matter. Nor do many inventories survive to provide a measure of the wealth of Pattingham constables, but the very few which are extant suggest that they were men of moderate prosperity.[141] Some Pattingham constables, like members of the farming families who held office in Branston and Waltham, combined their agricultural pursuits with other employments. The constables holding quarter yardlands included one man identified as a baker/victualler, another who was a tanner, and a third who was an ale-seller. One officer who possessed half a yardland, and who is identified as a yeoman, also possessed a shop with looms and clearly was a weaver as well. Another with a half yardland was an ale-seller.[142]

The sixty-three Pattingham constables listed among the landholders on local rating lists were joined in the position by a number of craftsmen and tradesmen. Twelve were taxed as cottagers, and nine of them can be identified as craftsmen or tradesmen, with a probable tenth in this category. Their number included three blacksmiths, all of whom were also identified as ale-sellers, at least one tanner, and probably another in this craft who is identified only as parish clerk, two shoemakers, one of whom was also described as a tanner, while the other sold ale, a glover identified as a husbandman too, a carpenter, and a shearsman who was also referred to as a husbandman. A butcher was chosen for the office, but he did not serve. While these men were taxed as cottagers, they do seem to have been among the more prosperous villagers in this category, some of them assessed for 8*d.* or 6*d.* for local levies as opposed to the 4*d.* or 2*d.* paid by most

[141] See the inventories of John Clempson (1583), John Cheese (1631), Thomas Keeling (1650) in Staffs. Joint Record Office, Lichfield.

[142] Social descriptions/occupations are derived from the sources listed in n. 134, while the landholdings of constables are based on the rating lists found with the constables' accounts.

cottagers.[143] In any case, some of them were probably as substantial as the office-holding farmers who possessed only quarter yardlands.

The village of Pattingham was economically more diverse than Branston and Waltham, and contained a much larger cottage population than did these communities. However, all three can be described as settlements of small farmers where most of the constables were men of only moderate prosperity. A majority, if not all, of the farmers in these villages held the office, while in the case of Pattingham some craftsmen and tradesmen who were taxed only as cottagers served as constable too. There were almost certainly some variations within these villages in the wealth and social status of those who filled the constableship. None the less, the officers do not display the range of ability found in Bushey, while the substantial yeomen who served as constables of Little Munden, Salwarpe, Stone, and Gissing are missing from the constabularies of these communities.

(5) Substantial Townsmen of Melton Mowbray

The small market town of Melton Mowbray, located south of Branston and Waltham and the major settlement in Framland hundred, was the most populous of the communities examined in this study. A local rating list of 1582 indicates that there were about 116 households in the town at that time, while 189 inhabitants were taxed for a local levy in 1602.[144] However, the town has been included not so much due to the difference in its size as because of its occupational and social structure. As might be expected in a larger settlement and a market town, the population reflected greater occupational diversity than most of the villages, with the possible exception of Pattingham; and there the non-farming population did not display the kind of prosperity found in Melton. A tax list drawn up in 1572, containing the names of those subject to contributions for poor relief, provides an excellent profile of the more substantial sections of the town at that time.[145] In addition to the vicar, who headed the list, there were 24 landholders farming from one to four yardlands, and 43 craftsmen and tradesmen as well as 5 men who combined holdings of one to four yardlands with a craft or trade. Over half of the 24 farmers, 15 of them, possessed three to four

---

[143] The occupations of these men are derived from the sources listed in n. 134; they appear as cottagers on the tax lists found with the constables' and churchwardens' accounts.

[144] Leics. RO, DG 36/191; DG 36/214; also see *VCH Leicestershire*, iii. 140, 166, 168.

[145] Leics. RO, DG 36/159/7.

yardlands, which suggests that many of the landholders in Melton were more substantial than those in the neighbouring villages of Branston and Waltham, where holdings of this size were uncommon. It is possible, however, that some of these properties had been subdivided by the early seventeenth century, the period covered by the Branston and Waltham evidence. Prosperous through they may have been, the landholders in the town in 1572 were outnumbered almost two to one by craftsmen and tradesmen. Seventeen different occupations appear on the list, some of them, like the shepherd, the two graziers, the three butchers, the wright, and the two smiths, in agriculturally related employments. Most numerous were the victuallers, the list including nine men in this trade, and one of them was also a baker. It also contained the names of four weavers, four drapers (three of whom combined their trades with farming), four tailors, four masons (two of whom were also farmers), three shoemakers, three glovers, two fullers, two chandlers, two carpenters, a fishmonger, and a salter.

Although the occupations of many of the constables of Melton Mowbray cannot be determined with certainty, and the list of 47 men who held the office between 1587–8 and 1617–18 is in any case very fragmentary, they seem to have reflected the economic diversity which existed in the town. Certainly the office was not confined to landholders. In addition to those known to have been farmers, the constables of this township included a grazier, a cordwainer, a vintner, and a mason, while another described as a yeoman mentioned a shop in his will.[146] James Shalcrosse, constable in 1609, is known to have been a grazier,[147] while a William Shawcrosse, butcher, appears on the 1572 list. Similarly, Thomas Blithe, cordwainer, was constable in 1606, and in his will of 1617 left to his son ten dozen pairs of shoes and the furniture of the shop and the brass pan 'wherein I do usuallie liquere my leather',[148] while a William Blithe, shoemaker, was on the tax list in 1572. It seems very likely that others among the constables also continued in the crafts or trades which their fathers or grandfathers had been pursuing in 1572. Four members of the

---

[146] The names of the constables are derived from some extant accounts, Leics. RO, DG 25/39/1/1–4; DG 36/186–9; receipts issued to constables, DG 36/196–8, 203, 219–20; and from the town book, DG 25/1/1. Unless otherwise indicated the information below is based on these sources and on the rating list of 1572, DG 36/159/7. For the yeoman with the shop, Thomas Owndell, c. 1591, 1612, see Leics. RO, DE 73/PR/T: 1620/2; the craftsmen and tradesmen will be discussed below.

[147] See his will, Leics. RO, DE 73/PR/T: 1642/44.

[148] Leics, RO, DE 73/PR/T: 1617/55.

Wormell family served as constable in the early seventeenth century, while there were three Wormells on the list of 1572, two of them chandlers and one a weaver. The Wormells who held the constableship were probably craftsmen or tradesmen. James Lovett, constable in 1589, was very likely the James, mason, farmer of two yardlands, who appeared on 1572 list. Another James Lovett, who held the constableship in 1612, perhaps carried on that craft. Three members of the Lacey family filled the office. John Lacey, draper, who farmed a yardland, and who also seems to have engaged in brewing, was constable in 1572 when the tax list was compiled. Two other Laceys appear on the document, one of them a gentleman farming four yardlands and another holding two yardlands. Of the two Laceys who held office in the early seventeenth century, John's son Matthew, constable in 1607, appears to have been a victualler and brewer. Andrew Lacey, who served in 1596–7 and 1615, perhaps came from one of the farming families of 1572, but he was a vintner.[149] Three members of the Trigge family also served as constable. William, who held office in 1587, was probably the 'William Trigge and his mother' listed as holding three yardlands in 1572. The later Trigges who filled the constableship, Robert in 1613 and William the younger in 1615, may have been members of this farming family. However, Robert was possibly descended from Humphrey Trigge, weaver, who appears on the 1572 list. Information about the occupational structure of Melton, and the rather fragmentary evidence about the occupations of men who served as constable, would both suggest that in market towns the office was frequently held by substantial craftsmen and tradesmen as well as by farmers.

On the basis of the settlements examined here it can be stated that constables were drawn from 'all sectors in society'[150] ranging from lesser gentlemen to cottagers. Although a few rather poor men apparently served in the office, there is little evidence to support contentions that substantial villagers escaped the constableship by thrusting it upon the meaner sort; and the most prosperous inhabitants too filled the office. While most constables were not gentlemen, neither were they, in a majority of cases, the 'meanest' and 'lowliest' villagers.

However, such generalizations disguise variations from settlement

---

[149] See the will of John Lacey, Leics. RO, DE 73/PR/T: 1590/3; for Matthew Lacey, DG 36/216; and the will of Andrew Lacey, DE 73/PR/T: 1635/34.

[150] Samaha, *Law and Order*, p. 87.

to settlement in the social composition of the constabulary. In villages such as Little Munden, Salwarpe, Stone, and Gissing many prosperous yeomen and a few minor gentlemen held the office, along with some husbandmen and an occasional craftsman who represented the middle range of wealth in the community. Men of some substance, whether they were farmers, craftsmen, or tradesmen, also filled the position in Melton Mowbray. The wealth and status of constables in these settlements were usually greater than those of the small farmers who most often filled the office in Branston, Waltham, and Pattingham, or of the craftsmen and tradesmen of moderate means who sometimes served in Pattingham. In Bushey too a majority of the officers appear to have been farmers and tradesmen of middling prosperity, despite the range of wealth represented among the constables of that village, and the fact that an unusually large number of gentlemen held the office there.

It is possible that there were some significant changes over time, at least in some villages, in the status of their constables. However, the information is so incomplete that any suggestions in this area must remain tentative. In Bushey and Little Munden, where a few of the constables do seem to have been men of rather slender means, all of these cases date from the 1630s. The contrast is particularly marked in Little Munden where in the first half of that decade an array of unusually substantial men seem to have filled the office, while between 1636 and 1641 some unusually poor villagers appear to have done so. Some evidence has been presented to suggest that there was growing reluctance to hold the constableship during the later 1630s,[151] when the duties of the office and especially the tax-collecting responsibilities became particularly onerous.[152] Perhaps at that time the position was sometimes thrust upon poorer men because others were unwilling to serve. Gary Owen suggests that in Norfolk the growing opposition to ship-money led courts leet deliberately to select the meaner sort as constables because they could be more easily intimidated when they attempted to collect the levy.[153] Although there is no evidence to suggest that the Gissing constables of this period were less substantial than those of earlier years, perhaps opposition to ship-money helps to explain the choice of some poor men in Little Munden and Bushey.

[151] See above, ch. 3.
[152] For further discussion of the difficulties constables encountered in fulfilling their tax-collecting duties during the later 1630s, see below, ch. 7.
[153] Owen, 'Norfolk, 1620–1641', pp. 278–9.

II. 'ESTABLISHED' FAMILIES VS. 'NEW MEN': POPULATION MOBILITY AND THE COMPOSITION OF THE CONSTABULARY

Variations among villages in the extent of population mobility also affected the composition of their constabularies. A number of historians have drawn attention to the amount of geographical mobility which existed in sixteenth- and early seventeenth-century England, and to the extent of the population turnover within rural communities during that period.[154] However, in this area too there seem to have been considerable variations among villages. While in some communities many of the same surnames appear in the records over several generations, in others there was a much more rapid turnover of families. These differences in the stability of populations helped to create variations among villages in the relative proportion of constables drawn from well-established families and from those that were newcomers to the community.

Pattingham was the most sedentary of the villages considered here. Although the cottage population displayed a higher degree of mobility than the farming households, cottagers who shared the surnames of these families often appear, along with their better-off relatives, on successive rating lists. The extent to which families were rooted in the village is reflected not only in the appearance of the same surnames in local records over a long period, but also in the fact that many of them were represented by a number of branches. While several of them might be farmers who possessed yardlands or half yardlands, others were engaged in crafts or trades, or sometimes were mere labourers. These extensive kinship networks were in turn interconnected by marriage, creating a complex web of relationships among the families who remained in the village over several generations. Apart from the mobile elements among the cottage population, almost everyone in

---

[154] For studies concerned with population mobility in early modern England see S. A. Peyton, 'The Village Population in Tudor Lay Subsidy Rolls', *English Historical Review*, xxx (1915), 234–50; E. J. Buckatzsch, 'The Constancy of Local Population and Migration in England Before 1800', *Population Studies*, v (1951), 62–9; Julian Cornwall, 'Evidence of Population Mobility in the Seventeenth Century', *Bulletin of the Institute of Historical Research*, xl (1967), 143–52; Peter Clark, 'The Migrant in Kentish Towns, 1580–1640', in Peter Clark and Paul Slack, eds., *Crisis and Order in English Towns 1500–1700* (London, 1972), pp. 117–63; Peter Laslett, 'Clayworth and Cogenhoe', in Laslett, *Family life and illicit love in earlier generations* (Cambridge, 1977), pp. 50–101; W. R. Prest, 'Stability and Change in Old and New England: Clayworth and Dedham', *Journal of Interdisciplinary History*, vi (1976), 359–74.

Pattingham seems to have been related, either through kinship or affinity, to almost everyone else.[155] Two residents of West Bromwich, who in 1598 brought suit for the possession of certain lands in Pattingham, described such ties in their petition to the Court of Requests. They claimed that they could 'hope for no indifferent triall eyther at the comon law or in the court baron' because the defendants were 'soe allied, acquainted, frended and neare kynne unto very many of the freholders and jurors . . . and in a manner to all the homages and tenants in the sayd mannor'.[156] Such claims may often have served merely as an excuse for seeking justice outside the manorial or common law courts, but in this case the plaintiffs offered an accurate description of the network of relationships in Pattingham. Before historians can entirely dismiss the extent and importance of kinship ties within English villages of the sixteenth and seventeenth centuries, it will be necessary to discover whether or not there were many other settlements which resembled Pattingham.[157]

As might be expected, in view of the stability of the population, a great majority of the Pattingham constables came from families who were firmly established in the community. Continuity among the landholders, and the existence of several moderately prosperous branches of many of these families, helps to explain the fact that only 34 different surnames appear on the list of 136 constables. The parish register reveals the presence of many of these families in the 1560s, and 22 of the 34 surnames are found on the hearth tax in the 1660s. Of the 81 different men who held the office, 13 of them came from families who apparently resided in the village rather briefly, and each of them served only once. The remaining 68 constables were drawn from families who provided successive generations of office-holders, son following father in the position just as he succeeded him in the possession of lands in the manor. The Hardwickes had the largest number of branches in the village, and the members of this family included farmers, tanners, smiths, and ale-sellers. Located in Rudge, Great More, Stone Head, Newgate, and the Fieldside, and with two

---

[155] Thirsk, 'Horn and Thorn in Staffordshire', 10, suggests that the population of Staffordshire may have displayed 'weaker migratory inclinations than most', and the evidence from Pattingham seems to confirm this. This discussion is based on information from Thomas, ed., *Pattingham Parish Register*; transcripts of the court rolls in Staffs. RO, D/1807, nos. 160–293; the tax lists included with the constables' and churchwardens' accounts; and the hearth tax, PRO, E 179/256/31.

[156] PRO, REQ. 2/231/44.

[157] See Wrightson, *English Society*, pp. 44–51.

branches in Nurton and Hale End, the Hardwickes provided no less than eleven constables. Another prolific family, the Deveys, which had branches in Clive, Copley, and Hardwicke, supplied eight constables. The even more numerous Perrys were represented in Clive, Great More, Little More, and the town of Pattingham, and seven of them served as constable. The Pitts too were numerous, and they supplied five officers. There were also five Taylors, four Sampsons, three Whites, and three Greenes who held the constableship, while eight other families provided at least two officers.[158]

Although they were not as sedentary as Pattingham, there seems to have been relatively little turnover of population among the landholders of Salwarpe and Stone. Many of the constables in these communities too came from well-established families, and sometimes from those with several branches resident in the village. The names of some of the yeomen families who provided constables are found in local records in the 1560s, and in some instances in the 1520s, while many of them were still there in the 1660s. The Hills of Stone, with major branches in Shenstone and Hoo and a number of lesser members also resident in the village, qualify as an established family. The Dolittles, Hornblowers, Clymers, and Thatchers had several branches and they too were 'old' families of Stone, the first three having been there at least since the early sixteenth century. The Oldnolls, Kyndons, and Bacons were present in the village throughout the late sixteenth and early seventeenth centuries, and they too can be classified with the established families who provided constables.[159] The Woodhouses of Salwarpe, who had major branches in Hill End, Ladywood, and Boycott, had roots extending back at least to Henry VIII's reign, and they were still there in the 1660s. A number of other constables of Salwarpe also came from families which had long been settled in the village. The Dugards, the Frenches, and the Walfords, along with the Smiths and the Brooks who probably served in the office, had lived there since the early sixteenth century. The families of Yarnold, Hodges, Tommes, and Ellis are known to have been present from the later sixteenth century to the 1660s, and they too seem to qualify as established families.[160]

---

[158] This discussion is based on the sources cited in n. 155.

[159] This discussion is based on the parish register for Stone, HWRO, BA 5660/1 (1); the subsidy roll of 16 H. VIII and the hearth tax of 1664, PRO, E 179/200/137; E 179/201/312.

[160] This discussion is based on the Bishop's Transcripts for Salwarpe, HWRO, BA

There also appears to have been little population turnover in Branston and Waltham, at least prior to the mid-seventeenth century. Just as in Salwarpe and Stone, most of the constables came from well-established households. All the families who provided officers in Branston were present throughout the late sixteenth and early seventeenth centuries, and nine of the thirteen surnames are still found on the hearth tax in the 1660s. Seven families provided two constables each during the period 1611–43, and this is another indication of the continuity among the landholders in that village.[161] The Waltham parish register reveals the presence from the 1560s of most of the families who served in the constableship in that village between 1609 and 1642. However, by the later seventeenth century there was a greater turnover of families in Waltham than in Branston, and the names of some of those which had provided constables disappear from the records by the 1660s. Only ten of the twenty-one surnames of constables of the early seventeenth century are found on the hearth tax of 1664.[162]

Some of the families who served in the constableship in Little Munden also had along associations with the village, but there was greater mobility in this community. In the 1630s some newcomers also held the office, and sometimes very shortly after their arrival in the village. A number of the yeoman families who supplied constables, the Faceys, Lanckthones, Kirbys, Rowleys, Cockes, and Irelands, were present in Little Munden throughout the late sixteenth and early seventeenth centuries. Some of the less prosperous farming families who filled the office, the Walkers, Woods, Goodwins, Colts, and Snells, were also well established there. Eight of these nine surnames still appear on the hearth tax in the 1660s, the Faceys disappearing from the records in 1641. However, the names of at least six families who had held the office between 1590 and 1610 are no longer found in local records by the 1620s and in the 1630s some new residents apparently served in the office only a few years after moving into the village. Daniel Nash, who leased the manor of Munden Freville, first appears in the records of 1629, and he was chosen constable in 1631.

2006/40, the subsidy roll of 16 H. VIII, and the hearth tax of 1662, PRO, E 179/200/137; E 179/201/325.

[161] This discussion is based on the parish register and local rating lists, Leics. RO, DE 720/1; DE 720/30, ff. 1–2, 55–7; and on the hearth tax of 1664, PRO, E 179/251/3.
[162] This discussion is based on the parish register, Leics. RO, DE 625/1; and on the hearth tax, PRO, E 179/251/3.

James Bardoll, constable in 1637, was not on a village rating list until 1632. John Kempton, constable in 1635, first appears on a rating list of 1632, while William Risdaile, constable in 1640, seems to have arrived in the village only in 1637.[163]

Population mobility was even greater in Bushey, the other Hertford-shire village considered here, and this fact is reflected in the character of the constabulary in that community.[164] There were some families with a number of branches who were firmly rooted in the village. However, many names appear briefly in the records and then disappear, while new names take their places on local rating lists. While some of the constables came from established families, many others belonged to families which had settled in Bushey quite recently. Just as was the case in Little Munden, such men often seem to have held office only a few years after their arrival in the village.

The Bonnicks, and the even more prolific Weedons, were established families with several branches who supplied a number of constables. The Weedons had lived in Bushey at least since Henry VIII's reign. The Huddells, Heywards, Adams, and Fells, also with more than one branch, and a number of other families of middling-sized farmers also seem to have been well ensconced in the village. So too were some of the yeomen and minor gentry who served in the office, such as the Blackwell, Nicholl, Francis, and Harte families.

However, some of the families who held the constableship in the late sixteenth and very early years of the seventeenth centuries had disappeared from the village by the 1620s. On the other hand, new surnames appear among the constables of the 1620s and the 1630s. Some of them remained only a few years, and many of these families were no longer resident in Bushey by the 1660s. John Hunt, the substantial yeoman who was taxed for 120 acres and who held office in 1632, probably had not been resident in the village much before 1628. He was on local rating lists throughout the 1630s, but there were no Hunts in Bushey by 1663. The Walkers were resident in the village even more briefly. Thomas Walker, miller, was present by the later 1620s and served as constable in 1629–30. He was taxed for Bushey Mills in 1632, but by 1635 a new miller had replaced him on the tax

---

[163] This discussion is based on local rating lists in Herts. RO, D/P71/5/1, D/P71/5/2, and the Bishop's Transcripts, Bundle 111, nos. 2–45; and the hearth tax of 1663, PRO, E 179/248/23, no. 43.

[164] The following discussion is based on local rating lists in Herts. RO, D/P26/7/1, D/P26/10/1, a subsidy roll of Henry VIII's reign, and the hearth tax of 1663, PRO, E 179/120/119; E 179/248/24, no. 19.

lists. Robinson also seems to have been a new name in Bushey in the
1620s, William Robinson first holding local office in 1620 and serving
as constable in 1625–6. William Morgan, gent., constable in 1626–7,
did not appear in Bushey records before 1625. The Fendalls, who
provided a constable in 1626–7, and the Davis family, which supplied
an officer in 1630–1, also seem to have arrived in the village during the
1620s. Some of the men who served in the constableship in the 1630s
apparently came from families which had settled in Bushey only during
that decade. Richard Backer, constable in 1630–1, Richard Ballard,
constable in 1635–6, Daniel Rose, who held office in 1633–4,
Thomas Buck, who served in 1638–9, and Nehemiah Knowlton,
constable in 1634–5, all appear to have been newcomers to the village.
The Robinson, Morgan, Davis, Backer, and Rose families were no
longer in Bushey in the 1660s.

At the opposite extreme from the rather sedentary village of
Pattingham was the Norfolk community, Gissing, which displayed the
greatest degree of population mobility of any of the settlements
examined here.[165] The farmers of Gissing were apparently distinguished
from their counterparts in the other villages considered in this study
not only by the proportion of their land which was freehold, but also by
their geographical mobility. Perhaps there was some connection
between the two factors. Not even the yeomen families, who elsewhere
seem to have been the least mobile elements in the village population,
appear to have had very deep roots in Gissing.

As a result of the rather steady turnover of population, many of the
constables were newcomers to the village. It seems to have been rare
for more than one member or one generation of a family to serve in the
office. There are almost as many surnames as individuals on the list of
constables between 1603 and 1643, 38 men and 34 surnames. Only
four families provided two officers. While this might be explained
simply by the short time-span covered and by gaps in the list of
constables, the pattern is in keeping with the extent of population
turnover in Gissing, and with the fact that some of the families who
provided officers resided in the village only briefly. The names of only
two of the forty-three families known to have filled the constableship
between 1592 and 1643 are found on the subsidy roll of 1523.
Furthermore, there was a considerable amount of movement in and

---

[165] The following discussion is based on local rating lists in NNRO, PD 50/36L,
nos. 63, 78, 80, 82, 84, 86, 88, a subsidy roll of 15 H. VIII, and the hearth tax (Chas. II,
n.d.), PRO, E 179/150/282; E 179/154/704.

out of the village during the late sixteenth and early seventeenth centuries. Eight of the families who supplied constables between 1592 and the very early years of the seventeenth century had left the village by 1624, while two others were represented only by lesser branches which do not seem to have held the office. A number of entirely new names appear among the office-holders of the 1630s and the early 1640s. Some who appear on one rating list as 'outsitters' apparently took up residence briefly, and even held office, and then they disappear or are found among the 'outsitters' once again. The names of seven families who provided constables in the 1630s and of three more who held office in the early 1640s are not found on a rating list of 1624, and some of them were not assessed for local rates as late as 1630–1. The little that is known about them, particularly their local assessments, would suggest that they were prosperous farmers; and presumably they took up tenements vacated by other yeomen who had held the office. Some of these new men who filled the constableship did not remain long in the village either. Only six of the thirty-one inhabitants on the hearth tax for Gissing shared the surnames of families which had provided constables between 1603 and 1643.

The constabularies of different communities thus varied not only in terms of the wealth and social status of those who held the office, but also in the extent to which officers were drawn from older families as opposed to new arrivals in the village. In some settlements it is appropriate to describe most constables as coming from 'established' families, but in other villages a greater number of them were relative newcomers to the community. The farming families of Salwarpe, Stone, Branston, and Waltham, and especially of Pattingham, appear to have been rather firmly attached to those settlements. In such cases a majority of constables had ties of some duration to the villages in which they held office. They must have been well known to their fellow inhabitants, and to many they were connected not merely by residential propinquity but also by bonds of kinship and marriage. On the other hand, in settlements which experienced greater population mobility, such as Little Munden, Bushey, and especially Gissing, a significant proportion of the constables came from families which did not have roots in these communities. Some of these men served as constables only a few years after their arrival in the village. Officers of this sort cannot have enjoyed the same kinds of ties with their neighbours as did those in more stable and sedentary settlements. These differences may well have affected the way in which the constableship functioned in various communities.

It was suggested above that a larger number of poor men may have been chosen constable during the 1630s,[166] and it is possible that the officers of those years also included a larger proportion of 'newcomers'. Settlements which experienced considerable population turnover would be expected to choose as constable some men who had not resided long in the village. However, a surprisingly large number of 'new men' appear among the Gissing constables of the 1630s and early 1640s. In Little Munden a majority of the cases in which men were put into office soon after their arrival in the village also date from this period. It is possible that the constableship was intentionally being thrust upon relative strangers during the 1630s because other inhabitants were becoming unwilling to serve. If poor men were chosen for office during that decade because they could be more easily intimidated, especially in the collection of ship-money,[167] the same argument may help to explain the selection of newcomers as constables. Probably it was easier to resist the demands of an officer who did not have long-standing ties to other villagers as kinsman, affine, or neighbour.

III. THE EXTENT OF ILLITERACY AMONG CONSTABLES

Historians have attributed some of the failings of constables to their ignorance and illiteracy,[168] and seventeenth-century writers too sometimes commented on the problems created by the inability of officers to read and write. A sheriff of Cornwall reported to the Council in 1637 that illiteracy of constables in that county had contributed to his difficulties in procuring the return of ship-money assessments.[169] William Lambard's concerns about the illiteracy of high constables would have been equally applicable to village officers. He warned that their dependence upon others for assistance in deciphering and penning documents was 'the breakneck of many a good business'. Lambard urged that no one be allowed to serve in the office unless he was literate, so that he could read and write warrants 'without discovery of his enjoined service to any other for help therein'.[170]

Cases can be cited in which both high and petty constables found

---

[166] See above, nn. 86–7, 107.

[167] See above, n. 153.

[168] See above, ch. 1, nn. 7, 23.

[169] PRO, SP 16/346/88.

[170] Conyers Read, ed., *William Lambard and Local Government* (Folger Documents of Tudor and Stuart Civilization, Ithaca, 1962), p. 138.

themselves in difficulties because of their illiteracy. The officer of one Wiltshire village asked to be relieved of the position on the grounds that he had to travel two miles to a scrivener to have warrants read to him.[171] A Hampshire hundred constable seems to have faced a suit in Star Chamber as a consequence of his inability to read and write. He was charged with drawing up a passport for a pregnant servant girl which falsely accused her former master of being the father of the child. The constable contended that he was illiterate and unable to write the pass; and he seems to have been unaware of the precise contents of the document, which had been drafted by a neighbouring schoolmaster.[172] A village constable of Chaceley, Worcestershire, appears to have suffered needless trouble and considerable embarrassment because of his illiteracy. A literate servant girl, dressed in male attire and carrying a dagger and pike staff, and 'having a purpose to be merry', appeared at the constable's door late in the evening with a sheet of paper on which she had written something. She apparently tricked the officer into believing that she was a neighbouring constable, and that the paper which she handed him was a hue and cry after robbers.[173]

Clearly illiteracy could present problems in holding an office such as the constableship, which entailed the reading and penning of various documents. Therefore, in examining the social characteristics of constables it seems appropriate to consider how many of them could read and write. The only measurement of literacy which can be applied uniformly to constables, as to others during this period, is the ability to sign their names. However, the possession of books does suggest an ability to read.

Evidence concerning the literacy of constables is very incomplete, and at best it is possible to obtain information for only about half of those whose names are known. Moreover, since most of the evidence comes from wills and inventories and from lists of those who approved assessments or authorized other village actions, the sample is probably biased toward the wealthier and more prominent among those who held the constableship. Although the findings may not be entirely representative, it appears that there were variations from village to village in rates of illiteracy among constables, just as there were

---

[171] *HMC Various Collections*, i. 89.
[172] PRO, STAC 8/95/6.
[173] Bund, ed., *Sessions Papers*, p. 161.

differences among settlements in the wealth and social position of such officers.[174]

Illiteracy apparently was highest among the constables of Branston and Waltham. This may not seem surprising since most of the officers in those villages were husbandmen and since historians have suggested that, as a group, they were less likely to be literate than were yeomen.[175] Of the 10 Branston officers for whom information is available, 7 were illiterate. The officers of Waltham prior to the Civil War displayed an equally high illiteracy rate, 7 out of 10 there too being unable to sign their names. However, during the 1640s and 1650s more of the officers in that village were literate. When the entire period 1608–60 is considered only 9 (40 per cent) of the 22 constables for whom there is information were unable to sign. There is evidence of books in the houses of only one Branston and one Waltham constable. Two bibles and 'other books', valued at £1.6s. 8d., appear in the inventory of the widow of William Robinson of Branston, husbandman and weaver, who signed his will of 1638.[176] A bible is also listed in the inventory of Thomas Lowe of Waltham, husbandman, who was described above as one of the more prosperous men of that village. However, Lowe made a mark on his will, and also many years earlier when he acted as witness to the will of another villager.[177] Constables and other inhabitants in these villages in the early seventeenth century appear to have depended on the writing skills of a few literate men. Abraham Bishop, yeoman, constable of Branston in 1619, 1631, and 1641, penned documents for other officers, and he also seems to have written a number of wills and inventories of his fellow inhabitants.[178] William Robinson too perhaps assisted other constables. His son

[174] For studies of literacy or illiteracy in the sixteenth and seventeenth centuries, which give some attention to the problems of the sources and the difficulties of determining literacy, see David Cressy, 'Levels of Illiteracy in England, 1530–1730'. *Historical Journal*, xx (1977), 1–23; Cressy, 'literacy in pre-industrial England', *Societas*, iv (1974), 229–40; and his book, *Literacy and the Social Order* (Cambridge, 1980), ch. 3; Spufford, *Contrasting Communities*, chs. 7, 8; also see Lawrence Stone, 'Literacy and Education in England, 1640–1900', *P and P*, xlii (1969), 98–102.

[175] See Cressy, *Literary and the Social Order*, chs. 5–7. The following discussion is based on evidence from wills and inventories, the signatures or marks of testators and witnesses and of those who took the inventories.

[176] Leics. RO, DE 73/PR/T: 1638/51, PR/I: 40/252.

[177] Leics. RO, DE 73/PR/T: 1669/8. PR/I: 69/9; and for his mark as witness to an earlier will, PR/T: 1634/40.

[178] For Bishop's writing for other constables, see Leics. RO, DE 720/30, ff. 20ᵛ, 23, 27, 36, 41, 42ᵛ, 44; he probably wrote the following wills and inventories: DE 73/PR/T: 1638/51, 1638/64, 1661/C27, PR/I: 40/257, 55/30, 55/31.

William, constable in 1638, is known to have kept the parish register in the 1650s and officers may have called on him for aid as well.[179] Villagers of Waltham also seem to have depended on a few men to assist them with their writing needs. William Hose, constable in 1640, was paid for making passes and doing other writing by some of his fellow constables, and he also seems to have written a number of the village wills and inventories.[180] Edward Baker, husbandman, constable in 1632, who signed and probably wrote his will in 1638, perhaps performed similar tasks. His son Christopher, who was constable in 1649, seems to have penned a number of village inventories in the 1660s.[181]

Much higher rates of literacy might be expected among constables in villages where the office was filled by substantial yeomen, but such men sometimes were not much more literate than the husbandmen. Of the 23 Little Munden constables for whom there is information, 15 of them (65 per cent) made marks rather than signing. Information is not available about the literacy of some of the substantial yeomen constables in this village in the 1630s, such as Daniel Nash and Robert Chapman,[182] and the figures are perhaps somewhat misleading. However, the absence of books in the inventories also suggests low levels of literacy; only John Facey, yeoman, who leased the manor of Libury, is recorded as possessing any.[183] The fifteen constables who were literate included some of the very large farmers in the village such as Michael and William Ireland, Henry Perry, and Thomas Rowley, but also lesser men like Edmund Walker, husbandman, and his son William, Robert Adams, and Simon Mitchell.[184] In some of the yeomen families changes between the generations are apparent. While John Rowley (*c.*1600) and John Cocke (*c.*1595) could not sign their names, their sons Thomas Rowley (*c.*1628–9) and Richard Cocke

---

[179] Leics. RO, DE 702/1; see entries for the 1650s.

[180] For references to Hose penning documents see Leics. RO, DE 625/60, ff. 27, 44ᵛ; he also appears to have written some of the constables' accounts and probably the following wills and inventories: DE 73/PR/T: 1640/60, PR/I: 53/114, 53/116, 61/134. In Waltham constables sometimes paid the rectors for writing their accounts and other documents; see Leics. RO, DE 625/60, ff. 17ᵛ, 20ᵛ, 21, 22ᵛ, 23ᵛ, 45ᵛ.

[181] For Edward Baker's will see Leics. RO, DE 73/PR/T: 1639/27; and for inventories probably penned by his son Christopher PR/I: 64/150, 67/105, 69/9.

[182] On these men see above, n. 46.

[183] Herts. RO, 41 HW 2.

[184] The evidence is derived from signatures and marks on wills and inventories and on the Bishop's Transcripts. For evidence about the economic position of these men see above, nn. 46–8, 82, 87.

(*c*.1635–6) could do so.[185] Many officers in Little Munden too must have depended upon the local clergyman and a few other men for their writing needs. Richard Newton, clerk, probably penned a number of the Little Munden wills and inventories since his signature is found on them, and he may have assisted constables in matters that required reading and writing skills.[186] Thomas Kitchin, very likely the man who served as churchwarden in 1642 and 1643 and who held 120 acres in the village, seems to have served as scribe on a number of occasions in the 1650s and 1660s, and probably there were other men who had performed such tasks in an earlier period.[187]

In Stone, another village in which a number of substantial yeomen served as constable, the illiteracy rate among such officers seems to have been similar to that in Little Munden. Since the names of so few constables in this village are known, the churchwardens, most of whom probably did serve as constable too, have been included. Of the 16 for whom there is information, 10 (63 per cent) were unable to sign their names.[188] Although John Oldnoll, a very wealthy yeoman, was literate (and his inventory listed a bible and a few small books), as was Humphrey Hill of Hoo, other prosperous farmers who served, or probably served, in the constableship were not able to sign their names. These included John Oldnoll's father Roger, once again perhaps indicating a generational difference, two John Hills, two John Dolittles, Richard Clymer, and John Bacon.[189] On the other hand, several weavers in the village were literate, and two of them, John Kyndon and Edward Salisbury, may have served as constable.[190] Many constables in Stone too probably depended upon the assistance of the vicar (who acted as witness to at least nine wills between 1626 and 1645 and who probably wrote most of them), and upon the skills of a few other literate neighbours.[191]

[185] On these families see above, nn. 46–7.

[186] Herts. RO, 3 HW 254; 21 HW 34; 4 HW 42; 4 HW 16 (will and inventory); 3 HW 196; 100 HW 60; Thomas Wood, HW (1630).

[187] Kitchen's own will, conveyed orally on his death bed, was taken down in note form on the back of a will of widow Kempton, which Kitchen apparently had started to draft; see Herts. RO, 75 HW 24; and for wills, and the inventories of the same men, which Kitchen probably drafted, see 80 HW 24; 119 HW 62.

[188] Evidence is derived from the signatures and marks on wills and inventories.

[189] For the inventory of John Oldnoll see HWRO, BA 3585: 240/94; on these families also see above, nn. 52–3, 55–6, 58.   [190] See above, nn. 59–84.

[191] William Spicer was probably vicar from 1622, succeeding William Roberts, who was buried in Stone in that year, having held the living since 1601; Spicer witnessed the following wills: HWRO, BA 3585: 214a/129, 207a/5, 206c/165, 203/104, 241/22, 219c/85, 222a/160, 240/94, 214b/181.

The illiteracy rate seems to have been slightly lower among the constables of Bushey, and this may seem surprising since the farmers who held the office there were, on the whole, less substantial than those in Little Munden or Stone. However, the gentlemen constables in that village skew the figures a bit. Of the 31 officers for whom there is information, 18 (58 per cent) could not sign their names.[192] These figures do not take into account William Morgan, gent., who was probably literate, nor John Fendall, butcher, who presumably could read if not write, since he was bequeathed money for the purpose of buying a bible.[193] Gentlemen such as the two George Hickmans and Robert and Thomas Nicholl were literate, as were Richard Blackwell, yeoman, and Thomas Harte, yeoman. However, other substantial men such as the elder Thomas Nicholl, yeoman, George Blackwell, yeoman, Henry Francis, yeoman, and John Hunt, yeoman, made marks.[194] Among the smaller farmers, two members of the Bonnick family, William and Thomas, could sign their names, but Ralph could not. At least one member of the Weedon family, William, yeoman (c.1622–3), was literate, but several other Weedons who served in the constableship, William (c.1586–7, 1601–2), Alexander, yeoman, and George, yeoman, could not write.[195]

Salwarpe officers displayed a significantly lower rate of illiteracy than the constables of these other villages. The sample for Salwarpe, where the names of relatively few constables are known with certainty, has been expanded to include the churchwardens, most of whom probably served as constable too. It also incorporates fathers or sons of those who held the office, since they almost certainly did fill the position as well. However, the inclusion of these men is not enough, in itself, to explain the difference in the Salwarpe figures. Of the 32 men for whom there is evidence, 15 (43 per cent) were unable to sign their names.[196] Several of the yeomen constables, John and William Woodhouse, John Tommes and his father Richard, and other yeomen who very likely served, Richard French, William Elly, Thomas and John Smith, were literate. French's inventory lists two bibles and other

---

[192] The evidence is derived from signatures and marks on wills, on rating lists authorized by the vestry or various assessors, and on the rather fragmentary collection of Bishop's Transcripts in Herts. RO, Bundle 3/1–7, 1A–1F, 2A–2C.

[193] See the will of Thomas Harte, Herts, RO, 81 AW 17.

[194] For these families see above, nn. 96, 98, 103–4.

[195] For these families see above, n. 106.

[196] The evidence is derived from signatures and marks on wills and inventories and on the Bishop's Transcripts.

books while that of Elly contained a bible and a psalter. However, some
men of similar status were unable to sign their names, including
Richard Walford the younger, Edward Yarnold, John Brooke, and
Thomas Shailer.[197] The husbandman families of Ellis and Dugard
who provided constables were also illiterate; at least that was true of
Robert Ellis senior and of John and George Dugard.[198] In this village,
as in Stone, some of the craftsmen were literate, and one of the parish
clerks, John Cowles, came from a weaving family. However, in
Salwarpe such men do not appear to have served in the constableship
or other major offices.[199]

Officers of Salwarpe apparently were more literate than those in
many communities, but the constables of Gissing take the prize for
their reading and writing skills. Only 5 (29 per cent) of the 17 for
whom there is information were unable to sign their names, and two of
the five who could not write were among the villagers who possessed
books and they could probably read.[200] The literate constables
included yeomen such as Thomas Blome, John Clipwell, Robert
Cobbe, Thomas Earle, James Freeman, and Thomas Froswell, whose
relative prosperity was discussed above,[201] while John Browne,
yeoman, and Edmund Smith, yeoman, possessed books, although they
could not write.[202] In no other village examined do so many of the
surviving inventories of the period mention books, and especially
bibles. Even more significant is the fact that wills so often included
specific bequests of books, which suggests that they were valued
articles. Nicholas Alden, yeoman, in his will of 1626 instructed that his
nephew and heir, William Alden, gent. (*c*.1633) be educated in his
books. When William died in 1635 he bequeathed his books to his
son.[203] Thomas Procktor, gent. (*c*.1620–1) also received books from
his clergyman father.[204] On his death in 1584 Henry Earle, yeoman,
left his bible to a son-in-law, while his other books were to be divided

<hr/>

[197] For these families see above, nn. 60–2, 64–8; and for the inventories of French
and Elly, see HWRO, BA 3585: 245/62, 180/84.
[198] For these families see above, nn. 80–1.
[199] HWRO, Bishop's Transcripts, 2006/40/211, which identifies Cowles as parish
clerk; his will contains no signature, BA 3585: 189/147. For other members of the
Cowles family and their identity as weavers, see BA 3585: 130b/92, 138b/20.
[200] This evidence is derived from signatures and marks on wills and inventories.
[201] On these families see above, nn. 76–8.
[202] NNRO, INV 52/36; Norf. Arch. Wills, original wills 1624, no. 107.
[203] NNRO, Norw. Cons. Wills, 46 Mittings; Norf. Arch. Wills, Register, 1635, ff.
73–5.
[204] NNRO, Norw. Cons. Wills, 62 Hudd.

between his two sons, John and Thomas (*c*.1592, 1620).[205] Edmund Smith, yeoman, left his bible to a daughter, while Thomas Froswell bequeathed his best bible and the prayer book with the parchment to one of his daughters.[206] A bible valued at 5*s*. was listed in the inventory of William Kidman, while the inventory of John Browne contained two bibles.[207] William Moore, who served as churchwarden in 1591 and who may well have held the constableship, possessed a bible and other books, listed in his inventory of 1591.[208] The inventory of William Roper, yeoman, who probably served as constable and who was the father of Thomas Roper (*c*.1611–12, 1612–13), also included a bible and other books,[209] as did the inventory of Peter Blome, yeoman, perhaps of the same family as Thomas Blome (*c*.1605–6, 1606–7, 1631–2).[210]

It is as difficult to generalize about the level of literacy among constables as about their wealth and social position. However, if the rather limited evidence presented here provides an accurate guide, there were not only individual variations in officers' abilities to read and write, but also differences from village to village in the literacy levels of their constabularies. These differences may owe something to the diversity among settlements in the prosperity of the men who filled the office. However, they cannot be explained entirely in such terms. Most of the constables of Branston and Waltham, the villages where the highest proportion of officers were illiterate, were men of middling prosperity; and this may suggest some correlation between illiteracy and lack of wealth. In Bushey many of the constables were also men of rather moderate means, and there too quite a high proportion of them were unable to sign their names. Gissing and Salwarpe, the settlements whose constabularies displayed the highest levels of literacy, were also villages in which many prosperous yeomen held the office. However, the officers of Little Munden and Stone seem to have been just as substantial as those of Gissing and Salwarpe, but the constabularies in these communities were much less literate.[211]

[205] NNRO, Norw. Cons. Wills, 335 Bate and his inventory, INV 2/69, which contains books valued at 26*s*. 8*d*.

[206] NNRO, Norf. Arch. Wills, original wills 1624, no. 107; Norf. Arch. Wills, original wills 1628, no. 34.

[207] NNRO, INV 44/84; INV 52/36.   [208] NNRO, INV 8/120.

[209] NNRO, INV 26/214.   [210] NNRO, INV 10/274.

[211] Margaret Spufford found connections between literacy and economic status in the village of Willingham, and suggests that it was the yeomen who benefited most from the school there, but literacy was less closely related to wealth in Orwell, where certain families had a tradition of literacy; see *Contrasting Communities*, pp. 199–200, 203.

The presence of schools may be more important than wealth in explaining the higher levels of literacy among the constables of Gissing and Salwarpe. A Mr Smith, schoolmaster, appears on a Gissing rating list of 1631, and the village may well have possessed a school long before that date.[212] The generosity of Thomas Trimnell, gent., made possible the establishment of a grammar school in Salwarpe in 1607.[213] He conveyed to the parish two bullaries of salt water, the profits of which were to be used to pay a master to keep a grammar school and to hire a woman to instruct girls in reading English as well as in needlework, knitting stockings, and weaving bone-lace. Since Trimnell's charity made no provision for teaching boys to read English, it seems probable that such instruction was already available in Salwarpe in 1607. While the existence of schools in the other villages cannot be entirely ruled out, the local records examined provide no evidence of such institutions.[214]

The high rate of literacy among Gissing constables may be explained not only by the presence of a school in the village, but also by the religious complexion of this community. Some have suggested that Puritans were particularly anxious to advance literacy,[215] partly in order to foster Biblestudy. The yeomen families of Gissing seem to have been quite well supplied with bibles, and there is some evidence that they had been exposed to Puritan influences. The rectors quite likely shared the religious outlook of their patrons, the Kemps; and Richard Kemp, in his will of 1600, expressed the belief that he would 'be receaived amonge the electe of god', a view usually regarded as 'Puritan'.[216] The phraseology in the preambles to many of the constables' wills is also strongly Protestant. In the disposition of their souls the testators emphasized salvation through the merits of Christ alone, and some of them expressed assurance that they would join the saints in heaven.

---

[212] NNRO, PD 50/36L, no. 84.

[213] HWRO, 850 SALWARPE, BA 1054/2, 'Parchments Belonging to the Parish of Salwarpe', no. VII.

[214] There was a schoolmaster in Pattingham who was paid for writing the churchwardens' accounts on two occasions (Pattingham Churchwardens' Accounts, 1596, 1605), but in the absence of wills and inventories there is little evidence about literacy rates in this village.

[215] e.g. Stone, 'Literacy and Education in England', pp. 79–81; Kenneth A. Lockridge, *Literacy in Colonial New England* (New York, 1974), esp. pp. 43–51, 97–100; Cressy, *Literacy and the Social Order*, pp. 3–6, but also see pp. 84–5, 181–3.

[216] NNRO, Norw. Cons. Wills, 44 Force; on the Kemps' presentation to the living see Blomefield, *Norfolk*, i. 163.

In terms of their abilities to read and write, clearly some constables were better qualified for office than others. At the same time, differences from village to village in literacy levels meant that some constabularies were better equipped than others to deal with the written communications which played a significant part in the duties of the office. Constables of Branston, Waltham, Little Munden, and Bushey would more often have been more dependent upon others for assistance in tasks which required reading and writing than would officers of Gissing or Salwarpe. Higher rates of literacy possibly made the constabularies of Gissing and Salwarpe more effective. However, illiteracy should not be weighed too heavily as a defect among constables, despite evidence of errors and problems which could result from their inabilities to read and write. It was necessary for constables to procure assistance in fulfilling many of their duties, and it will be shown that they often received a good deal of help from other villagers. Most officers who found themselves in need of a scribe could probably turn to a literate neighbour, or to the village clergyman, for aid in reading and writing, just as they were accustomed to seek local assistance with other kinds of tasks.

IV. EXPERIENCE IN LOCAL GOVERNMENT

Another measure of the men who served as constable is the extent of their experience in local government. Historians may be correct to describe constables as 'unprofessional', in the sense that they were ordinary inhabitants with no special training who were part-time officials. However, most incumbents were probably not as ignorant about their duties as sometimes supposed. Furthermore, those who held the constableship usually served in other local offices as well, and many of them accumulated considerable experience in running the affairs of the manor and the parish.

It has been shown that men often acted as constable more than once, sometimes as many as four or five times, and after their first term they would have brought experience to the position.[217] Even more important is the fact that villagers frequently assisted others who held the constableship before filling it themselves, while those in office sometimes received aid from former constables. The legal and customary provisions which entitled such officers to seek help from

---

[217] See above, ch. 3.

their fellow inhabitants thus worked to enhance constables' knowledge of their duties.[218]

Many of those who held the constableship also filled other local offices. Some have suggested that the positions of churchwarden and overseer of the poor were more prestigious and less onerous than the office of constable, and that the occupants were of higher status.[219] However, it will be shown that a high proportion of constables acted as churchwarden and, although the evidence is very fragmentary, some of them are known to have served as overseers of the poor and surveyors of the highways as well. Variations from village to village in the percentage of constables who held other parish offices seem to be accounted for largely by differences in the amount of information available.

Well over half of the constables in most townships are known to have served as churchwarden, and if the rather incomplete evidence about overseers and surveyors is included then an even higher proportion of them are found to have held office in the parish. At least 18 of the 20 men who were constables of Branston in the period 1611–43 are known to have served as churchwarden as well, and some of them filled the office for a number of terms.[220] One man who held the constableship twice served as churchwarden on seven occasions, while another who was twice constable was churchwarden for six terms. Three of the constables served as churchwardens at least five times and three others for three years each. Most of the Waltham constables too acted as churchwardens. Of the 42 men who held the office between 1608 and 1660, 37 are known to have served as churchwarden in the period 1610–60.[221] One acted as churchwarden on at least four occasions, while three others served three terms and eleven of them held the office at least twice. In Little Munden 22 of the 37 constables appear on the list of churchwardens, and 8 of these men are also known to have served as overseers of the poor. An additional five

---

[218] For constables' rights to assistance see above, ch. 2. The amount of assistance they did receive will be discussed more fully below, ch. 7; on this point also see Trotter, *Seventeenth Century Life*, p. 117.

[219] e.g. the Webbs, *The Parish and the County*, pp. 18–19 and n. 3.

[220] The churchwardens' names are found in the parish register, Leics. RO, DE 720/1; the names of 81 of them between 1596–7 and 1648 are known; 19 names are missing.

[221] Leics. RO, DE 625/18, for the churchwardens' accounts, which are extant for the years 1610–34, 1638–54, 1656–60; four years and 8 names are missing. The parish register, DE 625/1, gives the names of the churchwardens for the years 1565 to 1592–3 and 1599–1600 to 1610.

constables appear among the overseers, and another among the surveyors, so at least 28 of the 37 had served in another major parish office.[222] Many of the constables of Gissing too filled other positions; 18 of 38 are known to have served as churchwarden, and another 4 as overseers.[223] In Gissing the office of churchwarden, like the constable-ship during some periods, was held for two consecutive years. However, even when this is taken into account, some compiled rather lengthy records of service. One who served three times as constable was churchwarden for nine years, another was three times constable and churchwarden for five years. Two men with two terms as constable acted as churchwarden for five and four years, respectively. The materials from Salwarpe and Stone are even more fragmentary, but in those villages too many of the constables also served as churchwarden. This was true of all of the constables of Stone from 1570 onward who can be identified, while 11 of 20 Salwarpe officers are known to have served as churchwarden. In both villages some of the yeomen held the office on a number of occasions, and in Stone sometimes for several years consecutively.[224]

Fewer constables in Pattingham and Bushey appear to have served in parish offices; but in the case of Pattingham there is an explanation for this fact. Of the 81 Pattingham constables, 49 are known to have

---

[222] The names of the churchwardens are derived from the town book, Herts. RO, D/P71/5/2, ràting lists in D/P71/5/1, and Bishop's Transcripts, Bundle 111, nos. 2–45. The names of 39 churchwardens between 1590 and 1615 are known; 9 names are missing. A gap between 1616 and 1629 is unbroken except for 2 names in 1624; and for the period 1630 to 1644 22 names are known and 8 are missing. From the town book and rating lists the names of 18 overseers of the poor can be recovered, 2 of them serving in 1624 and the remainder in the 1630s and early 1640s. The names of 10 surveyors of the highways, a complete list for the years 1639–44, are recorded in D/P71/5/2.

[223] The list of churchwardens between 1570 and 1640 contains 114 names; 20 names are missing. The list was compiled from summary accounts in the town book, NNRO, PD 50/35, and from some detailed accounts and a few rating lists in PD 50/36L, nos. 27, 30, 50, 70, 73, 75, 80, 81, 84, 90, 95. The names of only 19 overseers of the poor are known, and all served between 1629 and 1642; their names are found in PD 50/36L, nos. 77, 80, 93, 102.

[224] The list of 118 churchwardens which it is possible to compile for Stone contains the names of only 43 different men and only 22 surnames. The names are found in HWRO, 850 STONE, BA 5660/2, nos. 219, 223, 223a, 223b, 223c, 224–6; BA 5660/3(1); BA 5660/7, nos. 42–3, 176–8; BA 5672/1, no. 22c. The names of Salwarpe churchwardens are derived from the Bishop's Transcripts, HWRO, BA 2006/40, nos. 191–202, 205–6, 208–9, 211–3, 215, 229–35, 237–8, 240–2; and from receipts, 850 SALWARPE, BA 1054/2, Bundle G, and BA 1054/1, Bundle A, no. 9. It is possible to compile a list of 54 churchwardens between 1608 and 1642, and this contains the names of only 28 different men.

served as churchwarden, 16 of them holding the office at least twice. It is highly probable that more of the constables in this village had been churchwardens, either prior to 1584 or after 1646–7.[225] However, in this township duplication on the two lists is reduced by the fact that at least 12 of those selected as churchwarden held their lands in the manor of Rudge. While liable for parish offices, they would not be found as constables in the manor of Pattingham.[226] In Bushey 30 of the 57 men known to have held the constableship between 1590 and 1643 are recorded as serving as churchwarden and 15 of them also appear on the list of surveyors of the highways. An additional 7 constables are also known to have been surveyors, making a total of 37 out of 57 who held a parish office.[227] Given the gaps in the records it is probable that more of the Bushey constables did act as churchwarden. However, it is possible that some of the smaller farmers who held the constableship in this village filled the lesser position of sidesman, but never served as churchwarden.

In some communities the names of other local officials are known, and these lists shed further light on patterns of office-holding and on the kinds of positions filled by men who held the constableship.

The townwardens, two of whom served each year, were the major officers in Melton Mowbray.[228] A number of those who filled the constableship are known to have held this position, as well as serving as churchwardens. At least 11 of the 44 constables were also townwardens, one for six years, two for five years, three for three years and another for two years. At least eight of these men served as churchwarden too, sometimes for lengthy terms, as many as nine or ten years.[229] While

[225] The names of the churchwardens are derived from their accounts, found in the same book with those of the constables, and they are extant for the period 1584 to 1647, with a few gaps. The names of 118 churchwardens are known; 7 names are missing from the list in the 1580s and 1590s.

[226] See above, n. 134.

[227] The names of many of the churchwardens can be recovered from the town book and rating lists in Herts. RO, D/P26/7/1, D/P26/10/1, and from the Bishop's Transcripts, Bundle 3. The names of 36 churchwardens between 1576 and 1600 are known; 12 names are missing from the list. After a gap in the records from 1601 to 1616, the list is nearly complete for the years 1617 to 1635; 36 names are known and 4 missing. The list of surveyors, containing 34 names, is complete for the period 1616–32; see Herts. RO, D/P26/7/1.

[228] See the discussion of the townwardens in Dorothy Pockley, 'The Origins and Early Records of the Melton Mowbray Town Estate', *Transactions Leicestershire Archaeological & Historical Society*, xlv (1969–70), esp. 28–9.

[229] A list of 70 townwardens can be compiled for the period 1576–7 to 1616–17, and it contains only 22 different names, while a list of 63 churchwardens between 1578–9 and 1615–16 contains only 28 different names; men often served a number of years in

terms as both townwarden and churchwarden seem to have become shorter by the early seventeenth century, some men in Melton Mowbray still compiled very substantial records of service. Consider, for example, Thomas Owndell, constable in 1591 and 1612, who between 1596 and 1617 also served three years as churchwarden and five years as townwarden, one of his terms overlapping with the constableship; or Robert Trigge, constable in 1613, who in the period 1608–15 served as churchwarden for two years and townwarden for six years.

While a number of constables of Melton held the major local office of townwarden, only a few of the Bushey officers served in the more minor positions of sidesman and headborough, one of them a lesser parish office and the other subordinate to the constableship.[230] Although some constables are found on these lists, the surviving information would suggest that the positions of sidesman and headborough were usually filled by lesser men in the community who did not hold major offices in the manor or the parish. A number of the tradesmen and craftsmen in Bushey, as well as men from minor branches of some of the leading families, are found in these positions.[231]

The manorial records of Pattingham provide additional evidence about the local offices held by men who served as constable in that township, and about positions which they did not usually fill. Jury lists

both offices. Twelve names are missing from the list of townwardens and 14 from the list of churchwardens. These lists were compiled from Leics. RO, DG 25/1/1; DG 36/140/18–30; DG 36/284/12–34.

[230] The names of some sidesmen (two served each year) are found in the town book and in Bishop's Transcripts, Herts. RO, D/P26/7/1, and Transcripts, Bundle 3. The names of 32 sidesmen are known for the period 1582–1600; 6 names are missing. There is a gap from 1601 to 1616, and then the list, containing 34 names, is complete for the period 1617–32. The names of the headboroughs of Bushey, not to be confused with those of the hamlet of Leavesden, are found in the town book, Herts. RO, D/P26/7/1, and in Bushey Court Rolls, nos. 6393, 6395–6, 6398–6407, 37140, 37142, 37145, 37148, 37149. The names of 32 headboroughs are known between 1624 and 1642; 8 names are missing.

[231] Examples of some constables who served in one or both of these lesser offices: Richard Ballard, h.b. 1633–4, c. 1635; Abraham Redwood, sid. 1628, h.b. 1637, c. 1639; Francis Heyward, sid. 1627, c. 1631; Henry Davis, sid. 1626, c. 1632; Thomas Robinson, sid. 1620, h.b. 1624, c. 1626; Daniel Dencom, sid. 1587, c. 1590; John Dooke, sid. 1598, c. 1602. More typical of the kinds of men who held these offices were William Adams, smith (sid. 1630); Thomas Marston, mealman (h.b. 1625); Robert Davis, miller (h.b. 1635); Thomas Adams, bricklayer (sid. 1617, h.b. 1623); William Carter, carpenter (h.b. 1636) and a Blackwell, a Hickman, and a Fells who came from families which provided constables, but who did not themselves serve in the major offices.

are defective for the period 1580–1622, only ten of them surviving, although complete for the years 1623 to 1648. Despite the fragmentary evidence, no less than 62 of the 81 constables are found serving as jurors in the courts leet and baron. Thirty-four of them did jury duty regularly, and an additional twelve probably did so, some of them serving from ten to twenty years without a break. When they were not on the jury their names sometimes are found among the 'six men', the frankpledge or *decenarri* as it was also called. However, only 42 constables are found on such lists, as opposed to 62 among the jurors. This position was also filled by lesser men who did not serve in the major offices in manor or parish, and whose names are much rarer among the jurors as well.[232] The position of ale-taster also appears to have been filled by lesser men, though the names of nine constables appear on the fragmentary list of such officers which it is possible to compile.[233] The surviving names of the leather-sealers were almost entirely those of tanners and shoemakers, most of whom never held major offices, and only two constables who were in the leather trades appear on the list.[234]

The Webbs, who suggested that the office of churchwarden was the most prestigious village position, cited as evidence the claims of an early seventeenth-century clergyman that there was a sequential pattern in local office-holding. He lumped together the positions of sidesman, headborough, and constable, and suggested that from these men might rise eventually to the office of greatest honour, that of churchwarden.[235] While the lists of office-holders are too incomplete to speak with certainty on the subject, there is little evidence to support the contention that service as churchwarden followed that as constable. Nor does any pattern emerge as to the order in which men filled local offices. Sometimes they served first as churchwarden, sometimes as overseer, and in other cases as constable. In Bushey some men did hold one or both of the lesser offices of sidesman or headborough and then moved on to be constable and sometimes churchwarden.

[232] Jury lists are extant for the years 1583, 1588, 1600, 1604, 1605, 1616, 1619, 1621, and in almost unbroken series for the years 1623–48, Staffs. RO, Transcripts Pattingham Court Rolls, D/1807. The names of the 'six men' survive for the years 1583, 1600, 1604, 1605, 1633–49, Staffs. RO, D/1807.

[223] The names of the ale-tasters survive for only four years prior to 1634–5: 1582, 1583, 1601, and 1606; but there is a complete list for the years 1634–5 to 1650, Staffs. RO, D/1807.

[234] The leather-markers can be identified only for the period 1635–6 to 1652–3, Staffs. RO, D/1807.

[235] The Webbs, *The Parish and the County*, n. 3, pp. 18–19.

However, it is necessary to recall that a majority of the constables apparently did not serve in these minor positions.[236]

The local political importance of many of those who served as constable is also reflected in the fact that their names appear among the dozen or so who agreed to various actions on behalf of the township or parish. In the case of Pattingham there are lists of those who authorized the levying of rates to pay the constables' expenses and for the repair of the steeple, who signed an agreement that constables be allowed reimbursement for the days and nights that they were abroad on the village's business, and who determined that the rent from the parish lands would be paid to the overseers of the poor.[237] Over half of the constables, 42 of the 81, at one time or another put their names to such documents, suggesting that political influence in this village was rather widely distributed. The names found on lists of those who approved various actions in Bushey were almost entirely those of men who served in the constableship. A document of 1632, specifying the acreage on which men were to be taxed for local levies, gives the names of seventeen members of the vestry who approved the assessment, while a constables' rating list of October 1632 contains the names of eighteen men who were present when the assessment was drawn up. The lists are identical except for the addition of Henry Hickman's name to that in October.[238] All except Hickman, lord of Bushey Hall, and William Ewer, whose major lands lay in the halmet of Leavesden, where he probably served as headborough,[239] are known to have held the office of constable. Some of the same names are repeated among the four or five assessors who signed other rating lists in Bushey during the remainder of the 1630s.[240] In Melton Mowbray too the names found on documents authorizing local actions are those of men who served as constable. For example, those who signed the constables' accounts to indicate that they had been accepted and approved by the township had themselves held the constableship or were to do so.[241] Evidence of this kind does not exist for many of the communities considered in detail in this chapter. However, to add a final example, in Shelton, Norfolk, nine of the thirteen men who

[236] See n. 231 above.
[237] These documents are contained in the same volume with the constables' and churchwardens' accounts.
[238] Herts. RO, D/P26/10/1, pp. 9, 11.
[239] See above, n. 100.
[240] See the rating lists in Herts. RO, D/P26/10/1.
[241] Leics. RO, DG 25/39/1/1, 3; DG 36/188, 189.

approved a local rate in 1629 are known to have served as constable.[242]

The office-holding records of men who filled the constableship, and other evidence of their participation in village and parish affairs, testifies to the local political experience and importance of many of them. Such records provide evidence that a majority of those who served as constable had an opportunity to glean some practical knowledge about the operations of local government, including the functions of constables. Most of them probably were less ignorant about the obligations of the constable's office, and more experienced in the conduct of government business, than some of their contemporaries and some modern historians believed.

V. OBEDIENCE TO THE LAW: COURT RECORDS OF PATTINGHAM CONSTABLES

Although constables were chosen from the wealthier segments of village society, and were men with considerable experience in local government, in their obedience to the law they often do not seem to have been more 'respectable' than other inhabitants. J. A. Sharpe has pointed out that many of those who served as constable in the Essex village of Kelvedon Easterford had previously been before the courts, though usually for minor offences.[243] An investigation of the constables of Pattingham suggests similar conclusions about those officers.

Neither ecclesiastical court records nor those of the assizes have survived for late sixteenth- and early seventeenth-century Staffordshire, nor have Pattingham men been followed systematically in quarter sessions records. However, in the court leet of the manor a number of them appeared as offenders rather than law officers. Although many of the leet rolls have not survived prior to the 1630s, and the record is thus very incomplete, at least 54 of the 81 men who served as constable are known to have been fined by the manorial courts.[244] Some of these illegalities could be regarded as rather minor in character, but many of them were breaches of laws which these same men would be expected to enforce when they served as constable.

[242] NNRO, PD 358/33, p. 214.

[243] Sharpe, 'Crime and Delinquency in an Essex Parish', pp. 95–6, 97–8.

[244] The following discussion is based on information from the Pattingham Court Rolls for the years 1583, 1599, 1600, 1604, 1605, 1633–54, 1659, Transcripts of Staffs. RO, D/1807.

The offences can be divided into a number of categories, and some were fined for more than one kind of violation. Sometimes they had broken only laws or customs of the manor. Twenty of them were involved in what might be termed 'agrarian offences', enclosing lands, overstocking the commons, encroaching on the waste, breaking hedges, or seizing stray animals. A further ten were fined for negligence in maintaining roads, gates, or ditches, and four for diverting or obstructing watercourses. In other instances they had broken statutory regulations as well as customs of the manor. At least twelve of them were fined for violations of laws concerning ale-selling, victualling, baking, and butchering, while eleven were charged with taking inmates or giving hospitality to wanderers, beggars, and vagabonds, six with playing unlawful games, and three with building illegal cottages. Perhaps most surprising is the fact that twenty-seven of the men who held the constableship, the largest number in any category, were fined for disturbing the peace, for 'affrays' on other villagers. In three cases these assaults were on men in official positions.

Some of the men who served as constable in Pattingham had been before the courts not just once, but were more frequent offenders. The gaps in the records almost certainly result in an understating of the number of times a man had been fined by the leet. However, despite such incomplete evidence, it is known that 44 of the 54 constables with court records had committed more than one offence. A few examples will illustrate the records possessed by some Pattingham constables. William Perry of Great More, constable in 1625–6 and 1629–30, was a rather regular offender in the years after he held office; and, if the records were more complete, earlier offences probably would be discovered as well. During the 1630s and 1640s he was penalized for selling ale without a licence and fined for three affrays, for giving hospitality to vagabonds, and for walking abroad at inappropriate times during the night. The constables' accounts indicate that he was also arrested and taken before a justice in 1632–3. Another frequent offender was George Parker, yeoman, of Woodhouses, constable in 1634–5 and churchwarden in 1636–7. He was fined for overstocking the commons, for giving hospitality to strangers, and for making an affray. The constables' records show that he too was arrested and taken before a justice in 1638–9. Walter Devey of Hardwicke, who served twice as constable and twice as churchwarden between 1621 and 1646, was fined for five affrays and failure to maintain a gate, and he appears to have been conveyed before a neighbouring justice on three occasions.[245] A John Taylor, either the yeoman who served three times as constable and twice as churchwarden, or the tanner and shoemaker who was constable in 1642–3, was fined for making an affray on the constable in 1635. Perhaps it was the same man who had erected an illegal cottage, encroached on the waste, obstructed a way, and given hospitality to strangers and wanderers. A final example is provided by William Ward, gent., constable in 1608–9 and 1615–16, whose offences follow a somewhat different pattern from those already described, but were none the less numerous. He was fined for only one affray, but on six other occasions he was penalized for agrarian offences such as enclosing lands or encroaching on the waste. His son, who served as churchwarden and probably would have held the constableship too but for an early death, and later his widow, were fined on twelve occasions for similar breaches of the laws of the manor.

Evidence that some of the men who were to hold, or who had held, the constableship were guilty of breaking the law adds a further dimension to the portrayal of such officers. It serves to emphasize that they were ordinary villagers; and although they were usually among the more prosperous, this did not assure that they would always obey the law. Even if their offences were only of a minor kind, the fact that some men who served as constable committed misdemeanours does preclude, as J. A. Sharpe has suggested, 'the formulation of an easy polarity between the lawbreaker and the forces of law and order'.[246] The selection as constable of men with court records would suggest that contemporaries' expectations of such officers, and of the system of law and order, were rather different from those which prevail in modern England. Moreover, the fact that constables themselves had sometimes previously been in trouble with the courts must be taken into account in assessing their conduct in office. It seems unlikely that ordinary villagers who themselves had committed breaches of certain economic and social regulations viewed their law enforcement duties in quite the same light as did higher officials such as the justices of the peace or the judges of assize.

VI. CONCLUSIONS: THE QUALIFICATIONS OF CONSTABLES

An examination of the men who held the constableship in a number of

---

[245] Pattingham Constables' Accounts, 1623–4, 1628–9, 1638–9.
[246] Sharpe, 'Crime and Delinquency in an Essex Parish', p. 97.

villages and one market town in various parts of England during the late sixteenth and early seventeenth centuries provides little support for the complaints of contemporary officials, or the contentions of some modern historians, that the office was being thrust upon poor men. A few cottagers did act as constable, and some men of lowly status were perhaps deliberately chosen for the position during the later 1630s. However, most constables in these townships were drawn from the upper half of society. There can be little doubt about the wealth and social standing of many of the yeomen who regularly took their turns in the office in villages such as Little Munden, Salwarpe, Stone, and Gissing, and in the market town of Melton Mowbray as well. In communities which contained lesser or parish gentry these men too sometimes are found serving as constable. Even the middling-sized or small farmers who held the office, and who in villages such as Branston, Waltham, and Pattingham constituted the wealthiest men in the community, cannot accurately be described as 'the poorest and weakest sort'. Nor was this true of the tradesmen and craftsmen who filled the position in Bushey, Pattingham, and Melton. Such men in Melton were substantial townsmen, and even in Bushey and Pattingham they were above the level of most of the cottage population.

Furthermore, a large proportion of the constables, whether they were yeomen, husbandmen, craftsmen, or tradesmen, held other local offices as well; and they were men experienced in the affairs of the manor and the parish. Many of the more substantial farmers, who in villages such as Little Munden, Salwarpe, Stone, and Gissing accumulated the greatest amount of service in other offices, seem to have constituted a political as well as a social élite in the village. Some of these yeomen regularly participated in local affairs, putting their names to decisions on village policies or signing local rating lists or the constables' accounts, even when they were not holding office.

In some settlements the extent of geographical mobility, even in the upper reaches of village society, resulted in continuous shifts in the membership of such local élites. A considerable proportion of those who served as constable in such villages did not have deep roots in the community, although these men probably had obtained experience in local office-holding elsewhere. The number of recent arrivals found serving in the constableship in Gissing and, to a lesser extent, Little Munden, in the 1630s and early 1640s may be explained in part by the fact that the office was thrust open newcomers because other inhabitants were unwilling to serve. On the other hand, some villages, especially Pattingham but also Salwarpe, Stone, Branston, and Waltham, displayed considerable continuity and stability in the landholding population. The same families were dominant in local affairs, providing constables and other office-holders over several generations.

Although constables usually seem to have been drawn from the more prosperous and more prominent sections of village society, these men none the less were 'ordinary members of their communities, subject to the prejudices, the strengths and weaknesses of their society', to adopt Keith Wrightson's well-chosen phrase.[247] While the duties of the office included tasks that required skills in reading and writing, many constables, like other men of similar status in their society, were illiterate. There were variations from settlement to settlement in the proportion of officers who could read and write, though these do not seem to correlate very closely with the wealth and social position of those who held the constableship. Such factors as the availability of local schooling and perhaps even the religious complexion of a community may have been more important determinants of the level of literacy. While in settlements such as Gissing and Salwarpe many constables could probably perform tasks which required reading or writing without assistance, in the other villages considered a large number of them must have been dependent upon the local clergyman or a literate neighbour to assist them in duties which presumed literate skills. Although constables' performance in office may have varied depending upon whether or not they were literate, in many cases they could probably manage to procure help when they needed it, without detriment to the proper execution of their duties. Moreover, it is difficult to see how higher rates of literacy among constables could be anticipated in view of the general levels of illiteracy which prevailed in late Elizabethan and early Stuart England.[248]

Similarly, it would be too much to expect that the ordinary villagers who filled the constableship, even if they were normally economically, socially, and politically superior to many of their fellow inhabitants, would always be completely law-abiding. Like other men, some of them had quarrelled with fellow villagers, and sometimes laid a hand on them in anger. In the course of their economic pursuits they had sometimes infringed local agrarian regulations or even statutory provisions governing the conduct of trades such as brewing, baking, or

[247] Wrightson, 'Two concepts of order', p. 26.
[248] See above, n. 174.

ale-selling. The fact that many of the constables of Pattingham had themselves been in trouble with courts for minor offences perhaps made them ill-suited to be police officers. However, to judge them in such terms is to apply twentieth-century standards to the sixteenth and seventeenth centuries, and to employ criteria for the selection of such officers which probably would not have been deemed appropriate even by those contemporaries who complained about the 'quality' of constables.

5

Constables at Work I: Tax Collecting and Military Duties

THE men who held the constableship were not only of higher status and often better qualified for the position than usually assumed; they were also more industrious and more effective in executing the office than some have suggested.[1] This does not mean that they were without fault. Court records contain a number of cases in which higher officials, private citizens, and sometimes groups of inhabitants accused constables of neglect of their duties, or sometimes an abuse of their powers. Reports and correspondence found in sources such as the State Papers, as well as precepts sent to constables, also contain complaints from their superiors about their conduct. Constables' own accounts too, and the documents which they submitted to higher authorities, sometimes raise questions about their effectiveness in performing a duty. However, the number of suits against them would suggest that only a tiny proportion of the officers in any county were formally charged with defaults. Other evidence of negligence or misconduct by such officers is not usually very plentiful.

The negative evidence should not be dismissed, and it is important to try to assess the kinds of failings which constables did display; but much of the surviving information attests to their industry and achievements. Although their own records sometimes reveal them to have been at fault, such materials would suggest that they very often did meet the demands that were placed on them. The detailed constables' accounts which survive for some villages, and which record their activities from month to month and year to year, provide evidence of how much time and effort some of them gave to fulfilling their duties. They also suggest the kinds of sacrifices constables sometimes made in order to meet their commitments. Although all of them may not have been as hard-working as the officers of the villages examined here, there is no reason to believe that they were particularly unique.

[1] e.g. Cheyney, *History of England*, ii. 408; Barnes, *Somerset*, pp. 76–7; Tate, *The Parish Chest*, p. 187; Morrill, *Cheshire Grand Jury*, pp. 32–3.

The conduct of these constables, which can be examined from duty to duty and over time, seems likely to be more representative than that of officers who are known merely from legal records, which capture them at only one moment in time and often in circumstances which show them in an unfavourable light.[2]

Detailed information about the activities of the constables of a number of villages will be combined with more general evidence from county records and other sources in order to provide an assessment of constables' performance in the major areas of their responsibilities. This chapter will consider their conduct in the area of tax collecting and their military duties, while the following chapter will focus on their administrative tasks and police functions. Attention will be drawn to instances of apparent negligence or misconduct by such officers as well as to the many occasions when they were conscientious and effective in executing their duties. Some were more diligent than others, and there were also variations from duty to duty and over time in the performance of such officers. However, it will be argued that on the whole constables were not as unreliable or inept as sometimes has been suggested.

I. TAX COLLECTING

There can be little question about the time and effort that constables often devoted to their responsibilities as tax-collectors. During most of the period 1580 to 1642 they seem to have been remarkably successful in gathering and returning the levies for which they were responsible, as well as in meeting the crown's demands for goods and services which were imposed on local communities. Only occasionally is there evidence that a constable was generally delinquent in his tax-collecting duties, and usually the failings of such officers consisted of their being in arrears for a particular rate. Precepts and accounts for particular villages suggest that it was the exception rather than the rule for constables to be behind in their payments. The quarter sessions records examined also indicate that in most years only a few constables in any county were prosecuted for such arrears, though in a few instances larger numbers were accused of negligence. There do appear to have been some significant changes over time in constables' performance of their duties as tax and rate-collectors, and in the later

---

[2] On this point also see Campbell, *The English Yeoman*, p. 324.

1630s there is increased evidence of their failure to assess and collect some levies, particularly ship-money and coat and conduct money.

(1) Constables' Achievements: County Rates and National Taxes

Constables' accounts testify to their general effectiveness in collecting county rates.[3] Quarterly payments for charitable purposes, yearly sums for provision, and in some shires for the muster master or the beacons, coat and conduct money and other military levies when soldiers were on active duty, and periodic rates for the repair of county bridges appear rather regularly in constables' accounts.[4] In addition to these normal levies, usually paid to the high constable, constables in some counties at some periods were also very much occupied in collecting county rates for victims of plague. Sometimes such payments were due every two weeks, or even weekly, thus entailing many additional journeys for such officers. During several months in late 1609 and early 1610 the constable of Salwarpe repaired to Worcester at least every two weeks to make payments for victims of plague in Foregate Street, while in 1611 similar sums were returned for plague victims in the tithing of Whistons, near Worcester.[5] Other officers too sometimes collected considerable sums for victims of plague, as did the constables of Branston and Waltham during certain years in the early seventeenth century. They were also probably obliged to make additional journeys to return such payments. The Waltham officer in 1610–11 collected levies for the 'visited people' of both Bottesford and Leicester, totaling £1. 10s. 8d., while between May and October 1631 the constable of that town paid £2. 18s. for plague victims in Loughborough, sums which exceeded the subsidy assessments in that village. The officer in 1631–2 gathered a further £2. 4s. for Loughborough and a smaller sum for 'the visited' of Plungar, while in September 1633 the constable paid £1. 13s. 4d. for the relief of the plague in Hinckley and during about twenty-eight weeks, beginning at Easter 1637, £5. 13s. 4d. was collected for victims of plague in Melton Mowbray.[6]

[3] For their responsibilities in this area see above, ch. 2.

[4] See esp. the detailed and almost continuous accounts of Pattingham from 1582 to 1640 (found in the parish church), and those of Branston and Waltham, Leics. RO, DE 720/30, DE 625/60; also see the receipts issued to Salwarpe constables, HWRO, 850 SALWARPE, BA 1054/2, Bundle G.

[5] HWRO, 850 SALWARPE, BA 1054/1, Bundle A, nos. 7, 10, 72, 73, 74, 162, 163, 185, 218, for precepts ordering such payments, and see the receipts issued to constables in BA 1054/2, Bundle G.

[6] Leics. RO, DE 625/60, ff. 6, 6^v, 36^v, 37, 38, 38^v, 42^v, 43, 54, 54^v.

Constables of Branston gathered similar funds for plague victims in Hinckley in 1626–7, in Loughborough and Plunger in 1631–2, in Melton in 1637–8, and in Whitston in 1641–2 and 1642–3.[7]

Constables also succeeded in levying a number of special county rates imposed by the justices, many of them collecting rather substantial sums toward the building of Houses of Correction, shire halls, and gaols, while in some counties they made smaller payments almost annually for a variety of other purposes. Officers of Waltham paid a levy of 13s. 4d. for the castle in Leicester in 1609–10 and £12 toward building a House of Correction at Leicester in 1610–11, while those of Manchester, in three separate payments in 1618 and 1619, contributed £24. 16s. 10d. toward building a House of Correction in that county. The constable of Salwarpe in 1633 made a smaller payment of 19s. 7d. toward building a House of Correction in Worcester, while in 1634 the officer of Gissing paid 13s. 6d. to the high constable for building a workhouse at the castle in Norwich.[8] Staffordshire constables appear to have been most occupied in collecting and paying miscellaneous county rates. Officers of Pattingham not only delivered to the high constable £3. 13s. 4d. in 1616–17 for a new gaol and House of Correction and finishing the shire hall, £3. 1s. 3d. in 1619–20 toward the new gaol, and 16s. 3d. in 1621–2 for the shire hall as well as smaller payments in 1634–5 for building a treasury house and in 1639 for the shire hall; but almost every year they collected small sums for other rates imposed by the justices. These included the maintenance of bastards born in the gaol or the House of Correction; children born in Ireland, who presumably had been deserted by their parents; children whose parents had been executed; on one occasion in 1636–7 for the maintenance of sixty children in the gaol; and in 1634–5 for conveying witches through the hundred.[9] Similar entries occur in the few surviving accounts for Gayton, Staffordshire.[10]

When the entire period 1580 to 1642 is considered, the records

[7] Leics. RO, DE 720/30, ff. 24^v, 31, 31^v, 42, 42^v, 51, 51^v, 52; also see Jonathan E. O. Wilshire, 'Plague in Leicestershire 1558–1665', *Transactions Leicestershire Archaeological and Historical Society*, xliv (1968–9), 45–71; Nicholas Griffin, 'Epidemics in Loughborough, 1539–1640', ibid., xliii (1967–8), 24–34.

[8] Leics. RO, DE 625/60, ff. 5^v, 6; Earwaker, ed., *Constables' Accounts*, i. 38, 39, 51; HWRO, 850 SALWARPE, BA 1054/2, Bundle G (receipt dated 2 Aug. 1633); NNRO, PD 50/36L, no. 89.

[9] See the Pattingham Constables' Accounts for the years cited; and similar entries in other years as well.

[10] Staffs. RO, D/705/PC/1/1.

would suggest that constables were usually successful in levying
national taxes, and that they devoted a good deal of time to this task.
Such duties normally required their attendance upon higher officials
on several occasions.[11] Constables' accounts show them trekking back
and forth to neighbouring villages or the county town to meet with
their superiors about assessments and to return local rating lists, as
well as to pay such levies. In the late Elizabethan and early Jacobean
period, when the collection of subsidies amounted very nearly to an
annual duty, the Pattingham constables' accounts record their
numerous journeys to Wolverhampton to consult with the commissioners
about assessments and to return local tax lists to these officials, as well
as to make subsidy payments.[12] Constables' accounts from other
villages and for later periods also show them busily engaged in the
assessment and collection of subsidies. For example, the constable of
Branston recorded no less than seven trips to Melton Mowbray about
the assessment of subsidies in 1621, as well as journeys to pay the tax.[13]
The Salwarpe accounts provide even greater detail about the busy
round of Francis Ellis, constable in 1641, in collecting taxes. On 16
March he appeared before the subsidy commissioners in Bromsgrove;
on 29 March he was off again, probably to Bromsgrove, to bring in the
names of those eligible to pay the levy; on 12 April he travelled to
Kidderminster concerning the assessment, while on 21 April he went
to Kidderminster again to return a subsidy assessment. He perhaps
had some respite from such duties in May, but by June he was engaged
in the assessment and collection of the poll tax, and during that
summer he travelled to Bromsgrove, Kidderminster, and Worcester in
connection with this levy. By October he was once more involved in
the assessment and collection of a subsidy, travelling three times to
Bromsgrove about this matter.[14] These examples are not untypical of the
evidence of constables' work in tax collecting, similar entries being found
in other constables' accounts, and in connection with benevolences,
loans, contributions for St. Paul's, and ship-money as well as subsidies
and the poll tax.

(2) Constables' Achievements: Goods and Services for the Royal Household, Saltpetre Men, and Postmasters

Even more impressive than their work in assessing and collecting

---

[11] See above, ch. 2. | [12] See the Pattingham Constables' Accounts for this period.
[13] Leics. RO, DE 720/30, ff. 18–18ᵛ.
[14] HWRO, 850 SALWARPE, BA 1054/2, Bundle D, nos. 8, 9.

taxes, and in paying county rates, was the amount of time and effort which constables in some counties gave to meeting the demands for goods and service required by the royal household when the monarch was on progress, or for other reasons travelling through a shire. The many entries concerning provision and carriage found in the accounts for Branston and Waltham suggest how busy and how hard-working successive constables of those villages were in meeting such responsibilities. For example, in August 1616 there are ten separate entries in the Waltham accounts concerned with provision and carriage. The constable attended the chief constable and cart-takers, he hired a cart to carry provision, procured oats and straw for the king, arranged for the threshing and tying of the straw, carried straw and oats to Belvoir on three different occasions, went to Nottingham with a cart of provisions, and on another occasion arranged for the carriage of provisions from Nottingham to Leicester.[15] There were many similar entries in 1619 when Waltham supplied capons and hens, malt and oats for the king at Belvoir, while the constable also carried boards and forms to Belvoir and back again, as well as supplying two carts to carry 'stuff' for the king from Belvoir to Rufford Abbey and another cart to go from Nottingham to Derby. He also provided hay and straw for the king's horses and hounds and arranged for the carriage of the hounds to Harby.[16] The summer of 1621 was an even busier one. The constable of that year made no less than twenty entries in his accounts concerning provision and carriage for the king, and such duties took him not only to Belvoir but to Melton and twice to Grantham.[17] There were similar, if fewer, entries in the Branston accounts for the same period, and the constables of both villages were also busy in fulfilling such duties during the 1630s.[18] While in some counties, such as Staffordshire, special rates were levied to cover the expenses of provision and carriage when the king was present in the shire,[19] in Leicestershire the king's arrival clearly created many additional duties for constables. However, on the basis of the evidence in the Branston and Waltham accounts it would appear that these officers were remarkably conscientious in meeting such responsibilities.

At some periods and in some townships constables can also be seen

[15] Leics. RO, DE 625/60, fo. 13.   [16] Leics. RO, DE 625/60, ff. 18, 19.
[17] Leics. RO, DE 625/60, ff. 23, 23^v.
[18] Leics. RO, DE 720/30, ff. 11^v–12, 16, 18–18^v; and both DE 625/60 and DE 720/30 for the 1630s.
[19] Pattingham Constables' Accounts, 1618–19, 1619–20, 1620–1, 1623–4, 1625–6, 1635–6; also see Staffs. RO, QS/O, ii. 48^v.

devoting considerable time to meeting the requisitions of saltpetre men. The constables of Branston and Waltham were very much occupied with such tasks in the later 1630s, while there are earlier references to these duties in Waltham in 1610–11, 1616, and 1634, and in Branston in 1619–20.[20] Both constables attended the saltpetre men when they came to test the grounds in 1635, and that year the officer of Waltham also provided a cart to carry ashes, arranged for the fetching of ashes from Grantham, for carrying saltpetre tubs to Thorpe, and for conveying a load of saltpetre to Melton. He also appeared before the justices in Branston when the coalmen of Harby came for coals, probably for the saltpetre works. Constables in other townships too recorded the assistance which they rendered to saltpetre men, the officers of Manchester providing carts and wagons to carry saltpetre, while a number of Norfolk officers also supplied carts or arranged for the carriage of ashes or coals or loads of saltpetre.[21]

Constables' accounts also provide evidence of their efforts to meet the demands of postmasters for coals, sometimes for oats, and primarily for horses. Officers of Waltham arranged for the carriage of loads of coals to the postmaster in Witham in 1619, 1620, 1632, 1634, and 1636; and from 1638 to 1642 they were very much occupied with the post. They went to Witham with oats, oversaw the taking of post-horses, accompanied neighbours and their horses to Witham, and attended the postmaster and his man when they came to Waltham.[22] Similar entries are found in the Branston accounts, and in both 1631 and 1639 the officers of that village travelled to Grantham about post-horses.[23] The Manchester constables in 1639 recorded expenses for staying overnight with horses at Rochdale, and on another occasion for fetching from Ripponden three horses which they had supplied to go post to Wakefield.[24]

---

[20] Leics. RO, DE 625/60, ff. 6ᵛ, 12ᵛ, 45ᵛ, 47, 47ᵛ, 48ᵛ, 49ᵛ, 56ᵛ; DE 720/30, ff. 15ᵛ, 31.

[21] Earwaker, ed., *Constables' Accounts*, i. 233, 240, 241, 242, 246, 250, 252; ii. 62; PD 358/33, pp. 11, 14, and the years 1622, 1637; PD 50/36L, nos. 83, 89; PD 219/126, 1636–7; PD 254/112, 1635, 1636, 1637. Also see the Wymeswold accounts, BL Add. MS 10457, ff. 26ᵛ, 28ᵛ, 37ᵛ; the Stockton accounts, Salop RO, 3067/3/1, p. 5; the Millington accounts, PR MIL. 10, 1634; and the Pattingham accounts, 1587–8, 1592–3, 1596–7, 1601–2, 1631–2, 1638–9.

[22] Leics. RO, DE 625/60, ff. 18, 19, 20, 40, 44ᵛ, 45, 51, 55ᵛ, 56ᵛ, 57, 58ᵛ, 60, 61, 61ᵛ, 62, 62ᵛ, 65, 65ᵛ, 66.

[23] Leics. RO, DE 720/30, ff. 29ᵛ, 34ᵛ, 44ᵛ, 45ᵛ, 47ᵛ, 48, 48ᵛ, 50, 52ᵛ.

[24] Earwaker, ed., *Constables' Accounts*, ii. 66; also see i. 201, 222, and ii. 64.

(3) Periodic Arrears vs. the Special Cases of Ship-Money and Military Levies in the 1630s

Although constables' accounts testify to the industry which they often displayed in their tax-collecting duties, both their accounts and the precepts sent to them do reveal that they were occasionally in arrears for a tax or rate. The periodic defaults of constables of Salwarpe in the early seventeenth century seem to be rather typical of the kinds of failings which such officers sometimes did display. Constables of this village usually do seem to have met their commitments, and the receipts issued to them provide some indication of their achievements,[25] but occasionally an officer had not paid a particular rate. A precept of January 1611 indicates that the constable of that year had not returned 20s. that was owing for victims of plague. The officer in 1614 had not, as of 20 March, paid provision money that was due on 22 February, and he was urged to levy it speedily since the high constable had already paid it for him.[26] In 1621 the constable was in default in his payments for the gaol, maimed soldiers, and the House of Correction, and he was warned that if he did not collect the money immediately he would be fined 20s. according to the statute.[27] The officer in 1624 was in arrears for the rate for the muster master. The high constable, who was about to leave office, threatened to penalize him unless he returned the money. Richard Walford, constable in 1625, was one quarter behind in payments for the gaol, maimed soldiers, and the House of Correction.[28] The officer of 1627 seems to have been somewhat more negligent than most and he was in arrears for several rates or taxes. He too was behind in payments for the gaol, maimed soldiers, and the House of Correction, and in the rate for the erecting and repair of the beacons, while he was also delinquent in gathering the loan of that year. Several precepts indicated that the loan money was behind, and the constable was ordered to return the names of those in default, and later to appear in Kidderminster with those who had not paid the tax, and to answer for his own activities.[29] Two precepts of 1628 suggest that the constable of that year had failed to

---

[25] HWRO, 850 SALWARPE, BA 1054/2, Bundle G.
[26] HWRO, 850 SALWARPE, BA 1054/1, Bundle A, no. 185; BA 1054/2, Bundle H (20 Mar. 1614).
[27] HWRO, 850 SALWARPE, BA 1054/1, Bundle A, no. 147.
[28] HWRO, 850 SALWARPE, BA 1054/1, Bundle A, nos. 25, 97.
[29] HWRO, 850 SALWARPE, BA 1054/1, Bundle A, nos. 117, 99, 204, 273, 183, 65.

pay the rate for the gaol, maimed soldiers, and the House of Correction.[30]

Some instances can be found in which constables were delinquent in paying a number of rates, as was the case with the officers of the constablewicks of Okeover, Ilam, and Castern, Staffordshire, who were reported to sessions in 1616 by the high constable of Totmanslow for their failure to return a long list of county rates in 1614–15.[31] However, occasional arrears, such as those displayed by Salwarpe officers, usually characterized the failings which are revealed in the constables' accounts of other villages and in quarter sessions records as well. Constables of Waltham are known to have been behind in their payments for plague victims in 1610 and 1637, and in payments for provision in 1631; and apparently they had also failed to pay a military rate of £5. 3s. 4d. in 1627.[32] The officer of Branston in 1631 was in arrears for provision too, and in 1642–3 for the rate for plague victims, and the village was two years behind in payments for the muster master in 1631.[33] The Pattingham constables had not paid all their provision money on time in 1610–11, and in 1629–30 they returned to the high constable on Shrove Tuesday rate money that had been due at Michaelmas.[34] Although all the arrears probably do not show up in constables' accounts, these seem to typify their periodic defaults in making payments.[35] The scattering of cases in quarter sessions records involving constables who were delinquent as collectors also usually entailed their failure to pay a particular rate, most often for charitable purposes or bridges,[36] but sometimes provision or a levy for a royal progress,[37] military rates,[38] or the subsidy and fifteenths.[39]

[30] HWRO, 850 SALWARPE, BA 1054/1, Bundle A, nos. 114, 21.
[31] Staffs. RO, Transcripts Sessions Rolls, Jac. I, Roll 51, no. 42.
[32] Leics. RO, DE 625/60, ff. 6, 55, 35ᵛ; PRO, SP 16/72/59.
[33] Leics. RO, DE 720/30, ff. 30, 52, 31ᵛ.
[34] See the Pattingham accounts for the years cited.
[35] For some other examples of such arrears see Earwaker, ed., *Constables' Accounts*, i. 34, 73; Somerset RO, D/P/West Monkton, 12/2/1, 1599; NNRO, PD 50/36L, nos. 15, 24.
[36] e.g. Burne, ed., *Staffs. Sessions Rolls*, ii. 255, 324; iv. 204, 327, 424, 442; v. 135; Salt, ed., *Sessions Rolls, Easter 1608 to Trinity 1609*, p. 105; Staffs. RO, Transcripts Sessions Rolls, Jac. I, Roll 24, no. 36; Roll 49, nos. 54–6; Roll 51, no. 42; Roll 74, no. 13; QS/O, ii. 67; iii. 15; iv. 157, 259; Atkinson, ed., *Sessions Records*, i. 17, 27, 33, 61, 69, 165–6, 205, 207, 227, 238, 244; ii. 57, 112, 159, 166, 179–80, 234; iii. 111–12, 126, 129, 164, 189, 191, 195, 269, 354, 359; iv. 28.
[37] e.g. Burne, ed., *Staffs. Sessions Rolls*, ii. 255; Staffs. RO, Transcripts Sessions Rolls, Jac. I, Roll 49, nos. 55–6; Atkinson, ed., *Sessions Records*, i. 250; ii. 57, 166; iii. 111–12.
[38] Atkinson, ed., *Sessions Records*, i. 238; iii. 195; Staffs. RO, Transcripts Sessions Rolls, Jac. I, Roll 51, no. 42.   [39] e.g. Tait, ed., *Sessions Records*, pp. 5, 219, 236.

In a few cases a larger number of constables than usual do seem to have been in default for a tax or rate, and occasionally all the officers in a particular hundred had apparently failed to make payment. For example, in 1623 seventeen constables in the North Riding of Yorkshire were in arrears for lame soldiers, hospitals, and bridges, while in most years only two or three officers were presented to sessions for their defaults in tax collecting.[40] There had apparently been fairly widespread negligence by Staffordshire constables, probably in collecting county rates, at about the same time. An order at Michaelmas sessions 1624 claimed that payments in Staffordshire were behind for three years, and directed that all high constables and petty constables attend the justices at their meetings for binding alehouse keepers for this matter to be considered.[41] Perhaps the defaults in both Yorkshire and Staffordshire in the early 1620s were due to the economic difficulties and scarcity of those years. In 1638 all the constables in the hundred of Offlow, Staffordshire, seem to have defaulted in the payment of a bridge levy, and the officers of the hundred of Lonsdale, Lancashire, had also failed to pay such a rate in 1604.[42] Similarly, many, if not all, the constables of the hundred of Birdforth in the North Riding of Yorkshire apparently failed to pay their levies for soldiers and bridges in 1621, and the high constable was issued a general warrant against them.[43] Another example of the officers of a whole division being delinquent in payment is found in a report on the benevolence of 1614 submitted by a high constable of the hundred of Totmanslow, Staffordshire. He informed the justices at Easter 1616 that he had sent warrants for payment to the nine constables within his division, in which the assessments ranged from 12s. to £6. 8s., but he claimed that he had received only 3s. 4d. given to him by one gentleman.[44]

Instances in which a number of constables, and not just an officer or two, had made default in paying a tax or rate do not seem to be very numerous during most of the period 1580 to 1642. However, materials for particular villages, and other kinds of sources too, suggest that officers were more often tardy or delinquent in paying their levies during the 1630s than in earlier years. During that decade the justices of a number of counties reported to the Council the difficulties they

---

[40] Atkinson, ed., *Sessions Records*, iii. 164.   [41] Staffs. RO, QS/O, ii. 13ᵛ.

[42] Staffs. RO, QS/O, iv. 259; Tait, ed., *Sessions Records*, pp. 209, 241.

[43] Atkinson, ed., *Sessions Records*, iii. 126.

[44] Staffs. RO, Transcripts Sessions Rolls, Jac. I, Roll 51, no. 42.

had encountered in securing the payment of contributions for the repair of St. Paul's,[45] though only the Berkshire magistrates attributed their problems directly to the negligence of constables. They claimed that they found 'much couldnes and remissness' in such officers.[46] Perhaps constables were negligent in gathering this levy, but most of the evidence of their failings concerns ship-money and military rates. During the years 1637 to 1640 higher officials sometimes accused constables in general of openly defying their orders and making no efforts to assess or collect ship-money. In some counties there were similar complaints about constables' negligence in regard to coat and conduct money in 1639–40. Constables' own accounts, and the precepts sent to them, suggest that they were more deliquent in collecting ship-money than any of the other taxes and rates for which they were responsible.

The repeated ship-money warrants sent to Robert Ellis, constable of Salwarpe in 1640, suggest that he was more tardy in paying this levy than earlier officers had been in returning any of their rates or taxes.[47] Nor does Ellis seem to have been as diligent in levying ship-money as was his brother, Francis, in collecting subsidies and the poll tax in 1641.[48] He was sent no less than six precepts concerning ship-money between January and July 1640, and probably others which have not survived; but he seems to have been slow in responding to the demands which they contained. He may or may not have attended a meeting in Bromsgrove, where he was commanded to appear by a precept of 10 January, and where it was to be determined how the ship-money would be divided among the townships within the hundred of Halfshire. Another precept sent to him on 17 January ordered him and the other assessors to make a rate on the parish for £19. 11s. 3d. and to return the assessment to the high constable by 28 January, or else appear personally before the sheriff in Worcester on the thirtieth of the month to answer for his neglect. However, by 10 March Ellis had apparently not even drawn up the assessment, let alone collected the money. The high constable accused him of having done nothing at all, despite the many warrants which had been sent to him, and of thus showing his disregard for the king's service and his

---

[45] PRO, SP 16/250/1; 252/42, 46; 285/67; 288/64, 87, 103, 104; 291/105; 298/38; 299/31; 300/56; 304/35; 311/97; 369/51.
[46] PRO, SP 16/236/36.
[47] HWRO, 850 SALWARPE, BA 1054/1, Bundle A, nos. 173, 180, 171, 174, 172, 169 for the precepts concerning ship-money; for the Ellis family see above, ch. 4, n. 81.
[48] See above, n. 14.

contempt for the sheriff and his authority. He was warned that his wilful neglect would not long be tolerated, and was advised to double his efforts in order to make amends for his former negligence. Ellis's accounts indicate that he travelled to Worcester on 1 April to pay ship-money.[49] However, he was still in arrears for some of the levy and a precept of 29 April ordered him to pay the money that was behind by 8 May. Despite this order 4*s*. was still outstanding on 13 June when another warrant directed him to levy this by distress or otherwise and to make payment by 20 June. By 16 July he still had not collected what was owed by the clergyman of Salwarpe, and he was ordered to do so or, if the man refused payment, to return his answer as to why he had failed to comply.

While more information concerning ship-money survives for Salwarpe than for the other villages examined, there is some evidence in the accounts of Pattingham, Branston, and Waltham that the officers of these villages too displayed greater negligence in returning this levy than in paying other rates. While in many instances these constables ultimately seem to have paid the money, or most of it, they appear to have been tardy in doing so. Apparent negligence by constables in Pattingham in collecting ship-money resulted in their being summoned before the undersheriff about the levy in 1636–7, twice before the sheriff in 1637–8, and again on two occasions in 1638–9. The officers of that year, one of whom was a deputy serving for a butcher who had declined the position,[50] travelled to Stafford on 27 April to pay the levy, but they still did not return the full sum. They went to Stafford about ship-money once again on 29 June, and the sheriff's officials seem to have distrained for some of the tax in the autumn of 1639. The constables in office in 1640, when the deputy of the previous year served once again for another villager, were also summoned before the sheriff in Stafford in March. On 23 July their accounts record a payment for writing an answer about ship-money. Perhaps in response to charges of negligence they were defending their actions, or rather their inaction. They were apparently summoned before the sheriff again on 11 August, when their accounts record that they spent two days in Stafford about ship-money; but there is no evidence in the accounts for 1640 that they paid the levy.[51] The constable of

[49] HWRO, 850 SALWARPE, BA 1054/2, Bundle D, no. 6.
[50] See above, 3, ch. 4, n. 143.
[51] See the Pattingham accounts for the years cited. The accounts for 1639–40 are incomplete.

Waltham in 1635 also seems to have been tardy in collecting ship-money, paying some of the tax in early November and the remainder later that month, while the officer of that village in 1640 was warned to appear before the High Sheriff about ship-money. There is no evidence that any of the levy imposed in that year was paid.[52] By 1639–40 the constable of Branston also seems to have been somewhat remiss in collecting ship-money. The chief constable and the king's bailiff distrained for some of the levy in 1639, while in 1640 the constable was summoned twice before the justices about ship-money.[53]

Evidence from the constables' accounts of particular villages of their laxity in paying ship-money receives more general confirmation in the reports which sheriffs submitted to the Council about such officers' deficiencies as collectors. Sheriffs of Worcestershire, Staffordshire, Hertfordshire, Leicestershire, and Norfolk all complained that constables had refused to obey their warrants concerning ship-money.

Some of the most damning reports came from sheriffs in Worcestershire, where as early as 1636 there were complaints that constables and others 'growe wearye and unwillinge to attend this service'. By 1640 Sir John Winford charged that many constables in that county were wholly opposed to the collection of ship-money. He claimed that they 'wilfully' absented themselves from their houses so that his officers could not meet them, and that in the whole week preceding his letter of 15 June they had managed to see only two constables. Some refused to make assessments or even to try to collect the money and Winford had committed to gaol a number who were in default. However, he reported that they remained defiant despite punishment.[54] A letter of 1640 from the deputy to the escheator in Worcestershire confirmed that constables were 'negligent and careless' and charged that some, like the officers of Cropthorne and Elmley Castle, refused to make any assessments or to collect the money. The letter added that others, like the officer of Tredington, kept the money they had levied, though claiming that they had been unable to gather it.[55]

Similar accounts of neglect poured in from Staffordshire. As early as 1637 the sheriff reported great 'refractoriness' in constables, which

---

[52] Leics. RO, DE 625/60, ff. 49, 58ᵛ.
[53] Leics. RO, DE 720/30, ff. 45ᵛ, 48.
[54] PRO, SP 16/331/12; 455/127; 457/22; 467/58.
[55] PRO, SP 16/467/11.

he attributed to the £1000 which had been added to the county's ship-money assessment, and he claimed that he could not get the local assessments signed. His successor reported that constables had tried to deceive him about ship-money when he first took office. By 1640, officers in that county too were accused of not returning any money and of refusing to distrain. Sir John Bellott, sheriff in that year, reported that he had tried to bring pressure to bear on negligent constables by summoning them before him, seeing six, eight, or twelve a day for a fortnight. However, despite their promises to pay ship-money they had not done so, and he too had committed a number of delinquent officers to gaol.[56]

Sheriffs of Hertfordshire too were increasingly loud in their complaints about the negligence of constables in levying ship-money. In February of 1638 Sir Thomas Coningsby claimed that they had not returned assessments. He had sent new warrants to the high constables, containing warnings to the petty constables that those failing to submit rating lists 'should finde sureties to answere there neglecte of the service att the Councill Table'. By April he was able to report that most assessments had been returned, but he claimed that little of the money had been collected, and that constables were 'colde in takeing of distresses'. The situation worsened in the following years. By May 1640 the sheriff, Sir John Gore, declared that constables 'refuse to doe their service as formerlie they have done upon the like occasion', and that he could not even procure local assessments of the levy. In June he repeated his protests that officers who formerly complied now refused to execute warrants or do anything to advance the service.[57]

There were complaints from Norfolk in 1638 about the difficulties in getting collectors there to take distresses. By 1640 Sir Thomas Windham reported that, although some constables were honest and industrious and brought in a large part of the money, others were remiss and obstinate and had done little or nothing.[58] On the whole, there seem to have been fewer accusations about the negligence of Leicestershire constables in levying ship-money. However, sheriffs from 1637 onward did complain about their difficulties in getting constables to return assessments.[59]

[56] PRO, SP 16/346/108; 371/78; 452/10.
[57] PRO, SP 16/381/71; 387/46; 414/162; 445/62; 455/85; 456/49.
[58] PRO, SP 16/385/1; 450/1; 456/21.
[59] PRO, SP 16/346/109; 351/91; 385/2; 415/39. For a discussion of the negligence of constables in other counties in collecting ship-money see Morrill, *Cheshire*, p. 28;

Some sheriffs did more than simply voice their complaints about constables' failures to assess and collect ship-money. Not only did they commit officers to gaol, but they, or their underlings, sometimes returned the names of delinquent constables to the Council. Some of them were attached by messengers and brought up to London to answer before that body.[60]

Occasionally there are indications that constables were rather defiant in their refusals to collect ship-money. The sheriff of Hampshire in 1636 reported that one officer, questioned by him for his failure to return the names of those who had not paid the levy, answered that 'I should never gather the mony while I lived'.[61] Two bailiffs in Northants claimed that the constables and a thirdborough of Long Buckby had refused to assist them in collecting ship-money, and that one of the constables had mounted considerable resistance when they went to distrain some of his goods. They were driven off by the constable's man, who attacked them with a flail, and by a crowd of women and children, including the constable's daughter, armed with pitchforks and with their aprons full of stones.[62]

In some counties constables were also in default for the military levies imposed in 1639–40. There had been occasional complaints about their negligence in paying such rates in the later 1620s, and it has been noted that the constable of Waltham in 1627 had not returned coat and conduct money for that village.[63] However, such failings seem to have become more numerous in 1639 and 1640. The constables of the particular villages examined, including Pattingham, Waltham, Branston, Salwarpe, Millington, Stockton (Salop), Manchester, Shelton, and Carleton Rode, all seem to have paid their military rates in these years.[64] A number of them however may have been tardy in doing so, as

Willcox, *Gloucestershire*, pp. 127–8; Barnes, *Somerset*, pp. 210, 228–30; P. Lake, 'The Collection of Ship Money in Cheshire During the Sixteen-Thirties: A Case Study of Relations between Central and Local Government', *Northern History*, xvii (1981), 60–1.

[60] e.g. PRO, SP 16/421/91, 427/113, 455/127, 467/58 (Worcs.); 395/111 (Herts.); 351/91 (Leics.); 306/55, 348/64, 350/2, 352/24 (Northants); 290/77 (Somerset); 341/20, 21 (Derbys.); 357/145 (Lincs.).

[61] PRO, SP 16/319/76.   [62] PRO, SP 16/379/132.

[63] PRO, SP 16/72/59; also see questions raised by the deputy lieutenants of Hertfordshire in 1626 as to whether they had power to impose such levies, SP 16/31/109 I.

[64] Pattingham Constables' Accounts, 1639–40; Leics. RO, DE 625/60, fo. 61; DE 720/30, ff. 44ᵛ, 47ᵛ; HWRO, 850 SALWARPE, BA 1054/2, Bundle D, no. 6; Borthwick Institute, PR MIL. 10, 1639–40; Salop RO, 3067/3/1, pp. 43, 47; Earwaker, ed., *Constables' Accounts*, ii. 63, for payment in 1639, but there is no such entry in 1640; NNRO, PD 358/33, 1639–40; PD 254/112, 1639–40.

was Robert Ellis, constable of Salwarpe in 1640, the officer whose delinquency in paying ship-money has already been discussed.[65] A warrant of 29 April ordered Ellis to set aside all excuses and delays and to make payment of the £7. 10s. 1d. in military rates due from his constablewick on 8 May. However, he apparently had not paid the levy by 2 June when he received another precept directing him to do so.[66] His accounts indicate that he ultimately did gather the coat and conduct money, his collection exceeding the sum required by 8s. 8d. The trip he made to Worcester on 4 June seems to have been for the purpose of paying the rate, even if he did so somewhat belatedly.[67]

From some counties there were reports of negligence by a number of constables in assessing as well as collecting coat and conduct money. The deputy lieutenants of Hertfordshire informed the Council in July 1640 that when they appeared in Hertford to gather in the rating lists from constables and to collect the money they found 'much disobedience' to their warrants. They claimed that few of the constables had made any rates let alone gathering the tax.[68] There were reports in June 1640 from Northants and Warwickshire too that some constables in those counties had refused to make assessments for coat and conduct money, and similar complaints were submitted in July by the Lord Lieutenant of Buckinghamshire.[69] The deputy-lieutenants of Somerset complained in July 1640 that many constables in that county had not brought in even a quarter of the levy, and that others had paid nothing at all.[70] Many constables in Middlesex in 1640 were in arrears for some of the coat and conduct money. At least one officer in that county was accused of hiding from higher officials who came to question him about those who were delinquent in payment,[71] just as Worcestershire constables apparently had gone into hiding when the sheriff's officers came in pursuit of them about ship-money.[72] Officers in some counties were also accused of refusing to

---

[65] See above, n. 47.
[66] HWRO, 850 SALWARPE, BA 1054/1, Bundle A, nos. 174, 170.
[67] HWRO, 850 SALWARPE, BA 1054/2, Bundle D, no. 6; a receipt in BA 1054/2, Bundle G, dated 4 June 1640, indicates that £3, part of a greater sum for conduct money, had been paid, while another receipt sometime during June reveals that £10. 10s. 1d. had been paid toward conduct money.
[68] PRO, SP 16/456/71.
[69] PRO, SP 16/458/32; 456/12; 461/69.
[70] PRO, SP 16/459/7.
[71] PRO, SP 16/459/47; 461/103.
[72] See above, n. 54.

return the names of those who had failed to pay coat and conduct money.[73]

Constables were not always diligent in tax collecting. Some of them were tardy in paying a particular rate or tax, and a few of them were hauled before the courts for their failure to do so. However, only in the case of ship-money and the military levies of 1639–40 does there seem to be widespread evidence of constables' delinquency in making payment. Until that time both their industry and their achievements as tax-collectors are far more evident than their failings.

(4) Financial Abuses and Financial Responsibility

Not only were constables sometimes negligent in paying a tax or rate, but occasionally there is evidence to suggest that officers abused their powers, showing partiality in their assessment of levies or lining their own pockets from the taxes they collected. Possibly constables more often showed favouritism to friends and neighbours, or alternatively over-assessed villagers with whom they were at odds, than the number of such accusations on record would indicate. However, the fact that other inhabitants joined in drawing up assessments probably did limit their opportunities for such conduct.[74] On the other hand, the likelihood of many of them growing rich as a result of their tax-collecting duties does not seem very great since they often had difficulty in levying the full amount for which a township was assessed.[75] Constables sometimes dipped into their own purses in order to meet their commitments, and evidence of financial responsibility, and even of sacrifice, by such officers seems to be more plentiful than signs of dishonesty.

In their assessment of taxes and rates constables were occasionally accused of favouring that part of the village where they lived and imposing heavier burdens on others, or of showing partiality to a particular socio-economic group.[76] Sometimes an officer apparently used his tax-collecting powers to do an injustice to a particular individual, probably someone with whom he was at odds. A Suffolk constable abused his authority in collecting fifteenths to penalize a yeoman neighbour. After he had collected the levy from all of the

---

[73] PRO, SP 16/456/12; 461/69; on constables' negligence in levying coat and conduct money in Gloucestershire, see Willcox, *Gloucestershire*, pp. 131–2.

[74] See above, ch. 2.   [75] See below, nn. 88–93 and ch. 7.

[76] Staffs. RO., QS/O, v. 83; PRO, SP 16/345/78; also see Willcox, *Gloucestershire*, p. 115.

inhabitants except this man, he got his superior to distrain the yeoman's cattle for the entire sum that was due from the township, reportedly out of mere malice. He was ordered to repay the money, except for the amount the man was normally assessed, and also to pay the charges which the villager had sustained as a result of this 'unjust vexacion'.[77]

Others were accused of using their tax-collecting powers to their own profit. In some instances it was alleged that they had extorted money that was not due, or had levied more than the assessment warranted and kept the surplus for themselves. An inhabitant of Eccleshall, Staffordshire, claimed in a Star Chamber suit of 1608 that the constables of that town were enriching themselves by collecting excessive lewnes through extortion. The plaintiff charged that the officers had received a warrant from the justices to gather 30s. to equip soldiers for service in Ireland, but that they had agreed to levy £6. 13s. 4d., planning to convert the money to their own use. Although some inhabitants allegedly had refused to pay, the constables were accused of having exacted most of the money through threats. These officers denied any wrongdoing, as did two constables of Loughborough, Leicestershire, who also were accused of extorting money, claiming that they were collecting for a fifteenth, but with the intention of keeping the proceeds for themselves.[78] Other constables were charged with extortion in collecting money to convey a prisoner to gaol, and for the transport of the king's timber, while a Cornish officer was accused of imposing unlawful levies of an unspecified nature.[79] A Wymeswold constable appears to have retained money collected for trained soldiers, and the town hired an attorney and took him to court over the matter in 1633.[80] Other officers were charged with embezzling money that had been collected for the watchmen[81] and for a benevolence.[82] A Yorkshire constable allegedly collected an extra 6s. 6d. in rates, an amount that scarcely can have made him rich, and a Somerset officer was accused of levying more than was due for ship-money, seemingly a rare feat, and keeping the overplus for himself.[83]

[77] PRO, E 124/1, fo. 158ᵛ.
[78] PRO, STAC 8/218/23; STAC 8/222/34.
[79] PRO, STAC 8/208/22; STAC 8/89/7; STAC 8/226/25; also see Trotter, *Seventeenth Century Life*, p. 116, who claims that constables sometimes were guilty of extortion in collecting rates.
[80] BL Add. MS 10457, ff. 57–57ᵛ.   [81] PRO, STAC 8/252/10.
[82] Staffs. RO, QS/O, ii. 88.
[83] Atkinson, ed., *Sessions Records*, iv. 69; Bates Harbin, ed., *Sessions Records*, ii. 249.

Occasionally inhabitants expressed general suspicions about the honesty of constables in collecting taxes, as did the inhabitants of Eccleshall in 1632. They claimed that when a precept was received from the high constable for a levy it was usual for the local officers to send out their warrants for a collection. On the basis of the high constables' directives the inhabitants could then determine whether or not they were being wronged in the levies. They complained that the present constables had 'found a way to blind us', charging that they concealed the high constables' warrants until they had accumulated a number of them and then collected a great lewne of £7 or £8. As a result the inhabitants did not know the purposes of the levy. However, the petitioners expressed their suspicions about where some of the money ended up when they asked for redress and alleged that otherwise the constables 'will make themselves gentillmen and us begers'.[84] Villagers sometimes complained to the justices that constables had not rendered proper accounts, and in some of these cases too they seem to have implied that officers had been dishonest in their financial dealings.[85] A constable of Carleton Rode whose claims of 8*d*. and 10*d*. for two dinners were challenged, and who was allowed a total of only 1*s*. rather than the 1*s*. 6*d*. he had demanded, was perhaps trying to pad his accounts a bit.[86] Possibly other officers did so as well.

In contrast to the few instances in which constables were charged with showing partiality or dishonesty in financial matters, there is substantial evidence to suggest that they often went to considerable lengths to meet their financial obligations. Sometimes they made personal sacrifices in order to do so.

Constables' conscientiousness is reflected in the fact that they returned the full sum demanded of them for a tax or rate even when they had not succeeded in collecting all the money.[87] Although there were various means by which they managed to meet their commitments, all of these might leave the constable himself out of pocket unless he eventually gathered the funds that were outstanding. Sometimes officers were authorized to borrow money from other village revenues to supplement their collections. This happened in Melton Mowbray on several occasions when the townsmen agreed to make good a

---

[84] Staffs. RO, Transcripts Sessions Rolls, Car. I, Roll 32, no. 35; QS/O, iv. 55.
[85] e.g. Staffs, RO, QS/O, iii, 47–47ᵛ, 73ᵛ, 75ᵛ, 84ʳ, 87, 95, 105; iv. 114; v. 78, 83, 93; Atkinson, ed., *Sessions Records*, iv. 215; Herts. RO, QS/B, 2B, fo. 8.
[86] NNRO, PD 254/112, 1623.
[87] For a fuller discussion of their difficulties in collecting some rates see below, ch. 7.

shortfall in the fifteenths from such sources, and in Wymeswold where the constable was permitted to take 20s. from the stock for the poor to add to the amount collected for a fifteenth.[88] In other instances they made good the difference between an assessment and their collections by drawing on their own lewnes, the money which they had collected to cover the expenses of the office. For example, constables of Pattingham supplemented the provision money from their lewnes in twenty-one of the twenty-three years between 1616 and 1640 for which their accounts survive, and by amounts ranging from 11d. to 12s. 4d. On one occasion Pattingham officers also paid from their expense money 40s. they were lacking for a bridge levy.[89] In the later 1630s the constables of this village even made good deficiencies in their ship-money collections from their lewnes, to the tune of 2s. in 1635–6, 28s. in 1637–8, and 16s. 10d. in 1638–9.[90] Constables of Waltham in the 1630s also drew on such funds on at least one occasion, in their case in order to pay the full sum assessed on the village for the repair of St. Paul's church.[91] Officers of East Harling, Shelton, and Carleton Rode also took money from their own revenues to supplement some levies. Usually the rates are not identified, but the constable of Carleton Rode in 1639 indicated that he had paid 9s. in ship-money from this source.[92] In other cases constables made good deficiencies in their collections by dipping into their own purses. An officer of Melton added 13d. to the provision money in 1597, and in the same year a constable of East Dereham, Norfolk, recorded that he laid out 'of myne owne money' 22d. toward the setting forth of soldiers.[93]

The fact that constables sometimes borrowed the entire sum that was due for a tax or rate, or paid all of it out of their own pockets, further attests to their diligence in fulfilling their obligations as collectors. The constable of Wymeswold in 1630 was able to borrow 40s. from the town stock to meet his payments until he could gather a levy,[94] but some officers apparently had to resort to money-lenders to secure loans. A Staffordshire constable who borrowed £10 in order to

---

[88] Leics. RO, DG 36/187, DG 25/1/1, p. 12; BL Add. MS 10457, fo. 2ᵛ.

[89] See the Pattingham accounts for this period; and for the bridge levy, the accounts for 1621–2.

[90] See the Pattingham accounts for the years cited.

[91] Leics. RO, DE 625/60, fo. 56ᵛ.

[92] NNRO, PD 219/126, 1630; PD 358/33, 1626; PD 254/112, 1639 for the case of ship-money in Carleton Rode; and PD 254/63 for other instances of borrowings there.

[93] Leics. RO, DG 36/189; NNRO, Accn. Sothebys, 11/7/67, P 182 D.

[94] BL Add. MS 10457, fo. 43ᵛ.

return a military levy was still paying interest fourteen years later on £5 which he had not repaid, and which he contended he had been unable to gather from the inhabitants.[95] During the 1620s and 1630s some other Staffordshire constables too claimed that they had borrowed money or had dipped into their own pockets to pay their rates, while a Worcestershire officer indicated that he had spent £3 from his own purse for a military levy.[96] Such cases usually seem to come to light only when officers complained because they had not procured reimbursement for funds which they had advanced; and they probably more often took such action in order to meet their commitments than the surviving records would indicate. The precepts sent to constables reveal that they sometimes received very little notice that a rate was due,[97] and in many cases they probably did not have time to collect the money by the date set for payment. This fact is attested to in one instance by a sheriff of Leicestershire, who claimed that constables in that county had received only a few days warning to pay military rates in 1640. Not having time to collect the levy, they used funds which they had already gathered for ship-money.[98] In other cases too constables probably advanced money in order to meet the deadline, obtaining it on loan or from their own purses, and hoping to gather it later from other villagers.

The financial responsibility displayed by constables is further reflected in the fact that many of them were out of pocket, at least temporarily and sometimes permanently, as a result of the expenses of the office. Constables, like all such local officials during the sixteenth and seventeenth centuries, were unpaid. Handbooks warned them that they must not accept anything from individuals for their work in the office because this constituted extortion, and was punishable by fine and imprisonment. William Sheppard claimed that their official expenses should be borne by the parish, but he suggested that constables themselves might be obliged to pay 'ordinary expenses', such as those for food and drink which they required in the course of

---

[95] Staffs. RO, Transcripts Sessions Rolls, Jac. I, Roll 66, nos. 26–7.

[96] Staffs. RO, Transcripts Sessions Rolls, Jac. I, Roll 75, nos. 34, 35, 70; QS/O, iii. 27–27^v, 39, 155^v, 158^v; iv. 258^v–259; Bund, ed., *Sessions Papers*, pp. 461–2; also see King, 'Vagrancy and Local Law Enforcement', 272, for evidence of Lancashire constables paying rates from their own purses.

[97] This is based on examination of the precepts sent to constables of Salwarpe, HWRO, 850 SALWARPE, BA 1054/1, Bundle A, and a few precepts to constables of Gissing, NNRO, PD 50/36L.

[98] PRO, SP 16/418/51.

their duties. He did conclude his discussion by indicating that in such matters local custom varied, and this was indeed the case;[99] but whatever the custom, constables might find themselves out of pocket at the end of their terms.

In some villages officers were allowed to claim not only for their official expenses but also for food, drink, horsemeat, and other private charges incurred in the course of their duties. Constables of Branston, Waltham, Wymeswold, and Melton Mowbray entered such charges in their accounts, as did those of Salwarpe, at least from 1619 onward. The officers of Pattingham, who were authorized in 1615 to claim 6*d*. for every day and 1*s*. for every day and night that they were obliged to be abroad on the business of the king or the parish, made numerous entries for such expenses.[100] Similar, though less frequent, claims for expenses were made by the constables in some Norfolk villages.[101] However, the fact that these officers were authorized to claim full reimbursement for both their personal charges and their official expenses did not assure that they would obtain what was owing to them, at least not immediately. Constables' accounts frequently were in deficit when they left office, in part because they had not succeeded in collecting from all the inhabitants the lewnes which were intended to cover their expenses. For example, in Pattingham the retiring constables were owed money by the village in 33 of the 53 years between 1582 and 1640 for which information survives, and in Waltham in 13 out of 22 years during the early seventeenth century.[102] Although the sum was sometimes only a shilling or two, in other cases it reached several pounds. The Waltham constables' accounts were in deficit for increasingly large sums during the 1630s; £1. 6*s*. 5*d*. in 1630–1, £1. 6*s*. 11*d*. in 1633–4, £2. 3*s*. 10*d*. in 1634–5, and £3. 19*s*. 8*d*. in 1639–40. In such cases officers usually had to wait for the new constables to levy a lewne to reimburse them, and sometimes it was months, and occasionally even years, before they were repaid. Meanwhile they must have been out of pocket, or in debt to someone from whom they had borrowed in order to cover their charges.

[99] Sheppard, *Offices and Duties of Constables*, pp. 177–9.

[100] Leics. RO, DE 720/30, DE 625/60; BL Add. MS 10457; Leics. RO, DG 25/39/1/1–4, DG 36/186–9; HWRO, 850 SALWARPE, BA 1054/2, Bundle D; Pattingham Constables' Accounts, 1615–40.

[101] NNRO, PD 50/36L (Gissing); PD 219/126 (East Harling); PD 254/112 (Carleton Rode).

[102] Pattingham Constables' Accounts, 1582–1640; Leics. RO, DE 625/60; also see King, 'Vagrancy and Local Law Enforcement', 272, who claims that Lancashire constables frequently ended their terms with their accounts in the red.

While some constables were apparently allowed reimbursement down to the last drop of ale which they consumed in the course of their duties, even if they had to wait some time to collect all that was due to them, others were expected to pay most of their personal expenses from their own purses. Sometimes constables were allocated a fixed sum for their 'office bearing' and this was but a token payment which would not have covered all their costs. The officers of Shelton, Norfolk, were granted only 2s. 6d. between them 'for their office' in addition to 6d. for writing; and they must have paid most of their expenses out of their own purses.[103] Constables of Gayton, Staffordshire, were allocated 20s. a year in 1642, and perhaps they had been obliged to bear even more of the costs of the office prior to that time. The officers of Hatherton in the same county were faced with the rather uncertain arrangement of being allowed toward their costs one quarter of each lewne which they collected, and they too probably had to pay some of their expenses themselves.[104] The fact that constables in such communities apparently did bear such burdens is further evidence of the conscientiousness of these officers in meeting the financial commitments of the position.

When the obligations of constables to supply produce and carriage for the royal household, and to meet the requisitions of saltpetre men and postmasters, are added to their responsibilities for assessing, collecting, and paying a wide variety of levies, it is apparent how very demanding these tasks could be. However, both constables' accounts and other sources suggest that many of them were both diligent and effective in fulfilling such responsibilities. Admittedly, it was not uncommon for officers periodically to be in arrears for a particular payment, and some of them were brought before the courts for their negligence. Occasionally a significant number of officers in a county seem to have been in default for a rate. Nevertheless, the overwhelming impression left by the evidence is of the remarkable success with which constables fulfilled their tax-collecting duties until the imposition of ship-money and of the military levies of 1639–40. Even then some of them returned payments, sometimes drawing on their own lewnes in order to do so. However, they displayed greater tardiness than in earlier years, and by 1640 a number of them defaulted in the payment of ship-money. While some officers probably did abuse their powers,

---

[103] NNRO, PD 358/33, p. 213.
[104] Staffs. RO, D/705/PC/1/1, p. 41; D/260/M/PV/1, 7 Nov. 1644.

displaying partiality or dishonesty in their assessment and collection of levies, and a few of them perhaps lined their own pockets in the course of their tax-collecting duties, they more often seem to have shown financial responsibility, and even to have made personal sacrifices in order to meet their commitments. The conscientiousness of a number of them is evidenced by the fact that they borrowed money or dipped into their own pockets in order to meet their obligations, both to pay taxes and rates and to cover their official as well as their personal expenses.

II. MILITARY DUTIES

The demands made upon constables in the area of their military duties varied considerably, depending upon the level of the government's concern about defence and whether or not England was engaged in war. In some years there were no trainings or even showings of the armour. However, during certain periods, particularly the later 1580s and the 1590s, the years 1613–15, the later 1620s, and the later 1630s, greater attention than usual was given to the trained bands and musters were held more frequently. Constables seem to have met the additional demands placed on them at such times, and to have been diligent in attending musters themselves and in assuring the appearance of the village's quota of soldiers. Their records also contain disbursements for the purchase and repair of military equipment. Despite an occasional accusation found in court records that a constable had neglected the communal arms,[105] and the complaints of some magistrates that such officers were so careless in their custody of the armour that it was often lost,[106] constables' accounts suggest that they devoted a good deal of time and effort to the maintenance of this equipment. When constables were required to press soldiers for active military duty they normally seem to have supplied the number of recruits required. Evidence from their own accounts, however, as well as from other sources, would suggest that their activities as press-men sometimes left much to be desired, both in terms of the quality of the soldiers they returned and the means by which they procured them.

[105] Staffs. RO, QS/O, ii. 88; Herts. RO, QS/B, 2A, fo. 167ᵛ.

[106] *Calendar State Papers Domestic*, 1595–7, p. 136, for the comments of Henry Cocke of Hertfordshire about the armour being in the custody of 'simple constables'; and Hamon L'Estrange, 'A Treatise Touching Imposicion or Finding of Armes', in BL Harleian MS 168, fo. 63ᵛ. Also see the comments of the Earl of Huntingdon, cited in Boynton, *Elizabethan Militia*, p. 23.

(1) The Communal Arms and Musters

Some historians claim that little money was spent on the communal armour. Gary Owen, for example, suggests that the 5*d*. paid for green cloth and green and white lace for the town pike of Tibenham, Norfolk, in 1625 was typical of the sums disbursed by small villages for the maintenance of the militia.[107] However, most of the constables' accounts examined contained entries for amounts much larger than 5*d*. There do appear to have been variations from village to village in the time and money which constables expended in maintaining the armour, but the officers of most of the townships examined regularly made some disbursements for the purchase of armour and for the storing, repair, and cleaning of the equipment.

In several of the villages examined there is no evidence of any major purchases of new armour,[108] but many officers did expend considerable sums in buying such equipment. Such disbursements sometimes may be explained by the fact that the old armour had not been properly maintained or had been lost. However, in view of the care that often seems to have been devoted to the arms,[109] this was probably not usually the reason for such purchases. Pattingham constables conscientiously replaced or added to the communal armour of that village. In 1587–8 they acquired a considerable amount of new equipment, two swords, two daggers, a pike staff and head, a headpiece, four girdles, two pairs of hilts, and two scabbards. There were further purchases in the later 1590s, a musket in 1594–5, perhaps indicating some modernization of the arms, and two swords in 1595–6 and 1596–7, respectively. Between 1613 and 1616 they purchased another musket as well as three new swords and belts for them and two headpieces. The officers of this village were somewhat delinquent in keeping the arms up to standard in the early 1620s. They borrowed a musket for trainings in 1621–2 and 1622–3, as well as for three trainings in 1625–6. However, that year they made three journeys to Bridgnorth, Salop, about the purchase of a musket, and eventually recorded an expenditure of 18*s*. to buy a new musket and for stocking an old one. There were further disbursements on military equipment in this village in the later 1630s, in 1635–6 a payment of £1. 9*s*. 6*d*. for swords and belts, while in 1638–9 the constables paid

---

[107] Owen, 'Norfolk 1620–1641', pp. 107–8.

[108] Leics. RO, DE 720/30; NNRO, PD 358/33; Salop RO, 3067/3/1.

[109] See below, nn. 117–24.

13*s.* 4*d.* for a musket, £2. 6*s.* 8*d.* for a corslet, and 5*s.* for a pike.[110]
More fragmentary constables' accounts for the early seventeenth
century also show officers in a number of other villages purchasing
new equipment in the years 1613 to 1618, the later 1620s, and the
later 1630s. Constables of both Melton Mowbray and Waltham
recorded substantial outlays on armour in 1613. Melton acquired two
new pikes, a musket, a corslet, headpieces, and bandoleers, while the
officer of Waltham spent £3. 10*s.* on undesignated military equipment.[111]
In Gissing in 1614 there were several expenditures on the common
arms, including the purchase of two swords and two daggers, and
another disbursement of 8*s.* 'for armour'.[112] The constable of Salwarpe
paid 26*s.* for a new musket in 1618, while the officers in East Harling
had purchased a musket in 1617.[113] Expenditures for new equipment
are recorded in the accounts of some villages in the later 1620s, the
officers of Carleton Rode buying a new pike in 1625–6 as did those of
Wymeswold in 1628.[114] In the later 1630s or early 1640s both Carleton
Rode and Stockton, Norfolk, acquired corslets and swords,[115] and the
officers of Millington bought a sword and two pikes as well as belts,
scabbards, and knapsacks.[116]

In addition to periodic purchases of new armour, constables more
regularly disbursed money for storage, repair, and cleaning of the
arms. Some accounts indicate that provision was made for keeping the
armour in one place. The Pattingham officers in 1582–3 acquired a
chest 'to laye the harnesse in', and this seems to have been replaced in
1598–9 when 2*s.* was paid for a coffer in which to store 'the harnes'.[117]
A payment of 4*s.* by the constable of Gissing in 1614 also seems to
have been to provide a storage place for the armour, while in 1632 an
officer of Cheddar, Somerset, made a disbursement of 12*s.* to set up a
frame in the church on which to hang the armour.[118] In addition to the
entries which appear in most constables' accounts for repairs to
particular pieces of equipment, some officers paid annual sums to an

[110] See Pattingham Constables' Accounts for the years cited.
[111] Leics. RO, DG 25/39/1/3, 2ᵛ–3; DE 625/60, fo. 31ᵛ.
[112] NNRO, PD 50/36L, no. 47.
[113] HWRO, 850 SALWARPE, BA 1054/2, Bundle D, no. 2; NNRO, PD 219/126, 1617.
[114] NNRO, PD 254/112, 1625; BL Add. MS 10457, fo. 37ᵛ.
[115] NNRO, PD 254/112, 1635, 1637; Carthew, 'Town Book of the Parish of Stockton', 178, 181.
[116] Borthwick Institute, PR MIL. 10, 1638–9, 1639–40.
[117] See Pattingham Constables' Accounts for the years cited.
[118] NNRO, PD 50/36L, no. 47; Somerset RO, DD/SAS, SE 14, fo. 32.

individual who was responsible for 'dressing' and sometimes storing
the armour. During the period 1613–14 to 1618–19 constables of
Branston several times made such payments to a William Armorie and
he probably was responsible for the equiment in other years too when
no name is mentioned.[119] In the 1630s the officers of both Branston
and Waltham paid one Francis Garland of Melton for keeping and
dressing the armour.[120] Pattingham constables too, from at least
1611–12 onward, made regular entries in their accounts for the annual
care of the armour, and between that year and 1620–1 it was
maintained for 2s. a year by a local blacksmith and alehouse keeper,
William Johnson, who himself served as constable in 1599–1600 and
1608–9.[121] During part of the 1620s the village's armour seems to have
been stored in Wolverhampton, and on one occasion the constables
noted that they had journeyed there to see that the equipment was in
order for the training.[122] By 1630–1 Henry Johnson, son of William,
also a blacksmith and ale-keeper, and constable in 1626–7 and
1635–6, had taken over the duties previously carried out by his father,
and he was receiving 3s. a year for 'keeping and dressing' the
armour.[123] In 1638 the constable of Cheddar, Somerset, also reached
an agreement with a man to keep, clean, and repair the armour during
his lifetime for 8s. a year.[124]

In addition to the maintenance of the communal arms contables also
were responsible for assuring that the shooting butts were kept in
repair, and to this matter too they seem to have given considerable
attention. Occasionally villages were fined for not having adequate
butts, as was Branston in 1624–5, 1629–30, 1640–1, and 1641–2 and
Stockton, Salop in 1641,[125] and in some constables' accounts there are
no references whatever to this facility. However, many officers
recorded fairly regular disbursements for the making of the butts. In

---

[119] Leics. RO, DE 720/30, ff. 7, 10, 14[v].

[120] Leics. RO, DE 720/30, ff. 29[v], 31[v], 34[v], 48, 50[v], 51; DE 625/60, ff. 42[v], 45[v], 47, 48.

[121] See Pattingham Constables' Accounts for those years.

[122] Pattingham Constables' Accounts, 1621–2, 1622–3, 1623–4.

[123] See Pattingham Constables' Accounts for this period.

[124] Somerset RO, DD/SAS, SE 14, fo. 44. On the storage and care of town armour also see Boynton, *Elizabethan Militia*, pp. 21–3. The fact that constables sometimes listed the arms which they passed on to their successors also suggests a sense of responsibility for this equipment; see, for example, Pattingham Constables' Accounts, 1582–3, 1587–8, 1598, 1599, 1604, 1620; Leics. RO, DE 720/30, ff. 8, 15, 19; DE 625/60, fo. 32[v]; DG 25/39/1/3, p. 4; DG 25/1/1, fo. 40.

[125] Leics. RO, DE 720/30, ff. 22[v], 28, 47[v], 49[v]; Salop RO, 3067/3/1, p. 49.

Manchester the constables made almost annual payments for the repair of the butts, while Branston and Waltham officers too recorded such expenditures in a number of years.[126] There are also some references to making the butts in the constables' accounts of Stockton, Salop, Melton Mowbray, Salwarpe, Carleton Rode, Gissing, Shelton, East Harling, and Stockton, Norfolk.[127] While it is clear from the records of these communities that constables often paid others to assist them in this duty, occasionally an officer can be seen devoting considerable personal attention to the task. An East Harling constable in 1617 made five trips with his own cart to fetch 'slaggs' for making the butts.[128]

Constables apparently were faithful in their attendance at musters, and they usually seem to have been successful in assuring the appearance of the 'common' soldiers for whom they were responsible. Sometimes no trainings or showings were held and in many instances there was only a single training a year. However, during the later 1620s and the later 1630s the bands were mustered more frequently and for longer periods. Although the burden on constables was considerably increased at such times, they none the less appear to have been diligent in fulfilling their responsibilities. Between 1613–14 and 1623–4 officers of Pattingham normally attended an annual training at Lichfield lasting three or four days. However, in 1624–5 the constables were present at a muster at Wolverhampton for two days, a training at Lichfield, and musters at Stafford for a week. Their successors in 1625–6 were even more occupied with the trained bands, attending seven trainings at Wolverhampton and one at Stafford for two days each, as well as travelling to Lichfield for two days to show armour.[129] The Melton Mowbray officers also gave a good deal of time to their military duties in 1625–6, attending five trainings that year, while the constables of Branston went to four trainings in 1626–7 and the constables of Wymeswold to four trainings

---

[126] Earwaker, ed., *Constables' Accounts*, i. 13, 43, 61, 68, 74, 83, 97, 113, 167, 223, 248, 282; ii. 6, 26, 35, 49, 65, 73; Leics. RO, DE 720/30, ff. 13, 26^v, 29^v, 34^v, 43^v, 47^v; DE 625/60, ff. 4, 25, 31, 33^v, 42, 44^v, 47^v, 51, 56, 61, 62^v.

[127] Salop RO, 3067/3/1, pp. 39, 49; Leics. RO, DG 25/39/1/2–4; HWRO, 850 SALWARPE, BA 1054/2, Bundle D, no. 9; NNRO, PD 254/112, 1621; PD 50/36L, no. 89; PD 358/33, 1619, 1624, 1632; PD 219/126, 1617, 1626, 1627, 1637–8; Carthew, 'Town Book of the Parish of Stockton', 169, 172, 176.

[128] NNRO, PD 219/126, 1617.

[129] See Pattingham Constables' Accounts for these years.

in 1628.[130] In the later 1630s and early 1640s some officers devoted even more time to the mustering of the bands. The constable of Waltham was present at three trainings in 1635, two at Leicester and one at Melton, while the officer at that village in 1639–40 was absent from home for no less than twenty-two days in the space of a few months to attend musters, and on one occasion for over a week at a stretch. He attended four trainings at Loughborough, from 6–8 May, 27–31 May, 9–11 June, and another, probably in September, for eleven days. The constable in office in Waltham in 1642 attended five trainings between mid- June and the end of August, though for shorter periods, at Melton on 15 June, at Leicester on 27 June and again on 20 July and 11 August, and at Loughborough on 26 and 27 August.[131] Constables of the neighbouring village of Branston were also very much engaged in fulfilling such duties in the later 1630s and early 1640s. They were present at two trainings in Melton and one in Leicester in June and July 1635, four trainings in 1638–9, two at Loughborough, one at Leicester, and one at Melton, three more in 1639–40 and three or maybe four at Loughborough in 1640–1.[132] Officers in some counties attended an even larger number of trainings at this time. The constables of Carleton Rode appeared at musters on six occasions in 1639–40, lasting for a total of twenty days. In the same year the officer of Millington appeared at eight trainings of the bands, four at Beverley, two at Newcastle, one each at Pocklington and Weighton, as well as showing armour at Beverley.[133]

(2) Constables as Press-men

During periods when soldiers were required for active military duty constables' accounts show them busily engaged in pressing such recruits. There may have been a few officers like a constable of Wilby, Northants, who in 1640 seems to have absented himself from his house so that he would not be available to receive a warrant for impressment,[134] just as others had made themselves scarce when higher officials had pursued them concerning ship-money or coat and conduct money.[135] However, constables usually seem to have been attentive to these duties. The officers of the villages examined

[130] Leics. RO, DG 25/39/1/4; DE 720/30, ff. 24ᵛ, 25; BL Add. MS 10457, ff. 37–37ᵛ.
[131] Leics. RO, DE 625/60, ff. 46ᵛ, 47ᵛ, 48; 61, 61ᵛ; 65ᵛ.
[132] Leics. RO, DE 720/30, ff. 38–38ᵛ; 44–44ᵛ; 45ᵛ; 47ᵛ.
[133] NNRO, PD 254/112, 1639–40; Borthwick Institute, PR MIL. 10, 1639–40.
[134] PRO, SP 16/461/53.
[135] See above, nn. 54, 71.

Their labours in connection with the militia may not have achieved the desired results, but their accounts show that they were far from idle when it came to military matters. Not only did they devote both time and money to the maintenance of the communal armour, and to keeping the butts in repair; but they also appear to have been regular in their attendance at musters, a duty which in some years required frequent absences from home, sometimes for a number of days at a time. Although constables usually seem to have supplied the number of soldiers they were required to press for military service, their record in this area probably was less commendable. They often returned recruits regarded as defective by their superiors, sometimes apprehending or hiring strangers to serve in place of the able-bodied residents from their own townships whom they were supposed to supply. Moreover, such negligence sometimes seems to have been compounded by dishonesty, some officers accepting bribes in return for releasing men from military service. However, such defects were not limited to petty constables. It is perhaps unreasonable to expect them to have behaved otherwise when the whole military system seems to have been riddled with abuse and corruption.[153] and when the conduct of high constables, captains, and conductors of troops, and even the deputy lieutenants, probably only encouraged delinquency in lesser officers.

[153] See Stearns, 'Conscription and English Society', 10–12, 14–15, for a discussion of abuses and corruption among deputy lieutenants and conductors of troops.

6

Constables at Work II: Administrative Duties and Law Enforcement

THE police duties of constables have received the greatest amount of attention from previous historians, but in fact it is more difficult to assess their work in law enforcement than in other facets of the office. The materials are more fragmentary, and the evidence which they contain often difficult to interpret. Constables' accounts are on the whole much less revealing about their activities as police officers than about their tax collecting or military functions, though they do contain considerable evidence about their appearances before higher officials to return presentments and to fulfill other administrative tasks. Surviving presentments, though not easy to evaluate, do shed some light on the nature of the returns which constables submitted. Legal records indicate that some officers were accused of negligence in returning presentments, and also in such duties as keeping watch, punishing vagrants, and the apprehension of other offenders. Such materials, however, usually contain no more than a brief charge of neglect, and they provide little evidence about the precise nature of the failings which constables displayed on such occasions. The number of officers indicted for defaults of this kind was not normally very large, although there were general complaints from higher officials about constables' negligence as police officers, and especially about their failure to punish vagrants.

Attention will be given first to constables' performance of some of the regular administrative tasks of the office, where there is considerable evidence to suggest that they were hard-working, if not always entirely effective in achieving what was expected of them. This will be followed by an examination of their conduct in returning presentments to higher authorities, punishing vagrants, and apprehending other offenders. In these duties they more often may have been found wanting, though their failings have probably been exaggerated. Constables were sometimes accused not merely of neglecting to enforce the law, but of abusing their police powers and also of committing misdemeanours themselves, and in a final section these charges will be considered.

I. ADMINISTRATIVE DUTIES

Court records contain very little evidence of constables being accused of negligence in carrying out many of the regular administrative tasks of the office, and their conscientiousness in such matters is often borne out by entries in their accounts. These record with some regularity their annual appearances before the clerk of the market with the village's weights and measures, attendance upon the justices with the churchwardens and overseers when they made their accounts, with ale-keepers for relicensing and rebinding, and with butchers, victuallers, and ale-keepers to enter recognizances against dressing and selling flesh during Lent. In some counties their accounts also show them appearing before the justices or the high constable annually or biannually with servants.[1]

The detailed records of constables of Pattingham, Branston, Waltham, East Harling, and Stockton, Salop, contain regular entries which show them travelling to neighbouring communities or the major town in the hundred to appear before the clerk of the market with the village's weights and measures. Sometimes they can also be seen responding to the clerk's demands that they supply another villager or two to serve on his jury.[2] The Pattingham constables travelled to Wolverhampton with their weights and measures, while officers of Branston and Waltham appeared in Melton, Stonesby, or Wymondham, though the clerk sometimes sat in Waltham. East Harling constables made annual appearances in Kenninghall with that township's weights and measures. Most of the Stockton accounts contain such entries too, though in 1605 the officers of that village paid 3s. to the clerk for not

---

[1] For a discussion of their duties in these areas see above, ch. 2. There are a few cases in which they were accused of default in their responsibilities for the selection of overseers of the highways or in determining days for communal work on the roads or being present at such work, but these duties receive no mention in their accounts; see Bund, ed., *Sessions Papers*, p. 130; Tait, ed., *Sessions Records*, pp. 7, 110; Atkinson, ed., *Sessions Records*, i. 171; ii. 32; iii. 337. The North Riding sessions records also contain two cases in which constables explicitly were accused of failing to present servants; see Atkinson, ed., *Sessions Records*, i. 108, 248.

[2] See Pattingham Constables' Accounts, 1582–1640; Leics. RO, DE 720/30; DE 625/60; NNRO, PD 219/126; Salop RO, 3067/3/1.

bringing in their measures.[3] The rather detailed Manchester constables' accounts contain only a few references to the clerk of the market, probably because he sat in Manchester and they thus did not incur expenses in appearing before him.[4]

Constables' accounts also record their attendance upon the justices with the overseers when they were required to render their accounts, and with alehouse keepers for relicensing and rebinding. These two items of business often seem to have been combined, and it is probable when accounts mention one or the other that constables' appearances before the justices entailed both matters.[5] The Branston accounts contain very regular entries attesting to officers' attendance upon the magistrates with the overseers, at Stonesby, Melton, Bottesford, or Stathern, or occasionally at Waltham. During six years between 1613–14 and 1628–9 there are also separate entries concerning their appearances with the alemen.[6] Waltham constables too accompanied the overseers to Somerby or Melton, though such entries appear less regularly than in the Branston accounts. Their more frequent journeys before the justices, usually in Melton, which mention only the ale-sellers probably included the overseers as well.[7] The Pattingham constables travelled to Wolverhampton about the relief of the poor in 1598–9; they procured a book of directions from the justices and also paid a villager to write a brief of the statute concerning the poor. Between 1606–7 and 1629–30 their accounts contain fairly regular entries indicating that they appeared before the justices for the selection of new overseers, and they too sometimes combined this business with the relicensing of ale-sellers. From 1607–8 to 1640 the constables made annual journeys, travelling to Wolverhampton or occasionally to Bobbington or Codsall, to bring the alemen before the justices.[8]

[3] Salop RO, 3067/3/1, p. 9.

[4] Earwaker, ed., *Constables' Accounts*, i. 4, 55, 56, 172, 251; ii. 35, 51. Other accounts too contain some references to appearances before the clerk; see NNRO, PD 254/63, 1621; PD 254/112, 1623, 1625, 1628; PD 50/36L, nos. 45, 47, 53, 55, 92; Borthwick Institute, PR MIL. 10, 1633–9; Leics. RO, DG 25/39/1/1, 3; HWRO, 850 SALWARPE, BA 1054/2, Bundle D, nos. 3, 4, 5; BL Add. MS 10457.

[5] Precepts sent to constables of Salwarpe, Worcestershire, indicate that the overseers and the alemen were to appear at the same time, and in that county in April; see HWRO, 850 SALWARPE, BA 1054/1, Bundle A, nos. 11, 20, 76; BA 1054/2, Bundle H (one unnumbered item). Also see one precept to constables of Gissing, NNRO, PD 50/36L, no. 57. Constables' accounts also indicate that these two items of business sometimes were combined.

[6] Leics. RO, DE 720/30.   [7] Leics. RO, DE 625/60.

[8] Pattingham Constables' Accounts for the years cited.

Some constables during the early seventeenth century made additional appearances before the justices with butchers, victuallers, and alemen who were required to enter recognizances binding them not to dress or sell flesh during Lent. These journeys are sometimes difficult to distinguish from those for relicensing ale-sellers. The Pattingham accounts make it clear that from 1618–19 to 1630–1 the constables of that township appeared before the justices each year before Lent, usually in Wolverhampton, at 'sittings' concerning the eating of flesh.[9] Perhaps during the 1630s this business was carried out at one of the monthly meetings of the justices, and therefore does not receive separate mention in the accounts. Similar, but much less regular, entries concerning constables' attendance with butchers, victuallers, and alemen are found in the accounts of Branston, Waltham, and Stockton, Salop, as well as those of Salwarpe, Gissing, and East Harling.[10]

In some counties constables also made annual or biannual appearances before the justices or the high constables with servants. The Millington accounts for the 1630s regularly record such journeys twice a year to Barmby, Pocklington, or Allerthorpe.[11] The officers of Branston, Waltham, and Wymeswold were accompanied by servants, and apparently submitted a bill of their names, at 'the statutes' which they attended annually in various neighbouring villages.[12] There is one specific reference to statute sessions, and a bill of servants' names being submitted there, in the accounts of Carleton Rode,[13] but there is no mention of such hiring sessions in the other accounts examined, not even in the very detailed Pattingham materials. It is, however, possible that some of the constables' appearances before the high constable or the justices did include the matter of servants.[14]

Although these administrative tasks were undoubtedly minor by comparison with some of the other duties with which constables were entrusted, neither the demands which they made upon such officials nor their importance should be underestimated. Not only did these

[9] Pattingham Constables' Accounts for the years cited.

[10] Leics. RO, DE 720/30, ff. 18ᵛ, 30; DE 625/60, ff. 20, 38ᵛ, 44ᵛ; Salop RO, 3067/3/1, pp. 16, 39, 41; HWRO, 850 SALWARPE, BA 1054/2, Bundle D, no. 5; NNRO, PD 50/36L, nos. 53, 71; PD 219/126, 1633–4.

[11] Borthwick Institute, PR MIL. 10, 1633–43.

[12] Leics. RO, DE 720/30; DE 625/60; BL, Add. MS 10457.

[13] NNRO, PD 254/112, 1623.

[14] Pattingham Constables' Accounts; the petty sessions mentioned in the accounts of East Harling, Carleton Rode, and Gissing may have included servants, NNRO, PD 254/112; PD 219/126; PD 50/36L.

tasks usually require constables to travel to other villages, but they were also responsible for the attendance of some of their fellow inhabitants. While constables themselves seem to have been diligent in making such journeys, whether or not they were able to assure the appearance of overseers, alemen, butchers, victuallers, and servants is another matter. In the case of ale-sellers at least it seems probable that they were not always successful, since so many unlicensed keepers appear in the records.[15] Occasionally there is evidence that constables did have to make a second trip before the justices because some of those who had been commanded to attend on the first occasion had not done so. The Pattingham officers in 1627–8 noted that they had appeared a second time with butchers and alemen to enter Lenten recognizances because some had not attended the justices the first time.[16] Sometimes constables' accounts contain two entries concerning their appearance before the justices with the alemen, and probably this is explained by the fact that they were required to bring in some who had been absent on the first occasion.[17] Such duties may not have constituted a major facet of the office. However, in serving as a link between the justices and the officers of the parish, and between the magistrates and the butchers, victuallers, ale-keepers, and servants whose occupations they regulated, these local officers made an important contribution to the routine administration of the county.

II. CONSTABLES' PRESENTMENTS AND THEIR CHARACTER

Constables' accounts also shed light on their activities in making presentments to higher authorities, a duty, as already noted, that was both administrative and judicial in character.[18] The officers of the villages examined here recorded many journeys to neighbouring villages to submit such returns, and their accounts would suggest that they were diligent in performing this duty. However, quarter sessions records do contain occasional cases in which constables were charged with failing to make presentments, and in the 1630s some justices reported that constables had neglected to appear at their monthly meetings to submit such returns. The presentments which are extant

---

[15] Constables' presentments frequently involved unlicensed ale-sellers; see below, nn. 58, 60.

[16] Pattingham Constables' Accounts, 1627–8.

[17] e.g. Pattingham Constables' Accounts, 1604–5, 1609–10, 1617–18, 1624–5, 1629–30, 1637–8; Leics. RO, DE 625/60, fo. 22ᵛ.

[18] See above, ch. 2.

in quarter sessions records or among the State Papers provide some evidence about the kinds of returns which such officers made. Although it is not easy to evaluate these materials, or to assess how representative they are, they do raise some questions about constables' thoroughness in reporting offences.

The detailed constables' accounts examined contain entries attesting to the regularity with which the officers of some villages appeared before higher officials to make presentments for quarter sessions and assizes. Between 1616 and 1642 the constables of Stockton, Salop, annually returned two presentments to assizes, and they normally made four presentments to quarter sessions.[19] Other accounts, even of a detailed nature, are not always as clear in identifying such returns. Certain patterns however, do become apparent and it seems safe to assume that many of the regular, but unspecified, appearances which constables made before the high constable or a neighbouring justice were for the purpose of submitting such presentments. Assize presentments made either to a justice or the high constable appear in many of the Branston accounts between 1612–13 and 1642–3, and sometimes sessions presentments are identified as well. Other entries which indicate that they had travelled to Bottesford to be 'examined on the articles' by a justice probably refer to assize presentments, while their appearances before the justices in Somerby, Bottesford, Croxton, Melton, or Stathern, and the bills which they returned on such occasions, were undoubtedly presentments for sessions or assizes.[20] The Waltham records also contain evidence of presentments to assizes, made to the high constable, and of some returns to quarter sessions. Other appearances by the constables before the justices at sittings in either Waltham or Melton, when the submission of bills is sometimes mentioned, were probably for the purpose of returning presentments for sessions or assizes.[21] The Pattingham accounts record presentments for assizes rather regularly between 1623–4 and 1639–40, and in some other years as well, while in most of the years between 1618–19 and 1639–40 there are also references to quarter sessions presentments returned to the high constable. Other unidentified presentments which they made to the high constable were almost certainly returns for sessions or assizes as well.[22]

Monthly meetings of the justices in the 1630s can also be identified in detailed constables' accounts, and these records show that officers

[19] Salop RO, 3067/3/1.   [20] Leics. RO, DE 720/30.
[21] Leics. RO, DE 625/60.   [22] Pattingham Constables' Accounts.

travelled rather regularly to neighbouring townships to make their presentments to the justices on such occasions. One of the Stockton constables in 1631–2 made presentments at eight meetings before the justices in Bridgnorth, and he identified the business as the punishment of rogues. Both constables appeared at two additional sittings to make presentments. By 1632–3 the constables of Stockton described these gatherings as monthly meetings, and their accounts for that year, and those extant for the period 1637–42, record their expenses to attend twelve such meetings each year.[23] Waltham officers too regularly made presentments at monthly meetings throughout the 1630s, often travelling to Melton or Saxby to do so, though occasionally the justices sat in Waltham.[24] Such meetings were perhaps somewhat less regular in the hundred of Seisdon, Staffordshire, or officers of Pattingham less diligent in appearing. However, they can be followed on journeys to at least six and sometimes as many as twelve monthly meetings a year at Wombourn, Over Penn, Wolverhampton, Sedgley, Spittal Brooke, Kinver, and Bobbington.[25] The Branston accounts show that these officers normally attended monthly meetings, usually at Stathern or Waltham. Their diligence is further reflected in the fact that they arranged for someone else to represent the village and make presentments for them on occasions when they were apparently unable to be present personally. Such entries appear in the Branston records in May, June, and July 1634, March 1636, and on five occasions in 1637–8.[26]

Constables' accounts also show them periodically answering special summons from high constables or the justices, and again travelling to neighbouring villages or the county town, to submit returns on particular matters. A number of these concerned the punishment of vagrants, and perhaps constituted the special sessions that were to follow the constables' privy searches for rogues, authorized in 1610.[27] Other special presentments concerned apprentices. The Branston and Waltham officers appeared twice before the justices concerning this matter in 1619, while the Waltham constable also submitted returns on

[23] Salop RO 3067/3/1, pp. 35 ff.
[24] Leics. RO, DE 625/60, ff. 35 ff.
[25] Pattingham Constables' Accounts, 1631–40.
[26] Leics. RO, DE 720/30, ff. 29 ff; and for references to others making presentments, ff. 36, 41, 42ᵛ.
[27] See above, ch. 2, n. 35; presentments on vagrants occur regularly in the Manchester accounts, Earwaker, ed., *Constables' Accounts*, i and ii, and there are some such entries in the Branston, Waltham, Melton, Wymeswold, and Pattingham accounts as well.

apprentices in 1630–1 and 1637, and both officers did so in 1640–1.[28] The Gissing accounts too reveal that the constables of that village appeared before the justices in Stratton or Diss concerning apprentices in 1620 and 1634 and on three occasions in 1631.[29] Sometimes constables seem to have made special appearances before the justices about recusants, though it is possible that some of these were sessions or assize presentments which focused on this one matter. The Melton officers responded to a summons to Leicester in 1613 about recusants' lands, while officers of Pattingham appeared in Wolverhampton and later before the high constable in Stafford in 1620–1 to present recusants, and also made returns on this matter in 1624–5 and 1635–6.[30] The Stockton officers travelled to Shrewsbury about papists in 1607, and their accounts contain further entries about the presentment of recusants in 1639 and 1640.[31] During periods of scarcity and high prices constables also responded to orders from the justices to make returns about supplies of corn. The Pattingham officers did so in 1607–8, and in 1622–3, when they appeared three times before the justices in Wolverhampton 'about corne'. They made similar returns in 1631.[32] In 1630–1 the Branston officer paid for a copy of 'the charge for corne' and after a two-day search of villagers' barns he returned an answer to the justices. The constable of this village made a further presentment on corn to the justices in Melton in 1631–2.[33] Officers of Waltham appeared before the justices in Melton about corn in October 1622, and made four trips to Melton between November 1630 and April 1631, presenting two bills on corn to the high constable or the justices.[34] Stockton constables spent two days before the justices in Bridgnorth concerning corn in 1622, and made another presentment on this matter in 1631–2.[35]

While the officers of the villages examined here seem to have been diligent in appearing before their superiors to submit presentments, other sources provide a rather mixed picture of constables' performance of such duties. Quarter sessions records usually contain only a scattering of cases in which constables were formally accused of failing to appear or to submit returns, but there do seem to have been some

[28] Leics. RO, DE 720/30, ff. 15ᵛ, 48; DE 625/60, ff. 17ᵛ, 36ᵛ, 53ᵛ, 62.
[29] NNRO, PD 50/36L, nos. 53, 83, 89.
[30] Leics. RO, DG 25/39/1/3; Pattingham Constables' Accounts for the dates cited.
[31] Salop RO, 3067/3/1, pp. 11, 43, 47.
[32] See Pattingham Constables' Accounts for the years cited.
[33] Leics. RO, DE 720/30, ff. 29ᵛ, 30ᵛ.
[34] Leics. RO, DE 625/60, ff. 26, 35.   [35] Salop RO, 3067/3/1, pp. 23, 35.

variations from county to county in the numbers returned for default in this duty. It is difficult to know how much faith to place in the justices' general comments in the 1630s about constables' presentments to them at monthly meetings, but these reports too suggest that officers in some counties, and even in some divisions, were more diligent than others in appearing to make returns.

The quarter sessions records of some counties contain very little evidence of constables being at fault in making presentments. Staffordshire high constables returned the names of some officers who had failed to appear before higher officials or to send presentments. However, such accusations occur very intermittently and the numbers involved in any year never reached more than eight or ten, at most, for the whole country.[36] The Worcestershire sessions materials indicate that a few constables in that county in the 1630s were summoned to sessions for failing to attend the justices' monthly meetings, but the numbers are very small. The records contain only seven such cases, all of them in 1636.[37] In the North Riding of Yorkshire larger numbers of constables were presented to quarter sessions for their defaults in making presentments. Almost every year between 1605 and 1620 a few constables were formally charged with failing to appear at the high constables' sessions to submit returns.[38] A number of them were apparently also negligent when they were summoned to quarter sessions itself to make presentments in 1611 and 1614. In a general order of April 1611 the justices directed that all constables who had not appeared at that sessions to present recusants be summoned to the next court to make good their default. A further order in 1612 authorized warrants to the bailiffs of all wapentakes to attach constables who had failed to present recusants and to bring them to the next sessions. In 1614 the justices claimed that many constables had not appeared when summoned to sessions to present recusants and alehouse keepers, and they ordered that a 10s. fine be imposed on each of them, and that they be called before the next meeting of the court.[39] The records reveal that in this case some constables were fined for their defaults, penalties of 20s. being imposed on officers of no less

---

[36] Burne, ed., *Staffs. Sessions Rolls*, i. 267; iv. 136, 327, 442; v. 231; Staffs. RO, Transcripts Sessions Rolls, Jac. I, Roll 24, no. 33; Roll 74, no. 13.

[37] Bund, ed., *Sessions Papers*, pp. 605–6.

[38] Atkinson, ed., *Sessions Records*, i. 1, 9, 24, 25, 46, 56, 88, 92, 112, 122, 127, 136, 137, 142, 151, 152, 153, 165, 186, 191, 201, 212, 214, 232, 233, 238, 254; ii. 9, 41–2, 123, 124, 209, 234.

[39] Ibid., i. 216, 262; ii. 49.

than twenty-two settlements in 1615, while another was summoned before sessions and several others were given additional time to make their presentments.[40]

Reports from the justices in the 1630s on their enforcement of the Book of Orders, although difficult to interpret, would suggest that there were variations from area to area in constables' diligence in making presentments to monthly meetings. The magistrates of the Limits of Worcester complained in June 1631 that some constables had failed to attend their meetings, and indicated that they had sent warrants commanding them to answer for their neglect at the next sessions.[41] However, in the counties examined here the justices seldom reported that constables had neglected to appear before them. The variations in their reports concern the nature of the returns which such officers submitted. Some justices stated or implied that constables were dutiful in this regard, but others claimed that officers had made few or no presentments or that they were negligent in fulfilling the tasks for which they were accountable on such occasions. The magistrates of Broadwater hundred, Hertfordshire, indicated in January 1633 and again in 1637 that the local officers submitted bills of presentment in answer to their directives. The detailed returns from the justices of other divisions in that county would also suggest that constables were fairly diligent in making presentments.[42] However, the magistrates of Cashio and St. Albans reported in May and October 1633 that they had punished a number of negligent officers.[43] Fewer returns survive for Staffordshire, but the justices of Pirehill hundred commended the local officers in that division for their care and diligence.[44] Leicestershire constables seem to have been dutiful in appearing before the justices, but reports from that county indicate that some were negligent in making returns and in performing the duties for which they were accountable at monthly meetings. The magistrates of Guthlaxton regularly reported that constables had attended their meetings in 1631 and 1632, but they usually indicated that few or no offenders had been presented; and in 1636 they claimed to have punished negligent officers.[45] The justices of East Goscote claimed in June 1631 that all officers in that division 'carefullie

---

[40] Ibid., ii. 96, 100–1, 104, 106.   [41] PRO, SP 16/194/63 III.

[42] PRO, SP 16/231/40; 351/113; also see below, nn. 78–80.

[43] PRO, SP 16/231/20; 239/52.   [44] PRO, SP 16/265/85.

[45] PRO, SP 16/193/20; 196/5; 197/52; 198/68; 200/24; 202/12; 203/52; 204/59; 210/28; 211/33; 215/14; 216/16; 218/7; 219/49; 221/50; 222/51; 223/42; 329/27.

behaved themselves in their severall places'. However, in September
1632 they reported that some officers had been fined for negligence,
and in July 1634 that they had penalized constables, churchwardens,
and overseers who were careless in their places.[46] The magistrates of
Framland hundred indicated that the local officers there appeared
before them to give an account of their proceedings, but they too
punished some who were remiss in fulfilling their duties.[47] The
justices of the Limits of Worcester not only recorded that some
constables had failed to attend their meeting, but they reported that
others who had appeared made no presentments.[48] Although a
systematic study has not been made of the returns of the justices of all
counties, an examination of these materials probably would reveal
considerable differences in constables' reliability in submitting returns,
and reports of much greater negligence by the officers of some areas.
To give but one example, rather explicit returns from Bolton and Dean
parishes, Lancashire, in 1633 and 1634 indicate that a majority of the
constables there either did not appear at the justices' meetings or failed
to make any presentments when they did attend.[49]

The fact that constables answered the summons of higher officials
did not always mean they returned any offenders, as some of the
justices' reports indicate. There remains the question of the kind of
returns which such officers submitted. Throughout the early seventeenth century constables were sent detailed directions concerning
their presentments,[50] but whether they responded to all of the articles
with which they were charged and how thorough they were in
reporting misdemeanours is another matter.

In most cases constables' presentments have survived only for short
periods or are rather scattered and fragmentary in character, and they
are difficult to evaluate. However, these documents do shed some light
on the character of such returns, though it is not easy to generalize
about constables' performance of this duty. While the brief returns
made by some officers give little indication that they had received a
series of articles on which to make their presentments, other officers
do seem to have been diligent in submitting detailed returns to the
justices. There is an occasional reference in the Staffordshire sessions

[46] PRO, SP 16/193/61; 223/51; 271/65.
[47] PRO, SP 16/215/54; 216/102; 271/66.
[48] PRO, SP 16/194/63 III.
[49] PRO, SP 16/265/86. Out of a total of 33 constables, only 5 made presentments.
[50] See above, ch. 2, nn. 45–50.

rolls to the fact that presentments were made in response to articles,[51] and it is evident from the Pattingham constables' accounts that officers in this county did receive successive sets of articles on which to make their returns. However, the documents which they submitted to quarter sessions give no indication of the range of matters contained in the warrants that were sent to them. Some constables' returns to monthly meetings in the 1630s were equally brief, though these officers too had received articles on which to make their presentments. For example, the returns submitted from forty-five villages in the hundred of Oswestry, Shropshire, to a monthly meeting in August 1632 reveal that none of these constables provided a detailed response. Nevertheless, they apparently had received articles, since one officer stated 'all good and faire accordinge to the artickles and hath nothinge to present to my knoledge'.[52] A substantial number of constables' presentments to quarter sessions in Worcestershire survive for the period 1633–7 and these documents reveal that a few officers in that county made detailed returns, referring to each of the articles with which they had been charged. Most however, presented an offender or two, and then added that for all the rest of the articles they had nothing to report.[53] Some Hertfordshire justices in the 1630s claimed that constables in their divisions were responding to all the articles sent to them, and there is some evidence in that county that they did so. For example, presentments made by constables, churchwardens, and overseers to monthly meetings in the Liberty of St. Albans, which were included with justices' reports on their execution of the Book of Orders, reveal that these officers had made written returns to sixteen articles, constables usually answering ten or eleven of them.[54]

Whether or not they submitted detailed returns in response to articles, constables often do not seem to have reported many offenders. Perhaps in some villages few or no misdemeanours had been committed, but the number of reports of *omnia bene* does raise some questions about the thoroughness of their returns. Of the 45 constables in the hundred of Oswestry who submitted presentments in August 1632, 33 of them reported 'all good and fayre' or other brief words to that effect.[55] A number of Worcestershire constables in the

[51] Burne, ed., *Staffs. Sessions Rolls*, v. 225; Staffs. RO, Transcripts Sessions Rolls, Car. I, Roll 28.   [52] PRO, SP 16/223/55.
[53] Bund, ed., *Sessions Papers*, pp. 500 ff. For detailed responses see esp. pp. 564–5, 566, 578–9, 643; also see pp. 567, 568, 595–6, 600–1, 645, 646–7.
[54] PRO, SP 16/344/30; 347/67; 418/21; also see n. 42 above.
[55] PRO, SP 16/223/55.

1630s presented roads and bridges in decay, but in only 54 out of 104 villages or parishes for which returns survive, and for some settlements there are several of them, did they report anything else amiss. A few indicated that all was well and that they had nothing to present, not even roads or bridges.[56] The amount of the fines levied by Worcestershire justices in the spring of 1631 would suggest that constables of some divisions returned a larger number of offenders to monthly meetings in the first few months after the Book of Orders was put into effect. The magistrates of Halfshire hundred reported in June 1631 that they had levied £15. 18s. 4d. in fines from offenders, while the justices of Doddingtree in their report of June 1631 had imposed £11 in fines on offenders in that division. The detailed presentments returned from the Limits of Worcester also reveal that constables in that division had presented a number of offenders.[57]

Constables' presentments indicate that when they did report misdemeanours these usually fell within only a few categories. Although some offences no doubt were more numerous than others, the evidence none the less suggests that officers were rather selective in their returns. Apart from decayed roads and bridges, unlicensed ale-sellers or other abuses in alehouses were most common in the Worcestershire returns of the 1630s, as they were among the more scattered presentments found in the Staffordshire sessions records of the late sixteenth and early seventeenth centuries. In both counties recusancy and failure to attend church took second place.[58] Staffordshire constables often reported too on the vagrants they had apprehended. A number of Worcestershire officers also answered this article, but few of them provided any specific information about the numbers they had punished. There are very occasional returns of other offences, in Worcestershire taking inmates and building illegal cottages, harbouring vagrants, playing unlawful games, refusing to keep watch and ward, and a few nuisance offences such as stopping a way or refusing to carry away a dunghill. According to the justices' reports from both Halfshire

---

[56] These figures are based on the returns in Bund, ed., *Sessions Papers*, pp. 500 ff.

[57] PRO, SP 16/194/63 II, IV, III.

[58] This is based on the returns in Bund, ed., *Sessions Papers*, pp. 500 ff; Burne, ed., *Staffs. Sessions Rolls*, ii. 255, 296–7, 336–7, 359; iii. 44, 47–8; iv. 75, 186, 205–6, 294, 433; v. 176, 225–36; Salt, ed., *Staffs. Sessions Rolls, Easter 1608 to Trinity 1609*, pp. 50, 84, 107; Staffs. RO, Transcripts Sessions Rolls, Jac. I, Roll 23, no. 59; Roll 24, nos. 32, 33, 34; Roll 35, no. 34; Roll 40, no. 45; Roll 41, no. 32; Roll 42, no. 25; Roll 47, no. 34; Roll 48, no. 23; Roll 59, no. 43; Roll 66; Roll 68, nos. 11, 12, 13; Car. I, Roll 28, nos. 114, 115; QS/O, ii. 129, 130.

and Doddingtree, the offenders returned to monthly meetings in 1631 included drunkards and swearers, but these misdemeanours are not found among the sessions presentments, with the exception of one drunkard reported by a constable of Salwarpe.[59] Staffordshire constables too returned a few who had built illegal cottages or who refused to keep watch and ward, and some who had committed affrays or assaults, but the number of such offences was small. The returns submitted by the justices of Hertfordshire in the 1630s would suggest that constables' presentments to monthly meetings in that county most often dealt with the number of vagrants they had punished, though they too seem to have returned a number of unlicensed ale-sellers or keepers who broke the assize, and some who were absent from church or who engaged in illegal activities on the Sabbath, as well as some drunkards.[60]

The system of hundredal presentment juries sometimes has been credited with leading to more regular returns of offenders than petty constables' presentments.[61] In Norfolk, where returns usually seem to have been made by juries rather than individual constables, there do seem to have been fewer responses of *omnia bene*. However, the range of offences presented was similar to that already described. A sample of seven years of presentments dating from 1615 to 1637 indicates that in Norfolk too abuses in alehouses and recusancy or failure to attend church were the most common misdemeanours reported, though in this county the order was reversed and religious offences far outnumbered others.[62] As in Worcestershire and Staffordshire other offenders were relatively few in number. The Norfolk presentments did include more drunkards than appear in the returns of those counties, and also the obstruction of highways, occasional affrays and assaults, illegal cottages and taking inmates, and some nuisance

[59] PRO, SP 16/194/63 II, IV; Bund, ed., *Sessions Papers*, p. 566.

[60] e.g. PRO, SP 16/188/43; 198/11, 14, 27, 30, 40; 206/72, 73; 210/16; 218/5, 22; 231/40; 238/37, 42; 239/52, 84; 247/47; 251/11; 262/71, 72; 266/4; 298/86; 319/26, 85, 107; 320/74; 344/30, 59; 347/67; 351/112, 113; 354/184; 364/73, 74; 383/57; 385/7, 8, 43, 55; 418/21.

[61] On the importance of presentments by hundred juries in Essex see Wrightson, 'Two concepts of order', pp. 35–6.

[62] This is based on presentments for the years 1615, 1617, 1618, 1620, 1621, 1629, 1637, NNRO, Sessions Records, Boxes 20, 21, 22, 23, 27, 31. Most of the surviving returns are from the hundreds of Freebridge, Holt, Wayland and Grimshaw, North Erpingham, Gallow and Brothercross, Clackclose, Mitford, and North and South Greenhoe.

offences such as throwing dead swine into a watering or leaving muckheaps in undesirable places.

It is difficult to provide an overall evaluation of constables' performance in making presentments. While some did not appear before higher officials when they were summoned to submit such returns, court records would suggest that only a few officers in a year were indicted for such defaults, at least in the counties considered in detail in this study. The constables' accounts examined indicate that they were busily engaged in such duties. They travelled to neighbouring villages to submit such returns for sessions and assizes, and in the 1630s to the justices at their monthly meetings, as well as making special presentments from time to time on a variety of matters. Furthermore, some constables in some counties, and especially during the 1630s, seem to have made detailed written responses to the charges they were given on such occasions, answering the articles one by one. On the other hand, the constables' presentments which survive, even those of a detailed nature, do raise some questions about the completeness of their returns, and suggest that they may often have been rather selective in the kinds of offenders they reported. Moreover, the number of reports of *omnia bene* among the presentments seem to indicate that, however regularly they may have appeared to make presentments, for some constables such returns were rather pro forma.[63]

III. THE PUNISHMENT OF VAGRANTS

It has been noted that the punishment of vagrants was one of the matters on which constables were often required to report to higher officials. In many cases they did answer the article concerning vagrants, and their accounts too show them at work in apprehending such offenders. However, they were frequently accused of neglecting this area of their duties. Constables' accounts and presentments, as well as reports from the justices, would suggest that there were changes over time in their diligence in punishing such offenders.

General orders issued by the justices in quarter sessions frequently charged that constables were negligent in apprehending and punishing vagrants, and these claims were sometimes combined with accusations

---

[63] Also see below, ch. 7, for an analysis of constables' conduct in making presentments.

that they had failed to keep watch and ward. The frequent repetition of such orders might suggest that the magistrates' directives met with little response. The fact that the judges of assize or the justices ordered the appointment of provost marshals or others assistants to constables also seems to indicate that constables themselves were not deemed very diligent or effective in rounding up vagrants.[64] Records of assizes or quarter sessions occasionally contain other general reports of constables' delinquency in performing such duties. The grand jury at the Hertfordshire assizes in 1624 claimed that the order made at the previous assizes for the apprehension and punishment of rogues had been 'much neglected' by petty constables.[65] A Wiltshire grand jury in 1633 also claimed that constables and tithingmen in general were negligent in keeping watch and ward and punishing wandering people.[66] Sometimes all of the officers in a particular hundred were accused of being negligent in punishing rogues.[67] Occasionally substantial numbers of constables were indicted for delinquency in apprehending vagrants, as in Wiltshire in 1633 when no less than thirty-three officers were returned for such defaults or in Staffordshire at Trinity sessions, 1603, when twelve faced such accusations.[68] However, quarter sessions records usually contain only two or three such cases a year.

In most instances the bare fact that constables were presented, and sometimes fined, for their failure to apprehend rogues is all that is known; but occasionally there is evidence to suggest that a local officer was rather defiant in his refusal to punish such wanderers. A headborough of East Grinstead, Sussex, was presented to assizes in

[64] Lister, ed., *West Riding Sessions*, ii. 7–8, 10–11; Atkinson, ed., *Sessions Records*, i. 119; ii. 206–7; iii. 314–15; Bates Harbin, ed., *Sessions Records*, i. 100; Hardy, ed., *Notes and Extracts*, pp. 58–9; Staffs. RO, Transcripts Sessions Rolls, Jac. I, Roll 71, nos. 23, 24; QS/O, iii. 124, 125; Bund, ed., *Sessions Papers*, p. 485.

[65] Cockburn, ed., *Herts. Indictments, James I*, no. 1369.

[66] Cunnington, ed., *Sessions Great Rolls*, p. 110.

[67] e.g. Atkinson, ed., *Sessions Records*, ii. 131–2 (East and West parts of liberty of Langbargh); NNRO, Sessions Records, Box 19 (hundreds of Freebridge and Wayland/Grimshaw).

[68] H. C. Johnson, ed., *Minutes and Proceedings in Sessions* (Wiltshire Archaeological and Natural History Society, Records Branch, iv, Devizes, 1949), pp. 71–3; Burne, ed., *Staffs. Sessions Rolls*, v. 13–14. For other cases in which constables were charged with negligence in punishing vagrants see, for example, Burne, ed., *Staffs. Sessions Rolls*, ii. 255, 296; Staffs. RO, Transcripts Sessions Rolls, Jac. I, Roll 30, no. 7; Roll 31, nos. 106–7; Roll 49, no. 53; Roll 62, no. 65; Bund, ed., *Sessions Papers*, pp. 38, 39, 65, 75, 112, 128, 133, 185, 499; Atkinson, ed., *Sessions Records*, i. 11, 56, 92, 136, 144, 148, 151, 163, 172, 186, 188, 193, 199, 212, 228, 240, 254, 258, 260, ii. 9, 32, 94–5, 103, 107, 214; iii. 309, 324; iv. 80.

1605 for punishing a vagrant 'very slenderly, as with a whip taken out
of the hedge', and for declaring that he would not punish any vagrants
sent to him in the future by Francis Chaloner, gent. He apparently was
not alone among the officers of that township in his reluctance to
punish vagrants. In 1590 the constable had been accused of allowing
rogues and idle persons to pass unpunished.[69] An officer of Preston
Bagot, Warwickshire, also seems to have been opposed to punishing
four vagrants who were turned over to him by a gentleman of that
township, who claimed that they had begged at his house and assaulted
his servants when they were denied alms. The constable placed them
in the stocks but, according to the charges brought by the gentleman in
Star Chamber, he had done so rather reluctantly, and even moved the
stocks into a barn when it began to rain. After imprisoning them very
briefly he allowed them to go their way. The constable reputedly told
one of the gentleman's servants to inform his master that if he wanted
the offenders taken before a justice 'that hee should then sende them a
horse or two to ride for that the wayes weare foule and unfitt for poore
people to travell on foote'.[70] A few constables who were alehouse
keepers by trade were charged with being so delinquent in their duties
as to entertain vagrants rather than punishing them. One officer in the
North Riding of Yorkshire was accused of allowing twenty rogues to
drink in his house at unlawful times.[71]

Some justices in the 1630s, in their reports on their enforcement of
the Book of Orders, still complained of constables' negligence in
punishing rogues, and indicated that they had fined them for such
defaults.[72] However, during that decade magistrates more often
commended the increased diligence of such officers in this particular
area of their duties. Sometimes they indicated that initially they had
found some constables to be negligent, but suggested that the
punishments which they had meted out to those who were remiss had
led to their reform. The justices of one Salop hundred claimed that as
a result of the fines constables had become so diligent that the area
was cleared of wandering beggars and the true poor were better
maintained.[73] The justices of the hundred of Totmanslow, Staffordshire,
claimed that the care and diligence of constables and tithingmen in

---

[69] Cockburn, ed., *Sussex Indictments, James* I, no. 54; Cockburn, ed., *Sussex Indictments, Eliz. I,* no. 1219.
    [70] PRO, STAC 8/252/10.   [71] Atkinson, ed., *Sessions Records,* iii. 290.
    [72] e.g. PRO, SP 16/191/53, 294/36 (Offlow, Staffs.); 210/83, 347/66 (Sparkenhoe, Leics.).
    [73] PRO, SP 16/263/47 (March 1634).

their division had resulted in the country being much less troubled with rogues, and they offered 'commendacions for their travaile and good service in this behalfe'.[74] The magistrates of several hundreds in Leicestershire also applauded the increased diligence of constables in punishing vagrants. Reports from Guthlaxton did indicate that officers there had presented few rogues, having punished only those that they had taken begging. However, the magistrates in Gartree hundred claimed that they had dealt 'soe strictly with constables according to law for there not punishing of vagrants that a wandering rogue abides not our hundred'.[75] Similar reports came from the division of Sparkenhoe where the magistrates claimed in June 1631 that as a result of the increased efforts of constables, who had punished 753 rogues, they had 'clensed the cuntry of vagrants comeinge from other places' as well as restraining idlers within the hundred.[76] The justices of Framland in June 1631 indicated that they had found some remissness and neglect in constables at first, and that they had fined negligent officers 20s. each. Nevertheless, they were able to report that 164 such offenders had been punished and sent with passes. By January 1632 constables in that hundred had punished a further 113 vagrants, according to their returns.[77]

Actual figures of vagrants punished are perhaps more convincing than general comments from the justices about constables' diligence, and in Hertfordshire a number of the magistrates' reports during the 1630s do provide these details. Returns from this county often give totals of the rogues punished since the previous certificate, and occasionally include presentments, village by village, giving detailed information about those apprehended and where they had been sent. The number of vagrants listed in such reports would suggest that constables in Hertfordshire were particularly diligent in rounding up such offenders during the 1630s. John Garrard, Charles Caesar, and William Prestley reported from Broadwater and the half hundred of Hitchin in August 1631 that 125 vagrants had been punished in Broadwater and 146 in Hitchin since April, while Garrard, John Luke, and William Cade in their returns from Dacorum in August 1631 indicated that 208 vagrants had been punished in that division.[78] Such reports continued through most of the 1630s, the magistrates in

[74] PRO, SP 16/266/17 (April 1634).
[75] PRO, SP 16/202/12 (Oct. 1631); 190/4 (May 1631).
[76] PRO, SP 16/193/89.
[77] PRO, SP 16/193/33; 210/37.   [78] PRO, SP 16/198/11, 14.

Broadwater claiming in April 1634 that 38 vagrants and 9 Irish had been punished since the end of January, while a return from that division in March 1637 indicated that 76 vagrants had been punished since the end of July 1636 and 154 more apprehended, probably between March and July 1636.[79] The justices in Dacorum reported 110 vagrants in March 1634, and in April 1636 they forwarded returns containing constables' presentments village by village listing 106 vagrants who had been punished during the last six months.[80]

While constables' accounts indicate that they may often have been remiss in punishing vagrants, these materials too contain some evidence to suggest that they were more diligent in the 1630s. There is little question that some constables were very much occupied with a variety of poor wanderers who appeared in their villages. This was particularly true during the 1620s, when many Irish joined the English who were on the roads, and during the 1630s, when some accounts reveal the presence of even larger numbers of poor migrants of all sorts.[81] Some of them were identified as vagrants brought with passes by neighbouring constables and they were conveyed to the next village. In other cases constables can be seen apprehending wanderers, whipping them and having passes made for them, and then conveying them to a neighbouring officer. A few pregnant women, who were not subject to corporal punishment because of their condition, some of them apparently at the point of giving birth, were conveyed rapidly to the parish boundary. The constables probably were concerned that the village, or they themselves, might be burdened with the upkeep of the child if it was born within their jurisdiction. However, only a small proportion of those who were on the roads were apprehended or punished, and many of them were given alms, sometimes provided with transportation to the next village, and occasionally given food or lodging. At no time did a very high percentage of the migrants receive punishment, and many of them may have possessed proper authorization for travel. However, in the 1630s there does appear to have been an increase over the previous decades in the numbers apprehended as vagrants by some constables, and such offenders were particularly numerous in 1630–1. For example, constables of Waltham punished 74 vagrants and conveyed 109 others in the 1630s as opposed to

---

[79] PRO, SP 16/266/4; 351/113.   [80] PRO, SP 16/262/71; 319/85.

[81] See my article 'Population Mobility and Alms: Poor migrants in the Midlands during the early seventeenth century', *Local Population Studies*, xxvii (1981), 35–51, from which the following material is drawn.

punishing 8 and conveying 6 in the decade 1611–20. In the single year October 1630 to October 1631, there were 49 vagrants listed in the Waltham accounts. Between April 1630 and April 1631 the constable of Branston recorded 29 such offenders, far more than in any other year between 1611 and 1640, and more than in the entire decade 1611–20. Poor harvests, economic depression, and plague no doubt contributed to a growth in vagrancy as well as to the general increase in the numbers of the mobile poor in the 1630s, but it is also probable that constables were more diligent at this time in apprehending those who should not have been on the roads.

It is not possible to draw very firm conclusions about constables' performance in the punishment of vagrants. There is considerable evidence that their superiors deemed them remiss in fulfilling this duty. Their own accounts too would suggest that on a number of occasions they may well have allowed wanderers simply to pass on to the next village rather than taking the trouble to apprehend them, whip them, have passes made for them, and then be obliged to convey them to a neighbouring officer. It would appear that during the 1630s constables in some counties, or at least within some divisions, were more vigorous in the apprehension of vagrants. T. G. Barnes claimed that constables in Somerset during this period were effective in clearing the roads of vagrants;[82] and both the reports from the justices and constables' own accounts would suggest that officers in other counties too displayed increased diligence in this area of their duties.

IV. THE APPREHENSION OF OTHER OFFENDERS

Constables' accounts contain some entries concerning their apprehension of other offenders, as well as disbursements for the maintenance of such facilities as the stocks, the cage, and the whipping-post, and very occasional entries concerning service on coroners' juries.[83]

---

[82] Barnes, *Somerset*, p. 182.

[83] There are regular entries in the Manchester accounts for repairs to the stocks, cage, pillory, and dungeon, and also references to the whipping-post and cuckstool, Earwaker, ed., *Constables' Accounts*, i and ii; and regular entries for repairs to the cage, and some references to the stocks, the cuckstool, and the pillory, in the Waltham accounts, Leics. RO, DE 625/60. For more scattered references to such facilities also see Leics. RO, DE 720/30, ff. 7ᵛ, 10, 14ᵛ, 38ᵛ, 45ᵛ, 52; DG 25/39/1/2, 3, 4; NNRO, PD 50/36L, nos. 9–9A, 45, 100, 103; PD 254/112, 1623, 1636; PD 219/126, 1635; HWRO, 850 SALWARPE, BA 1054/2, Bundle D, nos. 2, 4. For a few references to the coroner see Leics. RO, DE 720/30, ff. 17, 38ᵛ; DG 25/39/1/3; DE 625/60, fo. 6; Salop RO, 3067/3/1, pp. 15, 47; Pattingham Constables Accounts, 1622–3, 1637–8 (2), 1639–40;

However, items of this kind are not very numerous in most constables' accounts. In any case, due to the very nature of such materials they provide little evidence as to how consistently constables fulfilled these other peacekeeping duties. Court records contain some cases in which officers were charged with failing to apprehend offenders, or to assist in making arrests, and sometimes with allowing prisoners to escape their custody. Only a scattering of such cases appear in the records of assizes and quarter sessions for the counties examined. However, a number of constables who were accused of negligence of this kind are known to have been found guilty and fined, sometimes as much as £5 when they had permitted men to escape arrest.[84] Usually no more than the brief charge against a constable has survived in such instances, and little is known of the circumstances in which an officer failed to make an arrest or allowed a prisoner to go free. It is possible to make only a few general comments about their failings on such occasions.

Sometimes ignorance or carelessness probably account for their defaults. In a few instances when constables were asked to make arrests and refused to do so, they seem to have been afraid of exceeding their authority. The handbooks written for constables reveal some of the legal intricacies which such officers had to master in making arrests, and they sometimes were probably ignorant in these matters.[85] A constable of Walsingham, Norfolk, charged with refusing a woman's request that he apprehend a man who reportedly had nearly

Borthwick Institute PR MIL. 10, 1637; HWRO, 850 SALWARPE, BA 1054/2, Bundle D, no. 8.

[84] For cases in which constables were accused of failing to execute warrants or make arrests see Bund, ed., *Sessions Papers*, pp. 38, 50, 120, 135, 348; Burne, ed., *Staffs. Sessions Rolls*, i. 153–4; Staffs. RO, Transcripts Sessions Rolls, Jac. I, Roll 26, nos. 36–7; Roll 27, no. 14; Roll 51, no. 34; Roll 52, no. 35; Atkinson, ed., *Sessions Records*, i. 37–8, 64, 99, 165, 170, 210, 240, 268; ii. 13, 35, 47, 96, 115, 116, 132, 166, 191, 196; iii. 115, 365; iv. 35, 83, 117, 125, 212. For cases in which they were charged with allowing men to escape their custody, see Bund, ed., *Sessions Papers*, pp. 196, 237, 331, 462, 488, 610, 644; Burne, ed., *Staffs. Sessions Rolls*, iv. 203, 373–4; Staffs. RO, Transcripts Sessions Rolls, Jac. I, Roll 19, no. 16; Roll 22, no. 30; Roll 23, no. 49; Roll 30, nos. 34–5; Roll 77, no. 107; Car. I, Roll 24, no. 37; Atkinson, ed., *Sessions Records*, i. 42, 165, 245, 264; ii. 5, 48, 123, 226; iii. 117, 160, 169, 190, 201, 204, 225; iv. 68, 79; Cockburn, ed., *Herts. Indictments, Eliz. I*, no. 757; *Herts. Indictments, James I*, no. 1447; *Essex Indictments, Eliz. I*, nos. 332, 795, 1041, 1591, 2307, 2790; *Kent Indictments, Eliz. I*, nos. 1586, 1587, 1761, 2386, 2613; *Sussex Indictments, Eliz. I*, nos. 52, 1216, 1686; *Surrey Indictments, Eliz. I*, nos. 744, 1039, 1604, 1886, 2216; *Kent Indictments, James I*, no. 708.

[85] See Lambard, *Dueties of Constables*, pp. 11–19; Sheppard, *Offices and Duties of Constables*, pp. 33–63, 166–75; E. W., *Exact Constable*, pp. 15–25;) R. G., *Compleat Constable*, pp. 15–28.

murdered her husband, was perhaps afraid of exceeding his powers. He asked her if she had a warrant and, when she replied in the negative, stated that, 'I will not meddle in the apprehending of him.'[86] When a headborough of Flashbrook, Staffordshire, failed to execute a warrant procured by an inhabitant of that township for the appearance of a man before the justices, saying that he would not apprehend him unless he could charge him with felony, his action is perhaps explained by ignorance or uncertainty about his authority.[87] A constable of Powick, Worcestershire, summoned to sessions for negligence in executing a warrant, may have thought he was doing his duty when he kept the warrant and the prisoner until the next quarter sessions rather than conveying the man to gaol.[88] Some of the cases of 'negligent escape' brought against constables involved offenders committed to their custody for conveyance to gaol,[89] and in such instances they may sometimes have been remiss only in failing to secure sufficient help to keep the prisoner safe during the journey.

On other occasions constables seem to have been wilfully disobedient in performing such duties, and some of them quite unrepentant about their negligence. There are a number of cases on record of constables refusing to assist bailiffs in making arrests, and sometimes standing by while other inhabitants assaulted them. It was alleged that an officer of Marlborough did 'in a verye contemptible and scornefull manner walke upp and downe with his hands in his pocketts' while some of his fellow townsmen attacked a Wiltshire bailiff who had come to apprehend a man. This constable must have been quite aware that he was not fulfilling his duties.[90] An officer of Cley, Norfolk, accused of allowing the escape of a suspected felon, reportedly told the man to go away, and the other constable of the village was later seen drinking with the suspect.[91] A Yorkshire constable who was fined 20s. by quarter sessions for not executing a warrant also received an additional penalty

---

[86] NNRO, Sessions Records, Box 23 (1621–2).

[87] Staffs. RO, Transcripts Sessions Rolls, Jac. I, Roll 27, no. 14.

[88] Bund, ed., *Sessions Papers*, p. 348.

[89] e.g. Cockburn, ed., *Herts. Indictments, Eliz. I*, no. 757; *Essex Indictments, Eliz. I*, no. 1041; *Kent Indictments, Eliz. I*, no. 2386; *Sussex Indictments, Eliz. I*, no. 1686; *Surrey Indictments, Eliz. I*, nos. 1039, 2216.

[90] PRO, STAC 8/192/30; the constable was fined £20. For other cases of constables refusing to obey bailiffs or undersheriffs see STAC 8/61/61; STAC 8/189/1; STAC 8/179/10; STAC 8/210/19; Staffs. RO, Transcripts Sessions Rolls, Jac. I, Roll 23, no. 49; Roll 56, no. 30; Bund, ed., *Sessions Papers*, p. 83; Atkinson, ed., *Sessions Records*, iii. 149.

[91] NNRO, Sessions Records, Box 19 (25 Oct. 1614).

of 20s. and was conveyed to gaol for his 'scoffing, scornfull and distainfull speeches towardes the courte', and he apparently showed no repentance for his faults.[92] Sometimes officers confessed to having allowed a prisoner to escape, as did George Blackwell, yeoman, constable of Bushey, indicted at assizes in 1596 for permitting a labourer committed to his custody for conveyance to Hertford gaol to go free.[93] Others, like a Nottinghamshire constable who was summoned to sessions to answer for allowing a prisoner to escape his custody, defiantly refused to confess to their failings. He was not only punished for the original offence, but also fined 10s. for declaring in the presence of the justices, 'I will fynde another knave to execute my busynesse as constable.'[94]

Constables' accounts cannot shed much light on how consistently they carried out their police duties, and whether or not they apprehended all those who should have been taken into custody; but such records do indicate that some of them went to considerable trouble in such matters. Occasionally constables themselves recorded quite clearly what such duties entailed. The officers of Pattingham, who apprehended three men for the theft of a bullock, made the following entry in their accounts: 'for all charges with the trouble about John Perry, John Smallwood and John Fletcher in bringeinge them before the justice and keepinge them before we went to the justice with them'.[95] While some may have been negligent in such duties, 'charges' and 'trouble' often characterized the performance of the constables of the villages examined here. Many seem to have taken care that the offenders whom they arrested would not escape. Often they paid men to watch prisoners, sometimes keeping them guarded overnight or even for several days, until they could arrange to convey them before a justice or to gaol. They also procured assistants to help them safeguard prisoners during such journeys, and sometimes they were obliged to hire horses to make the trip to a neighbouring justice or to the gaol in the county town.[96]

Their accounts also provide some information about the kinds of offenders whom they did apprehend. Historians sometimes suggest

[92] Atkinson, ed., *Sessions Records*, ii. 96.
[93] Cockburn, ed., *Herts. Indictments, Eliz. I*, no. 757; on Blackwell see above, ch. 4, n. 104.
[94] Copnall, *Notes and Extracts*, p. 19.
[95] Pattingham Constables' Accounts, 1590–1.
[96] This is based on the Pattingham Constables' Accounts and those of Waltham and Melton Mowbray, in Leics. RO, DE 625/60; DG 36/186–9; DG 25/39/1/1–4.

that villagers were more likely to arrest strangers than to bring action against fellow residents;[97] but the offenders who appear in constables' accounts include substantial numbers of local inhabitants as well as outsiders. Some of them were accused of felonies, while others were conveyed before the justices for reasons which are not specified, and they probably were guilty only of misdemeanours.[98] Recent work on crime has shown that larceny was by far the most common felony tried at assizes and sessions in the late sixteenth and early seventeenth centuries,[99] and evidence about those apprehended by constables is certainly compatible with that finding. In most cases when detailed information is provided about the reasons for arrest, whether of local residents or strangers, the crime was simple theft or housebreaking. Most of the offenders listed in the Manchester accounts, where the crime often is identified, were accused of larceny. The hues and cries recorded by the constables of that township frequently were for thieves, often those who had stolen horses or cattle, though some offenders were being pursued for having wounded or even murdered others.[100] Accounts from other villages less consistently identify the nature of the crime, but those apprehended in Pattingham included a 'swine stealer', three local men who had stolen a bullock, three women suspected of breaking into a house in another village, a girl who broke into a house in Pattingham and a boy accused of the same offence, a man who stole a tablecloth from the church in another parish, and one who stole from a hedge.[101] Those arrested by constables of Waltham included a woman who stole a cloak, a man who broke into a house, another charged with theft of linens, and a local woman apparently accused of milking someone else's cows.[102] Officers of Melton are known to have apprehended a local man for stealing geese, a servant for theft of sheep, a stranger who stole swine, and a local woman accused of the receipt of stolen goods.[103] One more unusual entry occurs in the Melton accounts, when the constables arrested two men suspected of high treason.[104]

[97] See esp. Ingram, 'Communities and Courts', pp. 128–33.
[98] This is based on the accounts of Pattingham, Waltham, and Melton.
[99] See esp. Cockburn, 'The Nature and Incidence of Crime in England', and Samaha, *Law and Order*.
[100] Earwaker, ed., *Constables' Accounts*, i and ii.
[101] Pattingham Constables' Accounts, 1590–91, 1597–8, 1588–9, 1628–9.
[102] Leics. RO, DE 625/60, ff. 26, 42ᵛ, 45, 62ᵛ.
[103] Leics. RO, DG 36/188, 189, DG 25/39/1/3, DG 25/39/1/2.
[104] Leics. RO, DG 25/39/1/4.

The constables' accounts examined, with the exception of those of Manchester, never contain many entries concerning hues and cries or the apprehension of suspects; but the officers of both Pattingham and Waltham do appear to have dealt with more offenders during the 1630s than in earlier decades. In Pattingham there were at least 56 suspects or offenders, apart from vagrants, mentioned in the records of the 1630s, while the comparable figures for earlier decades are: 1591–1600: 22; 1601–10: 1; 1611–20: 6; 1621–30: 31.[105] Officers of Waltham recorded at least 51 suspects or offenders in the 1630s, while only 13 are mentioned in the accounts for 1611–20.[106] All of the forty-six hues and cries entered in the Pattingham accounts are also found during the 1630s.[107] The adverse economic circumstances of the time may well have fostered a rise in crime, especially larceny, and similar conditions might account for the smaller peak in the Pattingham records in the 1590s. However, the figures perhaps also reflect greater diligence by these constables in pursuing and apprehending offenders during the 1630s, just as some of them also seem to have been more rigorous in their punishment of vagrants.[108]

Some constables clearly were remiss in making arrests and also in assuring the safe delivery of prisoners to the gaol. While their defaults sometimes may have been a product of ignorance, in other cases they appear to have been wilfully negligent in fulfilling their duties. However, if quarter sessions and assize records provide an accurate measure of the failings displayed by such officers in the arrest and custody of offenders, such defaults do not seem to have been very numerous. Even if account is taken of instances when constables were required to answer at sessions for unspecified neglect of their duties, cases which may well have involved faults in law enforcement, such charges would still involve only a few constables in any year.[109] While the unreliability of at least a few officers cannot be dismissed, on the other hand constables' accounts sometimes show them to have been

---

[105] The figures were compiled from the Pattingham constables' accounts.
[106] The figures were complied from the Waltham constables' accounts, Leics. RO, DE 625/60.
[107] See Pattingham Constables' Accounts for this period.
[108] See above, n. 81.
[109] See a number of such cases in the Staffs. records, Burne, ed., *Staffs. Sessions Rolls*, i. 254, 297, 298, 353; ii. 242, 272, 303–4, 311, 312, 314, 347, 354, 373; iii. 24–5, 34, 35, 36, 65, 66, 96, 112; iv. 182, 219, 325, 401, 408, 448–9, 464, 465–6, 467, 482, 483; v. 10, 11, 51, 162. The same names are often repeated from sessions to sessions.

conscientious in their apprehension of offenders, and to have gone to considerable trouble to assure their safe delivery to a justice or to gaol.

V. BREAKING THE LAW: ABUSE OF THEIR POLICE POWERS AND PERSONAL OFFENCES

Some constables were accused not merely of neglecting their duties to present, apprehend, or punish offenders, but of actually breaking the law rather than enforcing it. Charges against them included exceeding their powers as police officers, accepting bribes for not presenting offenders, and warning suspects that they were wanted, so that they could flee. Others were accused of false arrests and/or prosecutions, unlawful imprisonment or other unauthorized punishments, unlawful searches, and occasionally illegal seizure of goods.[110] Most such suits against constables were brought by private citizens rather than higher officials, cases of this kind most often being found in Star Chamber. The outcome is seldom known and many of these cases may have been vexatious suits preferred against constables for legitimate actions which they had taken.[111] However, despite the uncertainty of the evidence, such accusations must be taken into account in evaluating constables' work as police officers. Some officers were also charged with disorderly conduct, and with committing misdemeanours that, when perpetrated by others, they were supposed to present to higher authorities.

Occasionally a constable was charged not merely with being negligent in making presentments, but with abusing his powers and accepting bribes in return for not presenting offenders. An officer of Woodbridge, Suffolk, allegedly procured the position for years on end in order to enrich himself by taking rewards for not returning offenders. The plaintiff in this case gave examples of the sums of money and the commodities which the constable supposedly had received for not presenting unlicensed ale-sellers.[112] Two Herefordshire officers were also charged with accepting money in return for not making presentments, in this case of recusants whose names should have been returned to quarter sessions. According to their accusers they had presented the recusants anyway; but on a later occasion when the justices issued a warrant for their apprehension the constables had

[110] For cases of illegal seizure of goods see Barnes, *Somerset Assize Orders*, pp. 2, 3; Bates Harbin, ed., *Sessions Records*, ii. 288; other charges will be discussed more fully below.

[111] See below, ch. 7, for a discussion of vexatious suits against constables.

[112] PRO, STAC 8/155/18.

given them warning that they were wanted, enabling them to flee.[113] The office clearly offered opportunities for dishonest conduct of this kind, and some perhaps took advantage of them; but if such behaviour was very widespread it does not often seem to have been detected, or official complaints to have been lodged.

There are occasional instances in which constables were charged not just with negligence in apprehending offenders, but, as in the case of the Herefordshire constables mentioned above, of giving them warning to escape. Two officers of Needham, Suffolk, and a deputy appointed by one of them, were accused of failing to take action in arresting two local men, Simon Daynes and Edward Guile, who were suspected of grand larceny by Edward Grimston, esq., Master in Chancery. One of the officers, who was alleged to be 'speciall frynde' to Daynes, was charged with misleading Grimston's servants who had come to procure the arrest, refusing to set watch on his house or to procure assistants to go and apprehend him, and of sending him warning that he was wanted so that he could escape. The other constable, whose wife was 'of kindred' to Daynes, allegedly had refused to come out at night, claiming to be sick, and had sent as his deputy a mere youth of 10 or 12 years of age. On the following morning when Grimston's servants discovered that Daynes had fled and sought to arrest Guile, they were told that this officer was not at home and had appointed a deputy. The deputy in turn was accused of delay in going to make the arrest, of sending Guile warning that he was wanted, and of refusing to enter the house to apprehend him. According to one of the witnesses in the case he had indicated sympathy for Daynes too, telling the deponent that Daynes was wanted and adding that 'it were a good turne the sayd Daynes had knowledge of it'.[114] Probably constables sometimes did behave in such a fashion in order to protect friends or kinsmen from arrest, but once again evidence of such conduct is not very widespread.[115]

Constables were also accused of false arrest or imprisonment. In some of these cases they probably had unwittingly exceeded their powers, or out of ignorance followed incorrect legal procedures. Not only did such duties require legal knowledge which some officers may

[113] PRO, STAC 8/304/30.

[114] PRO, STAC 8/4/15; 150/9; quotations from STAC 8/4/15. In another suit in the same year (STAC 8/210/19) one of the constables was accused of a long list of offences, apparently unjustly since the plaintiff was fined £66. 13s. 4d.

[115] For another case of this sort involving a thirdborough see Staffs. RO, Transcripts Sessions Rolls, Jac. I, Roll 30, nos. 34–5.

not have possessed, but there was discord and confusion, even among higher officials, about whether constables could imprison those who had broken the peace or even take sureties in such instances. Several cases involving charges of false imprisonment against constables, which were included in the law reports of the late sixteenth and early seventeenth centuries, reveal disagreements among the judges about the authority of such officers. The confusion was perpetuated in handbooks and legal treatises which cite these cases.[116] When even the judges seem to have been uncertain about constables' powers to detain offenders, it would not be surprising if these officers themselves sometimes committed errors or exceeded their powers as a result of their ignorance of the law and its procedures.

Sometimes, however, constables were charged with wilfully abusing their powers of arrest or imprisonment, of using the office for selfish purposes to make false arrests or bring unfounded suits against a party. Some plaintiffs claimed that officers had acted merely out of personal malice to do them some sort of injury. Sometimes it was even suggested that men had sought the position for that purpose. A Cornish constable was accused of seeking to overthrow a neighbouring husbandman by deliberately getting himself chosen for the office, falsely accusing the man of stealing sheep, and breaking into his messuage and seizing the animals.[117] Another officer, in Little Saredon, Staffordshire, allegedly abused his powers by bringing accusations of trespass, in King's Bench and Common Pleas as well as in the hundred court, against a man he wanted to force out of a tenement.[118] A constable of Audley, Staffordshire, apparently acted out of mere 'spleene' when he accused a man who should have served as headborough of the town of failing to pay provision money, though no such sum was due.[119] Another Audley constable, hired as a substitute by the man actually chosen for the position, was accused of acting on behalf of this man and several accomplices to procure an unjustified warrant of good behaviour against a gentleman toward whom they bore malice.[120] Sometimes constables were accused of bringing a long list of

[116] See esp. *The Reports of Thomas Owen, 1556–1615* (London, 1650), pp. 98, 105–6; also see George Croke, *Reports*, i. (London, 1669), p. 204; *Reports and Cases Collected by the Learned Sir John Popham* (London, 1656), pp. 12–13; *The Fifth Part of the Reports of Sir Edward Coke* (London, 1738), pp. 59–60; Sheppard, *Offices and Duties of Constables*, pp. 46–7; Dalton, *Country Justice* (1635 edn.), pp. 4–5; E. W., *Exact Constable*, pp. 15–19.
[117] PRO, STAC 8/89/1.
[118] PRO, STAC 8/194/20.
[119] Staffs. RO, QS/O, iii. 190.
[120] PRO, STAC 8/43/13.

false suits against personal foes in various courts. A Norfolk officer was charged with fomenting a quarrel between two men merely in order to take vengeance against one of them by apprehending him for an affray. He apparently also presented the man to assizes for witchcraft, and procured witnesses to give false evidence in the case, had him bound over to sessions to answer for riots and misdemeanours, and brought him before the court of the manor on charges that he had unlawfully cut down a tree. All were false and malicious suits, according to the plaintiff.[121] A Berkshire gentleman also claimed to have been subjected to a long list of vexatious actions by a constable who bore him malice because he had dismissed from his service the officer's stepson. Prior to becoming constable he reportedly had slandered the gentleman and lain in wait to attack him. On assuming office he used his position as a cover to inflict further injuries on his opponent. He allegedly presented the gentleman to the leet as a frequenter of alehouses and a drunkard, and when the jury refused to return the presentment he started a quarrel outside the court in order to arrest him for assaulting an officer. Reportedly he also bribed another man to prefer a false suit against the gentleman. Finally, he falsely procured a warrant of the peace against him, and arrested him in the churchyard in front of all of his neighbours to add to his humiliation.[122]

Other officers were accused of using their powers to imprison their foes or to inflict other unauthorized punishments on them. A Devon weaver claimed that a constable of Harberton had entered his house, under colour of carrying out his official duties, and dragged him off to the stocks and imprisoned him for eighteen hours. He attributed this unjustified action to the fact that the man had borne him malice for four years.[123] Two residents of Burton-upon-Trent, Staffordshire, also claimed that personal malice was the cause of their punishment by the constable of that township, who charged them with incontinence and who led other inhabitants in subjecting them to a noisy procession through the streets and imprisonment in the stocks.[124]

Occasionally constables were also accused of misusing their powers to conduct searches, of merely pretending to look for stolen goods in order to harass men or do injury to their good names. A Yorkshire yeoman claimed that a fellow villager who bore him a grudge, and who

---

[121] PRO, STAC 8/276/25.　　　　　[122] PRO, STAC 8/69/9.
[123] PRO, STAC 8/204/18.
[124] PRO, STAC 8/104/20; for another case of alleged false imprisonment see STAC 8/95/11.

had him falsely arrested for debt, later procured the office of constable in order to do him further harm. Under the guise of fulfilling his duties, he illegally broke into the man's house at night, apparently on the grounds of conducting a search, carried fire through the rooms, and caused such alarm that his wife became ill and his pregnant daughter-in-law lost the child she was carrying.[125] An Oxford constable was accused of breaking into the house of a butcher on the pretence of arresting him for felony and recovering stolen goods in his possession, and thus doing injury to his reputation.[126] In another case of this sort a Northumberland gentleman claimed that a constable had come to his house, on two different occasions, pretending to search for the flesh of stolen sheep, and he alleged that this was prompted merely by malice and a desire to spread evil reports about him.[127]

There is also evidence to suggest that the conduct of some constables was little better than that of offenders whom it was their duty to apprehend. They were sometimes brought before the courts for disorderly behaviour and for breaches of laws which it was their duty to enforce against others. In view of the court records constables sometimes possessed,[128] it is not surprising that a few of them displayed such traits. A year in the constableship probably often did little to transform the behaviour of a man who was prone to pick quarrels with his neighbours or to tipple a bit too much. Keith Wrightson gives examples of Lancashire constables who were 'so drunken that they had to be clapped in the stocks themselves', of an Essex officer who summoned the watchmen to join him in drinking and then led them in an affray on their counterparts in a neighbouring village, and of another constable in that county who ran a disorderly alehouse, although he does not regard such conduct as the norm among constables.[129] Some officers of similar ilk can be found in the records of other counties, though such cases do not seem to be very numerous.

Some officers were themselves accused of the breach of social regulations. Several Norfolk constables were presented to quarter sessions for haunting alehouses, while an officer of Bredon, Worcestershire, was accused of tippling during evening prayer on a

---

[125] PRO, STAC 8/82/1.
[126] PRO, STAC 8/189/20.
[127] PRO, STAC 8/217/29.
[128] See above, ch. 4.
[129] Wrightson, 'Two concepts of order', pp. 28–9.

number of Sundays.[130] Another officer in that county was presented for
playing bowls in the churchyard on May Day, contrary to the law, and a
constable of Pattingham who was an alehouse keeper was returned for
playing unlawful games.[131] A few constables were also accused of
joining in illegal assemblies or 'riots', usually directed against
landlords, or in some cases of standing by and allowing others to
engage in such actions. A constable of Belton, Leicestershire, was
charged with misusing his office when he led the inhabitants of the
township in tearing down the enclosure of a close which they claimed
was common land.[132] An officer of Knightley, Staffordshire, allegedly
supported a riot in which some of the inhabitants invaded a
gentleman's lands, assaulted his servants, and destroyed his fish-pond
by letting out the water. When one of the landholder's servants seized
their pikes and gave them to the constable, he returned them to the
rioters.[133] An officer of Culpho, Suffolk, also seems to have joined
other villagers in the harassment of a gentleman of that community.
They sang bawdy songs outside the man's house at midnight, made
slanderous remarks about his wife, and uttered threats to the
gentleman himself, and the constable apparently participated in the
activities rather than trying to disperse this disorderly assembly.[134]

Some men seem to have been as likely to commit affrays on others
while holding the constableship as to be attacked themselves.[135] While
such cases do not seem to have been typical of the behaviour of
constables, the conduct of some officers did place them in the category
of law-breakers rather than conservators of the peace. A Norfolk
officer was charged with assaulting and beating a man with a pitchfork,
and drawing blood of the man's wife as well, and another constable in
that county was accused of striking a man on the highway at harvest
time.[136] An ale-keeper in the same county allegedly siezed the
occasion, while constable, to quarrel with a man and 'strooke up [his]
heeles . . . and burst his legge', and another Norfolk officer was
presented to sessions because he 'cruelly beate' a man on the

[130] NNRO, Sessions Records, Box 20 (7 June 1615—c. of Beeston); Box 21 (3 June
1618—c. of Scarning); Bund, ed., *Sessions Papers*, p. 135.

[131] Bund, ed., *Sessions Papers*, p. 429; Burne, ed., *Staffs. Sessions Rolls*, iii. 44.

[132] PRO, STAC 8/71/6.

[133] PRO, STAC 8/289/19.

[134] PRO, STAC 8/176/14.

[135] For a discussion of attacks on constables see below, ch. 7.

[136] NNRO, Sessions Records, Box 19 (16 Dec. 1614 — c. of Dalling), (16 Dec.
1614 — c. of Tatterford).

Sabbath.[137] Sometimes when constables refused to assist other officials, such as bailiffs, in making arrests they were not merely passively disobedient but apparently joined other inhabitants in assaulting such officers, and helped to rescue the parties they were trying to apprehend. A constable of Weighton, Yorkshire, reportedly pulled out part of the beard of a bailiff and held it aloft, claiming that this was his warrant for arrest, and then joined others in an assault of the officer.[138] An officer of Chipping Barnet, Hertfordshire, apparently joined others in rescuing goods that were being seized by the underlings of a bailiff in that county, and then dragged the bailiff's officials off to the stocks. A constable of Burstall, Yorkshire, allegedly assisted in an attack on a bailiff of that county, freeing a prisoner he had apprehended, and later he reportedly bragged about the rescue.[139]

Cases in which constables were accused of abusing their police powers do not seem to be very numerous. However, their performance of such duties was probably affected sometimes by their use of the position for selfish ends, whether to extort money, to protect their friends, or apparently most often to harass their foes and take vengeance on them. In a society that was very litigious, even at the level of yeomen, husbandmen, and craftsmen, a man who was at odds with a neighbour, or who sought revenge for injuries real or imagined, would not necessarily put such contentions aside just because he had become constable. For a few the office may have offered the opportunity to pursue personal vendettas under colour of carrying out their official duties. Furthermore, some constables were guilty of disorderly behaviour, of drunkenness and other misdemeanours, and sometimes, while pretending to fulfil their duties, of committing assaults on others. However, while some of them do appear in the records as law-breakers rather than law enforcement officers, such illegalities do not seem to have been common among constables, or seldom seem to have reached the courts if they were widespread.

The constables of the villages examined here normally seem to have given a good deal of time and effort to fulfilling their administrative

[137] NNRO, Sessions Records, Box 23 (1621–2—alekeeper of Litcham); Box 27 (2 Apr. 1629 — presentment from Holt hundred). For other cases of assaults by constables see Atkinson, ed., *Sessions Records*, i. 264; S. C. Ratcliff and H. C. Johnson, eds., *Quarter Sessions Indictment Book, Easter 1631 to Epiphany 1674* (Warwick County Records, vi, 1941), p. 59.

[138] PRO, STAC 8/61/61; the constable was fined £20.

[139] PRO, STAC 8/189/1; 179/10. Also see STAC 8/210/19, probably a vexatious suit, against a constable of Needham, Suffolk; see above, n. 114.

and police duties, just as they did in carrying out their tax-collecting and military responsibilities. Their regular journeys before the clerk of the market with the township's weights and measures and their attendance on the justices with overseers, alemen, victuallers, butchers, and servants, as well as their numerous appearances before higher officials to submit presentments, all attest to their industry. Constables' accounts also indicate that they often went to considerable trouble in apprehending and guarding offenders and conveying them before a justice or to gaol, while many of them kept careful and detailed records of the poor wanderers whose appearance in their villages also made demands on their time. However, it would be false to suggest that such officers were always effective in the performance of their administrative and judicial responsibilities. Constables' presentments of *omnia bene*, and the apparent selectivity of their returns when they did present offenders, raise questions about their diligence in reporting on the misdemeanours of their neighbours; and a few of them may have turned a blind eye in return for monetary rewards. Nor can it be claimed that constables were always diligent in executing warrants and apprehending offenders. There are indications that ignorance or indifference, perhaps laziness, and in a few cases a desire to protect friends or relatives from the forces of the law, sometimes rendered them unreliable in such duties. Moreover, occasionally officers appear to have used their powers of arrest, search, and imprisonment for vexatious purposes, to pursue private quarrels with other inhabitants. Others committed breaches of the peace and engaged in disorderly conduct ill-befitting officers who were responsible for upholding the law. However, those guilty of such delinquency appear to have constituted only a tiny minority of constables. Larger numbers of them were probably negligent in punishing vagrants, the area of their duties where they most often received criticism. However, in this task, in their presentment of misdemeanours, and possibly in their apprehension of offenders as well, there are indications that constables in some areas acted with more than usual vigour during the 1630s. The praise of their performance by the justices of a number of counties during the first half of that decade may well have been deserved.

VI. CONSTABLES AT WORK: PERSONAL INADEQUACIES AND PERSONAL ACHIEVEMENTS

Evidence which suggests that some constables had neglected their duties or abused their powers cannot be dismissed. Many officers do not seem to have been very reliable as collectors of ship-money, especially in 1639–40, while some of them were also remiss in returning military rates at that time. Throughout the period under consideration there were often a few officers in a county who had failed to pay other levies, and occasionally larger numbers who were in arrears for a rate. There are indications too that the performance of constables as press-men, at least in terms of the quality of the soldiers they provided, left much to be desired. Despite evidence that such officers were, on the whole, fairly diligent in appearing before higher officials to return presentments, it is difficult to believe that the countryside was quite as orderly as might be suggested by the small number of offenders returned by some officers and the reports of 'all fayre and good' by others. It is also difficult to ignore the steady stream of complaints from higher officials, at least prior to the 1630s, about constables' negligence in punishing vagrants. A few officers, though probably only a tiny proportion of them, are known to have been remiss in pursuing and apprehending other offenders, or in assuring their safe delivery to a justice or to gaol.

The failings which constables displayed sometimes seem to be attributable, as historians have suggested, to the personal inadequacies of the incumbents. Some of those chosen for the position apparently were ignorant, lazy, or indifferent. A few of them probably were dishonest in their conduct, abusing their powers as tax-collectors, policemen, and press-men, and using the office for private ends or to serve the interests of friends. Occasionally an officer was every bit as disorderly as the miscreants whom it was his duty to apprehend. Some men who held the office clearly were personally unsuited to their duties as constables, although it will be suggested below that this was not the major cause of the failings which they displayed.[140]

Although the personal inadequacies of some officers must be recognized, it would be even more mistaken to ignore the positive qualities displayed by many of the constables whose accounts have been examined, even if they sometimes did not fulfil to the letter all their responsibilities. When the many duties of the office are considered, the surprising fact is not that these officers sometimes failed to carry out their obligations as royal officials, but that they so often were successful in meeting the demands placed on them. Many

[140] See ch. 7.

of them made personal sacrifices in order to do so. Daniel Defoe's comment during the early eighteenth century that the constableship 'takes up so much of a man's time that his own affairs are frequently wholly neglected' is equally applicable to the demands of the office during the late sixteenth and early seventeenth centuries.[141] Constables were expected to earn their livelihoods at the same time that they carried out their official responsibilities, and it must often have been difficult for them to co-ordinate their own economic pursuits with the demands of the office. In perusing the detailed records of constables of townships such as Pattingham, Branston, and Waltham it is difficult not to be impressed by the time, effort, and even financial sacrifice that was expected, and so often given, by the yeomen, husbandmen, and craftsmen who filled the constableship. As one follows them to neighbouring villages or the county town to convey offenders before a justice or to gaol, to make presentments, to bring in the weights and measures for inspection, to appear with alemen, butchers, overseers, or servants, to attend musters or deliver pressed soldiers, to confer with commissioners about tax assessments, and to return payments, it seems amazing that unpaid villagers, who had their own livelihoods to earn, could and did devote so much time to fulfilling their official responsibilities. At certain periods, and particularly during the later 1630s when the demands of the office were especially heavy, and when some constables were away from home for many days and sometimes for a week at a stretch for the single purpose of attending musters, they must have made personal sacrifices in order to fulfil their duties. Even though a number of petty constables in 1639–40 may not have been entirely diligent in their collection of ship-money and military levies, or in supplying able-bodied residents for the wars against the Scots, many would have been entitled to echo the complaints voiced by the high constables of one Norfolk hundred in January 1639. When these officers were charged with negligence in gathering ship-money they drew attention to the many directives which they had received, not only for the collection of this levy but for coat and conduct money and other rates as well, and to the orders which they had received to assemble the trained bands and to other warrants too. They protested that they had not had as much as a day to look after their own affairs, and in the course of a year they claimed to have spent £100 out of their own purses.[142]

---

[141] Cited in Campbell, *The English Yeoman*, p. 318.
[142] PRO, SP 16/410/65.

Petty constables did not expend sums of that size, but many of them did finance, at least temporarily, part of the expenses entailed in the office, and some of them also advanced money for rates and taxes. The fact that these men were able to bear such financial burdens, or to gain the credit which they required, and also to devote a good deal of their time to official business rather than their personal pursuits, seems to confirm the evidence presented earlier about the economic position and social standing of those who held the constableship. If constables normally were as poor and lowly as sometimes suggested it would have required more than personal sacrifices for them to have devoted to their duties the time, attention, and money given by many of the officers who have been discussed in these chapters. The social status of the men selected as constable, far from being the primary reason for their failings, often helps to explain their achievements in office.

7

Constables' Conduct: The Pressures of the Office

CONSTABLES appear to have been more industrious and more successful than often suggested, though they were not always reliable representatives of royal authority. The personal diligence displayed by many officers certainly contributed to their achievements, while the personal inadequacies of others made them unsuited to the position; but it is not sufficient to explain constables' conduct simply in terms of the qualities possessed by individual incumbents. If their behaviour in office and their achievements and failings are to be fully understood, it is necessary to take into account the dual nature of the position, and the dual and sometimes conflicting pressures which constables experienced.

An examination of the nature and duties of the constableship has revealed that such officers had obligations to their fellow inhabitants as well as to the state.[1] While they were required to represent the state to the village they were also obliged to represent the village to the state; and there were thus dual sanctions on them. Pressures exerted on them by their superiors, and the formal penalties which such officials might impose if they failed to fulfil their duties, were sometimes countered by local pressures, backed up by informal local sanctions. Although constables often seem to have been remarkably successful in juggling the demands that were placed on them by the state and by their fellow inhabitants, on some occasions they were likely to find themselves in trouble either locally or with higher authorities no matter what action they took. In the words of A. Hassell Smith they were confronted with the dilemma 'damned if I do, damned if I don't'.[2] A ballad of 1626 attributed to a Surrey constable described in rather vivid terms the dual sanctions experienced by such officers:

> The Justices will set us by the heels,
> If we do not as we should;
> Which if we perform, the townsmen will storm;
> Some of them hang 's if they could.[3]

---

[1] See above, chs. 1–3.
[2] Smith, *County and Court*, p. 113.
[3] James Gyffon, 'The Song of a Constable', (1626), in A. V. Judges, *The Elizabethan Underworld* (London, 1930), p. 489.

A few historians, including Smith, T. G. Barnes, and Keith Wrightson, have recognized the difficulties of such a mediating or 'interhierarchical' position, and they attribute constables' conduct on many occasions to their responsiveness to village interests or pressures rather than to their personal failings.[4] Such arguments seem to offer a better explanation of constables' actions in a number of instances than do claims about the personal deficiencies of individual incumbents; and especially when the character of the relationship between these officers and their fellow villagers is taken into account. Not only did constables have official obligations to the village, but it must also be kept in mind that they were local men, and usually chosen for office by their fellow inhabitants.[5] Like village headmen in other societies, they represented higher authority to communities of which they were 'in other respects full members', and their local political position was thus deeply enmeshed in the 'multiplex relationships' of the village.[6] Their ties to other villages were not just official but often personal in nature; they related to their fellow inhabitants as kinsmen, affines, friends, or neighbours, and not only as petty constables.[7] If, in their capacity as constables, they used their powers to act contrary to the interests of other villagers, they would endanger their local positions and risk destroying relationships within the community which would continue to be important to them long after their term in office had ended. Their place within the structure of social relationships in the village thus led them to be particularly subject to local influences on occasions when village interests conflicted with those of the state. As local men themselves however, they probably often shared the views of their fellow inhabitants. Furthermore, it must be recalled that constables were in many senses merely 'village headmen', and that they were heavily dependent upon securing the co-operation and assistance of

---

[4] Smith, *County and Court*, p. 112–13; Barnes, *Somerset*, pp. 222, 229, 230; Wrightson, 'Two concepts of order', esp. pp. 23–6, 29–32; Wrightson, *English Society*, pp. 157–9; also see Curtis, 'Quarter Sessions Appearances and their Background', pp. 145–8; Cheyney, *History of England*, ii. 415; Morrill, *Cheshire Grand Jury*, pp. 30, 32; Clark, *English Provincial Society*, esp. pp. 116, 251.

[5] See above, ch. 3.

[6] Gluckman, *Order and Rebellion*, p. 42; and for an elaboration of the concept of 'multiplex relationships', see Max Gluckman, *The Judicial Process among the Barotse of Northern Rhodesia* (Manchester, 1955), pp. 18–19.

[7] For a synthesis of recent work on the nature of relationships within local communities see Wrightson, *English Society*, ch. 2.

other inhabitants in carrying out their duties.[8] This factor too helped to make their actions subject to communal constraints.

Constables' conduct frequently does seem to be explained by their response to local pressures or obligations or by their local loyalties. However, the amount of pressure exerted on them by their superiors, and the extent to which these officials effectively supervised the work of the constabulary, also affected the behaviour of such officers. In contrast to the 'multiplex' ties which bound constables to their fellow villagers, their relationships with their superiors usually seem to have been formal in nature, 'single-interest linkages' to men with whom they were brought into contact as a result of their office. The pressures exerted on them from above were normally legal and official rather than personal in character.[9] The penalties with which they were threatened by higher officials, fines, imprisonment, or even summons before the Privy Council, must often have seemed rather remote by comparison with the more immediate pressures which such officers experienced within the village. Moreover, on certain occasions constables seem to have enjoyed something of an immunity to such sanctions because higher officials discovered that the punishment of negligent officers was no resolution to their difficulties, and even compounded their problems. However, the conscientiousness of their superiors in overseeing the work of constables could sometimes make a difference in their performance, and in some instances the diligence displayed by such officers seems to be explained by the increased pressures brought to bear on them by higher officials.

This chapter will consider constables' conduct in light of their relationships with higher officials and their local public. Consideration will be given first to the ways in which constables' performance could be affected by pressures from their superiors. Although this is a difficult matter to determine with any precision, some examples will be offered of occasions when pressures from above do seem to have had a marked influence on the conduct of such officers. Other instances will be cited in which higher officials seem to have been powerless in their attempts to command obedience from constables. This will be followed by a discussion of the local responses which constables encountered. Attention will be drawn to the amount of co-operation

[8] See above, ch. 2.
[9] On single-interest linkages as contrasted with multiplex relationships, see Gluckman, *The Judicial Process among the Barotse*, pp. 18–19.

and assistance which they often received from other inhabitants, but also to the resistance and pressures which they sometimes faced and to the kinds of local sanctions imposed on them. Evidence will be presented which suggests that constables' conduct on some occasions can be explained by their local loyalties or obligations or their response to village pressures.

1. CONSTABLES AND THEIR SUPERIORS: THE EFFECT OF PRESSURES FROM ABOVE

Higher officials had at their disposal various means of trying to keep constables up to the mark. Attention has been drawn to the fact that the precepts sent to such officers sometimes warned them of the punishments that awaited their failings and chastised them for their negligence.[10] It has been shown that on some occasions officers were summoned to appear before higher officials, and sometimes even the Privy Council, to answer for their neglect, while in other instances they were formally indicted in the courts; and many of those found wanting were fined or imprisoned.[11] Their military superiors threatened constables that if they were remiss in pressing soldiers, they themselves would be pressed for service, and sometimes this penalty was imposed on them.[12] The fact that higher officials had various ways of bringing pressure to bear on constables, and that they regularly did punish some officers for their failings, did not necessarily mean that they were always vigorous in their oversight of the work of the constabulary. Keith Wrightson seems to be correct in suggesting that throughout the early seventeenth century the central government was penetrating more deeply into the localities, and that local officers were under greater pressures from above. In general terms this does help to account for the diligence which constables often seem to have displayed in trying to meet the demands that were placed on them.[13] However, there were variations in the pressures exerted from above, and the extent to which their superiors could and did provide close supervision of constables affected their performance in office.

The relative vigour of the justices in overseeing the work of constables seems to have differed from county to county and over time,

---

[10] See above, ch. 5, nn. 27–9, 47, 66. [11] See above, chs. 5–6.
[12] See above, ch. 5, nn. 143–4, 146.
[13] Wrightson, 'Two concepts of order', p. 33; *English Society*, pp. 151–5.

and some variations in the conduct of such officers probably can be explained by this fact. When the magistrates in the North Riding of Yorkshire in 1612 did not even know the number of constabularies within their jurisdiction, let alone the names of the constables who served them, it appears doubtful whether they provided very close supervision of such officers.[14] In view of the justices' ignorance it is perhaps not surprising that townships in this county so often seem to have failed to select constables.[15] It also seems unlikely that these officers, at least in 1612, were subjected to very much magisterial pressure to comply with an order requiring them to make presentments on specific articles to the high constable before each of the quarter sessions.[16] In contrast to the situation in the North Riding in 1612, the justices of some counties at certain periods seem to have brought considerable pressure to bear on constables to submit such returns, and their vigilance seems to have made a marked difference in the performance of these officers. Historians of Essex have commented on the extent to which the increased vigour of the justices in the period 1629–31 affected the conduct of petty officers in that shire.[17] Keith Wrightson attributes the growth in regulative prosecutions during these years to new initiatives taken by the magistrates to foster greater efficiency in local officers. Not only did the justices require constables to make written returns to a specific list of articles of inquiry, and regularly prosecute those who were negligent in doing so, but they also provided closer oversight of the selection of such officers. They sent out orders for the appointment of sufficient constables and replaced those they deemed incompetent. Wrightson suggests that magisterial pressures brought to bear on constables in Essex during these few years resulted in 'spectacular' improvements in their diligence and efficiency in returning offenders.

Historians are not agreed as to whether the Book of Orders wrought any significant reinvigoration of local government during the 1630s.[18] However, in some counties the justices do appear to have displayed

---

[14] Atkinson, ed., *Sessions Records*, i. 256.   [15] See above, ch. 3, n. 50.

[16] Atkinson, ed., *Sessions Records*, i. 118.

[17] John Walter and Keith Wrightson, 'Dearth and the Social Order in Early Modern England', *P and P*, lxxi (1976), esp. 37–8; Wrightson, 'Two concepts of order', pp. 37–9; Quintrell, 'The Government of the County of Essex', p. 78.

[18] e.g. Barnes, *Somerset*, ch. 7; Owen, 'Norfolk, 1620–41', ch. 6; Morrill, *Cheshire*, p. 26; Quintrell, 'The Government of the County of Essex', esp. pp. 61–2; Fletcher, *Sussex*, esp. pp. 224–5; Clark, *English Provincial Society*, pp. 350–3; Holmes, *Seventeenth-Century Lincolnshire*, pp. 109–12.

increased vigilance in supervising the work of the constabulary, with effects on constables' conduct that were similar to, though perhaps not as great as, those in Essex in 1629–31. T. G. Barnes, who claims success for the government's programme in Somerset, suggests that the justices there used their monthly meetings to supervise more closely the work of inferior officials and to punish those who were negligent, and he comments that 'so long as the justices were zealous, the subordinate officers could not be otherwise'.[19] The apparent increase during the 1630s in counties other than Somerset in constables' diligence in punishing vagrants seems to be explained largely by the increased pressures which justices brought to bear on such officers at their monthly meetings. The fact that negligent constables were more regularly fined for their failures to apprehend rogues seems to have proven effective in spurring them to greater activity in this area of their duties.[20] During 1631, in their initial response to the Book of Orders, there are also indications that the magistrates of some divisions in some of the counties examined, particularly in Worcestershire, may have elicited the return of larger numbers of offenders as a result of the pressures they brought to bear on constables.[21] However, on the basis of their reports it would not appear that most of these magistrates kept up their vigilance after an initial flurry of activity. In Worcestershire the presentments which constables made to quarter sessions in the years 1634–7 do not suggest unusual diligence in returning offenders.[22]

Of the counties examined here only in Hertfordshire is there evidence of more thorough and more sustained supervision by the justices. Julie Calnan has directed attention to the general diligence of the Hertfordshire Bench in the period 1580–1620,[23] and during the 1630s the magistrates of most of the divisions in that county appear to have been particularly vigorous in their efforts to implement the Book of Orders and to instil greater diligence in their subordinates. The returns submitted from that shire would suggest that their actions did

[19] Barnes, *Somerset*, p. 184.
[20] See above, ch. 6; see also Silcock, 'County Government in Worcestershire', pp. 79–80.
[21] See above, ch. 6, n. 57; and Silcock, 'County Government in Worcestershire', p. 110, who also mentions the 'surprisingly high' total of fines levied in Halfshire hundred in 1631.
[22] See above, ch. 6, n. 56.
[23] Calnan, 'County Society and Local Government in the County of Hertford', esp. pp. 82, 165, 167, 290, 311–12.

have an impact on the conduct of petty constables and other local officers, though perhaps not to the same extent as in Essex in 1629–31.[24] In a report from Broadwater hundred in 1637 the justices of that division, John Boteler and William Lytton, contended that 'through our pressing them forward', the officers of every parish in the division were responding to all the orders and articles directed to them.[25] Similar pressures on local officers seem to have been applied by the magistrates of other divisions too. Not only did the Hertfordshire justices, like those in Essex, apparently require written presentments on a specific list of articles, but they too attempted to improve the quality of the constabulary by removing officers whom they deemed insufficient and replacing them.[26] The detailed constables' presentments which were sometimes included with the reports which they submitted to the Council or the judges of assize would suggest that the justices' actions did have a positive effect on the performance of officers in this county. However, in terms of an increase in regulative prosecutions they may not have achieved results as great as those of the Essex justices in 1629–31.

Returns from the liberty of St. Albans illustrate both the careful attention to their duties of some Hertfordshire justices and the detailed responses which their pressures elicited from inferior officers, although at the same time revealing that some constables none the less remained negligent in submitting returns. For example, the report by Robert Berkeley, William Grigg, and William Lemon of a monthly meeting held in February 1637, which includes presentments made by the townships, reveals that constables, churchwardens, and overseers submitted detailed returns to the justices on sixteen articles, although it must be admitted that they did not present many offenders at this particular meeting. When offences were reported the justices noted on the document the action to be taken in each case, and those against whom warrants were to be issued. They also recorded that both constables of East Barnet, and also the churchwardens and overseers of that township, had returned no presentments, and a warrant was to be issued against them to answer for their contempt at the next monthly meeting. The presentment made by Thomas Luke, constable of Elstree, was annotated with the comment 'a pore man — unfitt for the service'. A note was added that the steward of the leet was 'to be told of thinsufficiency of Luke', and that John Oxton alias Foxe, 'a fitt

---

[24] See above, ch. 6.   [25] PRO, SP 16/351/113.
[26] See above, ch. 3, n. 48.

man to be constable' was to be chosen at the next leet, after Easter.[27]

There are also indications that constables' performance of their military duties was sometimes affected by increased pressures from their superiors. While it has been suggested that many constables regularly gave attention to the maintenance of the communal arms,[28] most of the purchases of new armour occurred during periods when the Privy Council was particularly concerned about defence, and when directives were issued to the Lords Lieutenant ordering them to assure that the armour was up to standard and that musters were held regularly. The late 1580s, the later 1590s, and the years 1613–17, when the government feared Spanish invasion, the later 1620s, when Charles I was trying to create a 'perfect militia' and when England was engaged in the Thirty Years War, and the later 1630s, when the country was at war with the Scots, were all periods when the central government displayed particular concern about the country's military preparedness.[29] These were also the years when constables' accounts reveal that they were engaged in major purchases of new armour.[30] It seems probable that increased diligence by higher officials, particularly the deputy lieutenants, in mustering the bands and inspecting the armour did place villagers and their constables under greater pressure to remedy inadequacies in their equipment, and helps to account for their expenditures on arms at such times.

As important as was the oversight of the justices or the deputy lieutenants in influencing constables' conduct, it was not only officials at the county level whose actions had a bearing on the performance of village and parish officers. Much of the practical work of trying to assure their co-operation, whether in returning presentments, collecting taxes, or fulfilling their military duties, rested on the shoulders of high constables. They were responsible for transmitting orders to officers at the village level, and in many cases they were also charged with receiving the revenues and the presentments which had been demanded from the local officers.[31] While it is not possible to learn

[27] PRO, SP 16/347/67; also see SP 16/344/30; 418/21.
[28] See above, ch. 5.
[29] Boynton, *The Elizabethan Militia*, esp. pp. 169, 192, 195, 198, 210–19, 245; and for some of the state's orders concerning musters and equipment during those periods of the early seventeenth century, see PRO, SP 14/72/20; 86/159; 121/94; SP 16/13/43–9; 18/55; 31/34; 287/55; 365/90; 404/138; 455/19.
[30] See above, ch. 5, nn. 110–16.
[31] Precepts normally were sent by the high constables; see, for example, those sent to constables of Salwarpe, HWRO, 850 SALWARPE, BA 1054/1, Bundle A. Constables' accounts also provide evidence that county rates were paid to the high constable, as was

much about these intermediate officers, the extent to which they performed their duties probably had almost as great an influence on constables as the actions of higher officials.

Occasionally constables defended themselves against charges of negligence by claiming that they had received no order or precept to perform a task, and sometimes the delinquency of a high constable probably does explain the defaults of the petty officers. When one Staffordshire constable was bound over to assizes by the justices in 1626 for not making presentments, it apparently was discovered that the high constable had not given him notice to do so.[32] Ten Staffordshire constables who were indicted in 1603 for not punishing rogues claimed that they had done so, and professed ignorance that they were to certify this fact every month. Perhaps they had received no instruction from the high constable to make such returns.[33] When constables of a whole hundred were in arrears for a tax or rate,[34] it seems likely that the fault often lay with the high constable. In one such instance, when all of the officers of the hundred of Offlow, Staffordshire, had failed to pay a bridge rate in 1638, the justices returned the names of the high constables as well as the petty constables to the judges of assize.[35]

Defaults in the collection of ship-money sometimes were blamed directly on the negligence of high constables. While sheriffs' complaints about these officers may occasionally have been unjustified, the laxity of some of them in demanding assessments or the money itself from petty constables probably does help to account for their tardiness or failings. The sheriff of Leicestershire in 1637 attributed some of his difficulties in gathering the levy to the negligence of high constables. An officer of Guthlaxton hundred apparently refused to obey warrants to draw up assessments if the petty constables failed to do so, while a high constable of Sparkenhoe was charged with refusing to collect the money. In April 1637 the high constables of one division in that county were summoned to answer before the Council for their neglect.[36] A number of such officers in Norfolk were also charged with negligence in 1638 and the sheriff, Sir John Buxton, urged that some of them be summoned before the Council as an example to others. In

---

ship-money; and in some areas presentments for sessions and assizes also were delivered to them.

[32] Staffs. RO, QS/O, iii. 9–9^v.   [33] Burne, ed., *Staffs. Sessions Rolls*, v. 46–7.
[34] See above, ch. 5, nn. 40–4.   [35] Staffs. RO, QS/O, iv. 259.
[36] PRO, SP 16/346/109; 351/91; 354/144.

the case of the high constables of Blofield hundred, with whom he carried on a running battle during most of his year in office, he specifically accused them of being delinquent in calling upon the petty constables to demand or gather the ship-moeny.[37] Four high constables in Worcestershire in 1640 were charged with refusing to account for ship-money,[38] while there were complaints from Staffordshire too about the negligence of some of these officers. The sheriff in 1637 attributed his problems in securing the return of local rating lists to the delinquency of high constables, and he reported that he had threatened them that they would answer for their contempt at the council table. John Cocks, high constable of Seisdon, was accused of not bringing in any assessments or paying any money; and, if he was negligent in his duties, the constables of Pattingham and other townships in that hundred were probably not under much pressure to fulfil their duties.[39] The apparent faults of some high constables in the assessment and collection of ship-money, and the negative effect this probably had on the conduct of petty constables, can be contrasted with the seeming diligence of Gilbert Kimberley, high constable of Halfshire hundred, Worcestershire, whose actions can have left constables in his division in little doubt about their obligations to assess and collect ship-money. His persistence in trying to gather the levy is reflected in the number of warrants which he sent to Robert Ellis, constable of Salwarpe in 1640, and probably to other officers in that division as well. Even if these constables, like Ellis, were slow to respond, such consistent pressures do seem to have extracted the money in the long run.[40]

Although the extent of the pressures applied by their superiors, whether justices, deputy lieutenants, or high constables, could make a difference in the performance of constables, there sometimes were limitations on the ability of higher officials to exact obedience from such officers. This fact is well illustrated by the difficulties experienced by a number of sheriffs in dealing with constables who were negligent in collecting ship-money. While they sometimes may have been offering excuses for their own delinquency, there is a ring of truth to their cries of helplessness, and to their claims that the punishment of negligent officers merely compounded their difficulties while often having no effect on such officers. Several sheriffs claimed that they

[37] PRO, SP 16/389/9, 21; 397/46; 400/14, 55, 110.
[38] PRO, SP 16/455/127.
[39] PRO, SP 16/346/108; 349/88.   [40] See above, ch. 5, n. 47.

could have accused all the constables of negligence, and penalized them for their failures; but they pointed out the negative effects of doing so, and expressed the hope that, if they made an example of a few, others might be reformed. They claimed that they were dependent upon these local officers both in assessing the levy and identifying the lands and cattle of those from whom the money had to be gathered by distraint, and in such circumstances it was counter-productive to detain constables for their failure to return assessments or make payments.[41] In any case, not even a spell in prison was effective in reforming such officers, according to the sheriff of Worcestershire in 1640, while the sheriff of Staffordshire in the same year also vouched for the fact that constables, once released, soon forgot their promises to collect the levy.[42] Moreover, some sheriffs pointed out that if they attached constables for their failure to pay ship-money, other services would be neglected. In the spring and summer of 1640, when they were meeting with the greatest difficulty in getting constables to collect the levy, the chief service they had in mind was the provision of troops, horses, and money for the war against the Scots. As the sheriff of Norfolk pointed out, if he committed constables for their negligence in paying ship-money the country would be deprived of 'their attendance on other services and dutyes in their places, specially in matters of armes at this present'.[43] The sheriff of Worcestershire reported that he had released the constables whom he had imprisoned because of 'this great service concerninge the soldiers'.[44]

It must often have proven equally difficult for deputy lieutenants to implement their threats to impress for military service constables who had been negligent in returning able soldiers. If the officers who were pressed were quickly released, as sometimes claimed,[45] it was probably in part because the enforcement of such a penalty proved disruptive to the conduct of local government.

Clear and explicit evidence concerning constables' responses to pressures from higher officials is difficult to find. Nevertheless, in some instances, particular zeal by their superiors seems to have had an effect on constables' actions. Their diligence in punishing vagrants during the 1630s, and in certain areas in the return of presentments to monthly meetings, as well as their attention to the communal armour

---

[41] PRO, SP 16/457/22; 467/58; 456/21; 346/108; 455/85.
[42] PRO, SP 16/457/22; 452/10.   [43] PRO, SP 16/456/21.
[44] PRO, SP 16/457/22.   [45] See above, ch. 5, n. 143.

during periods when the government was especially concerned about the defence of the realm, appear to be responses to greater pressures from above. As Keith Wrightson points out in his discussion of the activities of the Essex magistrates, however, such initiatives by higher authorities 'required an enormous and exhausting effort and placed a considerable strain upon the machinery of local administration', and they could be maintained with full rigour only for brief periods.[46] Moreover, there were limitations on the ability of such officials to influence the conduct of their subordinates, particularly in certain of their duties. Sheriffs, and the high constables and bailiffs who served them, clearly were not always forceful in trying to keep constables up to the mark in collecting ship-money. However, what could they do when they called these officers on the carpet for their failures, and imprisoned those who were still recalcitrant, only to discover that they were unreformed? What recourse did they have when such officers made no attempt to procure their freedom, and were content to remain in gaol, according to the sheriff of Worcestershire in 1640, in order 'to avoid all other services'?[47] In their attempts to bring pressure to bear on constables higher officials also had to contend with the counter-pressures that sometimes were exerted on such officers by their fellow inhabitants, and with their local obligations and loyalties.

II. CONTABLES AND LOCAL COMMUNITIES: SUPPORT VS. SANCTIONS

In many cases the local pressures exerted on constables were probably greater than those which they experienced from their superiors. Several historians have drawn attention to the responses which constables encountered in trying to fulfil their duties, and to the informal local sanctions imposed on them. However, there is some disagreement among them about the extent of the obstruction and defiance met by such officials. Both Eleanor Trotter and Anthony Fletcher suggest that constables usually seem to have been obeyed.[48]

---

[46] Wrightson, 'Two concepts of order', p. 39.

[47] PRO, SP 16/457/22; also see Silcock, 'County Government in Worcestershire', p. 68, who also suggests that the collection of ship-money revealed the extent to which county government was dependent upon the co-operation of the parish officials.

[48] Trotter, *Seventeenth Century Life*, p. 91; Fletcher, *Sussex*, pp. 226–7; also see Sharpe, 'Crime and Delinquency in an Essex Parish', p. 103, who claims that cases of opposition to authority were not 'very common', though he suggests that 'parish officers can never have operated entirely free from fear of violence or the threat of obstruction'.

On the other hand, Mildred Campbell, William Willcox, and T. G. Barnes, as well as Keith Wrightson, lay greater stress on the physical danger, the ridicule, and the malicious actions to which such officers were subjected.[49] Willcox recognizes that constables were heavily dependent upon their neighbours for assistance, and he contends that they were often obstructed in their duties because these villagers proved uncooperative and unreliable.[50] Wrightson also draws attention to more subtle influences on constables, deriving from local conceptions of order which were sometimes at odds with the laws of the land and the expectations of higher officials. However, he suggests that by the seventeenth century many of the 'village notables' who held local office had assimilated the attitudes and values of their superiors.[51]

It is difficult to measure how often constables were subjected to such local pressures. However, if the number of cases found in court records provides an accurate indication of the extent of the obstruction which they encountered, it does not seem to have been very widespread. One of the most striking facts about the constableship was the amount of co-operation and assistance from their fellow inhabitants which such officers often managed to procure, and it will be argued that this, as much as their own diligence, helps to account for constables' successes in fulfilling many of their duties. Nevertheless, on some occasions they did meet with resistance and abuse and other kinds of local influences were brought to bear on them. In a number of instances constables' conduct seems to be explained by the fact that they were responding to such local pressures or acting out of concern for local interests.

(1) Local Co-operation and Assistance

Willcox is correct to draw attention to constables' dependence upon their neighbours for assistance in fulfilling their duties. Despite the existence in some villages of tithingmen or thirdboroughs who were their official aides,[52] the help of other villagers was extremely important. It is almost inconceivable that unpaid local men, who were obliged to earn their own livelihoods while holding the office, could

---

[49] Campbell, *The English Yeoman*, pp. 321–3; Willcox, *Gloucestershire*, pp. 52–5; Barnes, *Somerset*, p. 77; Wrightson, 'Two concepts of order', pp. 29, 30–1; also see Silcock, 'County Government in Worcestershire', p. 65, and King, 'Vagrancy and Local Law Enforcement', 270.

[50] Willcox, *Gloucestershire*, pp. 53–5.

[51] Wrightson, 'Two concepts of order'; *English Society*, pp. 155–9, 166–71.

[52] See above, ch. 1, n. 58.

have met the many demands of the constableship without some help
from their fellow villagers. However, it is also important to recall that
such assistance was formally necessary in assessing taxes and rates,
while in their police duties too constables were legally entitled to call
upon other inhabitants for aid.[53] Although there is evidence that they
were sometimes denied the help they needed, and that this could
constitute a rather effective kind of local sanction on such officers,[54]
many of them received a good deal of aid in performing their duties.
Admittedly, they often paid small sums to those who assisted them, as
well as covering their expenses, but even when this fact is taken into
account the time and labour which other inhabitants gave in aiding
such officers is none the less impressive. It seems evident that the
success of constables in executing many of their duties was due in no
small part to the active participation of other inhabitants in the work of
the office.

Although court records contain occasional cases in which constables
claimed that they had been denied the help to which they were entitled
in carrying out their police duties,[55] constables' accounts indicate that
some officers at least received a good deal of local assistance in
fulfilling such responsibilities. In Pattingham, for example, no less than
57 villagers assisted constables in apprehending, guarding, and
conveying before a justice or to gaol about 116 suspects mentioned in
their accounts.[56] The Melton Mowbray records for eight years during
the early seventeenth century show that at least 60 inhabitants assisted
the officers of that township with some 58 prisoners.[57] In these
communities, and others too, villagers sometimes also helped constables
to whip vagrants, to make passes for them, and to deliver them to the
next constable or occasionally to the House of Correction.[58] They
received assistance too in dealing with the larger numbers of poor
wanderers who were not punished, but who had to be moved along to
the next village; and in the case of disabled migrants other inhabitants

[53] See above, ch. 2.
[54] See below, nn. 105–11, 184–7.
[55] See below, nn. 184–7.
[56] These figures were compiled from the Pattingham Constables' Accounts,
1582–1640.
[57] These figures were compiled from the accounts in Leics. RO, DG 25/39/1/1–4;
DG 36/186–9. On the role of private individuals in capturing suspects see Herrup,
'New Shoes and Mutton Pies', esp. 814–20.
[58] e.g. Leics. RO, DG 25/39/1/2; DE 625/60, ff. 44, 44ᵛ, 45ᵛ, 46ᵛ, 49ᵛ, 50, 52; DE
720/30, ff. 20ᵛ, 23, 44. In this and the following notes examples are given and reference
is not provided to every relevant entry in all of the constables' accounts examined.

sometimes helped in transporting them to the parish line.[59] Occasionally during a constable's absence from the community another villager gave alms to poor travellers, and later was reimbursed for his expenses.[60] Others were involved in law enforcement in a more indirect fashion. In return for small payments they supplied the carts or horses which constables sometimes had to hire to transport prisoners or poor migrants; they provided food and lodging for prisoners who were kept overnight, and sometimes for poor wanderers as well; and they supplied sustenance and candles and sometimes fire to the watchmen who guarded such prisoners.[61]

In fulfilling the judicial and administrative tasks which required them to appear before higher officials, constables also received assistance from their neighbours. Sometimes their accounts show that another villager accompanied them before the justices or the high constable to make presentments,[62] and in some instances another inhabitant appeared before higher officials in their place.[63] Literate residents contributed their skills by penning the documents which constables were required to produce on such occasions.[64] Other inhabitants sometimes accompanied constables when they were required to appear before the justices for the licensing of ale-keepers, or the Lenten recognizances of butchers and ale-keepers, or with the overseers of the poor,[65] and they regularly accompanied such officers in their yearly appearances before the clerk of the market with the township's weights and measures.[66]

As tax-collectors constables also received a large amount of

[59] e.g. Leics. RO, DE 625/60, ff. 20, 24ᵛ; DE 720/30, fo. 26; DG 36/188; HWRO, 850 SALWARPE, BA 1054/2, Bundle D, no. 9; Pattingham Constables' Accounts, 1630/31 (4).
[60] e.g. Leics. RO, DE 625/60, ff. 12, 12ᵛ, 14, 14ᵛ, 15, 20, 23ᵛ, 24ᵛ, 25, 25ᵛ, 26; DE 720/30, fo. 32; NNRO, PD 358/33, 1622, 1637–8; Pattingham Constables' Accounts, 1614–15.
[61] e.g. Leics. RO, DE 625/60, ff. 23, 24ᵛ, 44, 44ᵛ, 45ᵛ, 54ᵛ, 55, 55ᵛ, 56ᵛ; DE 720/30, fo. 16ᵛ; DG 36/188; NNRO, PD 50/36L, no. 47; Pattingham Constables' Accounts, 1628–9, 1630–1, 1632–3, 1635–6, 1638–9.
[62] e.g. Pattingham Constables' Accounts, 1583–4, 1584–5, 1587–8, 1615–16, 1625–6; Leics. RO, DE 625/60, ff. 39, 39ᵛ, 50, 51ᵛ, 53; DE 720/30, ff. 2ᵛ, 11ᵛ.
[63] e.g. Leics. RO, DE 625/60, ff. 15, 16ᵛ, 22ᵛ; DE 720/30, ff. 36, 41, 42ᵛ.
[64] e.g. Leics. RO, DE 625/60, ff. 3, 12, 15ᵛ, 21, 27; DE 720/30, fo. 27; Pattingham Constables' Accounts, 1613–14.
[65] e.g. Pattingham Constables' Accounts, 1595–6, 1598–9, 1604–5, 1607–8, 1624–5; Leics. RO, DE 625/60, ff. 22ᵛ, 38ᵛ; DE 720/30, fo. 7.
[66] Constables' accounts regularly show other inhabitants appearing with the constable before the clerk; see especially the Pattingham Constables' Accounts for entries of this kind.

assistance from their neighbours during most of the period 1580 to 1642. Other inhabitants regularly accompanied them before higher officials to serve as assessors for subsidies, benevolences, and loans, and to represent the local community in giving their consent to county rates for the repair of bridges.[67] Another villager sometimes joined them in delivering payments to higher officials, and occasionally did so in the constable's place.[68] Villagers usually co-operated in acting as assessors to draw up local rating lists, though in the later 1630s they sometimes refused to do so,[69] and the signatures and marks of such men are found on surviving tax lists.[70] Sometimes they were also involved in such tasks as taking polls of sheep, in preparation for drawing up local assessments, and in helping to collect such levies.[71]

Constables in some villages and at some periods received a very considerable amount of assistance in meeting the collective obligations imposed on local communities for provision and carriage for the royal household, and in responding to the demands of saltpetre men and postmasters. Although they paid for the goods and services they received on such occasions, this did not negate the fact that such demands could be burdensome, nor did it eliminate the need for the constable to secure the co-operation of other villagers. Despite payment men cannot always have been eager to accompany a cart of provisions half a day's journey from home, or to fetch ashes or coals for the saltpetre man, or to hire out their carts, or to allow their horses to go post. Waltham was one of the villages most affected by such demands, and the constables' accounts show many inhabitants engaged in assisting officers with these duties, in return for small payments. They threshed and tied straw for the king's provision, supplied hay, oats, capons, and hens for the king and coals for the postmaster. They hired their carts to the constable to carry royal provisions or to remove the king to Newark or to fetch coals from

---

[67] Entries concerning the appearance of other villagers as assessors regularly occur in all of the detailed accounts examined; for the presence of other villagers to consent to bridge levies, see, for example, Pattingham Constables' Accounts, 1607–8, 1608–9, 1610–11.

[68] e.g. Pattingham Constables' Accounts 1582–3, 1584–5, 1592–3, 1607–8, 1621–2, 1625–6; Leics. RO, DE 625/60, fo. 2ᵛ; DE 720/30, ff. 24ᵛ, 48.

[69] See below, nn. 105–11.

[70] e.g. the local rating lists for Bushey and Little Munden in Herts. RO, D/P26/10/1; D/P71/5/2; and assessments for lewnes found amoung the Pattingham Constables' Accounts.

[71] e.g. Leics. RO, DE 720/30, fo. 45ᵛ; BL Add. MS 10457, ff. 2, 5ᵛ, 28ᵛ, 41ᵛ, 52ᵛ, which suggest that others assisted the constable.

Grantham for the saltpetre man. In return for the standard post fees they allowed the constable to take their horses to meet the demands of the postmaster in Witham. Others, who must often have been obliged to leave their own tasks in order to aid an officer, carried hay and straw to Belvoir for the king, coals to Witham for the postmaster, ashes to Leicester for the saltpetre man, or saltpetre and the tubs to Melton or Thorpe; and they assisted constables in such tasks as taking hens and capons to Leicester, in fetching ashes from Grantham, and in transporting provisions from Nottingham to Leicester and the king's hounds to Harby.[72]

Other residents also aided constables in their military duties. Villagers were not only paid for storing and cleaning the armour,[73] or for miscellaneous repairs to various pieces of equipment; but some of them also assisted in transporting the equipment to musters, and others seem to have received only their expenses when they accompanied the constable and the soldiers to trainings of the bands.[74] Inhabitants were called into service too when constables were required to press soldiers. The accounts of some officers record payments to villagers to help them in 'taking up' men for service, to guard the soldiers and to assist in conveying them to their captains or the point of rendezvous.[75]

In addition to the armour, there was other village equipment to be kept in repair, particularly in communities where constables had agricultural responsibilities.[76] In these tasks too officers received a good deal of assistance from their neighbours, assistance recorded in their accounts because they did pay for it. Some inhabitants were engaged in the seemingly endless repairs that were necessary to maintain such local instruments of justice as the stocks, the cage, the whipping-post, the pillory, and the cuckstool, and, in Manchester, the dungeon.[77] Others helped in the maintenance of the shooting butts, or

---

[72] Entries of this kind occur with some regularity in the Waltham accounts, Leics. RO, DE 625/60; see especially the accounts for 1614–21 and for the later 1630s.

[73] See above, ch. 5, nn. 119–24.

[74] The Pattingham accounts record regular payments for carrying the armour to musters, and the accounts for 1588–9, 1602–3, and 1620–1 name the villager who performed the task; also see Leics. RO, DE 625/60, ff. 12ᵛ, 26, 58ᵛ, 61ᵛ, 65; DE 720/30, ff. 51, 52; and for explicit reference to men accompanying constables to musters see Pattingham Constables' Accounts, 1601–2; Leics. RO, DE 625/60, fo. 61.

[75] e.g. Earwaker, ed., *Constables' Accounts*, i. 144, 145; Pattingham Constables' Accounts, 1598–9, 1638–9; Leics. RO, DE 625/60, ff. 58ᵛ, 61.

[76] On these duties, see above, ch. 2.

[77] Such entries are found regularly in constables' accounts; see especially those of

provided the sods or stones that were necessary for their construction.[78] In villages such as Branston, Waltham, and Wymeswold constables' accounts also contain numerous entries showing the aid which they received in the repair of gates, sheep dams, weirs, dykes, hedges, and pinfolds, as well as in the eradication of vermin.[79]

The records of some townships would thus suggest that it was not only constables themselves who gave their time and labour in order to fulfil the demands which the state placed on local communities. Although it will be shown that both individuals and groups of inhabitants occasionally proved uncooperative, defying constables and refusing them assistance, in many instances villagers gave them their support. Other inhabitants, many of whom had held or would hold the constableship, contributed time and labour, either freely or in return for small payments, to help constables in fulfilling responsibilities which continued to be partially communal in nature, and many of which could not have been fully carried out without such local aid. While the diligence of constables themselves merits full recognition, without the assistance of their fellow villagers it is unlikely that they could have achieved the degree of effectiveness to which their accounts often bear testimony.

(2) Local Pressures and Local Loyalties

While constables frequently seem to have commanded support and co-operation, on some occasions they were subjected to local pressures in the course of trying to fulfil their duties. Sometimes they met with disobedience and resistance; they were subjected to insults and ridicule or even to physical violence, and some of them were warned that they would regret their actions. Not all such threats were idle ones because men sometimes did seek retaliation against constables for official actions which they had taken. On some occasions constables also met with refusal when they called upon other inhabitants to render the assistance to which they were entitled, and this constituted another kind of sanction imposed on them. Pressures of a more subtle nature, verbal persuasions by other inhabitants or informal discussions within

Manchester where they are particularly frequent, Earwaker, ed., *Constables' Accounts*, i and ii.

[78] Such entries occur frequently in constables' accounts; see especially Earwaker, ed., *Constables' Accounts*, i and ii; and for other examples see Pattingham Constables' Accounts, 1596–7, 1635–6; Leics. RO, DE 720/30, fo. 34^v.

[79] See Leics. RO, DE 625/60; DE 720/30; BL Add. MS 10457.

the village, leave less mark on the records, but there is a good deal of indirect evidence to suggest that local influences of this kind were at work and were perhaps even more important than overt resistance or obstruction in shaping constables' conduct. The failings which they displayed sometimes are explained by the fact that they responded to such local pressures, or acted out of concern for village interests. However, it is not sufficient to label them as 'timorous' and 'powerless', nor to describe their conduct as 'disobedient' and 'negligent'.[80] Constables sometimes did fail to perform a duty because they were intimidated by the resistance which they encountered, or feared that they might encounter. However, their behaviour also reflects their local loyalties, and the fact that they shared village attitudes and interests which sometimes conflicted with the demands of the state and with their duties as royal officers.

(a) *Local Resistance to Ship-Money, Military Levies, and Burdens in Kind*

During most of the period 1580 to 1642 constables do not appear to have met with widespread resistance to their demands as tax-collectors, although this is not to imply that they had an easy time in gathering the taxes and rates for which they were responsible. On many occasions some inhabitants were in arrears for a levy,[81] and officers were sometimes obliged to gather such sums by distraint or to appeal to the justices for an order requiring inhabitants to make payment.[82] Occasionally they met with verbal abuse or violence in their attempts to collect taxes. A Yorkshire constable claimed to have been stabbed in the back while trying to gather a rate for victims of plague, while a Glamorganshire officer was apparently assaulted and wounded while he was trying to collect the subsidy.[83] Rates for the muster master

---

[80] Barnes, *Somerset*, p. 77.

[81] e.g. Pattingham Constables' Accounts, 1584–5, 1587–8, 1592–3, 1594–5, 1602–3, 1610–11, 1611–12; NNRO, PD 358/33, 1616, 1621, 1622; PD 50/36L, nos. 53, 101; HWRO, 850 SALWARPE BA 1054/2, Bundle D, no. 2; Earwaker, ed., *Constables' Accounts*, i. 37, 38, 101–3, 198, 229, 234–7; ii. 23, 79, 96, 163–5; Leics. RO, DG 25/39/1/1; also see above, ch. 5, nn. 88–93. The evidence presented by King, 'Vagrancy and Local Law Enforcement, 271, would suggest that the numbers in arrears may have been larger in the 1640s and 1650s.

[82] e.g. Earwaker, ed., *Constables' Accounts*, i. 38, 51, 82, 93, 106, 107, 129, 194; ii. 13–14, 29, 30; Bund, ed., *Sessions Papers*, pp. 336–7, 607, 608; Staffs. RO, Transcripts Sessions Rolls, Jac. I, Roll 35, nos. 38–9; QS/O, ii. 50ᵛ, 63, 81–2; iii. 19–19ᵛ, 36ᵛ, 39, 56ᵛ, 85, 117–117ᵛ, 132, 155ᵛ; iv. 24, 56, 100–100ᵛ, 143ᵛ, 196, 231, 234; v. 97, 139; Herts. RO, QS/B, 2A, ff. 49–49ᵛ, 87–87ᵛ, 90ᵛ, 91, 100–100ᵛ, 109ᵛ–110, 112, 165ᵛ; 2B, ff. 13, 14.

[83] PRO, STAC 8/192/8; 149/19; also see Atkinson, ed., *Sessions Records*, i. 244; iii. 342.

sometimes seem to have been unpopular, and some constables met with open defiance and abuse in trying to collect this levy.[84] There are occasional cases in which officers who had distrained for the subsidy were subjected to vexatious legal suits as a result of their actions. In a case brought against a Lincolnshire constable by a husbandman from whom he had distrained two oxen, it was alleged that the plaintiff, on hearing that the officer had spent £8 in defending himself against the suits in Common Pleas and the Exchequer, had said 'Lett him provide eight pounds more against the next term.'[85] The resistance offered by a few individuals, and sometimes the tardiness of larger numbers in paying a tax or rate, was probably often due to poverty or lack of ready cash, and in other cases to an inhabitant's belief that his assessment was unfair or even to resentment that a fellow villager had the right to make such demands. However, such disobedience does not seem to have constituted fundamental opposition to the taxes being imposed, nor do constables seem to have faced general local pressures which conflicted with their official duties as tax-collectors.

Although constables probably did encounter somewhat greater difficulties than usual, at least in some counties, in trying to collect the benevolence of 1622[86] and the forced loan of 1627,[87] it was only during the 1630s that they seem to have met with widespread disobedience, and even violence, in their attempts to gather taxes. A Waltham officer in 1633 was obliged to procure a warrant against some in that village who refused to pay their levies for the repair of St. Paul's, and other constables too may have encountered resistance in collecting this tax.[88]

[84] Calnan, 'County Society and Local Government in the County of Hertford', pp. 303–4; Owen, 'Norfolk, 1620–1641', p. 87; Willcox, *Gloucestershire*, pp. 82–3; Fletcher, *Sussex*, p. 186; Boynton, *The Elizabethan Militia*, pp. 179–80, 224–5; Silcock, 'County Government in Worcestershire', pp. 159–60; PRO, SP 14/97/104; SP 16/214/100; 247/26.

[85] PRO, E 133/8/1236; also see E 133/10/1466.

[86] For evidence of difficulties in collecting this levy see PRO, SP 14/130/34, 41, 48, 80, 81; 132/70.

[87] For evidence of inhabitants' failure to pay the forced loan in some of the villages considered here see PRO, SP 16/44/11; 58/11; 75/51; 76/24; HWRO, 850 SALWARPE, BA 1054/1, Bundle A, nos. 273, 183, 65. For other complaints about difficulties in collecting the loan in Staffordshire, Worcestershire, Leicestershire, Hertfordshire, and Norfolk see PRO, SP 16/33/8; 34/4, 23; 35/46; 36/41; 44/12; 49/76; 51/1; 52/70, 71; 53/33; 58/96; 59/48; 60/65; 65/77; 70/73, 80; 71/13, 49, 61, 62; 72/46; 73/31, 35; 74/58; 75/33, 62, 94; 76/24, 25; 77/3, 33; 79/70, 84; 89/5. On opposition to the loan also see Barnes, *Somerset*, pp. 165–8; Holmes, *Seventeenth-Century Lincolnshire*, pp. 105–7; Hunt, *The Puritan Moment*, p. 195; Clark, *English Provincial Society*, pp. 345–6; Conrad Russell, *Parliaments and English Politics 1621–1629* (Oxford, 1979), pp. 331–5.

[88] Leics. RO, DE 625/60, fo. 42ᵛ and also see fo. 56ᵛ; see above, ch. 5, nn. 45–6.

There are frequent reports of constables meeting with defiance in their attempts to collect ship-money, while there is also evidence of more widespread opposition to military levies in 1639–40 than had been the case during previous decades. By the end of the 1630s constables seem to have been subjected to considerable local pressure in trying to fulfil some of their tax-collecting duties. Moreover, at the same time there were also complaints from a number of counties about the exactions of saltpetre men and postmasters and, while such burdens may always have caused some protest, it seems probable that constables experienced greater difficulties than in previous years in gaining the co-operation of other villagers in meeting the demands of these officials.

A number of sheriffs testified not just to the delinquency of constables in gathering ship-money,[89] but also to the widespread refusal of inhabitants to pay this levy. They passed on to the Council accounts of the resistance encountered by constables and by their own officers who had been sent out to distrain for the tax. The sheriff of Worcestershire in 1636 claimed that he had received little or nothing except by distress because inhabitants refused to pay the sums assessed on them, while by 1640 it was alleged that no parish would pay until distrained. The sheriff of that year reported on the violence done to constables and other officers dispatched by him to take distresses, and also claimed that some were foiling their attempts to distrain by driving their cattle into other counties. In Hanbury the doors were shut against them, and when they did manage to distrain the goods were violently rescued. They faced even greater resistance in Borfield where villagers with staves and dogs frightened off the sheep they had taken as a distress, drew their swords and threatened the sheriff's officers that they would kill anyone who tried to take the sheep.[90] The sheriff of Staffordshire in 1637 claimed that whole regiments in that county came daily to his house saying 'distrain', and claiming that they had no money. In 1640 the sheriff reported that constables claimed that they had called for the ship-money but could not collect it, and that when they took distresses these were violently rescued.[91] Reports from the sheriff of Hertfordshire in 1638 indicated that his bailiffs had found the 'meaner sort' readiest to pay ship-money, but that others were backward until distrained. However, by 1639 and 1640 there were

[89] See above, ch. 5, nn. 54–60.
[90] PRO, SP 16/331/12; 455/127; 457/22; 467/58; also see Silcock, 'County Government in Worcestershire', pp. 225–7.
[91] PRO, SP 16/346/108; 452/10.

complaints from that county too of more general aversion to the levy, the sheriff claiming that few would pay until distrained.[92] Sir John Buxton, sheriff of Norfolk in 1638, claimed that the greatest part of the ship-money in that county had to be levied by distress, and there were similar reports from the sheriff in 1640.[93] Reports from Leicestershire in 1639 indicated that 'diverse' were unwilling to pay the levy, and the sheriff confirmed constables' claims that they could not collect the money due to the 'many taxes that have now lately bene [imposed] for souldiours and horses'.[94]

Reports from constables themselves sometimes attested to the resistance which they had encountered, and occasionally to the contempt and violence which greeted their efforts to collect ship-money. An officer of Ware, Hertfordshire, returned the names of thirteen inhabitants of that township who had not paid ship-money in 1638; while a Nottinghamshire officer claimed in 1637 that none of the inhabitants of North Muskham would pay the levy after the refusal of one woman to do so.[95] His experience seems to have been not untypical of the difficulties which constables sometimes confronted in trying to gather ship-money. He claimed that he had tried several times to collect the 50s. assessed on the woman, but had met with refusal. On the last occasion he was driven away by an attorney, who gave him 'ill language, bidding him packe the doores', and who claimed that the constable's authority 'was not worth a bitt of bread'. When he distrained a horse in lieu of the payment he was pursued and insulted, being called 'slave and base slave' and the animal was forcibly rescued from him. A number of officers of Northants reported the violence done to them when they distrained for ship-money or accompanied bailiffs to take distresses.[96] The officers of Burton Latimer indicated that there was a rumour circulating in that county in 1637 to the effect that sixty-six constables had been hanged by the inhabitants for their attempts to collect ship-money, and this rumour was perhaps as effective as violence itself in deterring officers from trying to gather the levy.[97] It has already been noted that constables of some villages supplemented their ship-money collections from their own lewnes, apparently being unable to gather the levy from a number

[92] PRO, SP 16/387/46; 414/162; 445/62; 455/85; 456/49.
[93] PRO, SP 16/400/55; 450/1; 455/36.
[94] PRO, SP 16/409/165; 418/51.
[95] PRO, SP 16/395/88; 362/83.
[96] PRO, SP 16/367/7, 32; 398/19.   [97] PRO, SP 16/313/111.

of villagers. Although they may not have met with violence or abuse they do seem to have encountered greater difficulty in gathering this tax than any of the others for which they were responsible.[98]

Some officers also appear to have encountered rather widespread resistance to the payment of military levies in 1639–40. An officer of Redruth, Surrey, returned the names of forty-two defaulters, apparently submitting a whole village rating list, and a number of officers in Hertfordshire reported that villagers had refused to pay any of the money.[99] Constables in Middlesex submitted long lists of those who denied payment, and the reasons they had offered for refusal.[100] Officers in Somerset too recounted considerable difficulty in collecting coat and conduct money in 1640, and when asked to return the names of those who had refused to pay they replied that 'they must bring in then the names of every man in some hundreds'.[101] Reports of the unwillingness of inhabitants to pay the levy also came in from Norfolk, Worcestershire, Hampshire, Northants, Dorset, and Buckinghamshire, among other counties.[102]

The extent of the local pressures which constables sometimes experienced in collecting taxes and rates during the later 1630s is reflected not only in the refusal of inhabitants to pay levies, and the more forceful resistance which they displayed, but also in villagers' refusals to assist these officers in drawing up local assessments. It has already been noted that they could not impose levies on their own authority, or at least that was not the customary way of proceeding, and they required the participation of other inhabitants in drawing up local rating lists.[103] Although villagers usually seem to have been co-

---

[98] See above, ch. 5, nn. 90, 92; the refusal of some inhabitants of Waltham to pay unspecified levies in the later 1630s probably concerned ship-money, Leics. RO, DE 625/60, ff. 48^v, 49^v, 50. On the opposition to ship-money in other counties, see Morrill, *Cheshire*, pp. 28–9; Willcox, *Gloucestershire*, esp. p. 130; Fletcher, *Sussex*, p. 208; Barnes, *Somerset*, esp. pp. 209–10, 222, 230–1; Clark, *English Provincial Society*, pp. 359–61; Holmes, *Seventeenth-Century Lincolnshire*, pp. 131–4.

[99] PRO, SP 16/458/33; 456/71.

[100] PRO, SP 16/459/47, 54, 55, 94; 461/103.

[101] PRO, SP 16/459/7; also see Barnes, *Somerset*, pp. 109, 274–5.

[102] PRO, SP 16/460/29; 461/13; 459/13, 53; 456/27; 461/69; also see Silcock, 'County Government in Worcestershire', pp. 171–2; Hurstfield, 'Wiltshire, c.1530–c. 1660', p. 249; Willcox, *Gloucestershire*, p. 131; Holmes, *Seventeenth-Century Lincolnshire*, p. 139. For some evidence of resistance to the payment of military levies during the later 1620s, see Stearns, 'Conscription and English Society', pp. 21–2; and for a discussion of the pressures of war on county administration in the 1620s see Russell, *Parliaments and English Politics*, pp. 70–84, 324–38. Clark, *English Provincial Society*, p. 251 draws attention to opposition in Kent to the military levies of the 1590s.

[103] See above, ch. 2, n. 91.

operative in acting as assessors,[104] during the 1630s they sometimes did deny constables' requests for assistance. Occasionally officers encountered refusal when they called upon inhabitants to draw up assessments for their lewnes. A constable of Standon, Staffordshire, complained in 1632 that when he had called a meeting for the purpose of assessing such a levy only four parishioners had appeared, and when he ordered them to lay a lewne for his expenses in the king's service they refused to do so.[105] However, it was in the assessment of ship-money and the military levies of 1640 that constables most often were denied assistance.

There are a number of reports of villagers refusing to assess ship-money. The sheriff of Cornwall claimed in 1637 that constables could not get other inhabitants to join them in drawing up rating lists, and in the same year the sheriff of Northants informed the council that many townships in that county had failed to make any assessments.[106] From Hertfordshire too there were reports in 1638 that some constables had made rates for ship-money without their parishioners, who apparently had refused to aid them. Later in the same year the sheriff notified the council that he had ordered constables to draw up rates themselves when inhabitants denied them assistance; but he claimed that it caused a good deal of disagreement when officers made assessments without the aid of the chief residents, who were knowledgeable about men's estates.[107] A constable of Suckley, Worcestershire, vouched for such difficulties when he was summoned before the Council in 1639 for his failure to collect ship-money. He claimed that the parishioners refused to make the assessments and that he had been obliged to draw up a rating list himself. However, he reported that villagers had refused to make payment on the basis of his assessments, apparently with the excuse that the sheriff had not signed the rating list.[108]

Some constables experienced similar difficulties when they attempted

---

[104] See above, nn. 70–1.
[105] Staffs. RO, Transcripts Sessions Rolls, Car. I, Roll 32, no. 38.
[106] PRO, SP 16/346/88; 367/7.
[107] PRO, SP 16/381/71; 387/46; on the difficulties encountered getting in ship-money assessments also see SP 16/346/108–9; 349/88, 92; 351/91; 384/2; 415/39; 455/85; 467/58. A sheriff of Northumberland reported that constables in that county were meaner than in other parts of the kingdom in quality and ability and so unsuited to apportioning the levy within their parishes, and in consequence he had called for meetings in every division with the justices, two of the ablest men in every parish and the parson being present, as well as constables. On the basis of the information he received from these meetings he had drawn up the assessments, SP 16/349/61.
[108] PRO, SP 16/427/113.

to assess coat and conduct money in 1640. A number of Hertfordshire officers claimed that other villagers had refused to aid them in drawing up local rating lists for this levy.[109] The constables of Kimpton, Aldenham, and Abbots Langley reported that they had given public notice of meetings to be held for the purpose of assessing the rate, but contended that villagers had refused to join them in drawing up tax lists. The officer of Kimpton claimed that nobody had even appeared at the meeting which he had called. Nine other constables also alleged that the inhabitants had refused to aid them in assessing coat and conduct money, though one of them, the officer of Norton, later withdrew his charge.[110] Several of them went on to explain that they were unable to draw up the rates without assistance from other villagers. The constable of Aldenham pointed out that he had only recently come into office, and claimed that he could not gain access to any old rating lists or procure any other assistance from the parish. The officers of Abbots Langley reported similar difficulties in securing a copy of any ancient rates, while those of Hitchin claimed that they were unfamiliar with men's abilities and thus unable to draw up the assessment themselves. There were complaints from Northants, Warwickshire, Buckinghamshire, and other counties too that no local rating lists for coat and conduct money had been returned, and perhaps in these cases too it was because constables had met with refusal when they called upon inhabitants to assess the levy.[111]

Not only were constables resisted when they attempted to collect ship-money and coat and conduct money, and even obstructed in their duties because other inhabitants refused to render the assistance they required in drawing up local assessments. They were also threatened with legal actions when they distrained for ship-money, and sometimes malicious charges of trespass were brought against them. In 1637 the sheriff of Cornwall claimed that constables in that county had been sued for taking distresses in lieu of ship-money, while there were reports from Devon in the same year that some 'have published their resolucions to bring their actions against the constables for takeing distresses'.[112] In Leicestershire too in 1639 those recalcitrant in paying ship-money apparently threatened to bring actions against any who distrained their goods or cattle.[113] The sheriff of Norfolk informed the Council in 1638 of the obstruction faced by constables in that county

---

[109] The following is based on PRO, SP 16/456/71, nos. 139–51.
[110] PRO, SP 16/457/57.   [111] PRO, SP 16/458/32; 456/12; 461/69.
[112] PRO, SP 16/346/88; 351/20.   [113] PRO, SP 16/409/165.

where villagers combined together 'to beare name and propertye of
one a nothers goods', and he claimed that officers were afraid to take
distresses 'for feare of suites by mistakinges'.[114] The narrow line
between vexatious suits and legitimate legal actions, and the difficulties
in which constables could find themselves, are well illustrated by the
fate of an Essex officer who assisted the sheriff's officials in distraining
a bullock from a man who refused to pay ship-money. He later was
sued for trespass in Common Pleas by the man's son who claimed that
the bullock belonged to him.[115]

T. G. Barnes has suggested that in the collection of ship-money
many constables bowed to local pressures because 'the Council had no
terrors to match those that the constables' neighbors threatened with
increasing frequency and, upon occasion, perpetrated'.[116] Constables'
defaults in collecting both ship-money and coat and conduct money
often seem to be explained by the extent of the local resistance which
they encountered, though as taxpayers themselves many of them were
probably ready to co-operate with other villagers in resisting such
collections. Whether men questioned the legal basis of these levies,[117]
or were influenced by the refusal of a leading inhabitant to make
payment or the pressures which he brought to bear on others,[118] or
refused to pay because they regarded the burdens as excessive and
unfair[119] the local pressures which constables experienced in 1639–40
in trying to gather ship-money and military rates seem to have been
greater than those which they faced in collecting any other taxes or
rates. Sheriffs themselves sometimes explicitly attributed constables'
negligence in gathering ship-money to the pressures exerted on them
not to collect the levy. The sheriff of Worcestershire in 1640 reported
that most constables there would 'doe nothinge in the service' because
they were 'soe threatened by the country'. He informed the Council of
his belief that these officers refused to make collections in response to

---

[114] PRO, SP 16/385/1.
[115] PRO, SP 16/380/35.   [116] Barnes, *Somerset*, p. 230.
[117] e.g. PRO, SP 16/318/75; 381/71; 395/9; 452/10 for suggestions that the legality
of ship-money was questioned; and for similar questions concerning coat and conduct
money, see SP 16/456/71, nos. 139–51.
[118] e.g. PRO, SP 16/313/111; 362/83; 387/46; 461/82.
[119] For the complaints of one Gloucestershire woman and her son about the extent of
the tax burdens in the later 1630s see PRO, SP 16/387/64. Entries in constables'
accounts reveal that the amount villages were assessed for taxes and rates in the later
1630s often was double the sum paid in the later 1620s, and the extent of the burdens at
this time probably in many instances explains ordinary villagers' resistance to ship-
money and coat and conduct money; also see Morrill, *Cheshire*, p. 28.

demands from their fellow villagers who could, and sometimes would, produce the money in order to get a constable released from custody. He had discovered that constables whom he had attached for their failure to make payment, and who accused their parishioners of refusing to pay the levy, could 'procure many of the best of the parishe to mediate for them'. This, he claimed, seemed to confirm the confession of some officers 'that they dare doe nothinge but what the parishe alowe of', and that 'the parishe promised to beare them out'.[120] The sheriff of Staffordshire in 1640 reported that constables in that county did not dare to distrain for ship-money because of the response of their fellow residents. He claimed that when he accused constables of negligence in distraining, most of them answered that they had not taken distresses because 'they were soe menaced by their neighbors'.[121]

While some officers may have been lazy in levying ship-money the tardiness of constables like Robert Ellis of Salwarpe in making payment was probably due largely to the difficulties which they experienced in gathering the money.[122] By 1639–40 when sheriffs were claiming that many constables refused to do anything, to draw up assessments, levy the money, or take distresses, and when some of them apparently absented themselves from home in order to avoid the sheriff's officers,[123] such conduct was very likely due to the pressures they were experiencing from their neighbours. Constables' tardiness in levying coat and conduct money too, or their failure to do so, was probably due more to the obstruction which they encountered, and to the local pressures brought to bear on them, than to personal defects such as laziness or indifference.

The burdens imposed by saltpetre men and postmasters, and sometimes the demands for goods and services for the royal household when the king was present in a county, also caused resistance on some occasions; and in these instances too constables can be seen reacting to local pressures. Villagers probably often responded rather grudgingly to the requisitions of such officials, and some constables who took horses to meet the demands of postmasters faced vexatious suits brought against them by the discontented owners of these animals. Several Lincolnshire constables who were subjected to such malicious actions were defended by higher officials, who claimed that they had acted correctly and who pointed out that such vexatious proceedings

[120] PRO, SP 16/467/58.
[121] PRO, SP 16/452/10; also see Holmes, *Seventeenth-Century Lincolnshire*, p. 134.
[122] See above, ch. 5, n. 47.   [123] See above, ch. 5, nn. 54–9.

against inferior officers discouraged them from doing their duty.[124] However, while there may always have been some resistance to requisitions of this kind, there seems to have been a growing outcry against the exactions of both postmasters and saltpetre men during the later 1630s. There were complaints that these officials were making excessive demands and abusing their powers. The grand juries at both the Wiltshire and Somerset assizes in the summer of 1638 registered protests about the activities of postmasters in those counties, and in the case of Somerset about saltpetre men as well, while from Hampshire and Hertfordshire too there were complaints in 1638 about the conduct of postmasters.[125] Villagers near posting stages claimed that postmasters took more horses than were needed for the king's service in order to discharge them for money or hire them out to others, and they protested that they were oppressed by such burdens. There were additional complaints from Hertfordshire that the postmaster of St. Albans came, unaccompanied by a constable, and broke open their doors at night and took away their horses without their knowledge, that he locked up the animals so that their owners could not see or feed them, and that he also took cart-horses that were unserviceable and returned them in a disabled state, to the great loss of the owners. Saltpetre men too were accused of abusing their powers. Inhabitants of villages near the coal pits in Somerset complained that when these officials moved their works to other counties they were required not only to carry the saltpetre and vessels but also to cart fuel to distant places. They contended that the saltpetre men's commission entitled them to procure the carriage of only their saltpetre and vessels and not more than twelve miles from their works.[126]

Although it has been shown that constables often received a large amount of local assistance in meeting such demands for goods and services,[127] sometimes villagers clearly did deem them excessive, and constables experienced pressures to act on behalf of the village to secure a reduction in these burdens. In the face of local resistance not

---

[124] PRO, SP 14/159/44; SP 16/196/89; also see SP 16/30/68, 69.

[125] PRO, SP 16/395/89; 395/9; 400/127; 388/77; on opposition to purveyance, and especially the activities of saltpetre men, in Essex in the 1630s see Hunt, *The Puritan Moment*, pp. 266–7. Clark, *English Provincial Society*, pp. 330, 358, draws attention to the opposition to purveyance in Kent between 1627 and 1640.

[126] On abuses of saltpetre men also see PRO, SP 16/103/31; 192/89; 124/11; and for other evidence of controversy about postmasters or allusions to their abuses also see SP 14/175/32; SP 16/124/11.

[127] See above, n. 72.

only to the demands of saltpetre men and postmasters, but sometimes to requisitions for the royal household as well, constables can be seem joining with other villagers and trying to procure concessions for the community through negotiations with higher authorities. Sometimes they were accompanied by other inhabitants when they conferred with such officials, and they thus acted as leaders of village delegations. When they attempted to compound for obligations in kind they occasionally noted that they did so on the instruction of the village.

Officers of both Branston and Waltham, who normally received so much assistance in supplying the king's needs while he was in the county, sometimes attempted to procure reductions in the demands for provision and carriage. In the summer of 1621, when there were so many such requisitions in Waltham, the constable negotiated to free the town from drawing a wagon to Newark, and in the company of two or three neighbours he also won the agreement of the high constable to spare a village cart that was supposed to carry a load of straw from Nottingham to Derby. When demands for carriage were particularly heavy in the summer of 1640 the officer of that year, along with neighbours, paid the high constable 11s. to excuse three horses and a cart with which the village had been charged for the king's carriage from Grantham to Tuxford.[128] The constable of Branston was engaged in similar activities to try to gain a reduction in the burdens imposed on that village in 1619. Accompanied by three of his fellow inhabitants he travelled to Belvoir 'to gett some parte of our gose abated', and he also persuaded the high constable to reduce the village's obligations for carriage to Derby.[129]

In Branston and Waltham, and in other villages too, constables engaged in similar negotiations with saltpetre men, particularly during the 1630s and probably at that time in response to growing village complaints about the exactions and abuses of these officials. In 1634 the constable of Waltham gained the agreement of the high constable to free three carts which should have fetched coals for the saltpetre man, and in 1635 he paid 2s. to gain release of carts that the village was supposed to provide to go to Ashby for the saltpetre man.[130] In 1619 a Branston officer, accompanied by three other villagers, went to the saltpetre man to negotiate a reduction in the carriages with which the village was supposed to supply him, and the constable of 1631 paid this

---

[128] Leics. RO, DE 625/60, ff. 23ᵛ, 61.
[129] Leics. RO, DE 720/30, ff. 15ᵛ, 16.
[130] Leics. RO, DE 625/60, ff. 45ᵛ, 48ᵛ.

official to excuse the town from carrying ashes to Nottingham. When the saltpetre men arrived in Branston in 1635 the constable paid them to leave town.[131] The accounts of Stockton, Norfolk, reveal that the officers there got the town discharged from carrying coals, probably for the saltpetre men, in 1632. In the same year the constable of Shelton paid 10s. for 'compounding with the saltpetre man for the carriage of too loads', while an officer of East Harling in 1627 paid 2s. 'for the carryinge away of the salt peterman'.[132]

Constables also conducted negotiations with postmasters to get them to reduce their demands or to accept money in place of the horses they requisitioned. The inhabitants of Branston appear to have become rather resistant to the continuous demands for horses in the later 1630s, and in 1639 the constable successfully negotiated with the postmaster to excuse some of the horses which he was demanding. The officer of that township in 1641 also gained the release of two post horses which the village was supposed to deliver to Witham.[133] In the spring of 1642 the constable of Waltham also travelled to Witham to negotiate with the postmaster, but he seems to have failed in his representations on behalf of the village. He recorded that he went 'to have agreed with the postmaster', and his lack of success is evidenced by the fact that he ended up taking ten post horses to Witham. However, later that year he did gain approval of the composition 'agreed by neighbours'. The postmaster apparently accepted £1. 12s. in place of horses, a payment which included 2s. for the postmaster's man, who probably had helped to expedite the settlement.[134] The officers of Melton Mowbray in 1625 also attempted to procure reductions in such burdens. They had taken ten post horses to Witham, and on hearing that the postmaster would send for more horses they retraced their steps in order to negotiate with him to excuse the town.[135] In 1614–15 the Manchester constables paid 5s. 'for sparinge post horses' to a captain who had a commission from the Council to be provided with them, while in 1639 they apparently

[131] Leics. RO, DE 720/30, ff. 15ᵛ, 31, 38.
[132] Carthew, 'Town Book of the Parish of Stockton', 171; NNRO, PD 358/33, p. 11; PD 219/126, 1627; also see Cox, *Churchwardens' Accounts*, pp. 333–4.
[133] Leics. RO, DE 720/30, ff. 46, 50.
[134] Leics. RO, DE 625/60, fo. 65ᵛ; in the same year the constable also paid 5s. to a man with a commission for seven post horses, probably to persuade him to look for horses elsewhere, (fo. 65).
[135] Leics. RO, DG 25/39/1/4.

252   *Constables' Conduct:*

gained no concessions, but they supplemented the post fees from their own revenues in order 'to spare our neighboures'.[136]

Horses were in great demand by 1643, but by then to supply soldiers rather than postmasters. The constable of Branston travelled to Belvoir 'to excuse the horses' and he also paid soldiers who had a commission to take horses 'for staying our horses at home', though on another occasion he did have to follow the parliamentary forces to Melton in order to retrieve some of the village's horses.[137] In the same year, and probably also in response to new kinds of burdens being imposed during the Civil War, the constable of Branston and several other inhabitants travelled twice to Melton Mowbray to 'make freinds for the tax'.[138]

The local obstruction and resistance which constables sometimes encountered in collecting taxes and rates reveals the extent to which the office could become a focus of conflict, with incompatible pressures being exerted on such officials by their superiors and by their fellow inhabitants. Constables usually seem to have met with open defiance from only a few inhabitants, although larger numbers of villagers were often somewhat tardy in paying their levies. However, in the later 1630s many officers appear to have experienced more general local pressures against the collection of ship-money and military levies. In view of the extent and the nature of the opposition to these rates, including the fact that other inhabitants sometimes even refused to assist in drawing up local assessments, it is not surprising that constables sometimes bowed to local pressures and made little attempt to collect them. Villagers who were normally co-operative in assisting constables in meeting the requisitions of saltpetre men and postmasters, and the demands for goods and carriage for the royal household, could sometimes prove reluctant to do so if these burdens became too great. On such occasions constables also responded to local influences and, putting their obligations to represent the village ahead of their duties as 'king's men', they acted on behalf of the local community to try to secure reductions in such demands or at least to compound for burdens in kind.

(b) Resistance from Offenders and Local Attitudes Toward Law Enforcement

Constables' conduct in law enforcement also appears to have been

[136] Earwker, ed., *Constables' Accounts*, i. 20; ii. 67; also see cases in which constables were accused of refusing to assist postmasters, PRO, SP 14/48/47; 169/53.
[137] Leics. RO, DE 720/30, ff. 52ᵛ, 53.   [138] Leics. RO, DE 720/30, fo. 54.

affected by the local pressures which they sometimes experienced and by their local loyalties. It was in the exercise of their police powers that these officers most often met with abuse. Although such cases apparently involved only a tiny proportion of the constables in any county, they are recorded throughout the period under consideration without any apparent chronological pattern. They were subjected to insults and violence, or sometimes more subtle verbal persuasions, by offenders themselves and sometimes their relatives or friends. Some law-breakers later sought revenge against constables for actions which they had taken in the course of fulfilling their peacekeeping responsibilities. On some occasions constables were obstructed in their police duties because other inhabitants refused to assist them. They also experienced more general local pressures which arose from the fact that villagers' attitudes toward law enforcement were not always in accord with those of higher authorities or with constables' official obligations as police officers. In their peacekeeping duties constables sometimes can be seen responding to local influences, while in other instances there are strong indications that their behaviour was shaped by local attitudes and concerns.

There is evidence of some constables being subjected to abuse or violence in fulfilling most of the police functions for which they were responsible, although some of their duties seem to have been more likely than others to be greeted with resistance. When they intervened in affrays to restore the peace, they were sometimes assaulted themselves, while constables engaged in searches also met with defiance and abuse. However, it was in serving warrants and in attempting to make arrests on their own authority that they most often appear to have been resisted. An examination of the abuses to which they were subjected by offenders, and sometimes by their friends or relatives too, will suggest that constables were sometimes prevented or deterred from fulfilling their police duties by such local responses.

Constables engaged in breaking up quarrels or other disturbances of the peace were sometimes forcibly resisted by the participants, probably in many cases simply because their anger was redirected at the officer who had intervened. Few seem to have met with resistance quite as serious as that encountered by an officer of Redbourn, Hertfordshire, who reported that he had been permanently disabled by the injuries he received when he was called out of bed to deal with strangers who were fighting in the streets. He claimed to have sustained ten wounds, lost the use of his limbs, and consumed his estate in seeking a cure; and he petitioned the justices for a yearly pension during life as compensation for his disability. Apparently there was some substance to his complaint since the Bench granted him an initial 20s. and ordered that the matter be considered further at the next sessions.[139] Although the consequences were less disastrous, other constables too reported that they were assaulted while trying to restore the peace. An officer of Darlaston, Staffordshire, who tried to break up a quarrel claimed to have received a wound in the hand while defending himself against one of the participants who attempted to stab him.[140] Others too reported that they had been beaten, and sometimes wounded, and one officer had the clothes torn from his back.[141]

Constables' powers to search, either for offenders or for stolen goods, also evoked an angry response on some occasions, and they were verbally abused or forcibly prevented from conducting a search. An Oxford constable claimed that the wife of a suspected thief ran at him with a knife when he accompanied some men to make a search for stolen goods.[142] A Staffordshire officer was kicked in the face and injured with a large stone by a man suspected of theft who tried to prevent him from conducting a search. In a petition to the justices he asked them to impose whatever penalty they 'thought fitte and expedient for a man contemninge the authority of your said orator beinge the kinges officer'.[143] Two Norfolk constables who possessed a warrant to search for stolen goods also reported that they had met with obstruction and abuse. The woman in question locked the doors, not allowing them to search for five or six hours, and when she finally did admit them she reportedly attacked them so violently that they could not conduct a search, and called them 'thefes and rooges and hooremasters and mor then heare is fittinge to be set downe'.[144] An officer of Shipston-upon-Stour, Worcestershire, seems to have encountered considerable violence when he attempted to search for thieves at a local inn. The innkeeper and several others present

[139] Herts. RO, QS/B, 2A, ff. 4, 9.
[140] Staffs. RO, Transcripts Sessions Rolls, Jac. I, Roll 31, nos. 98–9.
[141] Bund, ed., *Sessions Papers*, p. 249; and for other cases see Staffs. RO, Transcripts Sessions Rolls, Jac. I, Roll. 31, no. 66; Roll 49, nos. 68–9; Roll 73, nos. 29–30; Atkinson, ed., *Sessions Records*, iv. 71, 97; Cockburn, ed., *Essex Indictments, Eliz. I*, no. 3276; *Sussex Indictments, Eliz. I*, no. 2066; *Surrey Indictments, Eliz. I*, no. 2585; PRO, STAC 8/42/1; 62/18; 97/18; 124/2; 205/17; 250/3.
[142] PRO, STAC 8/189/20.   [143] Burne, ed., *Staffs. Sessions Rolls*, v. 14, 45.
[144] NNRO, Sessions Records, Box 21 (1617–18).

reportedly lashed out at him with 'outrageous and raylinge speeches', struck him and beat him to the ground, and swore the most 'fearfull oathes' that they 'would lett out the gutts of your said subiecte'. He claimed that he was forced to give up the search and flee for his life.[145]

Constables engaged in serving warrants seem to have been even more likely to encounter abuse and violence. One such officer was driven away with scalding water, stones, and mire, and another threatened with murder,[146] while others too were assaulted or received tongue lashings from the wanted parties or their relatives.[147] Even warrants for good behaviour or recognizances to appear at sessions sometimes elicited an angry response. One officer who was trying to deliver such a summons was labelled a rascal, beggar and tinker's dog and another called a thief and driven away with a knife.[148] Sometimes verbal abuse or violence were combined with attempts to persuade an officer to ignore the warrant. A Worcestershire constable reported that he had not only been greeted with contempt, but also subjected to pressures to disregard the warrant which he was trying to serve on two of the townships' overseers of the poor. One of these men allegedly had given him 'very bad words' and ignored the order, while the other scoffed at him and tried to deter him from doing his duty, saying 'I would do them a shrewd turn if I would not regard the same'.[149] When an officer of Longdon, Staffordshire, attempted to serve a warrant on three men, on a writ of attachment out of the Exchequer, they not only abused and attacked him, but tried to make him feel guilty about taking such action, presumably with the intent of persuading him to ignore the warrant. One of the parties told the officer 'that hee did marvayle that hee would bee made a speciall bayliffe to doe his neighbour that wronge'.[150] Sometimes when constables attempted to serve warrants

---

[145] PRO, STAC 8/176/18; for other cases of abuse of constables who were engaged in searches see STAC 8/217/29; Lister, ed., *West Riding Sessions*, ii. 159; Atkinson, ed., *Sessions Records*, i. 187.

[146] Staffs. RO, Transcripts Sessions Rolls, Jac. I, Roll 76, no. 6; Roll 22, no. 54.

[147] For other cases of constables meeting with resistance in serving warrants and making arrests see Staffs. RO, Transcripts Sessions Rolls, Jac. I, Roll 30, no. 46; Roll 36, nos. 40–1; Roll 54, no. 46; Roll 67, no. 27; QS/O, iv. 237ᵛ.; Bund, ed., *Sessions Papers*, pp. 196, 703; Lister, ed., *West Riding Sessions*, i. 87; ii. 11; Atkinson, ed., *Sessions Records*, ii. 2; iv. 48; PRO, STAC 8/53/21; 72/4; 143/8.

[148] Staffs. RO, Transcripts Sessions Rolls, Jac. I, Roll 65, nos. 61–2; Bund, ed., *Sessions Papers*, p. 44; also see Staffs. RO, Transcripts Sessions Rolls, Roll 49, nos. 66–7; Roll 56, nos. 39–40; Bund, ed., *Sessions Papers*, pp. 155–6.

[149] Bund, ed., *Sessions Papers*, p. 187.

[150] PRO, E 134/13 & 14 Car. I/ Hil. 17.

for arrest in a public place, such as an alehouse, a number of others who were present rallied to the defence of the wanted man and prevented the officer from apprehending him. When a constable of South Petherton, Somerset, appeared at a local alehouse to serve a warrant on three men he apparently was not only attacked with a sword by one of the offenders, but the ale-keeper ignored his appeals for assistance and the men escaped into the streets. There others joined in an assault on the officer and allegedly beat him to the ground.[151] A constable of Thirsk, Yorkshire, found himself in similar circumstances when he resorted to a tippling house to serve a warrant on a gentleman of that town. Others who were present rescued the offender and assaulted the constable, who claimed that he was grievously wounded and would have been murdered if he had not fled from the alehouse.[152]

Constables' authority seems to have been even more resented when they made use of their own powers of arrest, or sometimes simply warned men to cease activities which constituted misdemeanours under the law. A number of such cases on record involved defiance of officers who were trying to enforce social regulations, and constables seem to have been especially likely to meet with resistance from offenders of this sort.

Other historians have drawn attention to the fact that constables were frequently abused when they reprimanded or apprehended men for drunkenness.[153] Instances of this kind are found in some of the court records examined, especially those of Norfolk. Some officers in that county seem to have been particularly rigorous in enforcing the laws against drunkenness and disorderly conduct in alehouses, or else villagers in that county were especially resistant to such regulations. A constable of Grimston, Norfolk, presented to sessions a man who 'did raile and scandolize me by his fowle words for doinge my office and punnishinge him for his inordinate drunkenes', while another Norfolk officer claimed that a man whom he placed in the stocks for drunkenness 'used such unreverent speeches to him . . . as are not fittinge to be repeated'.[154] The words probably could not match the unpleasantness of the treatment meted out to a constable of Harpley, Norfolk, by a drunkard whom he had placed in the stocks. He reportedly abused the officer and those who had assisted him, with 'revilinge and skuffling' and 'threw his handfull of goare in the

---

[151] PRO, STAC 8/256/1.   [152] PRO, STAC 8/186/15.
[153] e.g. Fletcher, *Sussex*, p. 227.
[154] NNRO, Sessions Records, Box 22 (19 Sept. 1620); Box 17, pt. ii (17 Sept. 1610).

cunstables eyes'.[155] According to a constable of Hempstead a drunkard in that town 'grieviously beate' him, while an officer of North Wootton complained that he had been abused by several men who were in their cups.[156] A constable of Fincham reported that he had met with defiance when he had ordered the clerk of the village, who was carousing with travelling minstrels and other disorderly company at 10 or 11 p.m. on Midsummer Night, to cease his activities and depart from the alehouse.[157] Occasionally such offenders not only abused the constable, but made fun of the punishment which they had received. In another case from Grimston the constables reported that a man whom they had placed in the stocks for being drunk on the Sabbath was quite unrepentant about the offence, saying he cared nothing about it. After he was released 'he rayleth on the officers and laugheth at his correction in scorne'.[158] Sometimes an officer was reprimanded by others for taking action against a drunkard, suggesting that not only the offenders themselves were opposed to the enforcement of such regulations. When an officer of Wiggenhall, Norfolk, ordered home to bed a drunken man who allegedly had thrown a dumb boy into the river and threatened his sister with similar treatment, another man present admonished the constable, telling him 'Yoe doe offer us poore men wrong in troubling of us.'[159]

Constables who interfered with activities on the Sabbath often seem to have met with resistance as well. When the officers of Brancaster, Norfolk, ordered an ale-keeper and others in his house to cease playing cards on Sunday, they reportedly 'did rayle uppon the cunstables calling them knaves and other vile speeches'.[160] Some officers in other counties met with more extensive abuse when they attempted to disperse those gathered for Sunday sports or other kinds of popular festivities on the Sabbath. A Constable of Alton, Hampshire, complained to Star Chamber in 1615 of the treatment meted out to him when he attempted to suppress Sunday dancing in

---

[155] Ibid., Box 23 (1621-2).
[156] Ibid., Box 21 (1617-18); Box 17, pt. i (1611-12).
[157] Ibid., Box 20 (24 Aug. 1615).   [158] Ibid., Box 24, pt. ii (1624-5).
[159] Ibid., Box 20 (21 June 1615); for some other cases involving the abuse of constables by drunkards see Hardy, *Calendar to Sessions Books*, p. 6; Staffs. RO, Transcripts Sessions Rolls, Jac. I, Roll 31, nos. 102-3; Roll 58, nos. 81-2; Salt, ed., *Staffs. Sessions Rolls, Easter 1608 to Trinity 1609*, p. 31.
[160] NNRO, Sessions Records, Box 19 (1614-15); also see the case of a Staffordshire constable abused by men whom he had forbidden to play dice, though there is no indication in this instance that they were playing on the Sabbath, Burne, ed., *Staffs. Sessions Rolls*, i. 264.

the town, and to arrest the minstrel who was providing the music. According to his account the tithingman refused to aid him and the minstrel was forcibly rescued; he was struck over the head and his hat and jerkin torn; and one of the dancers called him a 'puritan', 'willinge him to goe to Chalton agayne to heare the devill', knowing that he had been there that morning to attend a sermon. Despite his reprimands to the dancers they defiantly carried on with their sport, crying out 'the towne ys ours, downe goeth the prieste, yt ys the better for us all.' In addition, the father of several of the participants apparently threatened the constable with gaol and expensive suits in Star Chamber if he did not depart and leave them alone. Having forcibly driven the officer away, the dancers posted someone on top of the 'somer howse', the scene of the dancing, to keep watch for him while they continued their activities.[161] A constable of Brinklow, Warwickshire, protested in a suit to Star Chamber about the abuse which he had received when he tried to disperse villagers who were setting up a maypole on May Day 1622, which fell on a Sunday, and to apprehend the minstrel who was playing for the occasion. He claimed that they had assaulted him, giving him 'greivous blowes, thrusts, hurts and wounds upon divers parts of his bodye', and that he had barely escaped with his life by fleeing into the fields and outrunning them to reach the safety of his own house.[162] Similar abuse was experienced by a constable of Longdon, Worcestershire, who in 1616 attempted to suppress 'May games, morrices and dancing' which he reported had occurred for several years on summer Sundays in that town. He too attempted to apprehend a minstrel who was providing the music, but one of the dancers allegedly did 'strake up your petitioner's heels and said he would break your petitioner's neck down the stairs there if he departed not from them and let them alone'.[163]

These constables got off lightly, however, by comparison with an officer of Wells, Somerset. John Hole, clothier, ultimately won judgment against twelve of the inhabitants whom he accused of defying his attempts to suppress the May games, morris dancing, and pageants which occurred in that town on Sundays and holidays in May and June 1607, and which during the last half of June coincided with a church-ale in the parish of St. Cuthbert's. However, he was subjected to considerable abuse before he finally gained redress. When Hole tried to put an end to the sports by reading the proclamation of 1603 against

[161] PRO, STAC 8/262/11.   [162] PRO, STAC 8/245/27.
[163] Bund, ed., *Sessions Papers*, pp. 254–5.

the profaning of the Sabbath, apprehending several minstrels who were providing the music, and ordering people to go to church or to return to their houses, he faced general opposition from the townsmen, including most of the leading burgesses. The minstrels were rescued from custody, some of the inhabitants harassed Hole in the streets and obstructed him in setting the watch, and the citizens defiantly carried on with their sport week after week. The townsmen responded to his attempts to suppress the festivities by staging three additional pageants which ridiculed Hole and several friends, and which cast aspersions on their moral character. When he tried to secure the punishment of the participants in these pageants they were released by the mayor and other burgesses. Moreover, Hole was made the butt of two widely circulated satirical ballads which poked fun at his attitude to the sports, and one of which accused him of adultery and at the same time ridiculed him for being a Puritan.[164]

The resistance which constables encountered in attempting to enforce the law did not always come to an end when they had apprehended an offender. Those whom constables placed in the stocks sometimes broke free or were rescued by friends or relatives, and on some occasions officers were abused and attacked in the process. A man imprisoned in the stocks by a constable of Brancaster, Norfolk, confessed that a fellow townsman released him at 3 a.m. after the watch had disappeared, while an offender who was stocked by an officer of Stourbridge, Worcestershire, was also rescued by another inhabitant. When the constable apprehended the second man he was assaulted by a woman whom he alleged to be 'the chief maintainer of many vices in our town'.[165] A group of armed men apparently tried to rescue a yeoman of Bosbury, Herefordshire, who was placed in the stocks because he violently resisted arrest. They reportedly threatened to kill anyone who would resist them, and they assaulted and wounded the constable.[166] A Wolverhampton man who broke free from the stocks verbally abused one of the constables, threatened to set fire to this house and to kill him with his dagger. Although he was recaptured and committed to gaol, he somehow procured his freedom and on his return to Wolverhampton showed his defiance of the constables by wearing the warrant for his commitment in his hat.[167] Some offenders could be rather persistent in their attempts to escape from a

[164] PRO, STAC 8/161/1.
[165] NNRO, Sessions Records, Box 19 (3 Oct. 1614); Bund. ed., *Sessions Papers*, p. 66.
[166] PRO, STAC 8/53/21.   [167] Burne, ed., *Staffs. Sessions Rolls*, ii. 110–12.

constable's custody. A man placed in the stocks because he had resisted arrest by a constable of Bromley Paggots, Staffordshire, called his son who helped him break free. He was recaptured by the constable, bound hand and foot and tied to a horse and taken to the town hall where, at the suggestion of neighbours, he was fastened to a post. However, he made another attempt to escape and pulled down all the plastered walls within in his reach in his efforts to do so.[168]

Not only did officers meet with immediate obstruction in trying to fulfil their police duties, but sometimes men later sought retaliation against them for action which they had taken. Some constables were warned that they would regret their doings; and while such threats often may have been issued in the heat of the moment and soon forgotten, they were not always empty words. Officers sometimes reported that they had been subjected to continuing harassment by men whom they had reprimanded or arrested or whose offences they had presented to higher authorities.

Such retaliation sometimes took the form of physical violence. A Staffordshire officer claimed to have been attacked in his own house by an offender whom he had presented for drunkenness, while a constable of Wellington, Salop, was subjected to violence by a yeoman of that township who reportedly bore a grudge against the officer for having assisted the bailiffs in arresting him. The man rallied some friends and they lay in wait for the constable when he was travelling on business outside the village, and they assaulted and beat him. On another occasion, when he was watching the bowmen practise, they apparently harassed him and pretended to have a warrant for his arrest.[169] It was reported that a man of Eldersfield, Worcestershire, had resorted to rather extreme violence in seeking revenge against an officer, allegedly having 'cut off his neighbours arm for doing the office of Constable upon him a little before'.[170] An alehouse keeper of

---

[168] Staffs. RO, Transcripts Sessions Rolls, Jac. I., Roll 40, no. 24; for other cases in which prisoners escaped or were rescued from constables' custody see NNRO, Sessions Records, Box 31 (Hindringham, 1636–7); Burne, ed., *Staffs. Sessions Rolls*, v. 64, 167–8; Staffs. RO, Transcripts Sessions Rolls, Jac. I, Roll 23, no. 48; Roll 30, no. 33; Car. I, Roll 21; Lister, ed., *West Riding Sessions*, ii. 29; Atkinson, ed., *Sessions Records*, i. 85, 113–14; ii. 175, 205; iii. 168, 253; Cockburn, ed., *Herts. Indictments, James I*, nos. 173, 270, 562, 1023; *Essex Indictments, Eliz. I*, nos. 2001, 3274; *Kent Indictments, Eliz. I*, no. 1488; *Sussex Indictments, Eliz. I*, no. 1447; *Kent Indictments, James I*, nos. 109, 611; *Surrey Indictments, Eliz. I*, nos. 278, 377, 1437, 1447, 2790; PRO, STAC 8/143/8; 245/27; 262/11.

[169] Staffs. RO, Transcripts Sessions Rolls, Jac. I, Roll 31, nos. 102–3; PRO, STAC 8/291/5.					[170] Bund, ed., *Sessions Papers*, p. 254.

Wymondham, Norfolk, apparently seized the opportunity to even the score with a constable who had tried to reform abuses in his house. He refused to lodge travellers brought by the officer, insulted him, and with the help of others dragged him into the street by the hair of his head. According to the constable's account he was assaulted with staves, clubs, and pitchforks, as well as having a large part of his beard torn out by the assailants, and was left languishing in peril of death.[171]

Constables also faced vexatious legal suits in retaliation for actions which they had taken in the course of their police duties. It is difficult to sort out charge and counter-charge in many of these allegedly malicious actions, especially since constables themselves sometimes were accused of bringing such suits against others.[172] Moreover, most of these are Star Chamber cases in which the outcome is not usually known, and in this court claims of malice and vexation constituted a common defence. However, in a few instances men are known to have been guilty of preferring such suits against constables in retaliation for arrests or other actions, and probably they had done so in other cases when officers claimed that they were being prosecuted out of mere malice for legitimate actions which they had taken.

John Hole, the constable of Wells who attempted to suppress the May games and other Sunday festivities in that town, was subjected to several malicious suits as a result of the legal actions which he took against the participants. When he had them arrested and brought before the assizes in Taunton, several of the offenders brought counter-suits against him, apparently vexatious in nature. In addition, the mayor and some of the burgesses, who had been spectators at these events and who had initially secured the release of the offenders, also brought suit against him. They claimed that he had infringed the liberties of the city by seeking legal redress in the courts of the county. This action too seems to have been essentially malicious in character, a means of causing Hole trouble and expense, and they lost the suit. Later, one of the burgesses brought other false charges against Hole, though the suit was preferred in the name of his servant. Eventually he was arrested in London, but by that time he had initiated action in Star Chamber against the offenders.[173]

Other officers too were apparently subjected to vexatious litigation in retaliation for arrests which they had made. A number of them complained of the trouble and expense to which they had been put by

---

[171] PRO, STAC 8/249/11.
[172] See above, ch. 6, nn. 117–22.   [173] PRO, STAC 8/161/1.

men who sought revenge against them for serving warrants. An officer of Chelmarsh, Salop, and two constables of English Frankton in the same county, all protested about having to travel to London as a result of malicious suits brought against them in the central courts by men whom they had apprehended. The Chelmarsh constable was put to additional trouble because the wife of the offender had procured a warrant of the peace against him, obliging him to appear at quarter sessions in Bridgnorth as well.[174] A wife, joined by neighbours, also sought retaliation against a constable of Bursledon, Hants, who had attempted to arrest her husband on suspicion of felony. She charged the officer with rape, in what appears to be a vexatious suit. He was bound over to appear at sessions, though the case did not come to trial. Meanwhile he had preferred a suit of defamation against her in the ecclesiastical courts, but that too seems to have been dropped. However, matters did not end there because the woman also brought suit against the constable in the court leet for the alleged rape, and from there the case went to assizes, where he was once more required to answer the charges. The bill was returned *ignoramus* by the grand jury, but meanwhile the officer had endured considerable trouble and expense as well as having aspersions cast upon his character, and he appealed to Star Chamber for redress.[175] Other officers too claimed that they had been hauled through the courts simply because they had done their duty in making arrests; and one Cornish officer protested that he had been removed from office as a result of a vexatious suit brought by a man whom he arrested for theft on a justice's warrant.[176]

Sometimes those whom constables presented for misdemeanours also sought revenge through vexatious litigation. A man of Advent, Cornwall, who was convicted of causing a nuisance by throwing carrion into the highway, retaliated by bringing the officer who had presented him for the offence before the court leet of the manor on charges of doing him an injury. The constable appealed to the assizes and the judges ordered that if the steward of the leet proceeded with the case he would be prosecuted at assizes as 'a disturber of the execucion of justice'.[177] A Devon gentleman was also found guilty of bringing a malicious suit against two constables who had presented him as a cornmaster who did not bring his corn to market. He charged them with riotous behaviour in searching his barn; but the judges

[174] PRO, STAC 8/101/16; 196/11.
[175] PRO, STAC 81/143/8.   [176] PRO, STAC 8/214/12.
[177] Cockburn, ed., *Western Circuit Assize Orders*, no. 663.

declared that the action had been brought against the officers merely for doing their duty, and the gentleman was ordered to pay double costs.[178] Several men of Audley, Staffordshire, who had been presented by the constable for the conversion of corn to malt and for building illegal cottages also appear to have sought retaliation by bringing a false suit against him. After he left office they apparently conspired with his successor to bring malicious accusations against him, had him publicly arrested in the parish church and conveyed before a justice where he was obliged to put in sureties to appear at the next quarter sessions. His failure to gain redress in a suit in Star Chamber, due to defects in the bill, had allegedly embolded them to take further action against him and procure another warrant for his arrest, and he appealed to Star Chamber for a second time.[179]

Most constables most of the time probably did not meet with such abuses in trying to enforce the law,[180] and historians are no doubt correct to caution against overstating the degree of lawlessness in early modern England.[181] However, some officers obviously did encounter men who did not respect the law or its agents, at least not in the person of the petty constable. Sometimes constables claimed that men who defied them had expressed contempt for the office itself, and even for the authority which it represented. They stated that they would not obey any 'base constable' in England, or that they did not 'reccon nor accompte of any constable in Devonsheere' or that they 'neyther cared for your Majesties name nor for my constables authorytye'.[182] Some such outbursts probably are attributable simply to the personal unpopularity of a particular officer or, as Anthony Fletcher has

---

[178] S. R. Gardiner, ed., *Reports of Cases in the Courts of Star Chamber and the High Commission* (Camden Society, new series, xxxix, 1886), p. 136.

[179] PRO, STAC 8/243/7; 243/8.

[180] In addition to the cases to which reference has been made here, court records also contain a number of other suits in which it was alleged that constables had been resisted or attacked, but there is no indication of which duty they were performing at the time. In many of these instances they probably were also engaged in police duties. See, for example, the following cases in the Staffordshire sessions records, Burne, ed., *Staffs. Sessions Rolls*, i. 271; ii. 137–8; iii. 102; iv. 194–5, 354, 462; v. 104; Staffs. RO, Transcripts Sessions Rolls, Jac. I, Roll 23, no. 59; Roll 31, nos. 26–7; Roll 37, no. 32; Roll 47, no. 25; Roll 54, no. 35; Roll 65, nos. 92–3; Roll 76, no. 66.

[181] e.g. Fletcher, *Sussex*, p. 226. For a general attack on the notion that early modern English society was a violent one see Macfarlane, *The Justice and the Mare's Ale*, esp. the Introduction and Conclusions. His view is challenged by Lawrence Stone, 'Interpersonal Violence in English Society 1300–1980', *P and P*, ci (1982), 22–33.

[182] Quotations from PRO, STAC 8/249/11; 250/3; also see STAC 8/115/9; 217/29.

suggested, to the fact that men sometimes were resentful that a fellow villager whom they regarded as 'no better than themselves' claimed authority to 'interfere with them or their livelihood'. Some officers may have been particularly tactless in the exercise of their powers.[183] On occasions when constables were trying to enforce laws regulating social conduct, it seems probable that some offenders, and occasionally their relatives or friends too, simply did not accept the need for such regulations. Whatever the reasons for the abuse to which some constables were subjected, in view of the resistance which they encountered it is not surprising that they sometimes failed to fulfil their obligations and simply fled the scene. Others may have been intimidated by the fear of violence or of vexatious legal actions, and on some occasions may have neglected their police duties as a result.

The refusal of other inhabitants to assist constables in their police duties sometimes constituted another form of local pressure on them, and such defiance helps to explain their failings in some instances. Although it has been suggested that constables received a good deal of help from their neighbours in fulfilling such duties, sometimes officers were denied the aid they required. The abuses and injuries which they suffered in the course of their police duties resulted at least in part from the fact that men sometimes refused their appeals for assistance and even stood by and watched them be assaulted by an offender. William Harrison in his *Description of England* attested to inhabitants' reluctance to assist constables in pursuing offenders, claiming that 'when hue and crie have beene made, even to the faces of some constables they have said: "God restore your losse! I have other businesse at this time." '[184] Occasionally constables claimed that men had refused to pursue hue and cry or keep watch and ward.[185] However, they more often seem to have been denied aid in executing warrants and making arrests or in quelling disorders, and they sometimes complained that they had been prevented from apprehending offenders because they were refused help. Furthermore, those to whom they entrusted prisoners for conveyance to gaol in some cases

[183] Fletcher, *Sussex*, p. 226; also see Sharpe, 'Crime and Delinquency in an Essex Parish', pp. 103–4.
[184] William Harrison, *Description of England*, ed. F. J. Furnivall (New Shakespeare Society, series vi, no. 1, 1877), p. 232.
[185] e.g. Burne, ed., *Staffs. Sessions Rolls*, iv. 75; v. 225–6, 232; Bund, ed., *Sessions Papers*, pp. 620, 645; Atkinson, ed., *Sessions Records*, i. 92, 231; ii. 96, 98; PRO, STAC 8/178/27.

proved unreliable and allowed them to escape.[186] In some instances inhabitants also refused to assist them in the punishment of vagrants. Villagers were accused of disregarding their statutory duty to apprehend such wanderers and turn them over to a constable, and sometimes of harbouring and relieving them. Those whom constables asked to aid them in whipping vagrants occasionally refused to do so, and even tried to prevent their punishment, while villagers who had been given custody of vagrants to convey them to the next constable or to the House of Correction sometimes allowed them to go free.[187]

As Harrison suggested, men sometimes probably refused to assist constables because they would be called away from their own tasks; and in the case of taking a suspect before a justice or to gaol they might lose half a day's labour or even be away from home overnight. Moreover, rendering aid to an officer in his peacekeeping duties could be dangerous, and there are some indications that villagers failed to co-operate in the apprehension of vagrants in particular because they feared such offenders.[188] Like constables themselves, their assistants were sometimes assaulted and injured, and occasionally seriously. A villager of Goodnestone, Kent, apparently received mortal wounds when he accompanied the borsholder to apprehend a disordered woman, and was struck by a stone she threw down the stairs.[189] On other occasions men may have been sympathetic toward offenders, particularly if they were fellow villagers, and even friends or neighbours, and have been reluctant to assist constables in their apprehension for that reason.

More general, and sometimes more subtle, local pressures also seem

---

[186] Burne, ed., *Staffs. Sessions Rolls*, v. 45; Staffs. RO, Transcripts Sessions Rolls, Roll 31, nos. 98–9; Roll 40, no. 24; QS/O, iii. 124; Lister, ed., *West Riding Sessions*, ii. 141, 217; Atkinson, ed., *Sessions Records*, i. 85, 91, 120, 196; iii. 112, 260, 262; iv. 44; Cockburn, ed., *Essex Indictments, Eliz. I*, no. 2072; *Sussex Indictments, Eliz. I*, no. 1407; *Sussex Indictments, James I*, no. 799; *Western Circuit Assize Orders*, nos. 595, 598; PRO, STAC 8/62/18; 178/27; 186/15; 256/1; 262/11.

[187] Burne, ed., *Staffs. Sessions Rolls*, iv. 265; Staffs. RO, Transcripts Sessions Rolls, Jac. I, Roll 25, no. 29; Roll 73, no. 36; Bund, ed., *Sessions Papers*, pp. 112, 133, 529–30, 565, 577, 640, 698; Hardy, ed., *Calendar to Sessions Records*, p. 235; Atkinson, ed., *Sessions Records*, i. 71, 72, 133, 171; ii. 49; iii. 119–20; Cockburn, ed., *Herts. Indictments, James I*, nos. 579, 1223, 1268, 1295, 1355, 1423; *Kent Indictments, Eliz. I*, no. 2458.

[188] BL Lansdowne MSS 80, fo. 115; 81, fo. 161ᵛ; Read, ed. *William Lambard and Local Government*, pp. 88–90; Bund, ed., *Sessions Papers*, p. 577; PRO, SP 16/467/79.

[189] Cockburn, ed., *Kent Indictments, Eliz. I*, no. 2458; for some other cases of assaults on constables' assistants see PRO, STAC 8/176/18; 256/1; 42/1; Bund, ed., *Sessions Papers*, p. 220; and for a case of vexatious litigation against an assistant, PRO, STAC 8/196/11.

to have affected constables' conduct as police officers, pressures which arose from the fact that villagers' attitudes toward law enforcement sometimes differed from those of higher authorities. Not only do local attitudes toward offenders in some cases seem to have been at odds with the laws of the land, but the costs entailed in peacekeeping and the fact that villagers had their own ways of settling disputes also helped to shape their response to offenders. Sometimes constables can be observed responding to pressures which were prompted by such local considerations, while on other occasions their conduct seems to be explained by the fact that village interests or local loyalties took precedence over their official responsibilities.

Historians have suggested that villagers sometimes did not agree that certain kinds of behaviour deserved the punishments prescribed by law. Some students of eighteenth-century criminal justice have drawn attention to the collective support accorded to some offenders, smugglers, coastal plunderers, poachers, and participants in certain kinds of riots, and to cases in which communities defended such actions as legitimate in defiance of laws which defined them as criminal.[190] Authorities on the seventeenth century have also pointed out that villagers tended to overlook certain misdemeanours or to enforce laws against them rather irregularly. Some have suggested that concepts of order in local communities were often very different from those to which legislators and moralists subscribed, and which were reflected in the statutes of the period. The strict enforcement of the law, which might set neighbour against neighbour, could be more disruptive in small communities than tolerance of certain behaviour, proscribed by law though it might be. Rather flexible local and customary definitions of acceptable conduct thus might come into conflict with more universal, impersonal norms of behaviour enshrined in the laws of the land. Keigh Wrightson contends that villagers were reluctant to prosecute those who had breached economic and social regulations unless their offences were particularly serious and they 'had stepped outside the moral community'; and he attributes constables' failure on some occasions to take action against offenders to 'studied negligence' which derived from such local attitudes. However, he does suggest that during the course of the early seventeenth century village élites came to share the values of their

---

[190] See the articles in Hay *et al.*, eds., *Albion's Fatal Tree*; and E. P. Thompson, 'The Moral Economy of the English Crowd in the Eighteenth Century', *P and P*, 1 (1971), pp. 76–136.

betters, and that 'local notables' were increasingly prepared to enforce the law and to regulate the conduct of their fellow villagers, especially their poorer neighbours.[191]

There is evidence to indicate that some constables, and probably more of them in some counties than in others, were rigorous in their attempts to enforce laws even though their actions met with defiance and sometimes aroused local hostility. Some of the Norfolk constables who seem to have been so assiduous in their punishment of drunkards, despite the resentment which their actions caused,[192] perhaps can be said to have assimilated the values of their betters, though the documents provide no evidence about their motivations in enforcing such laws. Officers like those of Alton, Brinklow, Longdon, and Wells, who met resistance in trying to suppress popular festivities on the Sabbath, appear to have accepted the need to reform popular culture; and perhaps the charges of Puritanism levelled at some of them provide the key to their actions.[193] However, cases of this kind must be balanced by other evidence which suggests that local considerations and village conceptions of order continued to influence the conduct of many constables in fulfilling their law enforcement duties.

There are indications that villagers sometimes viewed with sympathy fellow inhabitants who were wanted for debt, attempting to prevent their apprehension. The refusal of constables to assist the bailiffs who came to arrest such men seems to have been due to the local influences brought to bear on them.[194] Perhaps on some occasions they were merely intimidated by the violence when inhabitants assaulted such officers, and afraid that they too would be attacked if they came to the bailiff's assistance; but it seems probable that they often shared the attitudes of other villagers toward such arrests. A Yorkshire bailiff explicitly attributed the refusal of a constable of Weighton to assist him in the arrest of a man for debt to the fact that he bowed to local influence. He claimed that the officer, 'perceyving (as it seemed) that it was the desire of the said Robert Webster to be freed from arrest, and perceyving the inclinacon and disposicon of the inhabitants . . . there

[191] Wrightson, 'Two concepts of order'; also see Ingram, 'Communities and Courts', pp. 116–18, 127–32; Curtis, 'Quarter Sessions Appearances and their Background', esp. pp. 144–54; Sharpe, 'Enforcing the Law', pp. 105–17.
[192] See above, nn. 154–9.
[193] See above, nn. 161–4.
[194] See above, ch. 6, nn. 90, 138–9; for examples of villagers' attacks on bailiffs in Worcestershire, see Silcock, 'County Government in Worcestershire', p. 136.

present to rescue and free the said Robert Webster', had disregarded his oath of office and declared in the hearing of other inhabitants that the arrest was unlawful and might be resisted. The constable allegedly added that 'it was a shame for the inhabitants to suffer any such honest neyghbour as the said Webster was to be taken from amongst them by any knave bailiffe . . . or by ticketts and warrants which they had no reason to believe'. Acting on this principle, the constable and his fellow officer reportedly joined eighty others, some of them identified as 'of kindred and allyance' to Webster, in their assault on the bailiff and his assistants and in the rescue of Webster.[195] The conduct of a number of other constables who were accused of refusing to assist bailiffs or their underlings in such arrests and some of whom joined their fellow townsmen in assaulting the officers, is probably explained too by the fact that they acted in accord with village attitudes towards these offenders, attitudes which they may have shared.[196]

On some occasions when constables led or joined other inhabitants in certain kinds of social protest they were probably not being merely disorderly and disobedient to the law, but acting in response to pressures from other villagers who regarded these actions as legitimate. They were thus fulfilling local obligations, though these clashed with their official responsibilities. The constable of Belton, Leicestershire, who was accused of abusing his powers when he led other inhabitants in tearing down an enclosure was quite possibly urged by his neighbours to assume this role. In a county where such officers apparently continued to enjoy positions of local leadership in agricultural matters, he was probably not alone in directing such protests.[197]

The nature of constables' presentments to higher authorities, as well as the fact that they sometimes found no offences to present,[198] also seems explicable, at least in part, in terms of village influences brought to bear on them or local attitudes toward offenders which they may have shared. Inevitably there is little evidence about the number and character of offences which never reached the courts. However, the presentments themselves sometimes do contain hints that constables returned those whose conduct had been so disorderly or immoral as to arouse local indignation among many of the inhabitants, while others who were less troublesome or who did not threaten local order were

---

[195] PRO, STAC 8/61/61.   [196] See above, ch. 6, nn. 90, 138–9.
[197] PRO, STAC 8/71/6; and see above, ch. 6, n. 132. Also see ch. 2, nn. 96–7.
[198] See above, ch. 6, nn. 55–6, 58–60.

left alone. Wrightson regards the return of unlicensed ale-sellers as the 'litmus test' of constables' diligence in making presentments, and their willingness to regulate the conduct of their neighbours.[199] It has been noted that the returns made to quarter sessions in the 1630s by Worcestershire constables most often concerned alehouses,[200] and this might suggest that many officers in that county had allied themselves with the state in trying to bring these houses under control. However, a closer examination of these presentments would suggest that many of the offenders fall into Wrightson's category of 'those who had scandalized, threatened or alienated the greater part of the community', and that constables were rather selective in their returns.[201]

It was not uncommon for officers to report that they did not know whether some of the alehouses within their jurisdictions were licensed. The constable of Pershore, St. Andrews, who was ignorant about the seven alehouses in that town in 1635, may have had a valid excuse since he claimed that he had been in office only a month. However, it seems probable that in other cases constables were reluctant to return the names of unlicensed keepers; and whether or not such men possessed licences was perhaps not a matter of great local concern. Sometimes constables justified the existence of an alehouse in terms of the local needs which it served, while protesting their ignorance about the matter of a licence. Occasionally they even suggested that particular circumstances warranted the continuation of an alehouse which they presented as being unlicensed. The constable of Abberley, who in 1635 claimed that he did not know the status of an ale-keeper in that village, pointed out that the man sold ale and bread to many poor and labouring people. An officer of Northfield in 1637 noted that two ale-sellers in that community, whether or not they were licensed, were located in convenient places. The constables of Eastham in 1634 drew attention to the fact that one of the two unlicensed ale-sellers in that village was a poor, blind man. The constable of Holt in 1634 reported two women who sold ale despite 'being suppressed', but pointed out that they allowed no tippling during divine service, and in a later presentment he claimed that an unlicensed keeper dwelt in a convenient place. An officer of Upton-on-Severn who reported that

---

[199] Wrightson, 'Two concepts of order', p. 39.
[200] See above, ch. 6, n. 58.
[201] Wrightson, 'Two concepts or order', p. 29; see Silcock, 'County Government in Worcestershire', p. 100, who suggests that unlicensed ale-sellers were safe from prosecution as long as they kept good order, served local needs, and did not use excessive grain during times of dearth.

there were a number of unlicensed ale-sellers in that township pointed out, however, that they all kept good order, sold a full quart for a penny, and did not sell ale during divine service.[202]

When constables did call for action against unlicensed ale-sellers or those who had broken the assize, the presentments often seem to have been prompted not so much by these offences as by the fact that the keepers were guilty of disorderly conduct which had disrupted the community and probably had exceeded the bounds of neighbourly tolerance. Sometimes officers indicated explicitly that they were acting on behalf of the inhabitants in presenting such offenders. Four unlicensed ale-sellers reported by the constable of St. Michael's Bedwardine were accused of selling ale during divine service and also of entertaining all sorts of people in the night and at other times 'disturbing and disquieting their neighbours'. It was specifically on behalf of the inhabitants that the constable of Claines requested that four unlicensed ale-sellers in that township be suppressed in 1637 'during the time of this dreadful visitation', and presumably in this case the residents had taken action because they feared that strangers who might have the plague would resort to these houses. The constable of Whistons presented an ale-keeper who sold less than a quart for a penny, but it was probably not primarily this offence, but the fact that he was running a 'bawdy house' as well as an alehouse which aroused local opinion and got him into trouble. He had taken as an inmate a 'lewd woman' and reportedly allowed diverse persons to keep her company during the night, and had permitted her to be begotten with child on the very bed where he usually slept. His wife allegedly had put her apron in front of the window to hide these goings on, but this seems to have provided insufficient protection against the eyes of peering neighbours. A victualler of Shipston-on-Stour probably was presented not so much because he lacked a licence as because he kept disorder in his house, and allowed drinking at inappropriate times.[203]

Local opinion also seems to have been aroused by keepers who had been suppressed, probably often at the request of the village and because they were disorderly, but who sold ale again; and constables returned the names of a number of such offenders. The officers of Stone in 1637–8, one of whom was that very prosperous yeoman, John

---

[202] Bund, ed., *Sessions Papers*, pp. 601, 596, 641, 578, 567, 577, 567; also see returns from Bredon (p. 649), Eckington (p. 597), Hartlebury (p. 614), and Upton Warren (p. 565).

[203] Bund, ed., *Sessions Papers*, pp. 657, 639, 647, 597.

Oldnoll,[204] had acted at the request of the inhabitants of that township to gain the suppression of an ale-seller, and although the grounds are not known his conduct seems to have aroused considerable local hostility. When he continued to sell ale, despite being suppressed by the justices, the constables wrote to the clerk of the peace expressing the wish of the inhabitants that further action be taken against him.[205] Officers of Bayton, Bredon, Oddingley, and Tredington also presented keepers who had been suppressed but none the less continued their trades.[206]

Licensed keepers could also find themselves in trouble if they were so disorderly as to have aroused local antagonism, and especially if they had ignored earlier warnings to mend their ways. A tavern keeper of Pershore Holy Cross was presented because he entertained both strangers and townsmen all night, drinking and quarrelling, 'to the great disturbance of the neighbours', and he had continued such activities despite previous admonitions.[207] While the constable of Upton-on-Severn did not call for action against the unlicensed ale-sellers in that township, claiming that they all kept good order, he did present a *licensed* keeper whom he claimed sold ale at undue times during the night and who kept odious and loathsome drunkenness in his house at all times 'so that his neighbours cannot rest in their houses for the odious noise of drunkenness and voices of drunken men in the night time'.[208] The constable of Mathon returned a victualler guilty of similar behaviour; he allowed the parishioners to drink at all times, and for whole days and nights together.[209]

The selectivity of Worcestershire constables' presentments, and the extent to which they were affected by local considerations, is also suggested by the absence of returns of drunkards. Despite their reference to the drunken men who haunted the disorderly alehouses which they presented, only William Woodhouse, constable of Salwarpe,[210] reported a drunkard. The man whose name he returned seems to have had a long-standing reputation for quarrelsome and disorderly behaviour. It probably was the same man, Edward Bovey, weaver, who along with his wife was bound by recognizance to appear at sessions in 1619 and to keep the peace against a Salwarpe couple.

[204] On Oldnoll see above, ch. 4, n. 55.
[205] Bund, ed., *Sessions Papers*, p. 658.
[206] Ibid., pp. 645, 564, 567, 564 (2).   [207] Ibid., p. 648.
[208] Ibid., p. 567.   [209] Ibid., p. 578.
[210] On the Woodhouse family see above, ch. 4, n. 60.

An indictment of 1634, very likely against this man and in response to Woodhouse's presentment, though the name given in the sessions calendar is Edward 'Bayle', described him as 'a very drunken man and a mover of quarrels amongst his neighbours'.[211] It appears that Worcestershire constables were unlikely to present men for drunkenness except in cases when such offenders had a local reputation of this kind, and had long antagonized their fellow villagers.

Not only do villagers' views of offences and offenders sometimes seem to have differed from those enshrined in the laws of the land; their attitudes also seem to have been shaped in some cases by the cost that could be entailed in the pursuit, arrest, and punishment of offenders. It was not only those villagers called out to aid the constable who felt the burdens of peacekeeping. The community as a whole was often obliged to pay the expenses entailed in apprehending and guarding suspects and conveying them before a justice or to gaol, as well as the costs of preparing passes for vagrants or sending them to the House of Correction. The reluctance of inhabitants to bear such burdens was probably in some cases translated into pressures on constables to turn a blind eye to certain offenders. Walter J. King has suggested that Lancashire villagers were sensitive to the costs of law enforcement and especially to the expense of conveying vagrants to the House of Correction.[212] In other counties too inhabitants sometimes seem to have been uncooperative in meeting the costs entailed in dealing with vagrants and other poor wanderers.[213] Similar concerns may sometimes help to explain inhabitants' reluctance to arrest other offenders. The bill could mount up by the time the expenses of apprehending, watching, lodging, and feeding a suspect were added to those incurred in conveying him to a justice or the gaol, and in many instances the village had to bear such charges.[214] William Harrison claimed that he had 'knowne . . . that thieves have beene let passe because the covetous and greedie parishoners would neither take the

---

[211] Bund, ed., *Sessions Papers*, pp. 566, 279, 533.

[212] King, 'Vagrancy and Local Law Enforcement', 276–83.

[213] e.g. PRO, SP 16/255/47; Barnes, ed., *Somerset Assize Orders*, p. 32; Herts. RO, QS/B, 2A, ff. 53ᵛ–54; Bund, ed., *Sessions Papers*, p. 247.

[214] The tally for the arrest of one man in Pattingham in 1630–1 came to 15s., and it would not take many such arrests to substantially increase village taxes (Pattingham Constables' Accounts, 1630–31). A Cornish constable claimed to have spent the rather large sum of £7. 7s. 4d. in watching, keeping, and sending to prison a man accused of murdering his wife, but in that case he was reimbursed out of the man's goods (Cockburn, ed., *Western Circuit Assize Orders*, no. 649).

paines nor be at the charge to carrie them to prison if it were far off'.[215] In view of the local expenses that could be entailed, villagers, and in turn their constables, sometimes probably did think twice about the virtues of apprehending some offenders, or at least about the need to take cases before higher authorities if they could be settled locally.

It was not only that the official system of justice could be burdensome and expensive for villagers, but local communities had their own methods of dealing with offenders, and this fact too helped to influence constables' conduct in fulfilling their police duties.[216] Historians have drawn attention to the 'self-regulating' nature of village communities and have suggested that it was often only after 'neighbourly intervention' or 'communal censure' had failed to settle a dispute or reform an offender that the inhabitants were prepared to take a case to court. Sometimes there were pressures to allow disputes to be settled locally through arbitration rather than through the official channels of justice, and occasionally constables can be seen responding to such demands. On the other hand, inhabitants sometimes took the law into their own hands and employed folk punishments such as charivaris, skimmingtons, and ducking in the cuckstool to deal with offenders, penalties that were unofficial however traditional they may have been. In such cases constables could be under pressure to lend the weight of their office in imposing such unauthorized punishments on local offenders.

Occasionally constables who had apprehended offenders or brought suit against them can be seen responding to local pleas to show 'neighbourly tolerance' or to spare the community further trouble and expense by allowing these cases to be settled out of court. When a

---

[215] Harrison, *Description of England*, p. 232.

[216] The following discussion is based on Ingram, 'Communities and Courts', pp. 125–7; Curtis, 'Quarter Sessions Appearances and their Background', pp. 137–8, 142–3; Sharpe, 'Crime and Delinquency in an Essex Parish', pp. 107–8 and his 'Enforcing the Law', pp. 111–17; Wrightson, 'Two concepts of order', p. 30; Keith Thomas, *Religion and the Decline of Magic* (New York, 1970), pp. 527–9; Thomas, 'The Puritans and Adultery: The Act of 1650 Reconsidered', in Donald Pennington and Keith Thomas, eds., *Puritans and Revolutionaries* (Oxford, 1978), pp. 266–7 and the references cited there; E. P. Thompson, '"Rough Music": le charivari anglais', *Annales ESC*, xxvii (1972), pp. 285–312; G. R. Quaife, *Wanton Wenches and Wayward Wives: Peasants and Illicit Sex in Early Seventeenth-Century England* (New Brunswick, New Jersey, 1979), pp. 198–201; Lawrence Stone, *The Family, Sex and Marriage in England 1500–1800* (New York, 1977), p. 145; Martin Ingram, 'Le charivari dans l'Angleterre du XVIᵉ et du XVIIᵉ siècle', in Jacques Le Goff and Jean-Claude Schmitt, eds., *Le Charivari*, Actes de la ronde organisée à Paris 25–27 avril 1977 (Paris, 1981), pp. 251–64.

number of inhabitants of Upper Mitton in the parish of Hartlebury, Worcestershire, were called from haying to help the constable in apprehending and placing in the stocks an allegedly drunken husbandman/alehouse keeper who had assaulted him with a corn pike, they urged the officer not to take the offender before a justice for his misdemeanour but to allow the matter to 'be referred to neighbours without further trouble'. He accepted their suggestion, according to his account agreeing to 'stand to such order as neighbours should sett down' because he was 'unwilling to take advantage of the complainants weaknes, being his neighbour'.[217] An officer of Wellington, Salop, who had been assaulted and wounded by a villager while aiding the bailiffs in arresting him, and who had submitted a bill against the offender to the Council in the Marches, also responded to neighbourly pressures to settle the quarrel outside the courts. He apparently was persuaded to accept composition before the case came to trial, in his words 'beinge the rather induced to yeald thereunto' since the man was 'his neightboure'.[218] The officer of Hants who was maliciously sued for rape by the wife of a man whom he had apprehended as a suspected felon, and who in turn brought charges of defamation against her, also agreed to settle the dispute out of court and to 'stand to the order and arbitrement of certain freinds', probably also at the urging of some of his fellow villagers.[219] In view of the fact that constables bowed to village opinion to refer disputes to local arbitrators even when they were the injured parties, it seems even more likely that they often did so when other residents were engaged in disputes, and they had nothing to lose personally.

Sometimes when constables were accused of exceeding or abusing their police powers their actions seem to be explained by the fact that they had responded to local pressures to inflict punishment on an offender. The constable of Burton-upon-Trent, Staffordshire, who led about forty inhabitants in punishing two residents accused of cohabiting and having sexual relations without benefit of marriage was accused of personal malice. However, he seems to have taken this action in response to demands from other townsmen that communal censure be imposed on the couple. The officer was no doubt correct when, in defending his actions in a Star Chamber suit, he claimed that the punishment meted out to the couple was traditional for such offences; but they had not been found guilty of incontinence by due

---

[217] PRO, STAC 8/95/11.   [218] PRO, STAC 8/291/5.
[219] PRO, STAC 8/143/8.

course of law and he had no authorization from higher authorities to punish them. He had acted merely at the urging of his neighbours, claiming that he was 'very much pressed' by them to inflict punishment on the offenders.[220] Similar local pressures seem to account for the actions of a constable and tithingman of Nettleton, Wiltshire. They found themselves in trouble with the law because they had joined other inhabitants in ducking a woman as a scold, although charges against her in the court leet had been dismissed. When the villagers were dissuaded by the curate from apprehending the woman on her way to church, they persuaded the constable and tithingman to assist them; and they were able to gain access to the scold's house by virtue of the fact that these officers pretended to be searching for thieves. In an apparent display of contempt for the household the villagers, who had found some pottage, 'did pisse into the said pott and thereby spoyled the said pottage', and they also devoured two mince pies. After remaining on guard all night they carted the woman off to the river on the following morning and ducked her seven times. She and her husband claimed that she was in peril of her life due to the extreme cold, and no doubt it was a chilly experience on a December morning. In their defence the constable and tithingman claimed that they had only done their duty in carrying out the law against scolds. However, their actions seem to have been rather extreme, and their only authorization for inflicting such punishment was the demand of some of their fellow inhabitants.[221] Two constables of Prescot, Lancashire, who were hauled before the courts for ducking a woman of that town also seem to have acted in response to pressures from other townsmen. Rumours that she had been found naked in bed with a man other than her husband led to demands for her punishment.[222]

Local pressures of various kinds were thus brought to bear on constables in the course of their police duties, and there is evidence to suggest that their actions sometimes were affected by such pressures. It is difficult to determine how often they may have faced outright obstruction and abuse. However, at least some of them were prevented or deterred from fulfilling their police duties by the defiance which they encountered from offenders, and sometimes also from other villagers who refused to assist them in their peacekeeping tasks. Local

[220] PRO, STAC 8/104/20. For a further discussion of this case see my article ' "Folk Justice" and Royal Justice in Early Seventeenth-Century England: A "Charivari" in the Midlands', *Midland History*, viii (1983), 70–85.

[221] PRO, STAC 8/123/16.   [222] PRO, STAC 8/152/1, 152/26.

pressures of a more general nature, arising from the fact that villagers' attitudes toward offenders and their views of law enforcement sometimes clashed with the state's prescriptions and the demands of the official system of justice, were probably of even greater importance in influencing constables' conduct as police officers. On many occasions constables did fulfil their royal duties,[223] and some of them appear to have been particularly vigorous as 'king's men', enforcing social and economic legislation without regard to local considerations. However, the resistance which they sometimes encountered would suggest that these regulations were not always viewed within the village in quite the same light as they were by the parliamentarians who had enacted them. Officers often appear to have been rather sensitive to such local attitudes and interests, attempting to juggle the demands being placed on them by their fellow villagers and by their superiors. Such behaviour frequently seems to characterize their presentments of offenders to higher authorities. Sometimes, as in instances when they joined other villagers in thwarting the efforts of bailiffs to make an arrest, when they led social protests, or when they inflicted unauthorized punishment on an offender, they appear to have bowed more completely to local pressures, ignoring their obligations as royal officers.

(c) Resistance to Military Service and Local Attitudes Toward Impressment

There is also some evidence, though of a rather indirect nature, to suggest that the deficiencies attributed to constables in fulfilling their military duties sometimes derived in part from the resistance which they encountered and their response to local pressures. There are occasional reports of constables meeting with disobedience when they ordered men to attend musters, and a few instances in which they were subjected to verbal or physical abuse. An officer of Over Arley, Staffordshire, reported that a man who had refused to attend musters on three occasions resisted him 'with most opprobrious and thretninge wordes and stroke at me three or foure tymes and threwe at me two cuppes and hit me on the head with a paile'. Apparently unsatisfied with the damage he had inflicted on the officer he lamented 'that he had not made my puddinges a praye for the pies and the crowes'.[224]

---

[223] See above, ch. 6.

[224] Burne, ed., *Staffs. Sessions Rolls*, iv. 456; for a number of presentments by Staffordshire constables between 1593 and 1602, in which they claimed that men had refused to attend musters, see Burne, ed., *Staffs. Sessions Rolls*, ii. 340; iii. 130, 144–6; iv. 75, 294–5, 296–9, 352–3, 415–18, 444–5.

While evidence of men's reluctance to serve at musters is not very plentiful, there are suggestions of an indirect nature that constables probably met with greater resistance and disobedience in pressing soldiers for military duty. In fulfilling this responsibility they also seem to have experienced more general village pressures which help to explain their deficiences as press-men.

Military service appears to have been rather unpopular. There are reports of recruits escaping from their captains or conductors, sometimes after they had received their press money, and special watches occasionally were established in a county for apprehending them.[225] Constables too in some instances are known to have encountered such disobedience when they pressed men. Two Pattingham officers in 1598 were obliged to pursue a runaway soldier to Newport in Salop, having procured a warrant for his return to Staffordshire.[226] If constables were not often put to such trouble, it was probably because they usually kept under careful guard the soldiers whom they had pressed,[227] and not because men were co-operative about doing military service. However, placing them under watch was not always sufficient guarantee that they would be kept safe. Occasionally an officer seems to have been thwarted in his efforts to press soldiers because a friend came to the rescue of a recruit and helped him to escape custody.[228]

Although even more difficult to document, constables engaged in pressing soldiers probably also faced pressures from other villagers, who had their own ideas about the kind of men that it was appropriate to press. Local attitudes toward impressment are most apparent in 1640 when men from the trained bands were allowed to be recruited for the war against the Scots, and when in some counties there were protests about such substantial villagers being sent off to battle. The deputy lieutenants of Hertfordshire reported to the Council that the inhabitants were unwilling to press able men from the trained bands, while explaining that they had been able to raise soldiers the previous year because the county had sent men to whom they 'were willing to give theyre moneys to purge from amongst them'.[229] As long as men of this kind could be found all was well, but it seems likely that constables

---

[225] Earwaker, ed., *Constables' Accounts*, i. 145; PRO, SP 16/81/4; 459/7; NNRO, PD 50/36L, no. 66; and for refusals of men to receive press money see PRO, SP 16/461/2, 13. Also see Stearns, 'Conscription and English Society', 15.
[226] Pattingham Constables' Accounts, 1598-9.
[227] See above, ch. 5, nn. 137-8.
[228] PRO, STAC 8/238/33.   [229] PRO, SP 16/450/104.

met with local opposition if they attempted to recruit for service those 'able inhabitants' whom their superiors instructed them to supply on such occasions.[230]

T. G. Barnes suggests that in Somerset substantial farmers and their sons escaped impressment due to the connivance of constables,[231] and it seems probable that local pressures on them and their own local loyalties often did lead them to exempt such men, and in general help to explain their conduct as press-men. A few of them may have been dishonest and have accepted bribes in return for freeing men from service, or have used their powers for selfish ends and pressed their enemies;[232] but sometimes their actions are probably explained by the local circumstances they faced in trying to raise recruits. When they apprehended strangers or hired them to serve, rather than returning men from their own communities, such action seems attributable, at least in part, to the pressures which they experienced within the village and the opposition they encountered if they attempted to recruit local men.[233] The constable of Waltham, who in 1640 negotiated for a reduction in the number of soldiers being demanded from that village, was probably responding to local pressures too.[234] He appears to have represented village interests in this matter just as other officers did when they negotiated for reductions in provision or in the requisitions of saltpetre men and postmasters.[235] Like them he was placing his local obligations ahead of his responsibilities as a royal officer.

The nature and extent of the local pressures which constables experienced thus varied over time and from duty to duty. They often seem to have been remarkably successful in gaining both the co-operation and the active assistance of their fellow inhabitants in fulfilling their duties, whether in tax collecting, their administrative and judicial tasks, or their military functions. Their success in meeting many of the demands placed on them owed much to the amount of aid which they received from their neighbours. However, they sometimes met with disobedience, and even violence, from reluctant taxpayers, from law-breakers, and from men averse to doing military service; and

---

[230] See above, ch. 5, nn. 140–6; for instructions on pressing men for Count Mansfeld see PRO, SP 14/173/92, and for instructions in 1639 see PRO, SP 16/413/111; 414/157.

[231] Barnes, *Somerset*, p. 113.   [232] See above, ch. 5, nn. 147–52.

[233] On the pressing of strangers see above, ch. 5, nn. 140–2, 144–5. On conflicts between local interests and the demands of the state in pressing soldiers also see Stearns, 'Conscription and English Society', 5–7, 10, 22–3.

[234] See above, ch. 5, n. 136.   [235] See above, nn. 128–38.

such defiance prevented or deterred them from fulfilling their duties. Inhabitants who so often provided assistance to constables could also express their opposition to the demands of these officials by refusing to co-operate with them and by withholding such aid. They thus brought considerable pressure to bear on them to refrain from action or to give their obligations as village representatives priority over their duties as 'king's men'. Pressures of this kind help to explain constables' defaults in collecting ship-money and military levies in the later 1630s, and their actions in trying to procure reductions in the state's demands for goods and services, whether for the royal household or for saltpetre men and postmasters. Constables' conduct as police officers too was occasionally affected by the refusal of other villagers to assist them in their duties, while local reluctance to bear the costs entailed in law enforcement also seems to have had a rather dampening effect on the diligence of such officers. Moreover, local attitudes toward offenders sometimes differed from those of higher authorities, while the 'folk justice' of the village provided a partial alternative to royal justice. Constables' conduct as police officers was sometimes shaped by their attempts to balance these local concepts of order against official demands from their superiors for the apprehension and presentment of offenders. On some occasions their behaviour in pressing soldiers seems to have been affected by similar conflicts between village interests and those of the state. They were caught between the demands of higher authorities that they press able inhabitants for military service and pressures from villagers who regarded the press as a means of ridding the community of the disordered and unwanted.

III. CONCLUSIONS

The constableship was a demanding and difficult position due not only to the many duties which it entailed, but also to the conflicting pressures which constables experienced as a result of the very nature of the office, and of their mediating role in linking the village and the state. On many occasions constables were successful in fulfilling the demands that were placed on them by the state, and they often gained the co-operation of other villagers in doing so. However, in some instances they met with obstruction and abuse which prevented or deterred them from carrying out their duties, while in other cases they experienced other kinds of local pressures which conflicted with the demands imposed on them by the state. It often required a rather careful balancing act if they were to attempt to satisfy both their superiors and their fellow inhabitants, and in some instances it was impossible to do so.

Pressures from their superiors were applied rather unevenly, but in general terms constables were more regularly and more explicitly accountable to higher authorities during the early seventeenth century than they had been prior to that time. However, the pressures from above were considerably increased during some periods, and constables appear to have displayed particular diligence in performing certain duties as a result of closer supervision from their superiors. An apparent improvement during the 1630s in their performance in punishing vagrants, and in some counties in returning presentments to higher authorities, can probably be attributed to the pressures brought to bear on them by the justices at their monthly meetings. Such officers also seem to have given increased attention to the communal arms at certain periods in response to particular pressures from their military superiors. However, the ineffectiveness of the punishments which sheriffs imposed on constables who were negligent in levying ship-money illustrate some of the limitations experienced by higher officials in their efforts to influence the conduct of constables.

There were also variations in the character and intensity of the local pressures exerted upon constables. While villagers were often co-operative in meeting the demands imposed by the state, on some occasions they brought counter-pressures to bear on such officers and sometimes subjected them to various kinds of local sanctions. Constables appear to have experienced the greatest obstruction in their attempts to levy ship-money and coat and conduct money in 1639–40, but some officers also met with defiance in fulfilling their police duties and their military functions as well. In addition constables also experienced more subtle local pressures in the course of law enforcement and in pressing soldiers, pressures which arose from the fact that villagers' attitudes and interests sometimes were at odds with official regulations and requirements.

The extent of the local pressures on constables probably varied somewhat from community to community, depending upon the character of the settlement and in turn upon the nature of the relationship between constables and their fellow villagers. The survival of especially detailed constables' accounts for Pattingham, Branston, and Waltham is probably not in itself sufficient to explain the fact that the constables of these settlements seemed to have enjoyed the greatest amount of local co-operation and assistance in fulfilling their duties. In villages of this kind, with fairly settled populations and where economic and social differentiation were not very marked,[236] inhabitants seem to have joined together, under the leadership of constables who still acted as 'village headmen', to fulfil the demands imposed on local communities by the state. However, if constables in such villages were most likely to gain the support which they required in fulfilling their duties, such officers would also be particularly subject to communal pressures on occasions when local interests were in conflict with the demands of the state.

The constableship may sometimes have functioned rather differently in townships where population turnover, greater social stratification, and perhaps differences in religion and values, had undermined 'community', loosening ties among villagers and in some cases leading to a polarization of village society. In settlements such as Gissing and Bushey, for example, where newcomers often seem to have served as constable,[237] the relationship of these officers with their local public may have been rather different from that which existed in villages such as Pattingham, Branston, and Waltham. They presumably would not have enjoyed the network of ties within the village on which constables from established families could draw for support. It must have been easier for inhabitants to resist the demands of such constables, who at the same time may have been particularly subject to local intimidation. In villages such as Little Munden, Salwarpe, and Stone, where local society was more highly stratified than in Pattingham, Branston, and Waltham, and where many of the constables were drawn from the yeoman élite,[238] divisions within the community sometimes may have reduced both the local support and the local pressures experienced by such officers. These 'village notables' were perhaps more likely to align themselves with the state, either because they had come to share the interests and values of their superiors or because of their own 'social aspirations'.[239]

---

[236] See above, ch. 4.   [237] See above, ch. 4.

[238] See above, ch. 4.

[239] Morrill, *Cheshire Grand Jury*, p. 46, suggests that in the case of the substantial freeholders who served on grand juries their 'possible social aspirations might have set them slightly apart from the social pressures and the consensus of opinion in the community', and this may have been true of some of the yeomen constables as well.

8

The Localities and the Central Government: Constables, Communities, and the State

THE duties, selection, social characteristics, and conduct of the constables of a number of communities have been considered in some detail in this study. It remains to draw together the threads of the particular arguments presented here, and to suggest what this examination of the constableship reveals about the character of local government, and about the relationship between the state and the localities, under Elizabeth and the early Stuarts.

It is widely accepted that the central government attempted to increase its control over the localities during the late sixteenth and early seventeenth centuries, and historians have drawn attention to both legislative and administrative interventions during this period. Earlier writers often contended that these efforts met with limited success due to local resistance, and to the negligence and incompetence of local officials at all levels. However, recently it has been suggested that the state was relatively effective in tightening its control over local government and, at least in the area of law enforcement, in gaining implementation of its policies.[1] This success is attributed not only to the intensified pressures which the central government exerted on local officials, or to institutional improvements such as the monthly meetings of the justices, but also to growing local support for the government's policies. At the village level such co-operation is viewed as a product of growing social and economic differentiation and of the emergence of parish élites who, it is claimed, were increasingly distanced from their neighbours not only by their wealth and their style of life, but also by their attitudes and behaviour. Whether they were prompted by economic concerns about the growing numbers of 'the poor' or by a Puritan belief in the need for social and moral reform, or

[1] The following discussion is based primarily on Wrightson, *English Society*, esp. pp. 151–5, 164–71, 180–1; Wrightson and Levine, *Terling*, esp. pp. 2, 7–9, 115–16, 134–41; Wrightson, 'Two concepts of order', pp. 39–46; but also see Hunt, *The Puritan Moment*, chs. 2 and 6 and esp. pp. 79–83, 130–44; and Clark, *English Provincial Society*, esp. pp. 116, 120–2, 144–6, 155–7, 175–7, 180–1, 249–51, 352.

a combination of the two, it is suggested that the 'village notables' who controlled parish government often became anxious to enforce local order. As they distanced themselves from 'customary' behaviour and the disorders of traditional popular culture, they identified their interests with those of the magistracy and co-operated in the implementation of the government's policies. Moreover, it is suggested that administrative pressures from the state, combined with the desire by such élites to exercise social control within their own communities, led to greater formalization of parish government and often to the institutionalization of local oligarchies in 'closed vestries'. It is with these larger themes concerning the nature of local government and the relations between the localities and the state that this chapter will be concerned.

The central government's attempts to exert its power in the localities, and the growth in county administration during the late sixteenth and early seventeenth centuries, probably did contribute in some measure to more formal organization of parish government. By the end of the sixteenth century the parish had replaced the manor or the township as the basic administrative unit in many, if not all, areas of the country. It has been shown that even in cases when courts leet had survived and were responsible for the selection of constables, these officials often were regarded as 'parish' officers and presented their accounts to the vestry.[2] Moreover, legislation of the late sixteenth and early seventeenth centuries which brought constables into closer association with the churchwardens, overseers, and surveyors, and often conferred upon them joint duties, probably encouraged the formation of parish vestries dominated by these local office-holders.[3]

However, evidence presented in this study concerning the selection of constables, patterns of office-holding, and the execution of the duties of the position would suggest that there are dangers in placing too much emphasis on either the formality of local government or its oligarchical character. It has been shown that there were variations from community to community in the distribution of local offices, and also that village custom and rather informal institutional arrangements still affected the character of local government.

Although the economic conditions of the late sixteenth and early seventeenth centuries may have accelerated a trend towards growing

---

[2] See ch. 3.   [3] See ch. 2.

social differentiation in rural communities, it has been seen that such developments were much less marked in some villages than in others. In settlements such as Little Munden, Salwarpe, Stone, and Gissing a few prosperous yeomen, along with an occasional lesser gentleman, occupied the heights of village society, while there were substantial numbers of poor cottagers at the bottom of the scale in some of these communities. However, in villages such as Branston and Waltham wealth seems to have been much more evenly distributed among a number of middling-sized farmers. This was true in Pattingham too, although this settlement also contained a number of craftsmen and tradesmen of moderate prosperity, and during the early seventeenth century there were growing numbers of poor cottagers in the village. Bushey differed from all of these communities in the number of gentlemen which it contained, but below that social level wealth seems to have been fairly broadly distributed among a number of small farmers and tradesmen. Differences in manorial organization, in settlement patterns, and in the form of agriculture all contributed to variations in the character of local communities, as did the extent of population mobility which varied considerably from settlement to settlement.[4]

These differences in the economic and social characteristics of rural communities were matched by variations in the distribution of parish offices and in patterns of local government. While many earlier historians suggested that constables were lowly in status,[5] it has been shown that the officers of the communities examined here usually were chosen from among the middling and upper reaches of village society, including husbandmen, some craftsmen and tradesmen, yeomen, and a few gentlemen. The evidence indicates that these same men filled the other major local offices as well. However, there were some variations from village to village in the social status of constables, their levels of literacy, the extent of their connections with the settlements in which they served, and in the frequency with which men held office.[6] If constables were not usually of the poorer sort, neither was it the case that office-holding always came to be monopolized by 'village notables' or that parish government was in the hands of a self-perpetuating élite. Even when there was an inner circle of men who formed the vestry, they did not always dominate local offices, nor was membership necessarily confined to a small number of families who served on the

---

⁴ See ch. 4.   ⁵ See ch. 1.   ⁶ See ch. 4.

vestry year after year. A village such as Little Munden does fit the model of a community in which local government was dominated by a group of leading householders. At least this seems to have been the case in the 1630s and early 1640s when fourteen men filled fifty of seventy terms as constable, churchwarden, and overseer, some of them holding office five or even seven times during the fourteen year period 1629–30 to 1642–3. Were the information more complete, the extent of office-holding by these few men probably would prove even more striking.[7] A similar situation may have prevailed in Stone. The list of constables is very incomplete, though a number of prosperous yeomen are known to have held the office, and the names of the overseers are not known; but a small number of families did fill the office of churchwarden, and these men often held the position for a number of consecutive terms.[8] It is possible that parish élites also controlled local government in Salwarpe and Gissing, where a number of substantial yeomen held the constableship and regularly served as churchwardens as well.[9] However, such patterns are not found in all communities; and in considering the structure of local government it is necessary to give equal weight to villages such as Pattingham and Bushey where both wealth and local office appear to have been more widely distributed. In Pattingham thirty-nine different men filled fifty-six terms as constable and churchwarden in the years between 1629–30 and 1642–3, a pattern rather different from that in Little Munden during the same period. Although three men (and a substitute who held the constable-ship) served three terms during this period, and nine men held office twice, the evidence does not suggest that local government in Pattingham was controlled by a small group of householders.[10] There was a greater tendency in Bushey for a few men to hold office more frequently, but the lists of constables, churchwardens, and surveyors for the period 1621–2 to 1632–3 would not suggest that the government of the parish was in the hands of an élite.[11] Eight men did serve a combined total of 30 out of 72 terms during these twelve years, but 31 men holding office only once or twice filled the remaining 42 terms. In the smaller villages of Branston and Waltham local offices

[7] The names of the constables are known for the entire period, but the names of the churchwardens for only 11 of the 14 years and the names of the overseers for only 10 years. Also see ch. 4, n. 222.

[8] See ch. 4, n. 224.   [9] See ch. 4, nn. 223–4.   [10] See ch. 4, n. 225.

[11] The period 1621–2 to 1632–3 was selected for analysis because the lists of constables, churchwardens, and surveyors are complete for those years. Also see ch. 4, n. 227.

also seem to have circulated among the middling-size farmers in these communities, even if some men were selected for such positions more frequently than others.[12]

Not only were there variations in patterns of office-holding, but parish government often seems to have remained rather informal in nature. This fact is perhaps most apparent in the role played by ordinary inhabitants in the performance of 'official' duties. While villagers were obliged to assist constables in peacekeeping and the assessment of taxes, their participation was not confined to these duties. This study has shown that many other tasks of local government too were carried out by men who held no official position. Not only did inhabitants take over the contable's functions when he was absent from the village, but they sometimes acted in his place in paying rates or making presentments to higher authorities. Furthermore, villagers assisted constables, or acted under their direction, in fulfilling a host of other duties, ranging from the punishment of vagrants to the pressing of soldiers to meeting the demands of saltpetre men and postmasters.[13] The work of local government continued to be, to a significant extent, 'communal' in nature; and in the performance of their duties constables were as much executive officers of the village as they were royal officials.

Although many of the duties of the constableship were a product of common law or parliamentary legislation, and applied to all incumbents, there were still some local variations in the responsibilities attached to the office. Village custom often continued to play a role in shaping the character of the position. There were differences among communities in the division of responsibilities between constables and church-wardens, variations attributable only in part to legislation which made them alternate authorities in fulfilling certain duties, and which were probably more often a product of particular local arrangements.[14] Even more important, the kinds of local tasks which were attached to the office varied considerably from one village to another. It has been shown that in some cases agricultural duties within the village constituted an important part of a constable's responsibilities, as was the case in communities such as Branston and Waltham, while in other settlements some of these same duties were attached to the office of churchwarden. On the other hand, in some villages there is no

[12] See ch. 4, nn. 220–1.
[13] See ch. 2 and ch. 7.
[14] See ch. 2.

evidence of either constables or churchwardens enjoying functions of this kind.[15]

Furthermore, as long as constables were selected locally in accord with customs which varied from village to village, rather than by the central government or their administrative superiors, local government was unlikely to be entirely uniform or completely subordinated to higher authorities. It has been shown that constables were often sworn into office by the justices, although this was not invariably the case, and that the magistrates also made some attempts to intervene in the selection of such officers during the early seventeenth century. By the 1630s the justices in Hertfordshire, as well as in Essex, sometimes removed constables whom they deemed inadequate and replaced them; and in Kent the magistrates had apparently sought to gain control over the appointment of local officials as early as the first decade of the seventeenth century. During the later 1630s the justices in a number of counties also questioned the validity of certain customary procedures which had been used in the selection of such officers.[16] While these facts do suggest that county officials in certain parts of the country attempted to exert greater control over parish government, particularly during the 1630s, it is none the less the case that in the counties examined here constables normally did not become the appointees of the justices. Although the magistrates provided general oversight of the constabulary, it has been shown that they usually intervened in appointments only when disputes about the selection of such officers were brought to their attention. Even then they seldom resolved the matter by choosing a constable, and their orders normally showed respect for local rights and customary procedures.[17] Since in most cases constables were chosen locally, and were accountable to their fellow inhabitants as well as to their administrative superiors, they thus had dual obligations and were not exclusively officers of the state.[18] Moreover, it has been suggested that because they were members of the villages in which they held office, and bound to other inhabitants by many personal ties, they were likely to be influenced by local loyalties and considerations which sometimes clashed with their duties to the state.[19]

In a number of respects village government thus continued to

[15] See ch. 2.
[16] See ch. 3; on attempts to intervene in the selection of constables in Kent see Clark, *English Provincial Society*, p. 144.
[17] See ch. 3.   [18] See ch. 3.   [19] See ch. 7.

display diversity and informality, and to be shaped in part by local custom. However, an examination of the constableship suggests that the powers of the state did impinge more forcefully upon the localities during the late sixteenth and early seventeenth centuries than in earlier years, and also that the government was more successful in gaining the co-operation of local officials in the enforcement of its policies. The increase both in the duties of constables and in the number of occasions on which they were answerable to higher authorities attest to the state's interventionism.[20] At the same time the performance of these officers provides some evidence of the effectiveness of the government's efforts to exert its control over local communities. It has been shown that in many areas of their duties constables were remarkably diligent agents of the state, some of them apparently making personal sacrifices in order to fulfil their responsibilities. However, there were exceptions to this rule. In a few cases the deficiences which constables displayed can be attributed to the personal defects of those selected for the position. Some appear to have been ignorant about their powers and duties, others seem to have been lazy or indifferent, and a few were guilty of disorderly behaviour which accorded ill with their official positions. Officers were sometimes intimidated by the obstruction and violence which they encountered in trying to fulfil their duties, or by threats that were uttered against them. While such a response often seems to have been justified, in some instances they may have been rather easily deterred from the execution of an onerous or unpopular duty. Occasionally constables appear to have used the office for private ends, whether to pursue quarrels and to take vengeance upon their foes, to protect kinsmen and friends, or to line their own pockets. However, in many other instances cited here constables' behaviour seems to be explained by the fact that they aligned themselves with local interests, and as a result neglected or imperfectly fulfilled their duties to the state. Although constables were more reliable agents of the government than earlier historians contended, this study would suggest that on a number of occasions village pressures and local considerations continued to shape the conduct of such officers.[21]

The government's attempts to exert more effective power at the local level are particularly evident in the area of law enforcement and in the implementation of social and economic regulations; and it is

---

[20] See ch. 2.
[21] These conclusions are drawn from chs. 5–7.

these aspects of its policies which have recently attracted the most attention from historians. It has been shown that the judicial and administrative duties of constables increased markedly during the late sixteenth and early seventeenth centuries when a spate of legislation on economic and social matters added to their traditional responsibilities as conservators of the peace. Statutes concerning vagrancy, recusancy and church attendance, drunkenness, swearing, and the keeping of the Sabbath all conferred duties on constables. At the same time new administrative developments such as the institution of monthly meetings made them more frequently and more formally answerable for the enforcement of these and other laws. Moreover, constables also acquired additional responsibilities in the social and economic sphere when they became administrative agents of the justices in such matters as alehouse licensing.[22]

An examination of constables' performance in office has provided evidence to suggest that the central government was often successful in gaining local co-operation in the implementation of its economic and social policies and in the enforcement of law and order. Constables of the villages examined here normally seem to have been diligent in fulfilling such routine administrative tasks as bringing ale-keepers before the justices for relicensing and rebinding, appearing with butchers and victuallers to enter Lenten recognizances, and accompanying the churchwardens and overseers before the magistrates to give an accounting of their administration of poor relief. Such officers also appeared regularly before the clerk of the market with the village's weights and measures. In counties where the justices held annual or biannual 'hiring sessions' for the supervision of servants, constables attended such meetings and were accompanied by the servants of their villages.[23] Some officers were accused of failing to make presentments to quarter sessions or monthly meetings on their enforcement of the regulative statutes, and there were probably some variations from county to county and even from village to village in the regularity with which constables appeared to make such returns. However, dereliction in this duty does not seem to have been very widespread. Even during the 1630s, when the establishment of monthly meetings led to a considerable increase in constables' responsibilities for submitting such returns, few officers in the counties examined were accused of failing to appear before the justices. In the case of villages such as

[22] See ch. 2.   [23] See ch. 6.

Branston, Waltham, Pattingham, and Stockton, Salop, there is positive evidence of the regular co-operation of such officers in returning presentments. Moreover, it has been shown that some constables responded to the summons of the justices on a host of other, less regular, occasions to submit returns on matters ranging from the supplies of corn in the township to special presentments on alehouse keepers or recusants or apprentices.[24]

It is more difficult to assess how fully constables co-operated with the state in the execution of law enforcement duties which required them to pursue and arrest more serious offenders, and to convey them before a justice or to gaol. The apparent increase in the number of cases heard at quarter sessions and assizes during the later sixteenth and early seventeenth centuries may reflect improvements in law enforcement as well as a growth in crime,[25] and in turn greater diligence by constables in performing their police duties. However, Joel Samaha's claim that 'every offender who stood trial was the result of a constable's labours' must be modified in light of Cynthia Herrup's evidence that victims and their friends rather than constables were often responsible for the pursuit and apprehension of offenders.[26] Nevertheless, some constables are known to have gone to considerable trouble and expense to assure the apprehension and safeguarding of offenders, and their delivery to a justice or to gaol; and there is no reason to believe that they were particularly unique in the extent to which they supported the government's efforts to bring law and order to the countryside. Some officers were found guilty of failing to execute warrants or to make arrests or of allowing prisoners to escape their custody, though none of the court records examined contain more than a scattering of such cases. There is evidence to suggest that constables may have been rather remiss in punishing vagrants; but they seem to have become more diligent in fulfilling such duties during the 1630s, probably in response to pressures exerted on them by the justices at their monthly meetings.[27]

An examination of constables' performance in local administration and law enforcement thus provides considerable support for contentions that the central government received local co-operation in its efforts to

---

[24] See ch. 6.
[25] See esp. Samaha, *Law and Order*, and Cockburn, 'The Nature and Incidence of Crime in England'.
[26] Samaha, *Law and Order*, p. 88; Herrup, 'New Shoes and Mutton Pies', esp. 817–20.
[27] See ch. 6.

enforce its economic and social policies and to promote law and order. However, this study of the constableship also suggests some qualifications to such a portrayal of the relations between local communities and the state.

It has been shown that villagers sometimes sought to prevent the arrest of a fellow inhabitant and apparently brought pressure to bear on constables to place 'good neighbourliness' before their official responsibilities. In some cases they succeeded in winning the constable's support, particularly in instances when other law officers such as bailiffs arrived in the village with warrants for arrest. The fact that a number of constables who did assist bailiffs in apprehending men were subjected to physical attack, while a Staffordshire officer was accused of being unneighbourly when he served a warrant on behalf of a bailiff, suggests the extent to which constables faced conflicting pressures on such occasions. Sometimes their local loyalties took precedence over their official responsibilities. Attention has been drawn to a number of cases in which such officers apparently responded to local pressures and joined other villagers in defying bailiffs, either helping to rescue a party from arrest or standing by while these officials were assaulted by some of their fellow inhabitants.[28] There are other instances when constables themselves refrained from taking action against an offender and when, in response to pleas from other villagers, they allowed matters to be settled locally by arbitration.[29]

The character of constables' presentments casts some doubt on how completely they co-operated with the central government in the enforcement of the regulative statutes. Local officers in many Essex villages — constables, churchwardens, and jurymen — may have shown a growing willingness during the early seventeenth century to present their neighbours who breached the penal laws and may have used the courts to establish new standards of conduct, but how typical were such officers?

There was perhaps a similar readiness to make presentments, at least of certain kinds of offenders, among local officials in Norfolk during this period. The surviving hundred presentments for that county suggest a particular willingness by jurymen, many of whom may have been constables as well, to return the names of recusants and those who failed to attend church. It has also been noted that their presentments included a considerable number of unlicensed ale-

---

[28] See chs. 6–7.　　[29] See ch. 7.

sellers and victuallers, some cases of keepers who had broken the assize, and also instances of disorders and drunkenness in alehouses. Moreover, attention has been drawn to a number of cases in which constables of Norfolk villages risked and incurred the hostility of offenders, and sometimes their friends, in their efforts to suppress and punish drunkenness.[30] It seems possible that many local officers in this county, as in Essex, displayed a growing readiness to regulate the conduct of alehouse keepers and their clients. In Hertfordshire there are indications that many constables submitted detailed returns to the justices at their monthly meetings throughout the 1630s, probably at least in part as a result of the rather careful supervision of the constabulary provided by the magistrates in that county. It seems likely that there was some increase in regulative prosecutions in Hertfordshire during this period, although the reports which the justices submitted to the central government seem to have been more concerned with the punishment of vagrancy and the relief of the parish poor than with the enforcement of the penal laws.[31]

If many of the local officials in some counties did display increased willingness to return the names of offenders, and were prepared to place 'discipline' ahead of 'good neighbourliness', it seems unwise to generalize too broadly on the basis of this evidence. The presentments submitted to quarter sessions by Worcestershire constables during the 1630s would suggest that not all officers were imbued with a drive for greater order, and that in many instances concerns about personal relationships or local harmony probably continued to make such men unwilling to prosecute petty offenders among their neighbours. Some Worcestershire constables did give careful attention to the charges which they had received, and officers in some divisions in this county seem to have presented substantial numbers of offenders to the justices at their monthly meetings during the first few months after the issue of the Book of Orders. However, it has been shown that in their presentments to quarter sessions during the 1630s many of them returned nothing other than decayed roads or bridges, the most common offence reported. Although presentments concerning alehouses were numerically in second place, a number of officers claimed not to know whether the alehouses within their jurisdictions were licensed, while others defended keepers whom they reported to be unlicensed.

[30] See chs. 6–7.   [31] See chs. 6–7.

concern about the 'troble and chardge' of formal
n or who espoused the maintenance of 'good neighbourliness'.
es who employed communal sanctions to punish an offender,
llowed matters to be settled outside the courts through local
n, may have been as intent upon enforcing social discipline as
icers who presented offenders to higher authorities. For
the constable of Burton-upon-Trent and his fellow townsmen
cted punishment on a couple for incontinence appear to have
ite concerned to enforce certain standards of conduct within
n. Furthermore, higher authorities themselves sometimes may
nctioned such informal local methods of dealing with offenders.
r, it is none the less the case that the actions of constables in
stances were shaped by local considerations and pressures
han by the state's prescriptions for good order. It has been
that some of these officers found themselves as defendants in
uits because they had employed unofficial means of dealing with
rs rather than proceeding through the normal channels of
.[43]

lly, an examination of the personal conduct of some of the men
n as constable casts doubt on whether, in a number of cases, the
es and behaviour of local officers were markedly different from
of their less prosperous neighbours. Although constables were
y chosen from among the middling and wealthier segments of
society, it has been shown that men of this status were quite
le of breaking the law. They may have been guilty primarily of
r nuisance offences, but evidence from Pattingham has revealed
some of them had also committed breaches of the penal laws. It
noted that a number of them were punished for alehouse
alities, taking inmates, harbouring vagrants and wanderers, and
ling illegal cottages, the very kinds of offences that as constables
were supposed to present to higher authorities.[44] Moreover, J. A.
rpe has shown that some of the men who held office in Kelvedon
terford were also presented to the church courts for sexual and
al offences.[45] Several Pattingham constables and churchwardens
are known to have breached sexual mores, having fathered
tards, though there is no information as to whether they were

[43] See ch. 7.
[44] See ch. 4.
[45] Sharpe, 'Crime and Delinquency in an Essex Parish', pp. 95–6, 97–8.

On the whole the returns do not suggest a vigorous local campaign
against superfluous or unlicensed alehouses. It appears that ale-
keepers had to be guilty of particularly disorderly or immoral conduct,
which had occasioned considerable village hostility, before many of the
constables in Worcestershire were prepared to call for their suppression.[32]

Some have suggested that parish officers not only co-operated with
the state in enforcing the penal laws, but that they sometimes even took
the initiative in such matters. Keith Wrightson has drawn attention to a
number of Essex villages which petitioned the justices to suppress local
alehouses, and he argues that village élites often used the courts in an
offensive fashion to suppress the disorders of popular culture and to
promote new standards of behaviour within local communities.[33] Some
village leaders in other counties too took action in trying to gain the
suppression of popular disorders. Reference has been made to a
petition of the constables and other inhabitants of Stone, Worcestershire,
concerning the suppression of an alehouse in that village in 1638; and
similar documents were submitted to the justices from some communities in other counties as well. The constables, churchwardens,
and overseers and some other residents of Thursford, Norfolk,
requested the suppression of both alehouses in that village in 1620,
claiming that one of them was the scene of misrule and disorder and
that these houses drew many people into idleness and caused servants
to neglect their masters. Similarly, in 1621 eight inhabitants of
Shouldham, Norfolk, petitioned the justices about alehouse disorders
there, and complained that there were now three alehouses in the
village where in the past there usually had been only one such house.[34]
Such examples could be multiplied, and they do provide evidence that
the leaders in some villages were taking the initiative in suppressing
local disorders. Furthermore, individual officers in certain communities
seem to have been imbued with a similar spirit; and sometimes they
probably surpassed the magistrates in their eagerness to impose social
discipline. Attention has been drawn to the efforts of constables of
Wells, Somerset; Brinklow, Warwickshire; Alton, Hants; and Longdon,
Worcestershire to suppress popular sports and pastimes on the
Sabbath or other festivities such as May games and church-ales, and

[32] See chs. 6–7.
[33] See esp. *English Society*, p. 170, and his 'Two concepts of order', pp. 41–4, 46.
[34] See ch. 7, n. 205; NNRO, Sessions Records, Boxes 22, 23; also see ch. 2, n. 53.

their actions probably owed little to pressures exerted by their superiors.[35]

However, in contrast to communities in which local officers or parish élites initiated reform, there were other villages where officials continued to support traditional festivities or refused to co-operate with higher authorities in the suppression of popular disorders. If the officers of some parishes were hostile to 'festive sociability', and eager to reform popular culture, there were other parishes where local officials continued to give their support to communal celebrations and probably played a major role in organizing them. It has been noted that constables of Pattingham in 1603–4 paid for drink for those who gathered wood for a bonfire on the king's holiday and that Waltham officers recorded expenses for celebrations on Plough Monday, and on the occasion of a perambulation. These disbursements, and the sum spent by Abraham Bishop, yeoman, constable of Branston, 'amongst neighbours at the bonfyre' on 7 September 1641, like those of the Pattingham constables, were probably for ale.[36] These officers seem to have endorsed the kinds of communal festivities which some constables had earmarked for destruction as part of their campaigns to impose social discipline. Against local officials committed to reform it is necessary to set officers like the constable of Walsall, Staffordshire, who in 1610 refused to co-operate with the high constable in suppressing a wake in the town and in apprehending the minstrels and 'vagrant rogues' who had gathered for the occasion; or the church-wardens of Yeovil, Somerset, who were reported to quarter sessions in 1607 because they supported a church-ale and allowed minstrelsy, dancing, and carousing in the church house on the Sabbath.[37] It is clear that in some communities not even the parish officers could be counted on to support the enforcement of social discipline.[38]

It is also important to note that officers who were vigorous in their attempts to suppress popular disorders sometimes seem to have enjoyed little local support for their actions, and that divisions were not always between village leaders and the poorer sort. William Hunt suggests that 'the culture of discipline was resisted by a large fraction

[35] See ch. 7.

[36] See ch. 2, n. 98; and for the expenditure of the Branston constable see Leics. RO, DE 720/30, fo. 50.

[37] Staffs. RO, Transcripts Sessions Rolls, Jac. I, Roll 31, nos. 106–7; Somerset RO, Sessions Records, ii, no. 61.

[38] On this point also see Sharp, 'Enforcing the Law', p. 114.

of the populace', and he draws at[...]
came not only from Keith Wrights[...]
'Third World' or his own 'Hugh M[...]
the 'reforming' constables discussed[...]
from the 'better sort' when they atten[...]
popular culture. Most of the city fath[...]
Hole's attempts to suppress May gan[...]
town in 1607, and three of the six pe[...]
Brinklow, Warwickshire, as opposi[...]
popular festivities were probably mem[...]
were taxed for the subsidy.[40] These [...]
divisions with English villages were n[...]
élites and the disorderly poor; and tha[...]
government's attempts to enforce social[...]
took the initiative in such matters, somet[...]
isolated locally.[41]

Evidence of the continuing use of infor[...]
offenders also suggests some modificatio[...]
élites and local officers offensively using[...]
standards of behaviour. Several historians [...]
fact that a variety of procedures for dealing[...]
formal prosecution, existed during the early[...]
Sharpe accepts that the respectable elem[...]
century parish were concerned to enforce [...]
disorderly neighbours; but he points out tha[...]
only means of doing so and that it often seem[...]
only when other methods of control had fa[...]
enforcement officers had many alternatives t[...]
ment, and there is some evidence to suggest th[...]
alternatives.[42] It has been shown that constab[...]
the settlement of a matter through local action[...]
cited here apparently in response to pressures f[...]

[39] Hunt, *The Puritan Moment*, pp. 84, 144–54.

[40] See ch. 7; and for the subsidy roll for Brinklow see P[...]

[41] The conclusions in this paragraph are similar to those [...]
his 'Ridings, Rough Music and the "Reform of Popular [...]
England', *P and P*, cv (1984), 99–113. Also see his article '[...]
Moral Discipline in Late Sixteenth- and Early Seventeent[...]
Studies', in Kaspar von Greyerz, ed., *Religion and Society*[...]
1500–1800 (London, 1984), pp. 177–93.

[42] Sharpe, 'Enforcing the Law', esp. pp. 103–17.

punished for the offence.[46] Such evidence about the conduct of men who filled the constableship raises questions about the degree to which the behaviour and values of some local officers had distanced them from their poorer neighbours, and in turn about the extent to which such men had accepted concepts of order proclaimed by the state and its magisterial representatives.

Although constables were often reliable agents of the state in implementing its economic and social policies and in enforcing law and order, it is thus suggested that this statement needs to be qualified in certain ways and the extent of local diversity to be appreciated. If the constables of some villages, or even a majority of the officers in some counties, displayed increased diligence during the early seventeenth century in enforcing order, there is also evidence from other areas and other communities that local considerations and neighbourly ties could still affect the ways in which constables performed such duties. Moreover, various informal means of dealing with offenders continued to provide alternatives to the courts; and constables sometimes joined with their neighbours to resolve a case locally rather than taking official action and reporting the matter to higher authorities. While the officers of some parishes supported the government's drive for law and order, and even took the initiative in such matters as suppressing popular festivities, local officials in other settlements continued to organize and participate in these activities and sometimes ignored orders to break up such gatherings. Some village officers do seem to have assimilated the values of their betters and to have been ready to use the courts to impose discipline upon their poorer neighbours. In other instances, however, the men who filled local positions had themselves committed breaches of the penal laws or of the moral code of the church; and it seems unlikely that they viewed such wrongdoing in quite the same light as did their administrative superiors, or that they would be particularly vigorous in reporting or suppressing such offences.

---

[46] Thomas, ed., *The Pattingham Parish Registers*, reveals that the following constables and/or churchwardens fathered bastards: two men of the Perry family of More, who held the constableship, whose bastards were baptized in 1594 and 1602; George Sampson, constable and one of the more prosperous farmers of the village, in 1592; Richard Brooke, glover and constable, in 1593; Roger White of Nurton, yeoman and churchwarden, in 1594, and his son, Roger, in 1642. John Clempson junior of Rudge, who served as churchwarden, also seems to have fathered a bastard; the churchwardens' accounts in 1595 record a payment of 5*s.* to John Clempson senior to take care of this child.

298 *The Localities and Central Government:*

Some of the recent accounts of relations between the central government and the localities in England have focused almost entirely on law enforcement, and particularly on the implementation of the regulative statutes. However, it is important to bear in mind that the state impinged upon local communities not only as an agent of law and order, but also through its financial and military demands. In these areas too the central government increasingly made its weight felt during the late sixteenth and early seventeenth centuries, and such exactions were more likely than its interventions in law enforcement to provoke opposition in the localities. However, the response to government pressures at the village level, at least in England, seems to have been more complex than students of early modern state-formation have appreciated.[47] Even in cases of taxation and military demands constables were frequently successful in meeting the additional burdens imposed by the central government, and there was often co-operation between village communities and the state. It has been shown, however, that in some instances villagers were alienated by the state's policies, and that on such occasions constables often sided with local opinion. When the level or incidence of taxation or the extent and nature of military demands had disruptive effects within local communities, the integrative function which the constableship served on many occasions became untenable; and such officers could no longer act as both village agents and representatives of the state.

Taxation was no novelty under Elizabeth and the early Stuarts, but the burdens imposed by the state did increase during that period, at least for some segments of society, just as did the demands made upon constables and other parish officials as the government's local revenue agents. More frequent subsidies between 1590 and 1611, increases in purveyance as the Crown attempted to combat inflation, and apparently rising demands by saltpetre men and postmasters added to the tax burdens and to the duties of the state's local officers. In addition, there was probably an increase in military levies during the late sixteenth and early seventeenth centuries, such exactions being particularly heavy from the late 1580s to 1604, and as late as 1609 in some areas, in the 1620s, and in the later 1630s. Furthermore, the Crown attempted to collect several benevolences, gifts, or loans during this period, in 1614, 1622, 1625–6, 1627, and 1642, while Parliament authorized the collection of additional revenue in the form of a poll tax in 1641.

---

[47] See above, ch. 1, n. 28.

Various county rates for charitable purposes were enacted into law between 1593 and 1604, and during the 1630s the government also demanded 'contributions' for the repair of St. Paul's church. Lastly, and most important, there was ship-money which, in the form and manner in which it was levied during the 1630s, also constituted a new tax.[48] It was through the imposition of this rate more than any other that the localities came to feel the weight of the state as tax-collector. Ship-money touched many villagers who had not been assessed for the subsidy, and whose only previous experience of national taxation was in the payment of purveyance. For them ship-money did not replace other taxes; it was a wholly new burden imposed by the state.

Despite the increased financial demands of the period, in many of their tax-collecting duties constables do seem to have been effective agents of the state and to have enjoyed substantial local co-operation in fulfilling their responsibilities. When they did encounter difficulties in collecting a levy, it has been noted that they sometimes borrowed money, or even dipped into their own pockets in order to meet their commitments. Just as the churchwardens and overseers apparently displayed growing support for the government's policies in the sums which they levied for the provision of the parish poor, constables too appear to have been quite diligent in collecting the rates for charitable purposes for which they were responsible. Officers were sometimes accused of having failed to make such payments, and in other cases they were late in returning the money; but on the whole the evidence presented here would suggest that they were successful in making such collections. In the case of levies for victims of plague some villages contributed rather substantial sums, amounts in excess of what they paid toward the subsidy or toward the annual levy for provision. County rates for the repair of bridges sometimes remained unpaid, and they could be a contentious matter, probably often because a community disputed the share of the financial burden imposed on it. However, there does not seem to be widespread evidence of negligence by constables in collecting these levies. Rates for provision too were sometimes in arrears, as were subsidy payments, but in neither case do defaults by either taxpayers or constables appear to have been very numerous. The state received less local co-operation in its attempts to levy benevolences in 1614 and 1622 and to collect a forced loan in 1627. However, Leicestershire constables' accounts

[48] See ch. 2.

indicate that some officers in that county did succeed in collecting both of the benevolences, and in Staffordshire some constables are known to have returned the benevolence of 1622. In these counties, and in others too, constables usually seem to have been successful in gathering the forced loan, even if they sometimes did encounter resistance from a few of those who were assessed for the levy.[49]

However, the government's financial demands on some occasions did arouse considerable opposition, which left local officers confronted with a real dilemma. If they attempted to collect such levies they ran the risk of informal local sanctions being imposed on them, while if they failed to do so they risked punishment by their superiors. Peter Clark contends that military levies created such a situation for the leaders of village society in Kent during the crisis years of the 1590s, at the very time when the government was attempting to secure local support for the implementation of its social policies. He suggests that in this instance village oligarchies themselves were 'alienated . . . by Crown and gentry policy' and that in most cases they 'sided with local opinion', suspended their co-operation with county government, and even engaged in civil disobedience.[50] Quite possibly the military levies of the 1590s were greeted with a comparable response in other counties as well. Some village officers may have found themselves in similar circumstances when local communities were faced with the military rates of the later 1620s, while the evidence presented here suggests that the imposition of coat and conduct money and other levies necessitated by military preparations against the Scots in 1639–40 did meet with considerable local resistance. Confronted, in certain cases, with villagers' refusals even to assist them in drawing up local assessments for the levy, let alone making payment, constables in some areas once again seem to have bowed to local opinion and to have suspended their co-operation in implementing the government's policies.[51]

There are even greater signs of local opposition to ship-money. It has been shown that in the case of this levy too villagers sometimes refused to assist constables in drawing up local assessments, while officers who did attempt to collect the money, and especially those who distrained, on some occasions met with abuse and violence. Although there is evidence that some constables endeavoured to meet their commitments, officers of Pattingham even dipping into their expense

---

[49] See chs. 5 and 7.
[50] Clark, *English Provincial Society*, pp. 250–1.   [51] See ch. 7.

money in order to make up deficiencies in their collections, by 1639 and 1640 many of them ceased to co-operate with the government in levying ship-money. Faced with trying to exact revenues from unwilling villagers, and perhaps themselves alienated by the government's demands, constables once again sided with local opinion and ignored warnings and threats from sheriffs that they would be punished for their negligence.[52]

Purveyance, and especially demands for carts, as well as requisitions by saltpetre men and postmasters, could also occasion friction and undermine local co-operation with the central government. Historians of a number of counties have drawn attention to the grievances created by purveyance, and sometimes by the demands of saltpetre men as well. Although it has been shown that constables were often hard-working in meeting the demands of such officials, and that they received a good deal of local assistance and co-operation in doing so, it is also evident that in some cases communities regarded these burdens as excessive and unfair. Opposition to such demands seems to have been particularly marked during the later 1630s and early 1640s. On these occasions too constables experienced local pressures which conflicted with their duties as the state's revenue officers. They sometimes sided with local opinion to the extent that they attempted to gain concessions for the village, to procure a reduction in the demands being imposed, or at least to arrange monetary composition for burdens in kind. Occasionally, in the case of saltpetre men, officers went so far as to offer them a bribe to leave the village.[53]

The military demands of the central government also impinged more frequently and more forcefully upon local communities during the later sixteenth and early seventeenth centuries than in earlier years, and not only through the levies imposed for military purposes. The state perhaps made its presence felt more intermittently in military matters than in the collection of taxes or in its attempts to impose order on the countryside. However, during certain periods it did intervene to place extended military demands on local communities. The government's reorganization of the militia in the late Elizabethan period, which represented one kind of military intervention in the localities, was followed under James I by a period during which musters or trainings were held irregularly and infrequently, at least in the counties examined here, and when the state seems to have given little attention

<hr/>

[52] See chs. 5 and 7.   [53] See ch. 7.

to military matters. In 1613, however, the Privy Council issued directives ordering regular trainings and that the numbers and equipment of the bands be brought up to standard, and such instructions continued to be issued during the remainder of James's reign. The government's attempts in the later 1620s to create a 'perfect militia' constituted another phase of more intensive intervention by the state in military matters, and it has been shown that the frequency of musters and trainings at this time placed increased demands upon local communities and their constables. After another lull during the first half of the 1630s, the government renewed its directives concerning the proper training and equipping of the bands, and during the years 1638–40 the state's military demands were even greater than they had been in the later 1620s. The localities experienced the weight of central authority even more forcefully on those occasions when they were required to provide soldiers for active duty, as they were during the 1590s, and in some areas as late as 1608 or 1609 for Irish service, during the period 1624–8, and again during the years 1639–40.[54]

In the case of military demands, as of taxation, considerable evidence has been presented to indicate that the government secured local support for its policies. The constables of the particular communities examined here devoted a good deal of time and effort to the maintenance of the village arms and, probably in response to pressures from above, during some periods many of these settlements made substantial purchases of new armour in order to bring their equipment up to standard. There is evidence from Staffordshire of the failure of a number of village soldiers to appear at musters between 1590 and 1601, and perhaps there was similar delinquency in other areas at this time too. On the whole, however, both constables and the trained men from their communities appear to have been co-operative in fulfilling such duties, and they did so even when this entailed their absence from home for twenty days or more within the space of a few months, as sometimes was the case during the later 1630s.[55]

The impressment of soldiers for service in war was a different matter, however. Just as local communities were sometimes unwilling to meet the financial demands that were placed on them, on some

---

[54] See ch. 2; and on the increased pressures which the central government exerted on the counties in the later 1620s, see Russell, *Parliaments and English Politics*, pp. 70–84, 324–38.

[55] See chs. 5 and 7.

occasions they also apparently proved unco-operative in furnishing the soldiers they were supposed to supply. It is clear that the government's demands for soldiers could arouse local hostility, as was certainly the case in Hertfordshire, and probably in other counties too, in 1640 when officers were instructed that they could recruit men from the trained bands for the war against the Scots. Although the impressment of soldiers from the trained bands constituted a special grievance, it seems likely that the press created resentment on other occasions as well, and especially in small and fairly 'settled' rural communities where there may have been few inhabitants of the sort that villagers were ready to abandon to service in war. During most of the years when soldiers were being pressed there is some evidence of constables hiring strangers, or simply apprehending outsiders, and returning them as recruits in place of their own townsmen. In some cases they bribed the captain to release a local recruit or paid a more substantial sum as composition in return for the village being excused from providing a soldier. Such conduct may sometimes reflect personal negligence or dishonesty by particular officers, just as in cases when they took bribes for releasing men whom they had pressed, or when some of them allegedly used the press to pursue private quarrels and to take vengeance upon their foes. However, it seems probable that in many of these instances officers were responding to local opinion, and that in an effort to spare their fellow inhabitants from military service they risked incurring the government's displeasure and the rejection of the soldiers whom they did return.[56]

Although constables in many cases were diligent and successful in meeting the financial and military demands imposed by the state, and received local co-operation in doing so, there were thus some occasions when they failed to fulfil such obligations, or at least to perform these duties in the manner expected of them. Military levies, requisitions for the royal household or by saltpetre men and postmasters, and the impressment of soldiers all occasioned opposition at various times during the late sixteenth and early seventeenth centuries, and temporarily seem to have undermined local co-operation with the central government. However, it was apparently only in the later 1630s, when the imposition of ship-money coincided with demands for rather sizeable military levies, and when the exactions of saltpetre men and postmasters also seem to have been

[56] See chs. 5 and 7.

particularly heavy, that local resentment reached a point where large numbers of villagers resisted the government's financial demands. The fact that local communities were, at the same time, being required to supply and equip soldiers for the wars against the Scots, and that the state's instructions authorized the impressment of men from the trained bands, further undermined local co-operation with central authority. In the face of substantial village opposition to the government's financial and military policies during the later 1630s, constables were often either unable or unwilling to meet the government's demands. Some apparently attempted to juggle the conflicting pressures from higher authorities and their fellow inhabitants and probably often did not succeed in satisfying either. Others openly sided with local opinion and risked, and sometimes incurred, punishment by their superiors for failure to fulfil their duties.

To suggest that 'village' pressures sometimes led constables to neglect their obligations to the state is not to imply that English villages of this period were always united, or that relations within them were completely harmonious. It is evident that law enforcement could create divisions within local communities, particularly in cases when parish officers or leading inhabitants aligned themselves with the state in an effort to impose order on other villagers.[57] Taxation too sometimes could be a divisive matter, villagers being at odds with one another over the way the levy was to be distributed within the local community.[58] Moreover, it is apparent from the number of assault cases found in court records, and more generally from the extent of litigation among villagers, that in practice relations within local communities did not always match the ideals of harmony and concord that were so often espoused during this period.[59] However, it does appear that opposition to the demands of the central government could cut across the petty conflicts within the village and unite many of the inhabitants. The financial and military impositions of the later 1630s in particular seem to have evoked this kind of response within local communities. In such circumstances constables were placed under considerable pressure to withdraw their support of the state's demands and to side with local opinion.

[57] See esp. the work of Wrightson cited in ch. 8, n. 1; and see above, ch. 7.
[58] e.g. see ch. 5, n. 76, and ch. 7, n. 108, which probably reflect local disagreements about assessments.
[59] See esp. Wrightson, *English Society*, ch. 2 and pp. 161–2; Ingram, 'Communities and Courts', pp. 115–16; Sharpe, 'Enforcing the Law', pp. 101–2.

A consideration of men's willingness to serve as constable has also provided evidence of local co-operation with the state during most of the late sixteenth and early seventeenth centuries, while at the same time suggesting that this co-operation may have broken down during the later 1630s. It was found that some villages lacked constables and that others had not replaced men whose terms had expired, while individuals selected for the position sometimes claimed exemption from serving or refused to assume the office; but such cases do not seem to have been very numerous during most of the period 1580 to 1642. Nor was there much evidence of villagers trying to escape the office by hiring substitutes. Despite the rather onerous tasks entailed in the constableship, and the obstruction and abuse which officers sometimes encountered in trying to fulfil their duties, most of those selected for the position apparently did agree to serve. Some perhaps did so unwillingly, though others probably accepted a turn in the office as part of their civic duty. Villagers who were anxious to enforce greater local order, and especially those imbued with Puritan ideals, may even have sought the position because of the opportunities which it afforded to implement social and moral reform.[60] However, just as there were occasions when constables withdrew their support of the government's policies, there also seem to have been times when villagers were less co-operative than usual in agreeing to serve as constable. Peter Clark has pointed out that the opposition to military levies in Kent during the 1590s was reflected in the refusal of villagers to serve in local offices.[61] Information for this period is too incomplete to state whether or not there was a similar unwillingness to hold the constableship in the counties and villages examined here. However, some evidence has been presented which suggests that there was an increased reluctance to serve as constable in the 1630s, and particularly during the last half of that decade. The number of disputed constableships referred to the justices, along with evidence from individual villages that those chosen for the position were threatened with large fines if they did not serve and that men more often hired substitutes during this period, seem to indicate growing unwillingness to assume the office. The fact that in some communities a number of rather poor men were selected for the position during the later 1630s, and that in other villages the constables of this period included an unusually large number of newcomers, may also attest to

[60] See ch. 3.
[61] Clark, *English Provincial Society*, p. 251.

the increased unpopularity of the office.[62] Although the evidence is fragmentary, it would appear that local opposition to the government's financial and military demands in the later 1630s not only led officers to withdraw their co-operation, but also resulted in increased unwillingness by villagers to assume the constableship.

Despite some tendencies by constables to place village interests or local or personal loyalties ahead of their official duties, and the fact that they sometimes retreated from a duty in the face of violence or verbal threats, the constabulary provided a remarkably flexible and effective means of linking the state and local communities during most of the period 1580 to 1642. When consideration is given to the extent of constables' duties and the time and effort required to fulfil them, and also to the difficulties inherent in such a mediating position, the record of these officials is a surprisingly successful one. Their conscientiousness is evident on many occasions, and their sense of personal responsibility apparent in the lengths to which they sometimes went in order to meet their commitments. Although they occasionally faced obstruction or were heaped with abuse or were rewarded for their efforts by vexatious legal suits,[63] the resistance which they encountered should not be overemphasized. More striking, on the whole, is the amount of local co-operation which they enjoyed, and the active assistance which they received from other villagers in fulfilling their duties.[64] This local support, as much as their own abilities and efforts, helps to explain the extent of their success. On occasions when they did experience local pressures which conflicted with their official responsibilities, they often seem to have been quite adept in juggling these demands, and to have managed to carry out their duties, if sometimes only partially or somewhat tardily. However, it would appear that the demands imposed on local communities by the government of Charles I during the later 1630s substantially altered the situation faced by constables. The unpopularity of ship-money and the military levies of that period, along with resentment about the exactions and abuses of saltpetre men and postmasters and about the recruitment of soldiers for an unpopular war, greatly increased the local pressures brought to bear on constables. It became more difficult, and sometimes impossible, for them to mediate between the demands of the state and those of their fellow villagers. By 1640 some of them seem to have abandoned any attempt to do so and to have sided with

---

[62] See chs. 3 and 4.   [63] See ch. 7.   [64] See ch. 7.

village opinion on these issues. The sheriff of Worcestershire probably accurately depicted the attitudes of some constables when he claimed in 1640 that officers whom he had imprisoned for their failure to collect ship-money were content to remain in gaol in order to avoid all of their duties.[65] However, despite their negligence or tardiness in levying ship-money and military rates, even in 1639 and 1640 many constables continued to perform most of their duties, and it would be going too far to suggest that local government collapsed completely during those years.

Claims of historians such as the Webbs and T. A. Critchley that the constableship was already in decline by the late sixteenth century find little support in this study; but their depiction of the office and its occupants may be more applicable to the period after 1660.[66] In the absence of detailed county studies,[67] and of a clear picture of the duties of local officials during the later seventeenth and eighteenth centuries, one is not on very firm ground in suggesting why the quality and effectiveness of constables might have deteriorated. A few speculations can be offered, though detailed research may prove them to be in error.

The central government's withdrawal from the supervision of local government in the later seventeenth and eighteenth centuries may have had an impact upon the constableship.[68] Some recent studies emphasize continuity in the work of the justices, their industriousness despite the lack of central direction, and their use of petty sessions to

---

[65] PRO, SP 16/457/22.

[66] For that part of their discussion which deals explicitly with the constableship in the period after 1660 see the Webbs, *The Parish and the County*, pp. 62–4, 68–9; Critchley, *History of Police*, pp. 18–22. Also see Bryan Keith-Lucas, *The Unreformed Local Government System* (London, 1980), pp. 84–6, 90–1, 101–2.

[67] In a recent critical biography of seventeenth-century Britain, J. S. Morrill has emphasized the dearth of 'local studies' for the period after 1660; see his *Seventeenth-Century Britain 1603–1714* (Folkestone, 1980), p. 126. For brief studies of county government which deal with the later seventeenth century see G. C. F. Forster, 'Government in Provincial England Under the Later Stuarts', *Transactions of the Royal Historical Society*, 5th ser., xxxiii (1983), 29–48; W. R. Ward, 'County Government c1660–1835', in *VCH Wiltshire*, v. 170–94; D. C. Cox, 'County Government 1603–1714', in *VCH Shropshire*, iii. 90–114.

[68] On the central government's lack of supervision of local government see, for example, J. R. Jones, *Country and Court: England 1658–1714* (Cambridge, Mass., 1978), pp. 53–4, 55; Wrightson, *English Society*, p. 228; Ward, 'County Government c1660–1835', 172; Cox, 'County Government 1603–1714', 90; Forster, 'Government in Provincial England', esp. pp. 40–3; Norma Landau, *The Justices of the Peace 1679–1760* (Berkeley, 1984), pp. 2, 7–8.

supervise the work of parish officials.[69] However, without the prodding of the Council or the judges of assize the magistrates' oversight of the constabulary perhaps became less regular or less strict. If T. A. Critchley and the Webbs are correct in their claims that many of the justices by the eighteenth century sought the office largely for the profits which they could derive from it,[70] this probably affected the calibre of local government at all levels. The fact that the justices more often appointed constables after 1660 may thus have provided little guarantee of their quality, while at the same time depriving these officials of some of the local support which they had enjoyed when they were selected locally and could be regarded as village officers.

Economic and social changes of the later seventeenth and eighteenth centuries probably had an even greater impact on the way the constableship functioned and on the kind of men who filled the position. Historians draw attention to the decline of the yeomanry during this period and to 'the shrinking proportion of land owned by small occupiers'.[71] Such men had formed the backbone of village society in earlier years and had regularly served in local offices. Their disappearance must have made a difference. The tenant farmers of the later seventeenth and eighteenth centuries perhaps did regard the constableship as beneath them, and more often employed substitutes of mean status. By the eighteenth century population growth and industrialization were also altering the character of local communities in many areas;[72] and these changes, along with the growing differentiation of rural society into prosperous farmers and poor labourers, probably undermined the kind of communal co-operation which had contributed so much to constables' success in the sixteenth and seventeenth centuries. The constabulary had developed, and could be reasonably effective, in a rural society of small and fairly settled communities

[69] See Forster, 'Government in Provincial England'; and on petty sessions see esp. Landau, *The Justices of the Peace*, pp. 213–19.

[70] Critchley, *History of Police*, pp. 19–20; the Webbs, *The Parish and the County*, esp. pp. 321–37.

[71] For a recent survey of the social changes of the period 1660–1714 see Jones, *Country and Court*, Ch. 4; the quotation is found on p. 75. On the eighteenth century see W. A. Speck, *Stability and Strife: England 1714–1760* (London, 1977), Chs. 2 and 3 and esp. pp. 70–3, 77–9; Roy Porter, *English Society in the Eighteenth Century* (London, 1982), Ch. 2 and esp. pp. 83–5, 108–12.

[72] The Webbs and Critchley both attach considerable importance to the impact of such changes on local government; see the Webbs, *The Parish and the County*, esp. pp. 61–2 and Critchley, *History of Police*, p. 18. Also see Keith-Lucas, *The Unreformed Local Government System*, pp. 91, 101–2.

where most inhabitants knew one another and where communal customs and obligations were widely accepted. Such conditions were not always to be found even in the Tudor and early Stuart period, but they probably became less and less common during the course of the later seventeenth and eighteenth centuries as village communities were increasingly affected by economic and social change.

Changes in the criminal law and the extent of crime, in the level and distribution of taxation, and in the state's military requirements in the period after 1660 may be most important in explaining changes in the calibre and conduct of constables. Legal historians draw attention to the growing number of capital crimes between 1660 and 1800, and some suggest that crime was on the increase, at least during the latter part of the eighteenth century.[73] Constables' law enforcement duties may have become more burdensome, due to an increase both in crime and in the complexity of the law. Increased taxation and changes in its distribution probably had an even greater impact on the constableship, and perhaps help to explain the growing difficulties in filling the office in some areas as early as the 1640s and 1650s.[74] Although tax burdens of the 1630s may have been greater than in earlier years, taxes seem to have increased much more substantially after 1643 and, like ship-money, many of these levies affected sectors of the population which had not been subject to national taxes prior to the 1630s. It is not entirely clear which of these taxes were collected by constables, or for how long they continued to have such responsibilities; but it seems possible that their duties in assessing and collecting the state's revenues became more onerous after 1660, and that they more often met with opposition in trying to gather these levies.[75] If

[73] See esp. Beattie, 'The Pattern of Crime in England'; Douglas Hay, 'Property, Authority and the Criminal Law', in *Albion's Fatal Tree*, and his 'War Dearth and Theft'; but on the increase in capital crimes also see Langbein, ' "Albion's" Fatal Flaws'. Also see Critchley, *History of Police*, pp. 21–2.

[74] See King, 'Vagrancy and Local Law Enforcement, 269 and n. 13; and Fletcher, *Sussex*, pp. 141–2, whose evidence of greater intervention by the justices in the appointment of constables in the 1640s and 1650s may reflect reluctance by men to hold the office.

[75] The discussion of taxation is based on William Kennedy, *English Taxation 1640–1799: An Essay on Policy and Opinion* (Kelley Reprint, New York, 1968); and C. D. Chandaman, *The English Public Revenue 1660–1688* (Oxford, 1975), esp. pp. 81–105, 138–55, 170–2, 180–3, 188. The hearth tax was assessed and collected by constables between 1662 and 1664, and their presence was required during a forcible search for hearths or for distraint of the money even after the assessment and collection of the tax was turned over to officials appointed by the king. It is not clear whether they enjoyed similar responsibilities during the years 1666–9 and 1674–84 when the tax was

constables continued to be responsible for the collection of county rates, this task too probably became more difficult. Such rates appear to have increased during the later seventeenth and eighteenth centuries, particularly after the establishment of a consolidated county rate in the 1730s, and their collection was perhaps more rigorously enforced following the creation of semi-professional county treasurers.[76] Constables' military duties too may have become more burdensome, though in the current state of the evidence it is not possible to speak with any certainty on the subject. Under the militia acts of the late seventeenth and eighteenth centuries they continued to be responsible for raising and equipping village soldiers and assuring their attendance at musters. Even if trainings were held less regularly after 1660, and the duty was not so demanding in that respect, villagers were perhaps more reluctant to serve in the militia because of the uses to which it was put in suppressing religious dissent and political opposition.[77] If constables continued to have obligations for pressing soldiers, the wars of the later seventeenth and eighteenth centuries probably made considerable demands upon them.

An increase in the duties of the office, and in their complexity, may help to explain not only the reluctance of men to assume the position but the ineffectiveness attributed to those who did serve. It seems likely that by the later seventeenth and eighteenth centuries the weight of local government could no longer be borne by such part-time officials. Moreover, as central administration and to a lesser extent even county administration became more formal and more professional in character,[78] an office such as the constableship, staffed by impermanent amateurs, must have become increasingly obsolete.

farmed. Monthly assessments and subsidies after 1660 apparently operated much as they had in earlier years, though after 1671 the parish sub-collectors for the subsidy were to be chosen by the parish. Possibly constables often continued to act as collectors of these revenues. They were given responsibility for collection of the poll-tax in 1660, though after that date the commissioners could select any 'able and discreet' persons. After 1667 the sub-collectors of the poll-tax were chosen by the parish. Constables may often have remained as assessors and collectors of this tax, and they were required to assist in the execution of the commissioners' warrants under the poll-tax of 1678. (Chandaman, *The English Public Revenue*, pp. 81–5, 170–2, 180, 183, 188.)

[76] Cox, 'County Government 1603–1714', 100–2; G. C. Baugh, 'County Government 1714–1834', *VCH Shropshire*, iii. 120–2; Ward, 'County Government *c*.1660–1835', 174–5, 190–3.

[77] J. R. Western, *The English Militia in the Eighteenth Century: The Story of a Political Issue 1660–1802* (London, 1965), esp. pp. 10–11, 17–19, 30–2, 35–7, 48, 57–8, 248, 290–1, 372.

[78] Such developments are evident in financial administration by the second half of the

Whatever future studies may reveal about the failures of constables or about the general character of local government in the period after 1660, during the late sixteenth and early seventeenth centuries the absence of a bureaucracy in the provinces does not seem to have constituted as great a weakness in the English polity as some have suggested.[79] 'Government by the informal mechanism of consent', to use Penry Williams's phrase, appears to have worked during most of the period.[80] A system of local administation staffed by unpaid, part-time officials, who in turn were assisted by their friends and neighbours, functioned quite successfully in linking the village and the state; and although the system was subjected to strains during the later 1630s it was still in working order on the eve of the Civil War. The constableship under Elizabeth and the early Stuarts was a relatively effective embodiment of the principle of 'local self-government at the King's command', and constables of that period seem to warrant a much more favourable press than they have usually received.

seventeenth century, first in the case of the excise and then the hearth tax. In the case of the hearth tax a separate central organization for its collection was established in 1684 (though a central office had existed as early as 1670–4), and central officials were appointed to oversee local administration of this tax. This was accompanied by the transfer of its collection from local government officials to officers appointed by the king (Chandaman, *The English Public Revenue*, esp. pp. 84, 96–7, 104–5). For the development of some more permanent and professional elements in county administration, particularly the change in the character of the office of clerk of the peace and the creation of a semi-professional county treasurer, see Cox, 'County Government 1603–1714', 102; Baugh, 'County Government 1714–1834', 115, 128–9; Ward, 'County Government *c*.1660–1835', 173–5; Forster, 'Government in Provincial England', pp. 37–8. On the growing importance of the clerk of petty sessions see Landau, *The Justices of the Peace*, pp. 226 ff.

[79] e.g. Lawrence Stone, *The Causes of the English Revolution 1529–1642* (London, 1972), pp. 63–4; but also see H. G. Koenigsberger's comments in his review in *The Journal of Modern History*, xlvi (1974), 104–5, and Penry Williams, *The Tudor Regime* (Oxford, 1979), ch. 14, for alternative views.

[80] Williams, *The Tudor Regime*, p. 464.

Index